Arthur Gilman

The Story of Boston, a Study of Independency

Arthur Gilman

The Story of Boston, a Study of Independency

ISBN/EAN: 9783743322462

Manufactured in Europe, USA, Canada, Australia, Japa

Cover: Foto ©ninafisch / pixelio.de

Manufactured and distributed by brebook publishing software (www.brebook.com)

Arthur Gilman

The Story of Boston, a Study of Independency

CONTENTS.

		PAGE
I.—	A Declaration of Independence	1
II.—	Winthrop and his Companions	11
III.—	Getting Ready for a Voyage	23
IV.—	The Founding of Boston	33
V.—	Margaret Winthrop Comes over	45
VI.—	The Lay of the Land	56
VII.—	Sundry Troubles	63
VIII.—	The Government Becomes more Popular	83
IX.—	Welcome and Unwelcome Visitors	96
X.—	The Charter is Attacked	114
XI.—	The Times of the Mathers	129
XII.—	The Charter is Lost	145
XIII.—	An American Despotism	158
XIV.—	The King's Governors Begin to Rule	172
XV.—	The Governors and the Boston People	190
XVI.—	Strained Relations	207
XVII.—	Is it Lawful to Resist?	221

		PAGE
XVIII.—Tested and not Found Wanting		240
XIX.—A Maltster Enters Politics		256
XX.—Boston Opposes a Tax		273
XXI.—In the Grip of the Army		290
XXII.—Blood is Spilled		305
XXIII.—Stirring up a Continent		321
XXIV.—War		344
XXV.—Boston Besieged		363
XXVI.—Independence Declared and Won		378
XXVII.—The Old Order Changeth		396
XXVIII.—The Town Becomes a City		414
XXIX.—The Second Mayor		426
XXX.—The New Order Established		438
XXXI.—Changing Boundary Lines		448
XXXII.—Individualism and Other Isms		457
XXXIII.—Modern Boston		469
Index		483

ILLUSTRATIONS.

	PAGE
THE OLD STATE-HOUSE (1748) AS RESTORED IN 1881.	*Frontispiece*
JOHN WINTHROP	13
SIR RICHARD SALTONSTALL. FROM A PORTRAIT BY REMBRANDT	19
WINTHROP'S FLEET IN BOSTON HARBOR, FROM A SPOT BETWEEN BOSTON AND EAST BOSTON	39
BLAXTON'S LOT	43
THE GREAT ELM IN THE COMMON. DESTROYED IN 1876	47
COPP'S HILL AS IT APPEARED IN WINTHROP'S TIME. THE MILL WAS ERECTED IN 1632	57
TWO PAGES OF THE "NEW ENGLAND PRIMER" (SEVENTEENTH CENTURY). THIS WAS USED AS LATELY AS THE BEGINNING OF THE NINETEENTH CENTURY	71
THE FROG POND ON THE COMMON AS IT NOW APPEARS	75
INCREASE MATHER	133
THE FIRST KING'S CHAPEL (1688), SHOWING THE BEACON	166
THE FIRST CHURCH, OR "OLD BRICK." BUILT IN 1713, ON THE SITE OF THE PRESENT JOY'S BUILDING AND OCCUPIED UNTIL 1808. ITS BELL SOUNDED THE ALARM AT THE TIME OF THE "MASSACRE," MARCH 5, 1770	179
FURNITURE OF WEALTHIER TOWNSMEN IN PROVINCIAL TIMES	183
A MAP OF BOSTON IN 1722. THIS MAP, KNOWN AS THE "BONNER MAP," WAS MADE BY CAPTAIN JOHN BONNER, AND NO OLDER MAP IS KNOWN THAT GIVES THE STREETS AND PROMINENT PLACES. THE ORIGINAL IS PRESERVED AMONG THE ARCHIVES OF THE MASSACHUSETTS HISTORICAL SOCIETY	187
INTERIOR OF CHRIST CHURCH AT PRESENT (BUILT 1723)	203
BOSTON AND ITS ENVIRONS IN 1775. THIS SHOWS THE FORTIFICATIONS AROUND THE TOWN AT THE OPENING OF THE REVOLUTION; IT ALSO SERVES, SO FAR AS THE NATURAL FEATURES GO, TO ILLUSTRATE ALL STAGES OF THE EARLIER HISTORY OF THE CITY	209

	PAGE
SAMUEL ADAMS. AT THE AGE OF 45 YEARS. AFTER THE PORTRAIT BY COPLEY IN THE ART MUSEUM (1772)	223
THE SECOND FANEUIL HALL (1764)	235
INTERIOR OF THE PRESENT KING'S CHAPEL, (CORNER-STONE LAID 1749)	251
JOHN HANCOCK. AFTER THE PORTRAIT BY COPLEY IN THE MUSEUM OF FINE ARTS (1737–1793)	257
JAMES OTIS, (1725–1783) AT THE AGE OF THIRTY. AFTER A PORTRAIT BY BLACKBURN	267
THE OLD STATE-HOUSE IN 1801. THE STATE-STREET END, SHOWING THE OLD BRICK CHURCH (ON WASHINGTON STREET) BEHIND IT. BUILT IN 1748	315
GOVERNOR THOMAS HUTCHINSON, AFTER A PORTRAIT IN POSSESSION OF THE MASSACHUSETTS HISTORICAL ASSOCIATION, ONCE THE PROPERTY OF JONATHAN MAYHEW	333
THE OLD SOUTH CHURCH, IN ITS PRESENT CONDITION. (BUILT 1729)	341
JOHN HANCOCK'S HOUSE, FACING THE COMMON	401
CROSSING OF THE RAILROADS IN THE BACK-BAY REGION IN 1840	411
JOSIAH QUINCY (1772–1864). FROM THE PORTRAIT BY STUART NOW IN THE MUSEUM OF FINE ARTS	427
ADVERTISEMENT OF THE WORCESTER RAILROAD, FROM THE PAPERS OF THE DAY	450
THE REAR OF THE STATE-HOUSE, AND THE MONUMENT, SHOWING THE REMOVAL OF THE HILL. (1811–1812)	453
THE MONUMENT FROM TEMPLE AND DERNE STREETS (1811–1812)	455
MAP OF MODERN BOSTON, FROM THE LATEST AUTHORITATIVE SOURCES (1889)	463
THE PRESENT STATE-HOUSE (BUILT IN 1795)	471
THE PRIVATE LIBRARY OF GEORGE TICKNOR, UNTIL LATELY IN THE HOUSE ON THE CORNER OF PARK AND BEACON STREETS, IN WHICH LAFAYETTE WAS ENTERTAINED. (*Cir.* 1870)	477
THE PUBLIC GARDEN AND THE BUILDINGS AROUND IT IN THE "BACK BAY" REGION. THIS IS ALL ON "MADE" LAND, —THE SIDEWALK IN THE FOREGROUND MARKING THE EXTREME LIMIT OF THE ORIGINAL SHORE	481

THE STORY OF BOSTON.

I.

A DECLARATION OF INDEPENDENCE.

THE twenty-sixth of August, 1629, is an important date in the history of Boston. On that day the decision was taken that determined the settlement of the town. Had it not been for a conclusion then reached by a company of discreet gentlemen who met at Cambridge, England, the promontory called Shawmut might have been peopled by quite a different class of settlers from those who made it their first home on the American coast.

Up to that time England had done but little in the way of settling the new lands in the West, though she made great claims upon America, because, as she supposed, her sailor, Cabot, had been the first of Europeans to lay his eyes on the shores that he appropriately called *Prima Vista*. There had, it is true, been considerable exploration under Elizabeth; but it was not until the reign of James that any thing creditable and enduring was actually accomplished. On the third of November, 1620, the latter sovereign formed a body corporate known as "The Council for New England," the full name of which was "The Council Established at Plymouth, in the County of Devon, for the Planting, Ruling, Ordering, and Governing of New England in America," and it was upon its charter that most of the New England grants were based. The act of incorporation was essentially the giving of new and enlarged privileges to a body established in 1606 by the same king, which was known as "The Northern Colony of Virginia."

The Council for New England was an important company, comprising forty persons, most of them men of distinction, and some of them peers of the highest rank.[*] In March, 1628, it made a grant to another company of the territory in which Boston lies, known as "the Massachewset." The name had been conferred upon it by Captain John Smith, the explorer of Virginia, who considered it "the paradise of all those parts." There is some mystery about the granting of this charter, and there was indefiniteness about the extent of the territory conveyed; but without stopping to have all matters settled, the persons interested, who really formed a great land company, sent out a small colony under command of John Endicott, one of their number, which reached Salem, then called Naumkeag, in September, 1628, and that place became the first town in the colony.

[*] The facts about the Council for New England are given in detail by Charles Deane, LL.D., in Winsor's "Narrative and Critical History of America," vol. iii., pp. 295, 320, etc.

When the council for New England sold the territory just mentioned it gave the buyers no powers of government (though it had received rights for "ordering and governing"), and it became necessary to obtain them from the king, who at that time was Charles the First. By whatever means, a charter was obtained from him, and it was duly signed and sealed March 4, 1629. The territory was then defined as extending from three miles north of the Merrimac River to three miles south of the Charles River, and from the Atlantic Ocean to "the South Sea," as the Pacific was called. This seems an immense territory, but it did not appear so vast to the grantors as it does to us, because it was limited in two important particulars. In the first place, it was generally supposed that our continent was an island, the distance across which was not great[*]; and, in the second place, all territory that might prove to be occupied by any Christian state was excluded from the grant. The natives reported to John Smith that the river of Massachusetts extended "many days' journey into the entrails of that country," and in 1619, a bold explorer dreamed of getting through to the Indies by way of the Charles River, or the Mystic, which seems marvellously strange to us who know those little streams!

The persons interested in the Massachusetts wished to fish or to trade with the natives, and to

[*] The only exception to this belief known to the present writer is found in the "Records of the council for New England," edited by Charles Deane, LL.D., and published in the proceedings of the American Antiquarian Society for 1867. On page 124 it is said that the distance "from sea to sea is near about three thousand miles."

establish colonies for those purposes; but it was not long before the purposes changed. Many who were restive under the condition of religious and political affairs in England, who were discouraged at the prospect of ever accomplishing any thing in the way of certain reforms that they felt to be all-important, conceived the project of making a colony for religion under the purchase. Ferdinando Gorges,[*] in his book "America Painted to the Life," says that there were several kinds of these people, who did not agree among themselves; that some of the more discreet among them made plans to settle in New England, and that "in a very short time numbers of people of all sorts flocked thither in heaps"; but this anticipates our story.

The charter of Charles the First constituted the original purchasers, and some score of others whom they had admitted to their company, a political body corporate with the name "The Governor and Company of the Massachusetts Bay in New England," and gave them authority to enact laws and carry them out, provided they made none opposed to those of England. By the end of May arrangements had been made to send out a second company of settlers, under the general direction of the Reverend Francis Higginson. Five ships sailed from the Isle of Wight in that month, and reached Salem by the end of June; but our interest is not with them. The body corporate provided by the charter was far from complete in its political powers, though the

---

[*] Quoted by Hutchinson, in his "History of Massachusetts," chapter i.

governor, the deputy-governor, and the eighteen "assistants," which it mentioned, were authorized to make laws, and an annual gathering was provided for, in which all the " freemen " of the colony were to be brought together as " The Great and General Court."

The interest in the movement to which Gorges referred continued in England, and was destined to have a greater influence upon American affairs than he or any one else dreamed. Among the persons connected with it were several gentlemen of "figure and estate," as the old form of speech expresses it, who thought that there might be an opportunity in the distant land to manage affairs both of church and state in accordance with their own views. They became alarmed as they saw some of the principal liberal speakers in parliament committed to the Tower and to other prisons, and though they had hoped long, they at last gave up all expectation of being able to bring about a political and religious reformation in the father-land. To one of these, Matthew Cradock, who was governor of the Massachusetts company, a bold inspiration was suggested. It was no less than this: that the charter and the company itself might both be removed to the New World.*

In the history of America we find that at one time and another certain individual men seem to

* " He did not say, what he must have been clearly understood to mean, that in this way the king would have some difficulty in laying his hand upon the governor." " History of England, from the Accession of James I. to the Outbreak of the Civil War," by Samuel R. Gardiner, LL.D., vol. vii , p. 156.

preside over the destinies of the communities in which they live, and this is remarkably true in the history of Boston. Mr. Cradock appears now merely to make a suggestion, and it is another man who rises to prominence first, as the presiding genius of the settlement of our promontory. The characteristics and the very name of John Winthrop were strongly stamped upon much of the expression of life in the town during the early years of its existence, and their influence has not yet been lost. The meetings of the company had been held in London, but no particular place was mentioned in the charter, and they could be, and actually were at times, held elsewhere.

Perhaps this removal had been thought of before. In the year 1644, at a time when there was a good deal of political discussion in Boston, Mr. Winthrop wrote a formal "Discourse on Government," which has been printed.* In it he says that when the charter was at first drawn, it was the intention to "keep the chief government in the hands of the company residing in England," as was the case in the charter for Virginia, but that a clause to that effect was stricken out, "with much difficulty," and permission given to establish a government in America. Mr. Winthrop does not make it clear, however, that any thing more was intended than that such rights as had been given to Endicott might be

---

* In the following pages much use will be made of the "Life and Letters of John Winthrop," in which (ii., 443) this "Discourse," which came to light in 1860, among a mass of papers discovered in an old family residence at New London, Conn., will be found.

delegated to those who should go across the ocean, and that was quite different from the authority which he and his associates exercised in Boston after the actual transfer of the charter. As for the meetings, the gentlemen were free to come together, if they thought best, on a ship in the Thames, for all that the charter said; and if perchance that ship were to weigh anchor, and they should find themselves sailing away towards America, ought the meeting be stopped? If the proceedings should of right be stopped, how far might the vessel sail without making them illegal? Mr. Cradock was sure that there was room for a little profitable study in questions like these, and accordingly he made his momentous proposal, at a meeting held in London in July, that the charter and the government should be transferred to America, those members of the company being placed in its offices who should be willing to "inhabit and continue there" with their families.

Nothing in so grave a matter was to be done in haste and it was decided that before the next meeting, which was to be held on the twenty-eighth of August, the members should write out their views, both in favor of the proposition and against it, and they were desired "to carry this business secretly, that the same be not divulged," because, as they appear to have very well understood, taking a charter across seas was something very like setting up an independent government and placing it so remote from the king and parliament that they would find it difficult to interfere with it. There was, in fact, no reason for keeping the plan secret except this: that the scheme involved independence of king and parliament. In an address delivered on the completion of the second century from the settlement of Boston, Josiah Quincy, then president of Harvard College, declared that the idea of independence of the parent state was first conceived by Winthrop and Dudley and Saltonstall and their associates; that they, by their act in bringing the charter over the sea, indicated a settled purpose to obtain independence, and made as efficient a declaration of that purpose as was possible under their circumstances. They actually obtained, Mr. Quincy asserted, "an effectual independence under a nominal subjection." The historian, William Gordon, says of their motives (vol. i., page 42): "They meant to be independent of English parliaments."

Can we imagine the thought and conferences that occupied the four weeks after this meeting? These were earnest men, and though on the face of the records the matter seems to be new, there is reason to suspect, as has been remarked, that they had long held the secret intention of making such a transfer as was now broached. However, they took counsel of one another, and especially of a Mr. John White of their number, a man learned in the law, and after having satisfied themselves that it would be legal to make the transfer, they inquired who were willing to go to New England to "inhabit and continue there." Mr. Cradock had intimated that there were persons of worth and quality ready for the move. Now they appear.

On the twenty-sixth of August—two days before the meeting that was to settle the matter,—twelve men held the important conference to which reference has been made. Little did they foresee the importance of their unpretentious gathering. Perhaps they met in the room of Mr. John Winthrop's son, Forth, in Emanuel College. They failed to record the place, and we know only that it was in Cambridge. How long the men who met on that memorable day debated the subject before them we are not informed. We are certain, however, that " upon due consideration," having weighed the greatness of the work and the consequences of their action, they all agreed, and sincerely and freely promised and bound themselves one to the other, to " pass the seas (under God's protection), to inhabit and continue in New England," provided that the whole government and the charter should be legally transferred to remain there also.[*]

When the company met two days later, it was announced that the business to be attended to was to give answer to the gentlemen who had signed this agreement. There was no haste in this case.

[*] With regard to the transfer, Mr. Bancroft writes in his ninth chapter: "The lawfulness was at the time not questioned by the privy council ; at a later day was expressly affirmed by Sawyer, the attorney-general ; and in 1677 the chief-justices Rainsford and North still described the ' charter as making the adventurers a corporation upon the place.' " Dr. Ellis says that the imputation that the transfer was made illegally, in daring contempt of authority, and that the " company surreptitiously stole away from England with the patent to set up an unlicensed authority on the soil of New England," has been " satisfactorily set aside."—" The Puritan Age and Rule," p. 47.

Two committees were appointed to prepare arguments on the subject, the one for and the other against making the transfer. Accordingly the following morning the committees met. It was at the early hour of seven. They weighed each other's arguments—they turned them over and over again. Finally they discussed the points thoroughly before the whole company, and then a vote was called for. As many as desired to have the charter and the government of the plantation removed to America were asked to hold up their hands. Those who were opposed were likewise asked to do the same, and it appearing that it was the general consent that the removal should take place, it was formally decided that an order for the transfer should be drawn up. This, President Quincy calls " the first and original declaration of independence."

II.

WINTHROP AND HIS COMPANIONS.

OF the twelve men who thus boldly declared their independence, and expressed their willingness to become pilgrims, the first to fix our attention now, as we look at the list under the light of subsequent history, is Mr. John Winthrop. Probably his name would have attracted us if we had examined the list in the year 1630, for the man who bore it was evidently a person of no mean importance. He was a native of the little hamlet of Groton in Suffolk, a few miles west from Ipswich, a place so insignificant that it has faded from our maps, and its very name is dropped from the great gazetteers of our day. It is of importance to us in connection with the annals of Boston and of America, however, and will always be remembered as having given its name to other places in the New World.

John Winthrop was a late comer in the group of men interested in this scheme for colonization. His name does not occur in the records of the Governor and Company of the Massachusetts Bay until the meeting after that of August twenty-sixth, and we do not even know that he was actually present at any meeting until October, when he was appointed to make arrangements of a business nature for those who intended to emigrate. Though he comes thus suddenly into prominence, the course of his life, laid before us in his "Life and Letters," shows that he had been much engaged both in considerations of the progress of New England and old England. He felt (to draw from a carefully written paper known as "General Considerations for the Plantation of New England," which was circulated among some of the friends of the enterprise) that he had fallen upon disastrous times ; that fountains of learning in his native country were corrupted ; that all arts and trades were carried on in such deceitful and unrighteous ways that it was wellnigh impossible for a good man to live by any of them ; that the land was weary of her inhabitants ; that man had become of less importance than beasts, children, who ought to have been considered blessings, being counted the greatest burdens ; that the kingdom of antichrist was increasing ; that, in brief, the Lord had begun to frown upon England and to cut its inhabitants short. It seemed to Mr. John Winthrop that America was intended by Providence to be a place of refuge for the many who were to be saved out of the general calamity which seemed imminent, and that emigration was a work of God for the good of the church, which had no place left to fly into but the wilderness. The American continent was supposed to be the home of the arch-fiend and his angels, and a generation later Michael Wigglesworth, the typical Puritan poet, wrote in "God's Controversy with New England," that the region was

JOHN WINTHROP.

> " A waste and howling wilderness,
>   Where none inhabited,
>   But hellish fiends and brutish men
>   That devils worshipped.
> This region was in darkness placed,
>   Far off from heaven's light,
>   Amidst the shadows of grim death
>   And of eternal night.'

Mr. Winthrop did not fail to discuss the other side of the question in his "General Considerations"; probably that he might have a reply to give those who should differ from him in opinion. If it were said that Englishmen had no right to enter upon a land that had so long been occupied by others, he replied that the natives enclosed no land, and that if sufficient for their use were left to them, the remainder might lawfully be taken; that there were in fact but few of the natives left, since a great plague had overtaken them, and that those who were living would learn so much from Englishmen as to be able to obtain more benefit from what might be left them than they then did from the whole land. Was it urged that if good people were to leave England it would be more open to the judgments feared than it was before; he replied that the departing of the good people would only foreshadow and not bring on the evil, and might cause the remnant to repent; that the emigrants would do more good in the new land than at home; and that the barbarians might through them receive the gospel, the preaching of which had been one of the prominent purposes of every scheme of colonization that had been proposed since the days of Columbus and the

Cabots. The colony at Salem had already placed on its official seal an Indian erect holding an arrow in its right hand with the Macedonian cry, "Come over and help us!" indicative of its intentions in respect to the spiritual welfare of the savages.

John Winthrop was at the time forty-two years of age. His lot had been cast among men who had been associated with such statesmen and scholars as Bacon and Essex and Cecil, accustomed to discuss the highest matters of state. He was born the year that his country was threatened by the great Armada from Spain, and he had lived through the last part of the reign of Elizabeth, the whole of that of James the First, and the first years of King Charles. The discussions of vital topics of statecraft and theology were as familiar to him as household words. He was eleven years old when Spenser died, and doubtless he was acquainted with the almost puritanic allegory of that most poetical of poets. Doubtless, too, he was familiar with the "Divine Emblems" of Francis Quarles; perhaps he knew of the quiet life of saintly George Herbert, then hidden at Bemerton; and we may imagine that he had seen something of the brilliant promise of the youthful Milton, who had lately taken his bachelor's degree at Cambridge.

In the "History of the English People," by Green, and in the history of our literature, by Taine, we become acquainted with the most powerful influence upon the development of the English character at this time. In his history, Mr. Green says: "The small Geneva Bibles carried the Scripture into every home, and wove it into the life of every English family"; and he shows that the influence of this book was great also upon the intellectual development of the people, "that the mass of picturesque allusions and illustrations which we borrow from a thousand books, our fathers were forced to borrow from one," for, as he adds, " the Bible was as yet the one book that was familiar to every Englishman, and everywhere its words, as they fell on ears which custom had not deadened to their force and beauty, kindled a startling enthusiasm." Among the circle to which John Winthrop belonged the Bible was still the one great book, and as we consider this fact we shall, as Mr. Green says, " better understand the strange mosaic of biblical words and phrases which colored English talk two hundred years ago." The Geneva version was the one that the people still carried, but the translation known as " King James's" had appeared but a score of years previous to the time of the Boston emigration, and the fact that it was in progress, and finally that it had been completed, must have added to the interest in the volume.

The letters of Winthrop present us the picture of a loving husband and father, a careful man of affairs, a far-seeing statesman, and a most devout man of religion. He addresses the most affectionate messages to his " good wife," to whom he often writes in terms like these : " Yet I must kiss my sweet wife *; and so,

---

* It is Winthrop's third wife, Margaret Tindal, who is thus addressed. In her, according to the sympathetic historian Gardiner, " he found his mate ; she it was who made him what he now became. From the day that his faith was plighted to her, . . . he learned to step boldly out amongst his equals, to take his share in the world's

with my blessings to our children, and salutation to all our friends, I commend thee to the grace and blessing of the Lord." Every letter breathes the sweet sentiments of a faithful affection, as well as a deep religious spirit.

John Winthrop had among the acquaintances whose counsel he prized one Robert Ryece, a Suffolk antiquary, and to him he submitted the "General Considerations." Perhaps the arguments in it for and against the New England enterprise were the very ones that the Massachusetts company considered at its meetings. An interesting document has been preserved in which Mr. Ryece goes carefully over the ground these arguments present, writing like the conservative that he was. While guarding his friend against specious inductions, Mr. Ryece advises him, that in case affairs had gone so far that without his presence the chief undertakers of the plantation, who were men " of great goodness, quality, and wisdom," would in no way stir in the business without him, and if sundry divines of great understanding and good judgment had answered all impediments and objections which his Suffolk friends were not aware of, there seemed to him no reason, and less conscience, that he should by holding back overthrow a work of so eminent consideration and consequence ; " and, therefore," says Mr. Ryece, " your friends do now rather encourage you to

work. . . . In his letters of this period there is nothing to distinguish him from any other God-fearing Puritan of the time, excepting the almost feminine tenderness and sensitiveness of his disposition."
—" History of England," vol. vii., p. 154.

proceed, and do entreat the Almighty Lord of Hosts to go with you, to bless and govern you in all your ways."

Winthrop seems to have consulted Mr. Ryece a second time, for that gentleman writes again, this time just two weeks before the Cambridge meeting, urging his friend to leave the proposed business to younger men; and exclaiming: " How hard will it be for one brought up among books and learned men to live in a barbarous place, where is no learning and less civility," or, as we should say, civilization. " The pipe goeth sweet," he reminds Winthrop, " till the bird be in the net; many beautiful hopes are set before your eyes to allure you to danger. If in your youth you had been acquainted with navigation, you might have promised yourself more hope in this long voyage; but for one of your years to undertake so large a task is seldom seen but to miscarry. To adventure your whole family upon so manifest uncertainties standeth not with your wisdom and long experience. . . . I pray you pardon my boldness, that had rather err in what I think, than be silent in that I should speak."

Thus was the leading spirit in this great emigration warned and entreated by all considerations of prudence, and by reflections upon the advantages that might accrue to the church and the community if he would but remain at home; but arguments addressed to his prudence, and to his love for his wife and children, who might be left alone and unprovided-for in a strange land, far from all hope of receiving help; to his love of study, and to his

SIR RICHARD SALTONSTALL. FROM A PORTRAIT BY REMBRANT.

habits, adjusted to the conveniences of civilization, failed. In spite of every argument, John Winthrop, a hero in a heroic age, persisted in carrying out the design which Providence and his worthy associates in the company had, as he fully believed, called him to. Margaret Winthrop, the " dear wife," was also equal to the occasion, and wrote constantly to her husband words of cheer and sympathy, assuring him that the good Lord would certainly " bless us in our intended purpose."

The other members of the group of twelve require less attention at our hands, though they too were worthy men all, and doubtless they and their wives and advisers had gone through the same discussion that Mr. Winthrop so carefully followed. Sir Richard Saltonstall, whose name heads the list, was very largely interested in the enterprise. He was descended from a former lord mayor of London, and had for grandson a governor of Connecticut, and was the honored ancestor of many bearing the same name in Boston to-day. He is remembered as having left in his will a bequest to Harvard College, and he was the largest contributor to the company's funds. Thomas Dudley, also descended from ancestors honored in English history, and chosen into public office every year of his life in the new land (being for four years governor and often deputy-governor), was one of the older members of the emigrant group. John Nowell was related to the dean of St. Paul's in the reign of Elizabeth, was sometime ruling elder in the church at Charlestown, and again one of the magistrates at Boston. William Vassall bore a name afterwards honored among the colonists, but appears to have differed somewhat in religious matters from the majority at Boston, on which account he returned to England, though he came back again and lived a while at Scituate, in Plymouth colony. He made a fortune in Jamaica, when it was conquered by Penn and Venables, in the time of Cromwell. William Pynchon, a man of learning and piety, became the founder, first of Roxbury and then of Springfield, his family being still honored in Massachusetts. John Humfrey was one of the earliest persons interested in the company. He is described as a godly man of special parts, of learning and activity. He was chosen deputy-governor at first, but his departure from England was delayed until 1632, when he came over with his wife, Lady Susan, daughter of the Earl of Lincoln. He had been familiar with the conversation of patriotic nobles in the home of his father-in-law, who was the head of the now ducal house of Newcastle. Isaac Johnson was the man of largest estate among the group. He also was a son-in-law of the Earl of Lincoln. He rejoiced at the establishment of the colony, and considered his life well spent in its service. Governor Hutchinson calls him "the idol of Boston," and says that the people, when they died, ordered their bodies laid to rest around his in the grounds adjoining King's Chapel.* His wife is remembered as Arbella, after whom one of the vessels in which the party sailed for America was named. The other men of the Cambridge meet-

* This current fancy is, it must be added, disbelieved by careful investigators.

ing were Thomas Sharp, who did not remain long in New England, Michael West, Killam Browne, and William Colbron. Of them all it has been truly said that they were English country gentlemen of no inconsiderable fortunes, and of enlarged understandings, (measured by the standards of their time,) improved by collegiate education. They were most of them men who did not venture to America for the purpose of increasing their worldly goods, for they were too comfortable at home to make such an enterprise attractive to them.

III.

GETTING READY FOR A VOYAGE.

JOHN WINTHROP consulted his friends, but he did not forget his immediate family. That his wife sympathized fully in what he was about to do we already know. A few days before the Cambridge meeting John Winthrop, junior, wrote to his father that he, too, had given thought to the matter of "the business for New England," that he confidently believed it was "of the Lord"; and that he had seen so much of the vanity of the world that he esteemed no more the diversities of countries than as so many inns, whereof the traveller that hath lodged in the best or the worst findeth no difference when he cometh to his journey's end; and he called that his country where he could most glorify God and enjoy the presence of his dearest friends.* He mentions certain "Conclusions" sent to him by his father, which, he said, he had shown to his uncle and aunt, and reported that they liked them well; as for himself, he thought them unanswerable.

* John Winthrop, junior, had been an extensive traveller. He entered the naval service in 1627, going with the Duke of Buckingham to the relief of Rochelle; and he took a tour of Europe in 1628, in which he was absent more than a year, visiting Leghorn, Venice, Padua, Amsterdam, and many places of less importance.

These Conclusions of the elder Winthrop are in two parts, the first being general, relating to the plantation, and the second particular, relating specially to the writer's own case. It was probably the latter portion which was submitted to the members of the family circle. In it Mr. Winthrop says that "divers of the chief undertakers" of the plantation would not go to America without him; that his wife and such of his children as were come to years of discretion were voluntarily disposed to the same course, and that most of his friends consented to the change. We see that John Winthrop was thus fully settled in his mind. He entertained no doubts about his action; he was, as he believed, "called of the Lord," and of the company. Another incentive was to be added.

Mr. Matthew Cradock found that his departure was impracticable, and his name does not appear among those who had agreed to go, though he was one of the chief supporters of the enterprise. He therefore resigned his office, and the company was called together in October, only five days after Mr. Winthrop's first attendance at the meetings, to choose a new governor. The gentlemen spoken of for the office were Saltonstall, Johnson, Winthrop, and Humfrey. After serious deliberation it was "conceived to be for the especial good and advancement of their affairs" that Mr. Winthrop should take the chief office. It is said in the records that "extraordinary great commendations" had been received of him, both for his "integrity and sufficiency, as being one every way well-fitted and accomplished for the place of governor," and accordingly he was chosen with full consent, and immediately took the prescribed oath of office.

This was an unlooked-for turn in affairs, and the new governor wrote to his wife that he was called to a further trust in the business of the plantation than he either expected or found himself fitted for; but he added that he was cheerful and in health. Referring to the same matter a few years later, he said that there were other gentlemen of more ability and far greater adaptedness for the position than he; but his associates differed with him, and he modestly accepted their verdict. A few days were allowed for some necessary work, and then the governor returned to Groton for a brief visit to his wife; but even there his time was largely occupied with matters connected with the momentous step that he was about to take, and with efforts that he thought necessary to make to engage other suitable persons to go to New England with him.

The few days passed with his family were preliminary to still more severe labors in preparation. A circular-letter was addressed from London on the twenty-seventh of October, to sundry divines of the Puritan faith, inviting them to convene on the ninth of the following month for the purpose of selecting "able and sufficient ministers to join in the work" of colonization.* Plans were also made to provide a godly and able surgeon to go to New England that spring. At about this time there was a notable

* This letter is found in the "Life and Letters of John Winthrop," vol. i., p. 354.

change in the personality of the company. Those who had wished to have an interest in a business concern seem now to have desired to withdraw, and their places were taken by men of the serious and religious sort—the more discreet persons mentioned by Gorges.

The ninth of November came and passed, and apparently the proposed conference of ministers took place; at any rate, at a meeting of the company, held on the twenty-fifth of that month, two earnest Puritan divines, Mr. Joseph Archer and Mr. Philip Nye, were received as freemen, and Mr. Nathaniel Ward * was recommended for admission. Meantime Winthrop was writing to his good wife that he was pressed by "much business"; that "divers great persons" had been questioned, but the cause was yet uncertain; that official work came fast upon him, and he could set no time for his return to Groton; but he blessed God for giving him a wife who was a help and encouragement in his work, "wherein so many wives are so great an hindrance" to their husbands.

While the multiplied cares of the preparation were upon him, Mr. Winthrop was called to give advice to his sister-in-law, Priscilla Fones, about the delicate attentions she was receiving from the Rev. Henry

---

* This Mr. Ward afterwards compiled a code of laws for the colony, called the "Body of Liberties"; he is best known, however, as author of "The Simple Cobbler of Agawam," a quaint and pedantic treatise on the license that he professed to find in New England. He did not come over until 1634, being finally instigated by a sentence of excommunication pronounced upon him by Laud, Bishop of London.

Painter, of Exeter, afterwards a member of the celebrated Westminister Assembly of divines; and to his son Forth, who wished to marry Ursula, "my aunt Fones, her daughter." On the seventeenth of November widow Priscilla wrote that in her suitor she saw the traits that she chiefly aimed at in a husband, "grace and godliness, with gifts suitable to his calling," though in outward estate he came short of any that had yet been moved to her; but that in spite of all his virtues, she desired to hear no more of the suit, though all her friends persuaded her that it would be best for her to change her estate. The reverend man's importunity and "pains in coming so far" bred such distraction of mind in her that she knew not what to do, and she confessed that she was very fearful about changing her condition.

On the same day Fones Winthrop wrote to his father that he used his pen because letters could not blush, and that bashfulness would seal up his mouth in silence were he to attempt to speak on the tender topic. He plainly entertained no doubts about changing his condition, but expressed himself as not wishing to undertake any enterprise of moment without his father's knowledge, consent, and license, though he did desire to be blessed in time by the "holy ordinance of marriage" with his fair cousin. Alas for the hopes of poor Ursula and her loving cousin Forth, he died not many months later, and she was left almost a widow. The course of the loves of Priscilla and Henry seems to have run smooth, for, after a little diplomacy, they were duly married.

A week later Mr. Winthrop writes to his wife that the Rev. John Cotton, of Boston, might be expected at Groton on "Thursday or Friday," and that she ought to get him to stay a night if she could. At the Christmas-tide Winthrop was absent from London, presumably spending the time with his household at Groton; though he was again in the capital hard at work by the middle of January, but enjoying "fowls, puddings, etc.," that his good wife had sent to him. All his thoughts were turned towards the great venture, the time for which was fast approaching.

Winthrop promises his wife to leave fifteen hundred pounds with his friends for her support until she should be able to follow him to the New World, —an ample sum, surely, if we take into consideration the greater value of money at the time. John Winthrop, junior, who had been as we know a great traveller, and had an ingenious mind, writes to his father at this time about "a rude model" of a windmill that he had invented, which he thought might be "applied to many laborious uses, as any kind of mills, corn-mills, saw-mills, etc.," and he desired that New England should reap the benefit, "for whose sake," indeed, he said, "it was invented. *Et soli Deo gloria.*"

The letters from husband to wife become more and more tender as the moment for separation gets nearer; but in the midst of all the pathos of parting comes an intimation that good sister Priscilla hath written so earnestly to the reverend suitor not to trouble her more that she fears he will take her in earnest and not appear again, for which cause the grave president of the colony of Massachusetts Bay is besought to "send him word to come as soon as he can," for the coy widow would speak with him. The glimpses of courtship that we catch in the hurry of preparations for the serious enterprise of another sort, and among the tender and pathetic words passing from husband and wife, give a dash of humanity to the picture that is delightful to be observed in the life of the hero and the heroine of the tale of these stern Puritan pioneers.

February opens, and Winthrop says to Margaret: "My sweet wife, thy love is such to me, and so great is the bond between us, that I should neglect all others to hold correspondency of letters with thee. . . . I purpose, if God will, to be with thee upon Thursday come se'nnight, and then I must take my farewell of thee for a summer's day and a winter's day. The Lord our God will, I hope, send us a happy meeting again in his good time. . . . I wrote to Mr. P."

A few days later he writes: "My sweet wife, I wrote to thee yesterday, and this day our company hath spent in prayer and fasting, and the Lord hath been pleased to assist us graciously; blessed be his name; I doubt not but thou and all our family shall have part in the answer of our prayers. This evening, about ten of the clock, Mr. Painter came to me: he intends to be at Groton on Tuesday next." We may suppose that the matter between " Mr. P." and Priscilla was settled " on Tuesday."

The last week in February was the time that John

Winthrop made his final visit to Groton. Soon after, he went from London to Southampton, where he took ship for America on the twenty-second of March; but there were tedious detentions, owing to adverse winds, and it was not until April 8th that they weighed anchor and the long voyage actually began. All this time there was as brisk a correspondence between husband and wife as the circumstances admitted, and in one of the latest letters of the husband, written from aboard the *Arbella* off Cowes, March 28, 1630, among loving messages for many friends and relatives, there occurs this sentence: "Mondays and Fridays at five of the clock at night we shall meet in spirit till we meet in person." "And now, my sweet soul," he adds, "I must once again take my last farewell of thee in old England. It goeth very near my heart to leave thee. . . . Thine wheresoever, Jo: Winthrop."

While the ships were detained by adverse winds, the leaders of the company prepared a document which they left behind to be printed and distributed, for the removal of suspicions and misconstructions of their intentions. In this noble and pathetic paper we have the fundamental thoughts by which all their course was to be directed, by which it had already been guided. Addressing "the rest of their brethren in and of the Church of England," they express a suspicion that there may be among them some wanting in "tenderness of affection" towards them, or not having clear enough intelligence of their course to be able to appreciate their peculiar way, and to these they attempt to explain their course.

While devotedly attached to the church of their fathers, they evidently made a distinction between those traits in it which they conceived to be fundamental, and those that were of secondary importance, clinging to the one class and having no sympathy whatever with the other.*

Evidently the members of Winthrop's band felt much as those who went with Francis Higginson felt, when they united with him in saying they went to the New World not as "Separatists from the Church of England," though they owned that they could but separate themselves from the corruptions in it; in order that they might "practice the positive part of the Church reformation, and to propagate the Gospel in America." John Winthrop could truly write: "We esteem it our honor to call the Church of England our dear mother; and cannot part from our native country, where she specially resideth, without much sadness of heart and many tears in our eyes." He had been for too many years an humble and faithful worshipper in the parish church at Groton to renounce the communion of his fathers, and the very next year he refused to gratify Roger Williams, who wished the men of Boston to make a public declaration of repentance for having had communion with the churches of England. Winthrop not only never repented of this, but he doubtless gloried in it. The gentlemen of the Massachusetts colony were so careful in this respect that when the Rev. Ralph Smith desired to go to

* On this point see "The Puritan Age and Rule in the Colony of the Massachusetts Bay," by George E. Ellis, D.D., chap. ii., especially p. 54.

Salem with Higginson, he was only permitted to do so upon giving an agreement in writing not to preach in public or in private without the governor's permission, because there was suspicion that he was a "Separatist"; whereby, it appears, says the historian Hubbard, "how apprehensive the first founders of the Massachusetts were of any that might become an occasion of disturbance" on this ground.*

While the ships of the expedition were anchored off Cowes, the governor began a diary that became the mine from which the early history of Massachusetts has been dug. He dated the first entry "Easter Monday, March 29, 1629–30." This journal was continued up to a short time before its author's death, and though there are many gaps which were intended to be filled when an opportunity of leisure arrived, it is very full, and deeply interesting.

Eleven or twelve vessels of different sizes were provided to transport the company, among which were the *Arbella*, named in honor of Mrs. Johnson, and the *Mayflower*, which had carried the Pilgrims to Plymouth ten years before. Only four of these were ready to sail at the appointed time. The *Arbella* was one, and on its deck, on the sixth of April, Mr. Cradock said his last farewell to his successor in office, and from its "steerage" the captain fired three shots "for a farewell," before the party steered out into the broad Atlantic, not to cast anchor again until the seventy-sixth day, Saturday, the twelfth of June.

* Mr. Smith verified these suspicions. He went to Plymouth and "exercised his gifts," but even the Separatists there were forced to ask him to "lay down his ministry," and he returned to Massachusetts to give trouble.

IV.

THE FOUNDING OF BOSTON.

THE voyage to America was no pleasure excursion. We may well imagine the serious occupations of the passengers in the several vessels. It was a long time before such trips were taken with regularity and without trepidation. The laws of ocean navigation were not well understood; international law even was in its infancy, (Hugo Grotius had, in fact, laid its foundations but five years before this); pirates like Sir Francis Drake were universally honored; and vessels sailing on the broad ocean as those of Winthrop's fleet sailed were open to attack from any adventurous captain, carrying a different flag, who thought himself stronger than they.

The ten dreary weeks of the voyage of Winthrop were marked by Sundays sacred to the completest rest and the most earnest devotional services; and by "frequent and constant religious exercises of catechism, prayer and preaching, on Sundays and week-days," which Dr. Ellis thinks must have tried the patience of the sailors and servants as much as they "fed the joys of piety in the consecrated hearts of the exiles."*

---

* The "Puritan Age and Rule," p. 56.

Mr. Winthrop was wont to exercise himself in "prophesying," as sermonizing was then called, and he has left a discourse entitled " A Model of Christian Charity," which is probably a record of some of his efforts on board the *Arbella*. In this sermon there was an elaborate discussion of Christian charity, marked by the tender traits which we have observed in its author's correspondence, followed by careful deductions as to the mode of living by which its teachings were to be made the foundation of a commonwealth that should " be a praise and a glory," and not " open the mouths of enemies to speak evil of the ways of God, and all professors for God's sake." " We must be willing," he said, " to abridge ourselves of our superfluities, for the supply of other's necessities ; we must uphold a familiar commerce together in all meekness, gentleness, patience, and liberality ; we must delight in each other, make other's condition our own, rejoice together, mourn together, labor and suffer together, always having before our eyes our commission and community in the work."

There were dangers from violent storms, which might destroy greater vessels than theirs ; and on one Lord's Day we read in Winthrop's diary that the tempest continued all the day, " and the sea raged and tossed exceedingly ; yet, through God's mercy, we were very comfortable, and few or none sick, but had opportunity to keep the Sabbath, and Mr. Phillips preached twice that day." The greatest alarm overtook the *Arbella* soon after they left Yarmouth, where they had been told that ten sail of

"Dunkirkers"* were awaiting their coming. On a certain morning eight ships were seen astern, having more wind than the Winthrop fleet, and coming up apace. The gun-room and gun-deck of the *Arbella* were cleared, all hammocks were taken down, ordnance was loaded, powder-chests were made ready, twenty-five landmen were quartered among the seamen, appointed for muskets, and duly written down for their respective quarters. The race continued until noon came, and the pursuers were still gaining. Preparation was then made for a fight; cabins that stood in the way of managing the guns were taken hastily down; beds, and all other kinds of inflammable articles that were likely to take fire, were cast into the sea; the long-boats were heaved out; the Lady Arbella and the other women and the children were removed to the lower deck for safety; and the men were armed with muskets and other weapons and with instruments for fire-works. Then, for an experiment, the captain (Peter Milborne) "shot a ball of wild-fire, fastened to an arrow, out of a cross-bow, which burnt in the water a good time." All things being thus fitted," says Winthrop, "we went to prayer upon the upper deck," where they might watch as well as pray, doubtless, for these heroes never forgot that they needed not only to trust in God, but also to keep their powder dry. This was the traditional advice of Oliver Cromwell, though given some years later.

* "England was at war with Spain at the time; and Spanish cruisers seem to have been swarming about Dunkirk and other ports of the Spanish Netherlands."—"Life and Letters of John Winthrop," vol. ii., p. 14.

The approaching ships were eight against four, and the emigrants thought that the moments were serious ; but not a woman or a child or a man showed fear, for, as Winthrop writes, their confidence was in the Lord of Hosts, " and the courage of our captain and his care and diligence did much encourage us." It was about one o'clock in the afternoon when the captain found the strangers were within a league of him, and not wishing that the issue should come in the night, he decided to show that he had no fear. He therefore tacked about and stood to meet the eight vessels, when, to the great joy of all, they were perceived to be friends. " Every ship, as they met, saluted each other, and the musketeers discharged their small shot," and the dread and danger was turned into " mirth and friendly entertainment."

Thus the days passed, in prayers for blessings to come, in thankfulness for blessings received and dangers passed, in careful instructions and encouragement, in hope for and thoughtful discussion of the country they were going to and the biblical commonwealth they expected to found. Every changing phase of nature was carefully noticed ; and Mr. Winthrop sets down in his journal some of the phenomena that he observed, as, for example, that when they were at a distance of two hundred leagues from land, they encountered fowls flying and swimming ; that the sun did not give so much heat as in England ; that cold weather came with the winds from whatsoever direction they blew ; that the new moon, when it first appeared, was smaller than in England ; and that the pole star was much beneath what it was in England. They were not tedious days, we may suppose, though we may be sure that the adventurers were not sorry when at last, on the seventy-second day, " there came a smell of the shore, like the smell of a garden," and when, four days later, they were able to drop anchor in the harbor of Salem.

Firing off two pieces of ordnance, they sent a skiff to the ship of William Peirce of London, which they saw, and he came on board, and afterwards returned to bring Governor Endicott to them. There was a friendly welcome to the new-comers, and they were invited to go ashore, where the assistants and some other gentlemen and the women supped on a " good venison pasty and good beer." At night most of them returned to the ship, though the women, " like Noah's dove, finding sure footing on the firm land, returned no more to their ark floating on the unstable waves." The more common people on board took the occasion to go ashore on the other side of the harbor towards Cape Ann, where they had as good a feast on fresh strawberries as the gentlefolk had on their pasty and beer. The following day Governor Winthrop first saw the natives of the land, for Masconomo, sagamore of the Agawam, came on board and spent the day, bidding the party a cheerful welcome to the land from which the tribes of his fathers were fast fading away. Almost the first news received on landing was that there had been a general conspiracy among the natives a few months previous looking to the extirpation of all the white faces.

Though but two ships of the fleet had then arrived

at Salem, there was a formal "landing," and proper salutes were fired in honor of the governor and his party. The prospect was dismal for Winthrop. Higginson was wasting under a hectic fever; eighty of those who had come with him had died during the winter; many others were sick and weak; the supplies were almost exhausted, and the remnant of the emigrants, threatened by famine, now thronged about the new arrivals begging for bread. No wonder that we read that the place pleased Winthrop not, though the valiant and enthusiastic Captain John Smith had said of it: "Of all the parts of the world I have yet seen not inhabited, I would rather live here than anywhere."

Without delay the governor and some of the principal men started on foot to look for a more suitable place for the new settlement, expecting to find it "at the bottom of the bay." It was the seventeenth of June, now memorable for another event annually celebrated on that spot. They visited Mr. Samuel Maverick, who was well established in the first permanent house in the Bay colony at Winnisimmet, now Chelsea [*]; Mr. Thomas Walford, at Charton or Charleton; and, perhaps, Mr. Blaxton, or Blackstone, domesticated in a cottage on the western shore of Shawmut. These were Church-of-England men who had come out in 1623, under Robert Gorges, supported by the whole power of the Council for New

---

[*] It has long been held that Maverick erected his house on Noddle's Island; but Judge Mellen Chamberlain has shown that it was at Winnisimmet.—See Transactions of the Massachusetts Historical Society, Jan., 1885.

WINTHROP'S FLEET IN BOSTON HARBOR, FROM A SPOT BETWEEN BOSTON AND EAST BOSTON. FROM AN OIL PAINTING BY WILLIAM F. HALSALL, BASED ON A STUDY OF THE SHIPS OF THE PERIOD.

England.* The party returned by way of Nantasket, where Winthrop was called upon to settle a difficulty that had arisen between the emigrants who had come by the ship *Mary and John* and Captain Squeb, who, though under contract to deliver his human freight at the mouth of the Charles River, had left them at Nantasket at the end of May, in a merciless way, as they thought. At the governor's summons, the captain came ashore and the trouble was quickly settled. It was difficult at that day to determine where "the mouth of the Charles River" was, and it seems that there were obstacles in the way of navigating the river itself with a vessel of the size of the one the captain commanded.

The result of this little trip of three days was that Winthrop determined to settle at Charleton; but there was so much sickness and distress that the others did not all follow his example, but for one reason and another settled "dispersedly," as Thomas Dudley, the deputy-governor, wrote in his account of the beginnings of the Massachusetts colony. Some planted on the Mystic, at what is now Medford; some at Watertown; and still others at Roxbury † and Dorchester. This dispersion troubled the minds of some of them, "but help it we could not," said Dudley, and the time was "too short to deliberate any longer, lest the winter should surprise" them, before they had built forts or houses, to protect them from the Indians as well as from the wet and cold.

---

* Winsor's "Memorial History," vol. i., p. 75.

† Named Rocksbury on account of the rough and rocky surface of its territory.

The twelfth of July is given as the date of the beginning of Charlestown, where Winthrop, Saltonstall, Dudley, Wilson, Bradstreet, and others with their followers took up their abodes as promptly as possible, though it appears to have been several weeks before they all accomplished the work of removal. The governor and several of the members of the company occupied the " Great House," as it was called, which they found ready for them, and the multitude lived in uncomfortable tents and booths, which they set up on Town Hill. Those were dismal days : the long passage had fixed sickness and scurvy upon the emigrants ; the wet lodgings increased the distempers ; a lack of fresh water made matters worse, and now there was not a hut in which there was not lamentation and woe for the dying and the dead. Many graves soon marked the sides of the hill. In consequence of the great calamities, Mr. Winthrop recommended a fast to be kept on the thirtieth of July, at which time also the first church organization was made, according to the form already established at Salem, on the basis of separation, and Mr. John Wilson was chosen pastor.

Every thing seemed to indicate that Charleton was to be the capital of the colony,* but the kind heart

* Edward Johnson, in his " Wonder-Working Providence," chapter xvii., says that the settlers promptly determined to hold an election of officers, for what reason we know not, unless it was to assert their independence, and that accordingly a court was called for the twenty-third of August on board of the *Arbella*, on which occasion the form was gone through with of choosing Mr. Winthrop governor, and voting new commissions to the officers who with him had already been elected by the company in England.

of Mr. Blaxton, touched by the distress among the settlers, invited them to remove to the three-hilled peninsula (called Shawmut and Tri-mountain), where there was fresh water in abundance and other advantages. The invitation was accepted without hesitation; the frame of the governor's house was carried over, and the people transferred themselves as quickly as they could. The new site was an uneven rocky promontory, abounding with hollows and swamps, and connected with the mainland by an isthmus so narrow that the tide often washed completely over it. Mr. Blaxton won the thanks of generations by his polite and Christian invitation to the sufferers at Charleton.

The removal to Shawmut had so far progressed by the seventh of September that a court of Assistants was held on that day, and it was ordered that the name of the settlement should be Boston. Another court of Assistants was convened at Charleton on the twenty-eighth of September; but after that the courts were held at Boston.

We cannot tell exactly when the different settlers made the change of abode; we do not know even when the governor himself removed; but it is certain that the movement was hastened by the death of one of the most loved of the company. Lady Arbella Johnson, had died very soon after the arrival at Salem, "coming from a paradise of pleasure and plenty in the family of a noble earl, into a wilderness of wants," taking "New England on her way to heaven," as the quaint Cotton Mather expresses it. On the thirtieth of September the death of Mr.

Johnson occurred, and it cast a gloom over the colony. His lot as selected is that now bounded by School, Tremont, Court, and Washington streets, comprising the first place of burial in the town, and

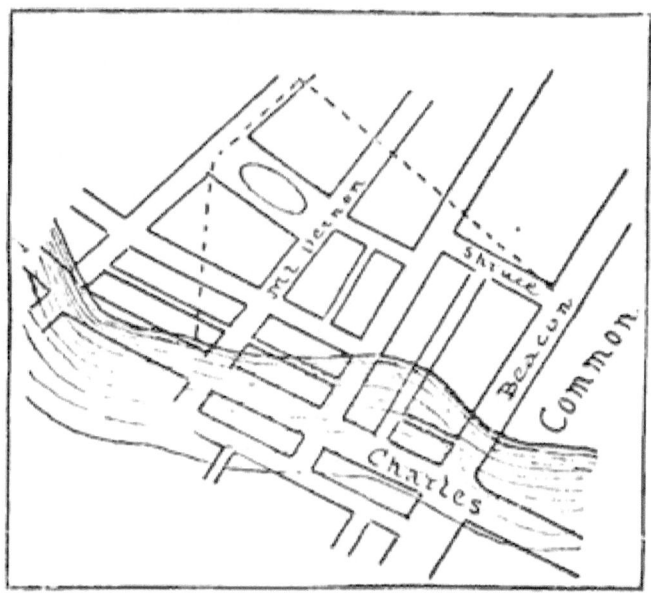

BLAXTON'S LOT.

in it he was tenderly laid to rest.* After this great affliction the work of removal from Charleton progressed rapidly.

* This account of Mr. Johnson's burial, given by Chief-Justice Sewall and repeated by Governor Hutchinson, is doubted; but whether Mr. Johnson was buried there or not, the spot became the first place used for such purposes, and for thirty years it was the only one.—See Shurtleff's " A Topographical Description of Boston," p. 184.

Thus the promontory of Shawmut became the capital of New England, and thus it received the name that it still bears, a name first written upon American maps by Prince Charles at the solicitation of John Smith, but placed by him at York, on the coast of Maine. It was evidently given to its present locality by reason of the attachment felt by many of the new inhabitants for Boston in England, over the parish church of which presided that John Cotton whom we have seen calling at the Groton home of John Winthrop, a man whom he loved so greatly that he wished him to rest awhile beneath his roof, even though absent at the time himself.

V.

MARGARET WINTHROP COMES OVER.

Governor Winthrop left behind him in England, besides his sons John and Forth, who were old enough to have accompanied him, but who intended to wait until Mrs. Winthrop would go with them, a son named Henry, who was to have been one of the passengers on the *Arbella*. This member of the family had been not in all respects a son after his father's heart. He had been quite an adventurer in his youth—he was but twenty-two years of age when his father left for America—and there are expressions in his father's letters which show some disapproval of his life and companionships. Henry was among the early planters on the island of Barbadoes, where he had been several years previously, and had become involved in schemes for trade and colonization, which appear to have proved unfortunate for his character as well as his purse and his good father's purse. Doubtless, however, he had gained experience that would have been of value in the new enterprise of the Massachusetts company.

Henry went ashore while the *Arbella* was detained by the adverse winds, for the purpose of obtaining an additional supply of provisions, and on account of the high sea was unable to regain the vessel before she sailed. He followed on the *Talbot*, another of the fleet, and reached Salem on the second of July. The passage was a very hard one, for the passengers were afflicted by the small-pox, of which disease fourteen died on the ocean, though Henry escaped. On the day of his arrival at Salem he was led by curiosity to visit some Indian wigwams, and seeing a canoe on the opposite side of a creek, he plunged into the stream to swim across to obtain it, in order to save several miles of walking. He was taken with a cramp in the water not far from the shore, and drowned.

Two weeks later John Winthrop wrote for the first time to his absent wife (from "Charleton in New England") by the hands of Arthur Tindale, her brother, who had come on the *Arbella*, but returned on the *Lion*, the first vessel that went back. In this letter he wasted no words, thinking that the details of the voyage would be given by the bearer. He said :

"We had a long and troublesome passage, but the Lord made it safe and easy for us. . . . I am so overspread with business that I have no time for these or other mine own private occasions. I only write now that thou mayest know that I yet live, and am mindful of thee in all my affairs. . . . My son Henry! my son Henry! ah, poor child! Yet it grieves me much more for my dear daughter. The Lord strengthen and comfort her heart to bear this cross patiently. . . . I shall expect thee next summer, if the Lord please, and by that time

I hope to be provided for thy comfortable entertainment. My most sweet wife, be not disheartened; trust in the Lord, and thou shalt see his faithfulness. . . . I kiss and embrace thee, my dear wife, and all my children."

Careful John Winthrop wrote no more than was necessary by Arthur; he feared the letter might

THE GREAT ELM IN THE COMMON. DESTROYED IN 1876.

miscarry, for he found him "the old man still," whatever his weakness was; but he took another opportunity, a week later, to give more particulars. Then he added that though the fare in the New World was but peas, puddings, and fish, quite coarse in comparison to what he had been accustomed to, it seemed sweet and wholesome to him, and he could truly say that he desired nothing better. Other matters did trouble him, however, for the relief from restraint that was felt by some of the emigrants made them restless; they were not at all bent on the establishment of a religious commonwealth, and could not all bring themselves to practise the good precepts of Winthrop embodied in his "Model of Christian Charity." "Satan," he wrote, "bends his forces against us, and stirs up his instruments to all kind of mischief, so that I think here are some persons who never showed so much wickedness in England as they have done here." Nevertheless, he urges Margaret not to be discouraged by any thing that she may hear, for he saw no cause to repent his coming, and experience had showed that the tenderest women and the youngest children might safely be brought over.

Mr. Winthrop gives careful instructions regarding the voyage; as that she should be warmly clothed, have a sufficiency of fresh provisions, meal, eggs (put up in salt or ground malt), butter, oatmeal, peas, and fruit, and strong chests, well locked, in which to keep them on the voyage. Margaret was to be sure to have two or three skillets, frying-pans and stewing-pans, large and small, drinking-vessels, pewter vessels, a case to boil a pudding in, a store of linen to use at sea, and a quantity of "sack," to be distributed among the sailors. For physic she was to provide a pound of Dr. Wright's electuary, and some other articles, as saltpetre and nutmegs, the latter to be grated or sliced when used. For use in the colony, Mrs. Winthrop was desired to bring bedding, linen and woollen; brass, pewter, and leather bottles; drinking-horns, axes (whatever they cost), candles, soap, suet, and great and small augers, " and many other necessaries which I can't now think of."

To his eldest son, Winthrop sends at the same time a journal of the voyage, besides a very long business letter, in which we find the reasons why it was necessary to send home so promptly for provisions, which one might have supposed a rich new land would have supplied, and particular directions about various members of the family and even dependents and others more remotely connected with him. As for the country itself, he observes that it differed little from England; that he had noticed but two days more hot than in Suffolk; that the land is as good as he ever saw there, and that he had observed none so bad as he had seen at home. " Here is sweet air, fair rivers, and plenty of springs, and the water better than in England. Here can be no want of any thing to those who bring means to raise out of the earth and sea."

No doubt Mr. Winthrop believed all that he wrote about the blessings he described; but sometimes it seems as though he did not find it quite easy to be entirely happy. On the ninth of September, for example, he wrote, " that though the lady Arbella is dead, and good Mr. Higginson, and my servant, old Waters," yet many mercies were mixed with the corrections of Providence, and he praised God that he had many occasions of comfort, though he *did* hope that the " days of affliction " would soon have an end, and he sustained himself by saying, significantly: "It is enough that we shall have heaven, though we should pass through hell to it." Winthrop magnified his mercies, and seems to have repeated his list of them frequently, to keep his heart from breaking under the combined load of care for the plantation, rendered hard by the instruments stirred up by "Sathan," his solicitude for his absent ones, and his sorrows for those whom he had lost. He writes: "I long for the time when I may see thy sweet face again, and the faces of my dear children," though he owned with sorrow that his much business "hath made me too often forget Mondays and Fridays."

It is interesting to read the family letters in connection with the records of the public meetings, and to see that while the governor was attending to the cases of discipline and doctrine, he was giving minute details to his wife and son about their approaching voyage. Thus, on the seventh of September, Thomas Morton was brought before the court for sentence, and it was ordered that he should be "set in the bilboes and sent prisoner to England," his goods seized to pay the charges of his trial and to satisfy the Indians whom he had cheated, and his house burned down in their presence as a sign of the displeasure of the well-meaning with his action. At the same time he was writing to his son to bring forty hogsheads of meal "well cleansed from the bran," and store of peas, cheese, malt, oatmeal, pepper, ginger, rugs, verjuice (the juice of unripe fruits), oil, pitch, tar, old cable to make oakum, cows, goats, sheep, garlic and onions, alum and aloes, oiled skins, "some worsted ribbing, several sizes," and conserve of red roses. While he was beckoning with one hand to good and true men to come over from England, he was signing a law to the effect that "No person shall plant in any place within the limits of this patent, without leave from the governor and assistants, or a major part of them."

There are many contrasts in the life of the governor as described in his letters and in the public records. On one page we read: "I have lost twelve of my family," whom he enumerates; the "Lord hath stripped us of some principal persons, Mr. Johnson and his lady," etc.; and yet, "My dear wife we are here in a paradise. Though we have not beef and mutton, etc., yet, God be praised, we want them not, our Indian corn answers for all. Yet here is fowl and fish in great plenty." On another we find the governor forming himself into the first American temperance society, as he writes under date, October 25, 1630: "The governor, upon consideration of the inconveniences which had grown up in England by drinking one to another, restrained it at his own table, and wished others to do the like, so as it grew by little and little into disuse."

At this period negotiations were in progress for the sale of the homestead at Groton, so that the family might be ready to leave in the spring unincumbered. In New England the supply of food was slowly running down, and there were anxious thoughts about the welfare of the ship *Lion*, which, we remember, had been hastily sent for supplies.

Six months passed and the *Lion* did not appear. Winthrop had his last batch of bread in his oven, and doubtless the poorer inhabitants of Boston were not so well off; in fact, we are told that at the time when the general stores had been so reduced that a fast had been appointed to pray for relief, Mr. Winthrop was in the act of giving the last handful of meal from his barrel to a poor man in distress, when a ship was spied entering the harbor with provisions enough for all. It was the *Lion*. The fast was turned to a thanksgiving, and the first regularly appointed Thanksgiving Day, held in 1631, is now celebrated as the birthday of Washington. On the *Lion* there came a young minister of whom we shall hear more, Roger Williams, an Oxford graduate.

The governor was now anxiously awaiting the arrival of his loved ones. The estate was at last sold for a price smaller than it was thought that it ought to bring, and Winthrop was still sending to his wife and son the detailed instructions about sheep-skins and lamb-skins and calves-skins and hats and woollen cloth and mill-stones, and all the increasing list of articles that greater acquaintance with the new life taught him might be needed. Meantime Sir Richard Saltonstall, the Rev. Mr. Wilson, and other good friends had left the plantation, some of them never to return, and the responsibilities of those who remained were increased.

On the fourth of July, 1631, the governor launched a bark named the *Blessing of the Bay*, from a place on the Mystic near his summer home, the "Ten-Hills Farm." It was on this farm that the governor took an after-supper walk on the eleventh of October, which came near having serious results for the plantation. He took his fowling-piece in his hand, apparently looking for wolves that had been killing his stock, and when distant not over a half mile from home it became so dark that he mistook his path, and was unable to find it again. In his unsuccessful wanderings he came to an Indian hut, where he made a good fire by means of a "match," which he always carried in his pocket, and laid himself down on some mats that he found. (He is careful to say that he always carried besides a match, a compass, and in summer some "snakeweed," one of the useful vegetable astringents.) Unable to sleep, he spent the night singing psalms, getting wood, and walking up and down. Near morning it began to rain, and the lost governor made shift by means of a long pole to climb up into the hut, where an Indian squaw found him; but he barred her out, though she remained a great while trying to get in. He managed to find his way home after daylight, and learned that his servants had been much perplexed for him, "having walked about and shot off pieces, and halloed all the night," but he heard them not.

The summer of 1631 was almost passed before the sale of the homestead and the settlement of the family affairs made it possible for Margaret Winthrop to turn her face westward. Just before that time she wrote to John Winthrop, junior:

"My dear Son: Since it hath pleased God to make a way for me, and to give me encouragement for my voyage, and uphold my heart that it faints not, I do resolve by his assistance to cast myself upon him, and to go for N : E ; as speedily as I can with any convenience. Therefore, my good son, let me entreat thee to take order for our going as soon as thou canst, for winter will come on apace."

It is evident that however much these good emigrants tried to keep cheerful in the face of such experiences as they expected to encounter, they always felt that it was a cross, or, as they said, a duty to " suffer what God hath laid out for us, and to be cheerful."

As Mr. Winthrop had been engaged, just before his voyage, in settling matters matrimonial, so his good Margaret was likewise employed before she sailed. She writes of the widow of Henry Winthrop:

"I rejoice much to hear that Mr. Cottington bears such good affections to my daughter ; I trust there will be further proceeding. I have heard him very well reported of, to be a religious man and one of good means. [We recollect that Mr. Painter was deficient in this respect.] Mr. Wilson had some speech with me about it, and did very much desire to know her virtues ; I gave her the best commendations that I could. I shall daily expect his coming. He shall be very welcome. P. S.—As soon as I had written these, Mr. Cottington came to see us, but would not stay all night. He hath not yet made his mind known to my daughter, but is gone to Sudbury to Mr. Wilson. I do verily believe it will be a match, and she shall be very happy in a good husband."

What " Mr. Wilson " said we are not told ; but the

fair widow did not become "Mistress Cottington"; one Robert Feake intervened and took her.

It was about the middle of August that the large remnant of the governor's family, with the exception of two sons, Forth and Deane, sailed for New England on the same ship, *Lion*, that had several times before made the trip. John Eliot, afterwards the apostle to the Indians, was one of the passengers. On the voyage Margaret's infant daughter, Ann, died and was committed to the deep. On the second of November William Peirce, captain, arrived off Nantasket, and was happy to be the one to present to the governor his good wife Margaret, his eldest son with his wife, and the other children, in good health, after the dangers of the passage that they had so much feared. The plantation was in sympathy with the loving husband and wife on their happy reunion; they were honored by volleys of shot as they landed on the fourth of November, and for divers days they were presented "great store of provisions, as fat hogs, kids, venison, poultry, geese, partridges, etc., so as the like joy and manifestation of love had never been seen in New England. It was a great marvel that so much people and such store of provisions could be gathered together at so few hours' notice." A week later there was a second Thanksgiving Day in Boston; and a few days after that the governor of Plymouth came up to offer his personal congratulations to his "much honored and beloved friends."

VI.

THE LAY OF THE LAND.

The physical aspect of Boston when Mrs. Winthrop and her family approached it in 1631 was quite different from its appearance now, for in the march of civilization the hills have been carried into the sea, the rough places have been made smooth, and many acres of superficial area have been added to the original measure. The area at that time was about 783 acres,—less than that of the territory bought by the city of New York in 1861 for its Central Park. The present dry land in original Boston measures 1,829 acres; and the total number of acres in the city limits is more than 23,000. Mr. Blaxton recommended the place on account of its good springs of water, and Winthrop established himself near the chief of these, which gave its name to Spring Lane, the water of which though long since disused is thought to have bubbled up anew when excavations were made in 1869 for the present Post-Office.

The chief features, however, that Mrs. Winthrop noticed, as she entered the harbor, were the hills at the feet of which the straggling houses of the hamlet were nestled. At the north end of the promontory

COPP'S HILL, AS IT APPEARED IN WINTHROP'S TIME. THE MILL WAS ERECTED IN 1632.

stood Windmill (now Copp's) Hill; to the south appeared Fort Hill, now completely cut away; and between them rose the three-topped Sentry Hill, which changed its name to Beacon Hill, when in 1635 the sentry who had had his post there gave place to the beacon which dominated the spot until about 1811.

The promontory itself was divided into two portions by coves which made into its boundaries; the first portion contained little more than Copp's Hill, and was separated from the rest by Mill Cove which put in at the north, and Town Cove on the south, the connection being made more complete by Mill Creek which very nearly followed the line of Blackstone Street, as now laid out. It has been supposed that at high tide the waters of the harbor may have swept quite over the slight connecting link of land, making an island of Copp's Hill and the small territory around its base.

The southerly and main portion of the promontory contained the other hills, and it was connected with the mainland by a neck much narrower even than that which has just been mentioned. Over this neck the tide sometimes flowed, making the whole promontory an island. Thus there was but one road leading from the town to the neighboring villages. It was at first known simply as High or Main Street, and at a later period, when it had become of sufficient dignity to receive names, it was called Cornhill, Marlborough, Newbury, and Orange Street, at different points. These names were attached as early as 1708, when the first list of streets was placed on the town records. The name of Washington was applied to a portion of this thoroughfare in 1789, on the occasion of the visit of the first President, who entered the town by it then, as he had at the time of the evacuation of the place by the British in 1776. Until 1872 it ended at Dock Square, but in that year, after a fire which opened the way for its extension, it was continued through that square, then re-named Adams Square, to Haymarket Square, a spot within the limits of the Mill Pond of the earliest days. For more than a century—for seven-score years indeed, there were no brick sidewalks except on that part of Main Street near the Old South, called Cornhill; and the streets were paved with pebbles. Foot-passengers took the middle of the streets, where they were the smoothest. King Street had no sidewalks before the Revolution, and the pavement extended from house to house. Of course there were no street lamps.

What "entertainment" Mr. Winthrop had provided for his family we do not know. His home was established at about this time on a lot nearly opposite the present School Street, on the principal thoroughfare, where at a later period it changed its name from Cornhill to Marlborough. It was a building of some capacity, but probably very rough and plain, and was surrounded by a garden, which extended as far as the present Milk Street, the Old South church being built on it. From Mr. Winthrop's house the walk to the water's edge was not more than one third of the present distance, and he was surrounded by unoccupied territory on all sides.

In fact the region beyond Milk Street was far out of town until a much later period, and was known as the "South End," for the chief portion of the town was found on the northern promontory, at the south side of Copp's Hill, and on the shore of "Town Cove," where it was under protection of a battery. The present North Street ran along the shore of this cove, and the Town Dock was at Dock Square, the site of Faneuil Hall being in early times covered with water. The appearance of the houses as they grew up on the line of the Town Cove was very agreeable from the water.

To the west from Mr. Winthrop's dwelling, a short space, was an open field running down to the waters that flowed thence quite to the higher land in Roxbury. It was the "Sentry Field," or the Common, and was, largely through the efforts of Governor Winthrop, kept open for the common use of the inhabitants. On it cows were pastured until about sixty years ago. At the time of Margaret Winthrop's arrival it was probably covered with boulders that were convenient, as building progressed, for use in the foundations. The whole promontory when Mr. Winthrop arrived was "very uneven, abounding in small hollows and swamps, covered with blueberries and other bushes," and doubtless its character had changed but little during the few months that elapsed before Margaret's arrival. There were, in fact, but a few cabins on the eastern side of the hill which sloped towards the bay.

"It being a neck and bare of wood, they are not troubled with three great annoyances of wolves, rattlesnakes, and musquitoes," writes one observer the first year, though Johnson, in his "Wonder-Working Providence," declares that at the time of Winthrop's landing the "hideous thickets" were such that "wolves and bears nursed up their young from the eyes of all beholders." It is a matter of dispute whether there was actually no wood on the peninsula, though there was but little, if any, and Winthrop wrote to his son in the winter of 1637, that Boston was "almost ready to break up for want of wood," the season being so severe, and the water about them frozen over. Most if not all of the firewood and timber was brought to the settlers by water, and so was the general supply of hay, for even when the blueberry fields had been subdued they did not prove sufficient for the agricultural purposes of the growing town.

We are left to imagine the slow process of making homes for the emigrants, and even the time when they provided the first meeting-house is not exactly known, though it was built on the street now called State, at first known as King Street, probably in 1632. It was near the first Town-House, standing at the head of that street, and was a small building, with walls of mud and roof of thatch. Before it was erected, the congregation of Mr. Wilson held service in private houses, or, perhaps, "abroad under a tree," as we know they did before they left Charleton.

Though the party that came with Winthrop was regaled by Endicott with venison pasty and beer, that was not the usual diet of the settlers, as we are expressly informed; and though we know that various kinds of "strong water" were brought over in the *Arbella* and other ships, it is related as among the privations of the New World that "it was not accounted a strange thing in those days to drink water," for "God did cause his people to trust in him, and to be contented with mean things,—nor to eat samp or hominy without butter or milk." Indeed, it would have been a strange thing to see a piece of roast beef, mutton, or veal, though it was not long before there was roast goat. The Indians sometimes brought them corn and bartered with the newcomers for clothing and knives, and Nathaniel Morton says that once he had a "peck of corn or thereabouts for a little puppy-dog." "Frost-fish, mussels, and clams were a relief to many." The "learned schoolmaster and physician, and the renowned poet of New England," Benjamin Thompson, wrote of these times in his "New England's Crisis" that

> "The dainty Indian maize
> Was eat with clam-shells out of wooden trays,
> Under thatched huts, without the cry of rent,
> And the best sauce to every dish, content.
> Deep-skirted doublets, Puritanic capes,
> Which now [about 1665] would render men like upright apes,
> Was comelier wear, our wiser fathers thought,
> Than the last fashions from all Europe brought."

VII.

SUNDRY TROUBLES.

TROUBLES arose in the colony at a very early period. It became necessary, in the opinion of the governor and assistants, to send some persons back to England, because they had come to Boston uninvited, and those who were thus punished naturally denounced the colonists, and gave evil reports of the land. There was one Philip Ratcliff, agent for Cradock, who thus reported that if the church-members were all like those with whom he had dealt, "he believed that the devil was the author of their church." For malicious and scandalous speeches he was sentenced to be whipped, to have his ears cut off, to be fined forty shillings and to be banished, the magistrates taking these barbarous measures not only because they were fashionable in England at the time, but because, as the old historian Hubbard says: "He that is mounted in the saddle had need keep the reins straight, unless he intends to be thrown down and trodden under foot. They that are the ministers of God for the good of mankind, should not bear the sword in vain."

Banishment was a favorite method of punishing evil-doers in those days, and of protecting the infant commonwealth. In 1629, Governor Endicott sent back John and Samuel Browne, who did not propose to secede from the English church, but set up at Salem a separate worship according to the Book of Common Prayer. The company in England saw the danger of this proceeding and gently warned Mr. Endicott that the act might be ill-construed in high quarters, and certainly it was ill-construed to the detriment of the Americans. Thomas Morton, represented to be a rollicking vagabond, of Mount Wollaston, was "set in the bilboes," and sent prisoner to England, his goods being seized and confiscated; and Sir Christopher Gardiner, a mysterious "knight of the Holy Sepulchre," who, as Hubbard says, very well became that title, "being himself a mere whited sepulchre," because he was suspected of being a "Romanist, an adulterer, and a spy," was sent home to be tried for imputed crimes. Ratcliff reported that the country was a "hideous wilderness, possessed with barbarous Indians; very cold, sickly, rocky, barren, unfit for culture, and like to keep the people miserable." One Henry Linn was, among others, whipped and banished for writing letters home full of slander against the government and the order of the churches; and Mr. Dudley said that many false and scandalous reports were spread abroad, it having been asserted that Massachusetts men were Brownists and Separatists. Worse than all, such "vile reports won some credit among those who once wished the colony well." Sir Richard Saltonstall has been mentioned as one of the principal supporters of the Boston colony.

He heard such rumors as these, and remonstrated against the intolerance of the colonists. Twenty years later, in 1651, when the evil reports became more "loud-mouthed," he wrote to the ministers:

"It doth not a little grieve my spirit to hear what sad things are reported daily of your tyranny and persecution in England, as that you fine, whip, and imprison men for their consciences. First, you compel such to come into your assemblies as you know will not join you in your worship; and when they show dislike thereof, or witness against it, then you stir up your magistrates to punish them for, such, as you conceive, their public affronts. Truly, friends, this your practice of compelling any in matters of worship, to that whereof they are not fully pursuaded, is to make them sin; for so the Apostle (Romans xiv., 23) tells us; and many are made hypocrites thereby."

No wonder that we read that only ninety came over in the twelvemonth after the great emigration, and but two hundred and fifty the year following.

Among the notable arrivals from England was that of Roger Williams, who came by the ship *Lion*, February 5, 1631, with those provisions which caused the public thanksgiving that was held on the twenty-second of that month. Mr. Williams was a Welshman, about eleven years younger than John Winthrop. He had been carefully educated after the fashion of the age, and had become a clergyman of the English church, in which he associated with John Cotton and other good men who afterwards sought our shores, but was then an enthusiastic Puritan. There are indications that he was not only pious and learned, but also that Mr. Cotton was correct, when he said that Williams looked upon himself as one who had " received a clearer illumination of and apprehension of the state of Christ's kingdom, and of the purity of church communion, than all christendom besides." At any rate, he felt that the Boston Puritans were not sufficiently purified from the corruptions, as he thought them, of the English church, and he determined to bestir himself to bring about a reformation in New England. He proved himself singularly eccentric and "heady," and Governor Bradford of Plymouth, though he thought him godly and zealous, considered him also "very unsettled in judgment." On the soil of England Williams was the friend and companion of Milton and Hampden, of Vane and Cromwell; in the New World he was a guest of the savages in their "filthy, smoky holes," and a sharer of the scanty and miscellaneous diet that they were able to provide him in the forest haunts.*

The deputy-governor, Thomas Dudley, was an older man than Winthrop, and of quite a different character in some respects. He was "of approved wisdom and godliness," to use the language of the time, but he had been in the English army, and was, perhaps from his training there, of a somewhat stern and rigid disposition. Probably it irritated him to be second in office to a man so much his junior, and it did not lessen this feeling to know that the governor felt that in the infancy of the state justice

* " The Puritan Age and Rule," chapter viii., and the " Life of Roger Williams," by Professor William Gammell, p. 54.

ought to be administered with more lenity than he approved. These constitutional differences made it easy for Dudley to fall out with Winthrop on small occasion. Accordingly, when Winthrop decided that he would not make New Town the capital, as he did in 1631, after Dudley had built a dwelling there, and when Winthrop himself had erected the frame for his own, Dudley complained a good deal. In the spring Mr. Dudley went away abruptly from a meeting of the court, declaring that he would no longer serve as deputy-governor; and though his resignation was not allowed, there was much discussion about the relations of the two men.

Mr. Winthrop complained that Mr. Dudley made his dwelling too costly for a building in a new plantation, because he ornamented it and put wainscoting in it. The quarrel that grew up seems small at this distance of time; but apparently Dudley had some cause to complain that Winthrop removed the frame of his house from New Town to Boston, and Winthrop does not seem warranted in finding fault with Dudley's house as too elaborate, for the "wainscoting" appears to have been nothing more than "clapboards nailed to the wall in form of wainscot," for purposes of warmth. However, the unpleasantness was not removed for some years, and kept breaking out at intervals. Doubtless it was an important matter to the young community, and all were happy when in 1638, after previous deceptive reconciliations, the governor and deputy met at Concord, where they were laying out farms, and were reconciled. They named two stones there the

Two Brothers, in memory of the reconciliation, and to remind themselves also that they were connected by the marriage of their children, Mary Winthrop and the Reverend Samuel Dudley.

There was a good spirit shown at one time in the controversy, when Dudley sent a bitter letter to Winthrop and Winthrop returned it, saying that he was not willing to keep by him a letter that might tend to make him angry. He also offered Mr. Dudley a present of a fat hog, as a testimony of good-will. Upon this Mr. Dudley said to the governor, " Your overcoming yourself hath overcome me." The angry and threatening quarrel, though it lasted years, ended happily. It was not settled, however, until it had been considered by the ministers, who were general advisers in those days. They differed from Mr. Winthrop, and told him that strict discipline in criminal offences and martial affairs was more needful in a new community than in an old one ; and he replied that " he was convinced that he had failed in overmuch lenity and remissness, and would endeavor (with God's assistance) to take a more strict course " thereafter.

The people at this time were very busy in all the occupations that one would expect the settlers of a new town to be engaged in. They did not generally feel acquainted enough with the art of government to take much part in its details, and the governor and his assistants were permitted for some time to attend almost alone to such matters. A great many small police regulations were found necessary, and the assistants were busy with petty offences. Josias

Plastowe was, for instance, fined five pounds and ordered to make twofold restitution for stealing corn from some Indians, and thenceforth he was to be called Josias, and not Mr. Plastowe as formerly. Captain Stone, for calling a justice "just-ass" was fined one hundred pounds. Corn was ordered to be accepted instead of gold and silver, unless money or beaver skins were expressly named in bargains; a day was appointed for the monthly "training" of the militia; certain offenders were fined for "abusing themselves disorderly with drinking too much strong drink"; Captain Lovell was admonished to take heed of "light carriage"; the price of boards was fixed; Henry Lyon was whipped and banished "for writing against the government and the execution of justice"; a ferry was established between Winnesimmet (Chelsea) and Charlestown; pastor Phillips of Watertown was disciplined for speaking of the Church of Rome as a true church; the wages of servants was settled; no person was allowed to leave the jurisdiction by sea or land, or to buy provisions from any vessel without permission from a magistrate; the sachem Chickatabot was fined a beaver skin for shooting a swine of Sir Richard Saltonstall's*; the time for burning over ground for corn was fixed; there were assessments for making the creek at the New Town "twelve feet broad and seven feet deep," and for fortifying the same place; and a fort was built on what has since been

---

* On the contrary, Sir Richard was directed at another time to give Sagamore John a hogshead of corn for the hurt his cattle had done to the Indian's corn.

called Fort Hill in Boston. In 1632 a windmill that had done service at New Town, but would not grind except when the wind was in the west, was taken down and set up on Copp's Hill. Boston was formally declared to be the fittest place for public meetings, and the court ordered that a House of Correction and a house for the beadle should be erected speedily. The beadle was charged with the correction of petty offenders.

Laud had now become archbishop of England, and his furious dealings with the Puritans led to new emigration of men of means and of learned divines, in 1633. The arrival of Mr. John Cotton, for more than a score of years minister of St. Botolph's Old Boston, who had journeyed to Southampton to say farewell to Winthrop in 1630, was an event of note. His was the most stately parish church in England. The beautiful tower rises to the height of two hundred and eighty feet. Though the church contains no galleries, it is estimated to accommodate five thousand persons. With Mr. Cotton's arrival is connected an incident showing that however great the influence of the clergy may have been at the time, and undoubtedly was, it did not overawe the careful Puritans enough to lead them to give up any political power that they thought was by right theirs. Mr. Cotton had renounced Episcopacy, but he was not so advanced as the colonists had become in the short time that had passed since they had been under the king's immediate rule. He came to Boston with a reputation which his great learning and ability increased. Hutchinson says of him that

THE
New-England
PRIMER
Improved.

For the more easy attaining the true
Reading of English.

To which is added,

The Assembly of Divines,
and Mr. COTTON's
Catechism.

BOSTON: Printed and Sold by
S. ADAMS, in *Queen street*. 1762.

A. In ADAM's Fall,
We sinned all.

B. Heaven to find,
The BIBLE mind.

C. CHRIST crucify'd,
For Sinners dy'd.

D. The Deluge drown'd
The Earth around.

E. ELIJAH hid,
By Ravens fed.

F. The Judgment made
Felix afraid.

he is supposed to have been more instrumental in the settlement of the civil and as well as the ecclesiastical polity of New England than any other person.* He was ordained pastor of the First Church in October with peculiar ceremonies, which have been essentially followed in the Congregational body since. The next day, in like manner, Mr. Hooker was formally placed at the head of the church at New Town.

When Mr. Winthrop's term of office came to a close in May, 1633, Mr. Cotton preached an election sermon, in which he urged that a magistrate ought not to be turned into the condition of a private man without just cause; whereupon the independent voters proceeded to relegate Mr. Winthrop to private life, and to place Thomas Dudley in the office of governor, coolly referring Mr. Cotton's arguments to "further consideration." Winthrop had held the chief office since his election in England before the emigration, had performed its heavy duties without remuneration, and had, indeed, paid many expenses from his private purse that might properly have been charged to the public treasury; but latterly he had lost some favor, and now at four elections a change was made with regularity. The last change, however, was to Mr. Winthrop again. Mr. Cotton did not reflect that the voters were the ones to settle the question as to whether there was just cause for not re-electing an officer. Though Winthrop was out of office, he did not cease exerting an influence upon the town. He was at the head of a committee

* "History of New England," vol. i., p. 32.

appointed to dispose of all the common lands of the town, in December, 1634, and he induced the people to reserve forty or fifty acres for the perpetual use of the public. It seems that but for Mr. Winthrop's determined stand, in the face of much opposition, the region which is the beauty and the pride of the city would now be covered with buildings.

The promoters of the Boston emigration seem to have had grand visions of the creation of " a transatlantic English empire," which should include all that was best in the land that they left behind ; perhaps they saw a New Atlantis rising on our shores, such as Bacon and others before him had imagined. So, at least, Burke seems to have thought that they felt.* Now there came from London a direct proposition on the part of some " persons of great quality and estate, and of special note for piety," for the establishment of a social system comprising two ranks of men, the one called " princes, or nobles, or elders," and the other " the people." The colonists willingly acknowledged two distinct orders, both " from the light of nature and Scripture," and that they should be hereditary,—members of the first having the right to attend parliament or public assemblies personally, and members of the second having the right of meeting and voting by deputies whom they should choose.

Nothing came of this proposal except discussion, which probably settled the minds of many and gave more full knowledge to the people as to what they might safely and properly try to do in the new land.

* Palfrey, " History of New England," vol. i., p. 308.

One person of "quality" came over, "Harry Vane," afterwards Sir Henry Vane, and it is said that Pym, Hampden, and Oliver Cromwell would have followed but for "an express order of the king" forbidding them. These facts show that the charter was thought to give the colonists power to establish any sort of government that they pleased, if it was not antagonistic to that of England. We shall see that the tendency was toward making the government more popular rather than towards any sort of hereditary nobility, in spite of the tempting propositions of the persons of quality.

Certain new-comers, Williams, Vane, Hugh Peter,* and Mrs. Anne Hutchinson, caused great disturbance for several years, into the details of which we cannot go ; but a few facts concerning them are necessary to enable us to understand the story. Mr. Williams refused to unite with the church at Boston on his arrival, because it would not profess repentance for having had communion with the English church, and from that time he proved the correctness of the judgment of those who thought him "eccentric." He went to Salem, where he was asked to become teacher of the church. He remained a while, and then went to Plymouth, becoming associate with that Mr. Ralph Smith of whom the Boston colonists had been afraid that he was a Separatist. Soon Elder Brewster, of Plymouth, was anxious to be rid of Williams, on account of the restless disputes which he excited, and was

---

* This person always spelled his name thus, though a final s is often added by others.

THE FROG POND ON THE COMMON
AS IT NOW APPEARS.

happy when the Salem people called him to them again.

Back at Salem, Williams began to stir up discussion upon various subjects. Cotton Mather said, rather more wittily than truly (using the proverbial expression), that Williams had " a windmill in his head." He gave out that women ought to wear veils when they went abroad, and especially when they appeared in public assemblies; upon which Mr. Cotton spent a Sunday at Salem and preached a sermon to the women, which " let in so much light into their understandings that they who before thought it a shame to be seen in public without a veil were ashamed ever after to be covered with them." Williams was so much of a zealot for reform that he thought that the cross should be taken from the flag because " it was a relic of anti-Christian superstition," and Governor Endicott cut it out accordingly. "What that good man would have done with the cross upon his coin (if he had any left) that bore the sign of superstition," says Hubbard, slyly, " is uncertain." Williams maintained that it was unlawful for an unregenerate man to pray or to take an oath, especially the oath of fidelity to the government, and that a godly man ought not to have any communion with such as were considered unregenerate, and therefore he refused to take the oath of fidelity, and taught others to refuse. He urged that the magistrates ought not to have to do with matters relating to a man's duty to God, but only with his duties to man, and that " there should be a general and unlimited toleration of all religions, and for any man to be punished for any matters of his conscience was persecution.*

Probably the worst feature in the case of Williams was what Cotton calls " his violent and tumultuous carriage against the patent." He declared that King James told a " solemn public lie " in that document, and that it gave the colonists no right to the territory it described, but that the natives were still the true owners of it. This doctrine, if not " violent and tumultuous" itself, tended to promote violent and tumultuous carriage, for it would have upturned all civil order in the colony, would have rendered invalid all titles to land, and would have relegated the community to a state of anarchy. No wonder the magistrates were alarmed to have a man not only carefully writing such things down in a book (which, though unpublished, was probably known to many, as other unpublished books were at that time, when printing was not yet introduced into the colony), but also, as Winthrop expressly declares, " publicly teaching against the king's patent," and the great sin of the colonists in claiming rights under it. The magistrates spared no pains in warning Mr. Williams and in endeavoring to lead him to give up his offensive practices ; but when their efforts failed, they treated him as they had other offenders, and ordered him to " depart out of the jurisdiction within six weeks now ensuing." The remainder of the life of this remarkable man belongs to the history of another community.

Pages of the history of this period are covered

* Hutchinson, " General History of New England," p. 206.

with details of the "Antinomian controversy," so called—a discussion which began in the First Church, and apparently should have been confined to it. It was more threatening than the trouble with Williams, and permeated the whole Puritan fabric, and, if peace had not been brought about, would have involved the whole town, and perhaps the colony, in dissension and ruin. "Hitherto the beauty of the Lord had been upon the primitive plantations of New England," wrote Mr. Hubbard; "but the wicked one stirred up several of his instruments, as the Pequod Indians and the preachers of antinomianism, who infested the plantation."

The fears of the men of Boston were not imaginary. They had read the story of the split in the Reformed Church of Münster in 1534, and remembered the horrible excesses that it led to—the decapitation of citizens by the score by the fanatic draper Knipperdolling, the wild and degrading vagaries of "King" John, the head of the Anabaptists; and the hideous circumstances of the subsequent siege of the city.*

Some had been heard to say, so Mr. Hubbard reports, "that they believed the church of Boston to be the most glorious church in the world," mainly, doubtless, on account of the presence of "that burning and shining light," Mr. John Cotton. Now it was about to go under a cloud, all by reason

---

* The story of these troubles was given in all its repulsive details in a pamphlet entitled "The Dippers Dipt; or the Anabaptists ducked and plunged over head and ears," written by Daniel Featley, who died in 1644. See also "The Story of Germany," chapter xxxvi.

of the insinuating efforts of one Mrs. Anne Hutchinson, a gentlewoman " of a nimble wit, voluble tongue, eminent knowledge in the Scriptures, and notable helpfulness to her own sex, to which especially she addressed herself." Antinomianism was a doctrine much feared by the ministers of Boston, and by all who had any interest in the Puritan church. The sect to which it was attributed originated just before the beginning of the reign of Queen Elizabeth, and held that under the gospel dispensation the moral law is of no use or obligation. Another sect, known as the Family of Love, or Familists, arose about sixty years later, receiving its name from the affection that its members professed to bear to all people, however wicked. The errors of these sects were attributed to both Mrs. Hutchinson and her brother, the Reverend John Wheelwright, and even the "loving and gentle" Mr. Cotton found that many of them were attributed also to him, though all three denied that they were Antinomians. The colony was thoroughly stirred up by these opinions; Mrs. Hutchinson gathered a company of some sixty women in private houses, and expounded to them her views; Mr. Winthrop says that most members of the church were carried away by the errors, and that the five or six who held to the old views were desired to withdraw. A synod was called to meet at New Town in 1637, composed of the elders of the churches throughout the country, to consider the matter.

The synod, which had been called, not by the ministers only, but also with consent of the magistrates, met at New Town in November, in the church of the Reverend Mr. Thomas Shepard, and for three weeks patiently listened to tedious discussions, eighty-two opinions being finally condemned with apparent unanimity. A basis was thus presented for further proceedings. Mrs. Hutchinson was formally tried by the court, and sentenced to banishment. The church took up the case again afterwards, and pronounced sentence of excommunication. Thus banned, both Mrs. Hutchinson and her brother left Boston, the one going to found Exeter, New Hampshire, and the other taking her way to Rhode Island. She afterwards met a tragic death at the hands of the Indians somewhere near the present Astoria, whither she finally went. To prevent tumults, a good number of citizens of Boston were now required to give up their arms, and a law was passed threatening fine and imprisonment or banishment, upon all who should defame any court or any sentence passed by one. Many persons removed from the jurisdiction of the Massachusetts magistrates, going to Rhode Island and elsewhere; some were banished and others disfranchised. It was a long time before the wounds then made were healed. Two years later, Mr. Winthrop, who had opposed Mrs. Hutchinson's views when they were popular, was received into even greater esteem than before; and in 1644, the decree of banishment that had been made against Mr. Wheelwright was withdrawn.

There were two men of note exceedingly prominent in Boston affairs at this time, to whose strange and tragic careers a few words must be given. Harry Vane and Hugh Peter, of whom we have spoken, arrived there in 1635, and had scarcely been on the shores of the New World three months before they undertook to "revise the administration of the government"; a fact which shows that the pleasantries about the too prompt interference by new-comers in American affairs, which are seen nowadays in our journals, might have found appropriate place in correspondence before the daily newspaper was thought of. Mr. Vane rushed through his brief course in Boston in a short time. His high birth, and the fact that he sympathized with the colonists against the wishes of his father, gave him prominence, and he was incontinently chosen governor at the first election after his arrival. He was defeated by Winthrop the following year, and on the third of August, just before the synod met at New Town, he left Boston forever.*

Mr. Peter had suffered for his opinions under Laud,† and had been for six years a pastor at Rot-

---

* He had proved, to use the language of Governor Hutchinson, "young and inexperienced, but obstinate and self-sufficient," and gave offence to the greater part of the people. It was thought at the time that he had left behind him dissensions that would trouble the colony for ages.

† "New England has perhaps never quite appreciated its great obligations to Archbishop Laud. It was his overmastering hate of non-conformity, it was the vigilance and vigor and consecrated cruelty with which he scoured his own diocese and afterwards all England, and hunted down and hunted out all the ministers who were committing the unpardonable sin of dissent, that conferred upon the principal colonies of New England their ablest and noblest men."—"A History of American Literature," by Professor Moses Coit Tyler, vol. i., p. 204.

terdam, whither he went for safety. He took the place of Williams in the church at Salem, and engaged with energy both in religious and business affairs, going from place to place inciting men to public spirit, raising money to develop certain kinds of industries, working with John Winthrop, junior, in the matters of the Connecticut colony, and at one time rebuking Vane for his "peremptory conclusions," which, he said, he perceived the young governor to be very apt unto. In 1641 he went to England as agent for the colony, remaining there. He became chaplain to Cromwell, and walked by the side of his secretary, John Milton, at his funeral. At the Restoration he was executed.

VIII.

THE GOVERNMENT BECOMES MORE POPULAR.

The Company of the Massachusetts Bay was at first a pure democracy; every member was authorized to vote for the governor and assistants. It was not at all the intention of the promoters of the colony, however, to establish a democracy on the shores of America. John Cotton said in express terms that he did not conceive that God ever ordained democracy to be a fit government, either for church or commonwealth. The form of civil polity in the new colony was determined by the circumstances as they arose; and the fact that loyalty to the king was not so strong when a broad ocean rolled between him and his subjects, and when weeks were occupied in conveying orders from him to them, as it was when the sovereign was near to them, and could cause his commands to be quickly conveyed to them, had a considerable effect in making a gradual change.

The supreme authority in Boston was at first in the hands of the governor and assistants, and they were chosen by all the freemen; but on the occasion of the first general court, which was held October 19, 1630, it was determined that the freemen should choose the assistants, and they should, from their own number, elect the governor and deputy-governor. More than a hundred men were admitted to the privileges of freemen at that time, and among them were some who did not belong to any of the churches. This fact shortly became the cause of serious consideration, for, the purpose of the colonists being to build up a biblical commonwealth, it was found necessary to establish some basis of character which would ensure the continuance of its desired traits. It was of paramount importance, as the voters expressed it, May 18, 1631, to make sure that the body of the commons should be "honest and good men," and accordingly the only steps known to them to make this sure were taken. It was voted unanimously that no man should be admitted to the freedom of the body politic who was not a member of one of the churches within the limits of the colony. By this vote all members of the Church of England were excluded, though naturally Mr. Blaxton, Mr. Maverick, and others, who had not renounced connection with it, were permitted to retain the privileges that had previously been voted to them. It was the first time in history when such terms for the franchise had been laid down in any civil state.* A kind of aristocracy hitherto unknown was established, based not upon birth, nor learning, nor wealth, but upon personal character, so far as the real worth of a man could be determined by human tests.†

The methods of election were modified from time to time, and it was not very long, indeed, before the

---

* Ellis, "The Puritan Age and Rule," p. 201.
† Palfrey, "History of New England," vol. i., p. 345.

general court ordered that the right to choose the governor should be taken from the assistants and conferred upon the whole body of the commons. It was also agreed that, instead of calling all the freemen at the general court to settle taxes and assessments, two deputies should be chosen from each plantation to confer with the governor and assistants in regard to such matters. Thus there appears to have been a steadily growing desire on the part of the freemen to enlarge their share in the government, which, by every change that was made, became more popular in its character. Speaking of this period, Governor Hutchinson says that "the people began to grow uneasy," and no longer wished to allow the whole management of public affairs to rest in the hands of the governor and assistants, though apparently their experience had at first inclined them to assume as little responsibility as possible. In May, 1634, the freemen, assembled as the fifth great and general court, voted that the deputies, when they met, should have all the powers they themselves enjoyed, except as to the choice of magistrates, which they retained. It was at this time prescribed that the freemen should swear allegiance to the government in the use of the following words:

"I, A. B., being by God's providence an inhabitant and freeman within the jurisdiction of this commonwealth, do freely acknowledge myself to be subject to the government thereof, and therefore do here swear, by the great and dreadful name of the Everliving God, that I will be true and faithful to the same, and will accordingly yield assistance and support thereunto, with my person and estate, as in equity I am bound, and will also truly endeavor to maintain and preserve all the liberties and privileges thereof, submitting myself to the wholesome laws and orders made and established by the same ; and further, that I will not plot nor practise any evil against it, nor consent to any that shall do so, but will timely discover and reveal to lawful authority now here established for the speedy preventing thereof. Moreover, I do solemnly bind myself in the sight of God, that, when I shall be called to give my vote touching any such matter of this state, wherein freemen are to deal, I will give my vote and suffrage as I shall judge in mine own conscience may best conduce and tend to the public weal of the body, without respect of persons, or favor of any man. So help me God, in the Lord Jesus Christ."

There were other reasons for this establishment of a representative body. The freemen had much increased in number, and the plantations had become more widely scattered ; so that it was not only a matter of some difficulty to get the men of the different settlements together in Boston often, but it was really dangerous for them all to leave their homes at the same time, on account of their private business, but more particularly because the Indians were likely to take advantage of such occasions to make raids upon the defenceless wives and children. Thus it was that the first legislative body arose in Boston. It was the second in point of time in America, having been anticipated by the General Assembly of Virginia, convened in 1619, which consisted of the governor and council and two burgesses from each plantation.

There were now about three hundred and fifty freemen in the colony, the majority of whom lived in Boston, which remained not only the chief settlement in the Massachusetts colony, but also the largest place in all the colonies until about the time of the revolutionary war. This numerical importance of Boston in comparison with the other places in America for so long a period must be carefully remembered, for it accounts for many acts on both sides of the ocean that cannot otherwise be understood. In comparison with the body of freemen in the colony at this time, the number of magistrates was very small indeed, for, though the charter permitted the election of twenty assistants, only about one half as many had actually been chosen each year, in order that there might be place for those "men of rank" who were expected to come over. There were now some thirteen ministers, who had great influence in secular matters, though not permitted to hold office. It was natural that their advice should be highly prized in the public councils, for they were usually the most fully educated persons in the community; but it is evident that in some cases their views had altogether more weight than was best for the people.

Thus the settlers built up an original form of government under their charter, and they repeatedly proved by their acts that they were not at all averse to measures that looked towards independence of the king of England. This is shown in the form of the Freeman's Oath, just quoted, for not a word was said in that about loyalty to the king, from under whose authority they professed never to have betaken themselves. The home government did not fail to notice these assumptions of independent authority; and trouble came from them, aggravated as they were by the representations of those disaffected persons who were from time to time sent home as unfit to dwell among the colonists. In 1635 the Council for New England surrendered its charter to the crown, and complained that it was unable to control its own colonists, who had "framed unto themselves both new laws and new conceipts," in order that they might make themselves "absolutely masters of the country and unconscionable in their new laws." "Such," writes the historian Gardiner, "was the view of the proceedings of the Massachusetts settlers which prevailed in the English court."

An amusing circumstance gave rise to another change in the management of public affairs, and Winthrop, in his diary, gives many pages to an account of it, very properly calling it a "great business upon a very small occasion." It happened that in the year 1636 there was a stray sow in Boston. It was against the rules of the town for vagrant sows to go about the streets, and accordingly this one was taken to Captain Robert Keayne, at the time charged with the care of estrays, and now remembered from the more significant fact that he was the first leader of that famous body of military men called the Ancient and Honorable Artillery Company. Captain Robert gave as wide notice as he could, through the town-crier and otherwise, that the owner might come and take his property; but no claimant appeared, and more than a year passed, he the meantime feeding the estray among his own swine. At the proper time, Captain Robert guilelessly proceeded, as usual, to slaughter one of his swine; and not long after, good-wife Sherman, consort of a worthless fellow, who was not at the moment in the colony, called upon Captain Keayne to see if the sow that he had taken care of so long were not one that she had lost months previously. Her pet had "a black spott vnder the eye of the bignesse of a shilling & a ragged eare," which traits the specimen in the captain's pen had not; and it occurred to the good-wife that it was her animal which had been slaughtered! She therefore brought the matter before the "elders of the church" of Boston, who patiently heard her plaint, and then exonerated the captain, whereupon she took the case before a jury, and, in spite of the fact that the captain was unpopular "for the hardness of his dealings," he was again victorious. Whereupon he turned upon his accuser with a suit for defamation of character, and recovered fifty pounds damages. The never-to-be-satisfied goodwife then took the matter to the great and general court, and seven weary days were occupied by that honorable body in hearing testimony about the spots under the eye, and the raggedness of the ear, after which it appeared, upon a vote, that the majority of the magistrates supported the captain, while the majority of the deputies were so prejudiced against the doughty man of war that they inclined to be on the woman's side. Seven of the deputies, however, declined to commit themselves either way, and the result was a decision that the case was "not determined," because the votes of five magistrates and sixteen deputies were required to settle the question, and these neither party had.

Much contention and earnestness of argument followed, and the members of the court, but especially the magistrates, were so irreverently spoken of that Winthrop and the others found it necessary to issue a true declaration of the case. Even this did not satisfy all; and Winthrop was obliged to write further that "the sow business not being digested in the country," it had started another question, which was the right of the magistrates to a veto in the general court. Another long discussion followed; much was written on both sides, and in March, 1644, it was voted that the two branches of government should sit separately, and that each should have the right of veto upon the action of the other; that is, that an act, having been passed by the deputies, should not be effective unless it also passed the magistrates. Thus was established a principle which has obtained in all subsequent governments formed in America, and all our legislative bodies are composed of two houses voting separately.

There are two other movements connected with the political organization of the colony of the Massachusetts Bay, which exerted great influence over American affairs ever afterwards. At the time that the town of Boston was stirred to its foundation by the pre-revolutionary struggle, Governor Hutchinson wrote:

"By an unfortunate mistake, soon after the charter, a law was passed which made every town in the province a corporation perfectly democratic, every matter being determined by the major vote of the inhabitants ; and, although the intent of the law was to confine their proceedings to the immediate concerns of the town, yet for many years past the town of Boston has been used to interest itself in every affair of moment which concerned the province in general." *

The name " town " occurs in the second meeting of the assistants, September 7, 1630, when Boston, Charleton, and Watertown were named ; and it is said that the first " town-meeting " was held in Dorchester the following year, for the purpose of making orders for the control of the affairs of that particular community.† Very soon thereafter it became customary to choose annually certain members of the plantation into whose hands the execution of the orders of the meeting should be entrusted for the year ; these were first called " selectmen," at Charleton, in 1635, and the title was afterwards adopted throughout New England.

The gatherings of freemen in town-meeting at the " beating of the drum," or otherwise, became an important item in the education of the New Englanders in the art of self-government, and Governor Hutchinson was right, from the point of view of a royalist, in thinking it " an unfortunate mistake "

* March 7, 1772, in a letter to General Gage.

† To give the towns the necessary compactness, it was ordered that houses should not be erected at a greater distance than a half-mile from the meeting-house in new plantations.

that established such hotbeds of patriotism. In those meetings, which are purely democratic, men are taught to stand up for their opinions, to think upon their feet, and to exercise many of the talents that are vitally necessary for the legislator on a broader platform. It is because of these town-meetings that New England, the colony of the Massachusetts Bay, and especially the town of Boston, obtained and kept such great influence in the colonies during all the earlier period of American history. They are themselves a heritage from our Anglo-Saxon ancestors of a remote period.

The next fundamental action on the part of the New England colonists, in which, as interesting herself in every thing that was connected with the public weal, Boston took her share, relates to the treatment of the Indians. These creatures, which the colonists seemed truly to have desired to bring to the Christian faith, were looked upon as the veriest ruins of mankind, showing, in the words of Cotton Mather, how hard a master the Devil is to his most devoted vassals. Connecticut was, at the time of the settlement of Boston, more thickly occupied than any other portion of New England by the savages, and they had, in 1633, murdered one John Stone, who had been banished from Boston for immoralities. They afterwards murdered others. There was great uneasiness in Boston, and it was thought necessary to take positive steps for the protection of the two hundred and fifty Englishmen in Connecticut, many of whom had gone from Boston and the vicinity.

A frightful war against the Indians was entered upon, in which Governor Endicott, Captain John Underhill, and Captain John Mason led the forces of the colonists. The campaign was short and terribly earnest. The Pequods were exterminated, those that were not killed being sold into slavery in New England and the West Indies; no mercy was given them, for the soldiers verily believed themselves agents of the God whom they worshipped in punishing the savages as enemies of the saints. And the land had rest from the Indians forty years.*

The Indians were not the only enemies against whom the colonists had to protect themselves. The attempt was made to divide the councils of the savages by making friends with one tribe, in the hope of thus being protected against the others; but this involved the colonists in many difficulties, and it was a policy not possible in the case of the French and Dutch colonists on the east and on the west, who were much feared. The colonists nearest the settlements of the Dutch felt that they were in an unprotected condition, and in 1637 some magistrates and ministers from Connecticut being in Boston in attendance upon a synod, called to take action in regard to the spread of the dreaded Antinomianism, a meeting was held to agree if possible upon a confederation for the purpose of mutual protection:

* For the details of this bloody struggle the reader who is curious on the subject is referred to the "Life of John Mason," by Dr. Geo. E. Ellis; to Palfrey's "New England," vol. i.; and to Winsor's "Memorial History of Boston," vol. i., p. 253.

but it failed to settle any principles of union.
Massachusetts was ready for union, but Connecticut
did not approve of the plan which was proposed.
The following year the governor of Connecticut and
the Reverend Mr. Hooker, the most prominent minister there, were in Boston for a month upon the
same business; but no action was taken then. In
the autumn of 1642 Connecticut made new overtures,
and a consultation between the magistrates of Boston and the deputies from Boston and the neighboring towns, and commissioners from Plymouth,
Connecticut, and New Haven was planned, but
nothing was done until spring. Then the general
court appointed a committee for the same purpose,
and articles of confederation were agreed upon.
The document which was drawn up recited the
objects of the league to be, to preserve and propagate the truth and liberties of the gospel, and to
ensure the mutual safety and welfare of the colonies.
A preamble gave the reasons for the union. It
said that all the colonists came from England for the
same purpose; that they were then scattered upon
the sea-coasts and rivers farther than had been intended; that they were encompassed by people of
several nations and of strange languages; that the
natives had committed "sundry insolences and outrages upon several plantations," and were at that
time combined against the English; that there were
distractions in England which made it difficult to get
advice or protection from that quarter, and that for
these reasons the colonies formed themselves into
one nation, to be called the United Colonies of New

England. Here was another of the signs of independence that may be noted in the history of the colonists of Boston. It was the first combination of the sort in American story, and it pointed out to the children of the men who entered into it a mode by which they could make still more comprehensive and durable unions.

IX.

WELCOME AND UNWELCOME VISITORS.

From the first settlement of the promontory of Boston the population increased in a promising way until the year 1640, when certain events in the mother-country caused emigration almost to cease. Laud, "the great enemy" of New England, as Winthrop properly stigmatizes him, with many others of high condition, had been imprisoned and called to account by parliament, and it seemed that there was to be a reformation in both church and state, so that it would not be necessary for any to remove themselves over seas for the sake of peace. It has been estimated that during the ten years of great activity in emigration some twenty thousand persons had found their way to New England, a large number of whom made Boston their home. In 1638 alone it is said that twenty ships brought three thousand passengers to that port.

These immigrants made business brisk in Boston; they brought articles that the colonists needed, and they made a market for all that the colonists produced. When the incoming flood stopped there was a small financial panic; small in comparison with many that have afflicted American cities since, but great enough to give much solicitude to Governor Winthrop, the patriarchal father of the town and the colony. A cow worth twenty pounds in 1640 would bring not more than four or five pounds the following year; and the man who was accustomed to spare one cow a year from his herd and to clothe his family with the price of it, was now in a strait. There had, of course, been straits and difficulties at the beginning of the settlement; but they had been manfully overcome, and industry had produced provisions enough for home consumption and an overplus for exportation. The trade for the first seven years was small; consisting of bartering toys, tools, and clothing with the natives for furs and skins. When the settlers found themselves able to produce a surplus, a trade sprung up with the Barbadoes, the West Indies, and other places from which a profit was made that permitted the importation of manufactured goods from England. Then one vessel ventured to the coast of Guinea and brought away slaves, for which its owners were called to answer, the general court bearing witness to "the heinous and crying sin of man-stealing," and ordering the return of the negroes. By degrees it was found possible to spare some hands from farming, and they were employed in getting out lumber for houses, in the fisheries, or in building vessels for the coasting trade. Merchants were in time tempted to come to Boston and commerce began. As the usual supplies of manufactured goods became less and less, it was seen that articles of that sort must be produced by the colonists themselves, and they "fell to a manufacture of cotton, whereof they had store from Barbadoes, and hemp and flax." Then the now ancient spinning-wheel began to whirr, and the thump of the drowsy loom was heard day by day in the dwellings of the Boston housewife. For two hundred years these homely implements of industry were familiar objects in all quarters of New England. All of these steps were taken in the most natural process, and not by any calculation on the part of the colonists. The extent of the suffering that followed the cessation of immigration may be guessed at from the correspondence of the town.

Corn was made legal tender in the payment of debts, and chosen men were sent to England to apologize for the slowness with which obligations were paid. Some of the less stable of the colonists returned to England; others betook themselves to the West Indies or to the Dutch settlements. Mr. Winthrop was harassed by all this, and there was much disputation about the righteousness and liberty of removing "for outward advantages." Winthrop thought it would be hard to make it clear to one's conscience that it was right for those who came together in a wilderness where were nothing but wild beasts and beast-like men, and confederated themselves in church and state, thus impliedly at least binding themselves to support one another and the society they had formed, to break away without the consent of those who remained. He said to himself: "Ask thy conscience if thou wouldst have plucked up thy stakes, and brought thy family three thousand miles, if thou hadest expected that all or most would have forsaken thee there."

The rise of the trade spirit led to a curious complication with the French of Acadie, to which early historians have given a prominence that proves its great importance in their estimation. By the treaty between France and England in 1632, France received back all of the territory in America of which England had despoiled her, and very soon after that time two rival and unscrupulous "governors of Acadie" appear on the scenes, the one of whom, La Tour, professed to be a Protestant, and the other, d'Aulnay, was evidently a zealous partisan of the Catholic church. There was an opportunity for Boston to increase the trade which it had already begun in that quarter, and though Endicott wrote to Winthrop that he feared there would be "little comfort in having any thing to do with these idolatrous French," the interests of Boston were so strongly involved in making alliance with one party or the other that in process of time a treaty was entered into with the professed Protestant.

It was in June, 1643. The governor and his family were on the island in the harbor known as the Governor's Garden, now Governor's Island, enjoying the summer air; in a boat on the water was Mrs. Gibbons, wife of Captain Edward Gibbons, going down with her children to her husband's farm at Pullen Point, in the present town of Winthrop. A French ship from Rochelle came up the harbor, bringing La Tour, the Protestant Acadian governor. One of his gentlemen recognized Mrs. Gibbons as one at whose house he had been hospitably entertained, and La Tour sent off his shallop to go to speak to her; but she, afraid when she saw so many foreigners coming towards her, caused her boat to be turned towards the Governor's Garden and hastened to the land. There she found Winthrop, with his wife, two of his sons, and the wife of another son. La Tour landed and explained to the governor that he had come from France, intending to make land at his fort at St. John's, but that his enemy had blockaded it, and he now came to ask help to enable him to force an entrance. Meantime Mrs. Gibbons was sent to Boston in the governor's boat, and she gave information of the sudden coming of the French. Winthrop declined to answer La Tour until he had consulted other members of the magistracy, and the party took supper together, after which all started to Boston in La Tour's boat; but the towns of Boston and Charleton, having learned the condition of affairs, and knowing that the governor was quite in the Frenchman's power, fitted out three shallops of armed men to guard him and accompany him home. The Frenchman was sent to lodge at Captain Gibbons's; but the facts of the day showed the citizens how defenceless their town was, for the strangers, had they been so disposed, might have captured the governor and his family, and Mrs. Gibbons and her attendants, as well as all the ships in the harbor, if, indeed, they had not sacked the little town.

The reply that was made to the request of La Tour created much ill-feeling in the colony. It was determined not to afford him any help, though he was given to understand that he was at liberty to make whatever bargains he pleased with owners of ships that he could find in the harbor. La Tour remained in Boston a little more than a month, behaving himself like a gentleman and a Protestant; going to meeting with the governor; receiving entertainment at the hands of many of the town " in their houses and at table"; and at last sailing away with four ships and a pinnace, the chiefest of which had sixteen pieces of ordnance and was very well manned and fitted for fighting, and " the rest proportionable."

The governor was overwhelmed with correspondence upon the matter of this decision; and a meeting of neighboring magistrates, elders, and deputies was held to consider " whether it were lawful for Christians to aid idolators, and how far we may hold communion with them." Indeed, weighty questions of neutrality and intervention were involved, and doubtless Winthrop's action would not stand the test of modern international law. The contemporary discussion brought into the consideration the cases of Jehoshaphat, Solomon and the Queen of Sheba, Ahab and Ahaziah, the king of Babylon and Pharaoh, but it did not change the practical policy that Winthrop had adopted. The rivals kept up their warfare for several years, until, in 1650 or 1651, d'Aulnay died, and in 1652 his widow married her husband's enemy. Though La Tour and the widow disappear from history, they left a number of descendants, and the race still lives in Nova Scotia.*

* The story of the negotiations with La Tour and d'Aulnay is given with much detail in Hutchinson (ed. 1755), pp. 128-135; in Hubbard, chapter liv.; and in Winsor's " Memorial History of

The Puritans of Boston were Protestants of the Protestants, and though they were jealous of having among them any persons who held and taught other doctrines than their own, they were naturally most of all jealous of those who professed the "religion of the court of Rome," and of those holding to this, the "old religion," a member of one of the orders of the priesthood, especially the Jesuit order, was the most feared and hated. For this reason, taking into consideration "the great wars, combustions, and divisions" in Europe, which seemed to be chiefly "raised and fomented by the secret underminings and solicitations of those of the Jesuitical order," the general court of the Massachusetts Bay ordered that no Jesuit or spiritual or ecclesiastical person ordained by authority of the Pope of Rome should at any time be allowed within the colony; that if any such found entrance, he should be banished, and on returning he should be put to death. Survivors from shipwreck, and public messengers behaving themselves inoffensively and departing promptly, were excepted. Some "papistical" persons were in the company of La Tour and d'Aulnay, but they were carefully watched, and apparently no harm came from them, save the discussion that has been mentioned. On one occasion two of these characters were brought to Boston from their vessel to confer with Mr. Cotton, which was certainly safe.

There was a devoted Jesuit missionary heroically

Boston," vol. i., pp. 282-295; but it must also be said that almost every thing that one wishes to learn is found in Mr. Winsor's storehouse of Boston history.

laboring among the Abenaquis in Acadie at this time. Governor Winthrop wrote to the governor of Canada proposing free trade between the colonies, and in 1650 this missionary, whose name was Gabriel Druilletes, was sent to Boston to confer on the subject. He appeared to the English first near the present site of Augusta, Maine, where he met John Winslow of Plymouth, then in charge of the trading post of his colony at that point. The conference between the two was agreeable, and the Jesuit believed that the Protestant was as much interested in the conversion of the Indians as he was himself. Continuing his journey, the father reached Charlestown, where he was commended to the hands of the same Edward Gibbons, of whom we read in the account of the sojourn of La Tour. This hospitable and not very radical Protestant gave the Jesuit a key to a private apartment in his house where he was at liberty to "exercise his religion" without disturbance, and there doubtless the first mass in Boston was said.

Druilletes presented his credentials in due time to Governor Dudley, who afterwards received him at dinner, and listened to his message in company with other magistrates and one deputy. From this interview, Druilletes went to Plymouth, where he lodged with one of the persons interested in the Maine trade. He felt encouraged here, as he had in Boston, and on the day before Christmas he returned to the capital of the Bay colony, stopping at a place that he calls "Rogsbray," better known to us as Roxbury, where he was entertained by the minister, who was giving instruction to some savages, just as Druilletes had been accustomed to do in the northern woods. This minister he calls "Master heliot." It was no less a person than the Reverend John Eliot, the apostle to the Indians, who had arrived on the same ship that brought Mrs. Winthrop, and was at this time full of zeal in his new work of preaching to the Indians. Mr. Eliot urged his guest to spend the winter with him, in order to avoid the severe journey through the wilderness to Canada; but the Jesuit declined, and after resting one night, resumed his journey to Boston, where again he was guest of Captain Gibbons. The purpose of the governor of Canada in sending Druilletes to Boston was to gain the help of the colonists in his war with the Iroquois; but the settlers both there and at Plymouth, saw that to take such a step would involve them in difficulties with other tribes that had been friendly to them. They gave the Jesuit diplomatic encouragement, and entertained him very hospitably, but that was all. They were ready for trade, but they were determined to avoid an Indian war, if possible.

When the Antinomians had been silenced there was still no rest to the colonists from intruders holding heterodox views; and in the year 1644, it was thought necessary to take sharp action against another class of heretics. A man named Painter refused to have his infant baptized; said that the custom was antichristian; and when the church, of which his wife was a member, enjoined him to submit the child to the ordinance, he still refused; upon which he was brought to court. He was sentenced to be whipped, the magistrates specially insisting that it was not for holding an opinion, but for "reproaching the Lord's ordinance," and for bold and evil behavior, some men his neighbors testifying that he was very loose in his conduct, and given to much lying and idleness.

The court determined to be armed in time against offenders like Painter. They had read, as we have seen, of the terrible work wrought by "Anabaptists" in Münster; how they had been "incendiaries of commonwealths," and "troublers of churches"; and how with the error about baptism of children they had usually held others, which they adroitly concealed until "they spied out a fit advantage and opportunity to vent them." It was therefore ordered that any persons who held such views wilfully and obstinately, should be sentenced to banishment. The "Anabaptist" of those days was simply a Baptist: he was one who believed in the necessity of being baptized in adult years, and as it was supposed that all persons had been baptized in infancy (as all children of Catholic parents had), this was a rebaptism. The Anabaptists of Münster "denied the authority of magistrates, the lawfulness of taking oaths, and almost all the Christian doctrines, and were guilty of several gross enormities, such as polygamy, rebellion, theft, and murder," and all their extravagances were charged upon the opposers of infant baptism. No wonder the colonists were alarmed, if they believed such stories as were told of the Anabaptists; and yet they are the people of whom Judge Story said that in Rhode Island they were the first to declare in laws that "conscience should be free and that men should not be punished for worshipping God in the way that they are persuaded he requires." The people of Boston had good authority for fearing the Anabaptists, for Jeremy Taylor, the great and mild divine, wrote in his "Liberty of Prophesying," that their doctrines were as much to be rooted out as the greatest pest and nuisance to the public interest.

The men of Boston were not, however, all agreed in the matter of punishing Baptists, though there was not very much dissent. The town showed that the character which Governor Hutchinson gives it was deserved at this early period, for in 1649 the court addressed a letter to the brethren at Plymouth pathetically remonstrating with them for harboring Baptists in that sister colony, which, they urged, was not in accordance with the articles of confederation. To this the Plymouth men sent no very hearty response, and the court at Boston was accordingly grieved. The story of the dealings of Boston with the Baptists is a disagreeable one, and may be passed over after mentioning one notable case, which brings us to the origin of the college of the colony.

In the year 1636, the court ordered that a public school should be established somewhere. The following year it was decided to put it at New Town, and a committee was appointed to carry the order into effect. This committee was composed of Governor Winthrop, John Cotton, Thomas Shepard, and four others, who were either ministers or elders. In

1638 it was ordered that New Town should be called Cambridge, in consideration of the fact that a number of the persons interested in the school were graduates of the University at Old Cambridge. In March, 1639, it was voted that the " colledge " to be built at Cambridge should be known as Harvard College, in consequence of the fact that the Reverend John Harvard had become its benefactor. One Nathaniel Eaton was appointed " Schoolmaster," for the name college was not immediately adopted in common usage. It was not long before Eaton was accused before the court for " cruel and barbarous beating " of his usher, Mr. Nathaniel Briscoe, and he was in consequence fined heavily, discharged from keeping the school, and directed to give Mr. Briscoe thirty pounds for the wrong done him.

It appears that Mr. Eaton's ideas of proper corporal punishment allowed him to beat Mr. Briscoe for the space of about two hours with a " walnut-tree plant, big enough to have killed a horse, and a yard in length." Not unnaturally, during the two hours of this unscholarly exercise, Mr. Briscoe thought that he was about to be murdered, whereupon he " fell to prayer," and Mr. Eaton only rained his blows the harder, accusing his poor usher of " taking the name of God in vain." It came out, upon the trial which ensued, that it was Mr. Eaton's usual custom to beat his pupils in this way ; and besides, that he ordinarily furnished them but " porridge and pudding, and that very homely," for their diet, though their friends gave him large allowance for their board.* The reprobate schoolmaster fled from the jurisdiction, and was reported to have gone to Virginia, where "he was given up of God to extreme pride and sensuality, being usually drunken, as the custom is there."

This was not a good beginning for the college of the colony; but the error was soon rectified, and, in 1640, the able and engaging, though perhaps litigious, Henry Dunster was made president of the young institution, just after he had arrived in Boston. He was, like John Harvard, a graduate of Emanuel College, Cambridge, and he adopted the course of study of the English university, aiming at the education of a learned ministry. The school soon earned a reputation sufficient to draw students from the other side of the sea. In its twelfth year the college was made a corporation, Mr. Dunster being confirmed in his office as president; but doubts in time began to be expressed regarding his soundness in the faith, and clouds were rising about his path.

Mr. Dunster was a member of the church of the Reverend Thomas Shepard, and when that "soul-ravishing" preacher died, in 1649, Dunster occupied his pulpit until a successor was found. By insensible degrees the president of Harvard College came to hold doubts regarding the doctrine of baptism, and, in 1653, he found himself unable to agree with

---

* Eaton's wife confessed that the flour of which the porridge was made was not "so fine as it might be, nor so well boiled or stirred"; and that when the pupils called for more butter and cheese, they were denied; and she confessed her sin in giving them "bad fish," and for "letting the blackamoor sleep in Sam Hough's sheet and pillow-bier," and in giving them bread made of heated sour meal.

his church on the subject. A young minister named Mitchell, who succeeded Shepard, remonstrated with the president for his "intolerable offence," but, as he found misgivings arising in his own mind, he withdrew, with such a "strange confusion and sickliness upon his spirit" that his study for the following Sabbath was interrupted. He was thereafter afraid to go needlessly to Mr. Dunster, because he detected "venom and poison in his insinuations." When Mr. Mitchell's discoveries came to the knowledge of others, it was found necessary for Mr. Dunster to vacate his office as teacher of orthodox youth, and he accordingly resigned his position and withdrew from Cambridge.* Ten years afterwards the First

* Any one curious in regard to Mr. Dunster's ability as a literary critic should read the "Bay Psalm Book," the first American printed book, prepared by others, but afterwards submitted to the president that he might "use a little more art upon it" (1650). The verses are, the authors confess, "not always so smooth and elegant as some may desire or expect," even in their refined state. The nineteenth Psalm began thus:

> "The heavens do declare
> The majesty of God;
> Also the firmament shows forth
> His handiwork abroad."

Joseph Addison did better threescore years later, when he wrote "The spacious firmament on high." The third edition (which is the one "revised and refined" by Dunster) contains some spiritual songs, in one of which the following lines occur:

> "Gad the Kenite, Heber's wife
> 'bove women blest shall be,
> Above the women in the tent
> a blessed one is she.
> He water ask'd, she gave him milk:
> in lordly dish she fetch'd
> Him butter forth; unto the nail
> she forth her left hand stretched."

Baptist Society was organized in Boston, and, much to the dismay and scandal of many, it proved strong enough to keep on in its way. Its services have endured to this day.

The next intruders upon the Boston colonists were much more troublesome, and the story of their sufferings is so sad that one hesitates to revive it, and we must be permitted simply to sketch some of its traits. In the middle of the summer of 1656 it was rumored that a ship in the harbor was bringing to the town two women, from England, by the way of the Barbadoes, who had embraced the heretical doctrines of George Fox. There had been fears that some of the Quaker sect might come to Boston, and in May there had been a day of fasting on this account. A Quaker says of the occasion: "Two poor women arriving in your harbor so shook ye, to the everlasting shame of you, and of your established peace and order, as if a formidable army had invaded your borders."

This was true, for the authorities took almost as great precaution against harm from Anne Austin and Mary Fisher as they would have taken to preserve the town from an armed invasion. Acting probably under the law by which Mrs. Hutchinson was condemned, the master of the ship was directed to take the women back to the Barbadoes, their books and papers were to be burned, and they themselves to be confined in the jail until the ship *Swallow*, in which they had come, should sail away. Hardly had these intruders been gotten rid of when another vessel arrived from the same place with four men and four women of the like stripe, and they received the same treatment. This was the most merciful dealing that was meted out to any of the Quakers. As soon as the general court could meet, a stringent law was passed, threatening fines, imprisonment, banishment, and whipping against any "Quakers, ranters, or other blasphemous heretics"— "fit instruments to propagate the kingdom of Sathan." The banishment was, at a later period, ordered to be enforced by pain of death in case of the return of the condemned. This law, it ought to be said, was passed by a majority of one, and an absent deputy cried out in horror that he would have crept to the meeting-place on his hands and knees to have prevented it.

Banished Quakers found that they could go to Rhode Island and be safe, whereupon the New England Confederation advised that plantation to send them off; but the president of Rhode Island replied that there was no law in his jurisdiction by which these persons could be punished, and that he found that they did not care to go to places where they were opposed by argument only; that they delighted to be persecuted, and that they were the most dangerous where they were the most hardly used. Roger Williams, though acknowledging that the Quakers were "insufferably proud and contentious," would not persecute them. Doubtless, too, a feeling of pity for the sufferers was rising among the people of Boston, which increased as their fate became more and more severe. We find that, in 1659, when there was to be an execution of two Quakers after the Thursday lecture,* great precaution was taken to "see things carried peaceably and orderly," and the procession from the jail to the Common was by a back way, "lest the people should be affected too much" if it went through the chief thoroughfare. This feeling of humanity seems to have increased, as the atrocious acts of the magistrates continued to shock the townsmen, and it led to more merciful treatment of Quakers. The end came for a while in 1660, and the prison doors were opened for such as had been confined; but it happened that at the same time a letter was received in Boston from the king, Charles II., commanding this very action. It has long been supposed that the king's missive opened the Quakers' prison doors; but it is at least possible that public opinion in Boston had anticipated it. Let us hope, for the credit of humanity, that it had.

The respite was, however, temporary. Quakers were suffering by the hundred in England, and they were not free from persecution in Boston until 1677, when Margaret Brewster, who came from the Barbadoes, like the first invaders, having entered the Old South meeting-house in sackcloth, with her face blackened, her feet bare, and with ashes on her head, was whipped for the offence. A few days later others were treated in the same way for attending upon their own meetings. Public opinion could then be no longer aggravated, and the lash was not

---

* Wm. Robinson and Marmaduke Stephenson were hanged October 27th. Mary Dyer, who stood with a halter about her neck, was reprieved, but she suffered the next year. See Ellis's "Puritan Rule," pp. 463, 472.

again flourished over the defenceless Quakers. With its disuse the objectionable acts of the sect diminished. The number of those who can be called "turbulent" was never large, and it is difficult for us, who know the quiet Friends as the modest and lovable citizens that they are, to connect any sort of disorder with the sect to which they belong.

X.

THE CHARTER IS ATTACKED.

DURING most of the time that we have thus far reviewed, Mr. and Mrs. Winthrop lived together in their modest but commodious dwelling on the present Washington Street. Mrs. Winthrop died there in 1647. Two years later the governor, who had meanwhile married a fourth time, followed her, and was buried in the graveyard of King's Chapel. For twelve of the nineteen years of his life in Boston John Winthrop held the office of governor, and during the other years he was entrusted with official duties of almost equal importance. While he sat among the elders, his faithful Margaret followed the example of the good wife described in Scripture, seeking wool and flax and working diligently with her hands. They were wakened from sleep in the morning at half-past four o'clock by the sounding of the public bell, and the curfew bid them to cover their coals and retire at nine in the evening. In 1649 Richard Taylor agreed with the selectmen to ring the bell for four pounds a year.

The Winthrop household was always well supplied with the comforts of the time, though the dwelling was probably itself not the most elegant of those that adorned the growing town in the governor's later years. Information gathered from early inventories and other sources shows that there was much comfort and elegance in many of the Boston dwellings. The principal hall was often ornamented with pictures and lighted from a great lantern, while there might have been a velvet cushion in the window-seat that gave upon the well-kept garden. There was a great parlor and a small one,—the latter being sometimes known as the study,—which were supplied with large mirrors, tasteful curtains, portraits and maps, brass clocks, chairs, which we now like to copy, with high backs covered with red leather, and in the ample fire-place stood the bright brass andirons. In the chambers were bedsteads with high corner-posts, often richly carved, and supplied with feather-beds, warming-pans, and all the luxuries of the day. The pantry was filled with good fare, with dainties, prunes, and marmalade, and the sideboard was ornamented with silver tankards and wine cups and other articles of silver and glass; while the cellar was stored with good ale, and with materials from which to brew the smoking punch that was brought before guests on the occasions of festivity, when there had been an ordination, perchance, or a meeting of the clergy, for the clergy in the olden time, rigid as was their theology, were not at all averse to the good creatures of sense, and enjoyed their punch and pasty as much as any layman of them all. There were servants enough in the Boston families, though in 1634 it was permitted the governor by vote of the court to " entertain " an

Indian as additional help in this capacity. Mrs. Winthrop was, however, not above going to the spring conveniently near (on the present Spring Lane) to draw water, and we know that the governor gave his people a good example by "putting his hand to any ordinary labor with his servants."

Twice every Sunday for ten years the family followed the custom of the colony by walking around to the meeting-house, which stood on the present State Street near the corner of Devonshire; but in 1640 the humble building there was replaced by a new structure, which stood on Washington Street near by, and was the only meeting-house during the rest of the lifetime of the first governor. This edifice was not only used for religious services, but also for meetings of the magistrates, and, naturally enough, for there was a close connection between the two in a theocratic government, which based its proceedings largely upon precedents found in the Bible.

Twice each Sunday the drum-call summoned the townspeople to the meeting-house, where the men took their places on one side, and the women on the other, the boys being relegated to the supervision of a special officer charged with the by no means unimportant duty of keeping them in order through the long sermon. Below the high pulpit, and just in front of it, sat the elders, and still nearer the body of the people were the deacons, both groups looking over the demure assembly. The men of the congregation were armed, as if in fear of interruption by the Indians. When all was ready the services began. They included singing, perhaps at first from the Psalter of Sternhold and Hopkins,* renowned for its adherence to the original Hebrew, of which Montgomery said that it was "the resemblance of the dead to the living." There was no instrumental help to harmony, and the tunes seldom counted more than five or ten for eighty or ninety years. There was extemporaneous prayer, sometimes of great length, and a sermon, which it was thought ought not to be less than an hour, measured by the sand-glass visible to the hearers on the sacred desk, though it was often much longer. Mr. Winthrop mentions, that on one of the few occasions when he was absent from his accustomed congregation on the Lord's Day, he went with many others to Cambridge to hear Mr. Hooker, who, after having preached for a quarter of an hour, found himself deprived both " of his strength and matter"; but he " went forth, and about half an hour afterwards returned again,

* The new version of the Psalms, which was revised by President Dunster ten years later, appeared the year that the second meeting-house was built, and then the good Bostonians, who abhorred the help of "cornet, flute, dulcimer, sackbut, psaltery, and all kinds of [instrumental] music," joined their tuneful voices in singing to some one of the half-a-dozen melodies then in vogue such words as these:

> "I in my streights, cal'd on the Lord,
> and to my God cry'd : he did heare
> from his temple my voyce, my crye
> before him came, unto his eare. . . .
> And he on cherub rode, and flew :
> yea he flew on the wings of winde,
> His secret place he darknes made
> his covert that him round continde,
> Dark waters, and thick clouds of skies."

and went on to very good purpose about two hours." This was in 1639. These were heroic days.

In the church that the Bostonians had left, the Bible was read in the hearing of the congregation without note or comment; here it was called "dumb reading" to read it so, and the text was accompanied with explanations and applications, according to the learning or the peculiar spirit of the clergyman. Occasionally a minister from another congregation was present, and at such times, after the Psalm had been sung, the elder would rise and say: "If this present brother hath any word of exhortation for the people at this time, in the name of God let him say on." It was called prophesying if the stranger then preached. The regular feasts of the Church were utterly ignored; but in their place there was the Thursday-forenoon lecture, besides other week-day meetings, and fasts and thanksgiving-days were appointed by the authorities from time to time.

The families of Boston were possessors of a good many books, all of which had been brought from the other side of the ocean, of course, until Stephen Daye came over in 1638, and set up widow Glover's printing-press in Cambridge. The following year it began its work with an almanac and an oath intended for the freemen to set their names to; these being followed by the Bay Psalm Book, which President Dunster "refined" in 1650. He had, in 1641, married the widow Glover, and the press had in that way indirectly passed under the control of the college.*

---

* Mrs. Dunster died two years after her second marriage. She left several children by her first husband, two of whom married sons of Governor Winthrop.

It was not till 1674 that John Foster had permission from the court to set up a press "elsewhere than in Cambridge," and thus he became the first Boston printer, his office being established the last month of that year, at "the Sign of a Dove," where he printed, as his first book, a sermon by Increase Mather, entitled "The Wicked Man's Portion." These presses did not, however, greatly increase the number of books; but many pamphlets and sermons appeared from time to time, and in 1678 the first American edition of the poems of Anne Bradstreet was issued from this the first Boston press.

Boston and the Bay colony had for ten years no laws except the common law of England, and the court was well occupied in framing ordinances aimed at evil-doers as their acts required repression; and in this connection the promptness with which "that ould deluder, Satan," managed to get his emissaries among the select band that sought to flee from his influence strikes one as not a little strange. The Bostonians had scarcely settled upon the promontory of Shawmut, when it was found necessary to enact laws against some of the most bestial offences, and the necessity for a statute law was soon apparent. In 1636 John Cotton was asked to give suggestions on this matter, and in October he presented a draft of "Moses, his Judicials," amply fortified by "proof-texts" in the margin,* the whole being supported by the words, quoted from Isaiah: "The

---

* Thus :—" The governor hath power . . . to send out warrants for the calling of the general court." (And Joshua gathered all the tribes of Israel to Shechem. Josh., xxiv., 1.)

Lord is our Judge, the Lord is our Lawgiver, the Lord is our King; he will save us." This effort was in accordance with the plan of a biblical commonwealth which the founders of the colony desired to establish, but it was not accepted.

The following year it was ordered by the court that the freemen of the several towns should gather and prepare such laws as they thought necessary under the circumstances of the colony, which were to be digested by the council and three elders, and the result presented to the court; but it proved that the people were inexperienced in such work, and probably thought that the method which had been pursued—of making laws as they were called for—would suffice. There was, however, in New England at the time a scholar of ripeness and eccentricity able to do the work. He was a graduate of Emanuel College; had practised law some years in England; was an acquaintance of Francis Bacon and of Archbishop Usher; had been in somewhat familiar intercourse with other men and some women in high life; had served as parish priest for ten years in England, until ejected by Laud; and was then for a while pastor of a parish in the raw settlement at Agawam—now prosaic Ipswich. At the moment when Cotton was compiling his Judicials, this scholar—Nathaniel Ward—was meditating on the badness of the times upon which he had fallen, and grumbling at the profaneness of many about him and the "foul shame of religious toleration," which he berated not long after in one of the raciest books of the day, "The Simple Cobbler of Agawam."

Nathaniel Ward decided to prepare the needed statutes, and accordingly presented to the court a "Body of Liberties," consisting of one hundred laws. After a discussion lasting three weeks these were adopted, as a response to a popular clamor that arose for something settled which would bring the "interminable consultation of the towns" to an end. The biblical character of the legislation is evident from a provision that in case of any defect of the body of liberties, the Law of God should be the ultimate rule of administration. The law of Ward was more merciful than that of the mother-country, and mentioned but ten capital offences, though there were thirty such in England at the close of the reign of Elizabeth, and more than twice that number at a later period. Ward supported each of his capital penalties with a scriptural text, though in the rest of the code he did not imitate the compilation of Cotton in that respect. These laws were to be considered annually by the court for three years, and such of them as were not altered or repealed were to stand.

The establishment of the fundamental laws just mentioned was a most important step on the part of the colonists. It has been called almost a declaration of independence, for the code began with an assertion that neither life, liberty, honor, nor estate was to be invaded, except by virtue of an express law established by local authority; and it certainly verged closely upon opposition to the rule of the sovereign. It declared to the world that while the charter allowed no laws to be enacted under it "repugnant to the laws of England," the colonists felt themselves empowered to build up such a system as the circumstances of the people demanded.

Those persons who had been sent out of the colony as unfit to live there had, as we know, carried prejudicial reports home regarding the spirit of independence that was growing up, even before Winthrop's arrival, and these were repeated frequently from time to time. The first efforts to lead the government to interfere proved signal failures; but they were only the beginning of a long struggle which lasted more than fifty years, and finally succeeded. In 1634, there was a direct demand by the English government that the charter should be delivered up, but the governor and council declined to surrender it. There seems to have been a feeling in Boston, as well as elsewhere, that the possession of the actual parchment, signed and sealed by the sovereign or his agent, was necessary to the preservation of liberty, and we find that after a while it was ordered that two or three persons should be appointed by each house to "keep safe and secret the said patent."

The colonists were fully determined not to give up their charter without a struggle, but they also decided that the best policy for them was to make long consultations and discussions, and thus to avoid a direct reply whenever possible, while using diplomatic words that were intended to be received as professions of loyalty to the powers that happened to be uppermost in England at a given time.

There was great alarm in Boston on the occasion of this very demand for the charter, for it was rumored that the rights of the colonists were to be invaded by a governor and commission from England authorized to make laws, call in patents, and levy taxes. A meeting was held at which all the ministers (except Mr. Ward) were present, and it was voted that such a governor if sent over ought not to be accepted, but that the colonists should defend their lawful possessions. The court appropriated six hundred pounds towards fortifications and other charges at Castle Island, at Charlestown, and Dorchester, and captains were directed to train skilful men, while a committee, comprising Winthrop, Dudley, and others was appointed to " consult, direct, and give command for the managing and ordering of any war that might befal." Forts were begun; a beacon was set on the Sentry hill, " to give notice to the country of any danger "; musket-balls were made a legal tender; and every man older than sixteen years was obliged to take the freeman's oath; while a military commission was formed with power to imprison or even to put to death, " any that they should judge to be enemies to the commonwealth," or who " would not come under their command or restraint." This was the reply, and the only reply that the court made to the demand for its charter, in 1635, and it looked much like a threat.

The English government was not idle, and after many other movements on both sides, another, and a very strict order, was sent to Governor Winthrop for delivering up the charter; upon which the court directed that a letter should be written to " excuse our not sending it." Accordingly Winthrop wrote a very dignified letter, in which he said that the colonists would like to know what charges had been made against them, and urged reasons why the demand should not be insisted upon. He expressed a desire not to question the proceedings up to that point, but to "open the griefs of the colonists," so that the king might judge how to remedy them. The reply to this letter was a peremptory repetition of the demand; but the order was sent to Mr. Cradock, through his agent, and the court did not respond, since the demand had been received "in a private letter" and not in official form. The mother-country was by this time in so much confusion that no more notice could be taken of the remote colonies, and for thirty years matters went on in Boston and the Bay colony as though the people there were independent.

The year 1640 is to be remembered for an attempt that was made by Lord Say and Sele to dissuade emigrants from America, and to turn them to the West Indies; in fact to break up the colony of the Massachusetts Bay for that purpose. Governor Winthrop wrote a letter on this subject which must have been very forceful, for it drew from Lord Say and Sele a reply of the most spirited description. Winthrop showed, to his own satisfaction at least, that it was evident that God had chosen America to plant his people in, and that it would be dangerous and displeasing to try to change such a plan, and that his lordship ought not to "abase the goodness of the country." It is interesting to note in passing that when Cromwell had conquered Ireland, in 1649, and wished to keep that country in subjection, he bethought himself of the few thousand Englishmen in New England, and invited them to come over and occupy the land. Some persons expressed a wish to learn more of the project; but there was no general desire to change their abode. Similar offers were made by Cromwell in 1655 to the New Englanders, if they would go to Jamaica which his fleet had reduced. The Massachusetts court read Cromwell's letter, after a delay of eight months, and composed a reply in which reference was made to the great mortality of the English in Jamaica, and the intention of the Americans to remain where they were, though they assured "his Highness" that they would never cease to pray for him. They had written to him in 1651 that during the ten years of his trouble with the late king they had constantly adhered to him, not even wavering in the times of his weakest condition, but by their "fasting and prayers for your good success," and our thanksgiving after the same was attained, in days of solemnity set apart for the purpose, as also "by our sending over useful men," they had done him acceptable service and suffered hatred from other English colonies, and damage from the king's party, from the king of Scots, and the king of Portugal. Neither of these schemes was further urged by Cromwell, who, by the way, was otherwise engaged pretty soon.

Boston was meantime prosperous. The wigwams, huts, and hovels of the first days were changed into "orderly, fair, and well-built houses, well furnished";

it was a "city-like town," wharfed out with great industry and cost, the buildings beautiful and large, some fairly set forth with brick, tile, stone, and slate, and orderly placed with comely streets, "whose continual enlargement presages some sumptuous city." There were " streets filled with girls and boys sporting up and down" with a great concourse of people, where once were "wolves and bears nursing their young" far from the eyes of all. Dr. Ellis has drawn a picture of some of the wants and needs of the inhabitants of Boston at this time in his work on the " Puritan Age." He says:

"A grim wilderness environed them, with real and visionary dangers in its dark shadows. Marshes, morasses, unbridged streams and devious trails made intercourse difficult and all travel tedious. The numerous inventories left to us of household goods, of farm implements, and of apparel, are often amusing illustrations of simple thrift, and of the frugality, paucity, and rudeness of their furnishings, which still were of such relative value as to be carefully appraised. The tortures of the medical and surgical practice of those days were fearful for endurance. Our light foot-gear and water-proof protection for snow-storms and tempests found substitutes for them in boots of hide smeared with grease, and doublets of leather which drank in the water so that they had to be cast aside as the weight increased. The spoils of the hunter and safety from the Indian foe were won by the long gun supported by a ' rest,' and fired by a matchlock. What would the housewife and the forest-traveller of those days have been ready to give for a bunch of friction-matches, the cost of which for us is one cent! The lack of any currency, save Indian shell-peage, caused all traffic to be by barter of produce or labor at shifting values. The entire lack of all the delights of intellectual intercourse and of literature, save those of the most lugubrious character, must have had a most depressing influence upon the spirits of those who were so intently brooding over dismal theological problems." *

There was nothing, or little, to make the citizens think of the tumultuous doings that history records as going on in the mother-country; but they came to the knowledge of them in time.

John Winthrop died, in 1649, and was buried in the yard of King's Chapel, where his sepulchre may be seen to this day. He had been governor of "the considerablest part of New England," as Mather said, and "he maintained the figure and honor of his place with the spirit of a true gentleman." He let his moderation be known to all men; he "abridged himself of a thousand comfortable things" that he had been accustomed to, for the sake of those who were about him. He was a true father, not only to Massachusetts, and to the New England Confederation, of which he was chief, but also to Boston, and by his cheerful courage sustained the spirits of his companions when they were ready to droop. He was mild, magnanimous, and firm; he was benevolent and sympathetic; mildly aristocratic, but consistent and well-balanced; the noble founder of a state and a civilization. He had nourished the church, the school, the college; he had laid the

* "The Puritan Age and Rule," page 38.

foundation of a system of laws that was to endure; he was mourned by the Dutch Stuyvesant, at the New Netherlands, and by the governor of New Haven, who wondered who could be chosen to take his place in the arbitration of differences that might arise in the future, as they had in the past.

The place left vacant in Boston was occupied at first by Thomas Dudley, who did not long survive, and then by John Endicott, who lived through the time of the Commonwealth, and died during the struggle with Charles the Second for the charter.

XI.

THE TIMES OF THE MATHERS.

When Winthrop had been in Boston five years there arrived an emigrant who was the first of a family destined to furnish political and ecclesiastical leaders to the town for the whole of the colonial period. Richard Mather, for fifteen years minister of the church at Toxteth, finding himself in danger on account of his dissent, fled to America in 1635, and as his reputation was already known, he was immediately accepted as a "mighty man," and several parishes strove for his services. Mr. Mather relates that on his long and dangerous voyage he saw "mighty whales spewing up water in the air like the smoke of a chimney, and making the sea about them white and hoary," and they were "of such incredible bigness" that he exclaimed, "I will never wonder that the body of Jonah could be in the belly of a whale."

When put to the proof in Boston this mighty man was found to be as learned in the classics and in the Scriptures as his fame promised; his voice was "loud and big," and he uttered his words with a "deliberate vehemency" which, in the language of the day, "procured unto his ministry an awful and very taking majesty." He went to Dorchester and remained there until his death in 1689. He wrote many of the ponderous tomes of the period, composed the preface to the Bay Psalm Book, as well as some of its marvellous verses; showed himself a voracious reader and an indefatigable student; and established his fame on a lasting foundation both as a leader in church and state.

There were preachers of note in Boston besides Mr. Mather, and among them Mr. John Cotton and Mr. John Norton are to be especially remembered for the influence they exerted upon the town in its impressionable stage. Mr. Cotton was for twenty years minister to the congregation that gathered in the great church of St. Botolph, at old Boston; but in the year 1633, when Laud became archbishop, he found it necessary, like so many others, to seek the American shores. He came to Boston with Thomas Hooker and Samuel Stone, also distinguished lights in the New England pulpit, and was preacher to the First Church until his death in 1652. He has left behind him nothing that gives to the present generation any strong impression of the "insinuating and melting" style in which he is said to have preached—a style that is reputed to "have carried away every adversary captive after the triumphant chariot of his rhetoric," and it seems to us often, as we shake the dust from the volumes in which the ponderous pulpit oratory of those days is embalmed, that Boston audiences must have been very easily "captivated" by dry disquisitions; though it must be allowed that in the printed page we lose all the earnest fervor which a preacher, loved by his flock for his social virtues, threw into his formal utterances, and we are apt to forget, too, that an emigrant people who esteemed themselves persecuted for righteousness' sake, felt that there was a reality and an appropriateness in doctrinal discourses that cannot be appreciated by their descendants who have for generations enjoyed the peace that resulted from their tribulations. Mr. Cotton's death was brought on by a cold caught in consequence of exposure in crossing the ferry on a visit to Cambridge, whither he went to preach to the students of Harvard College.*

John Norton appeared in Boston three years later than Mr. Cotton, and immediately attracted attention by his scholarship, eloquence, and wisdom. He reluctantly accepted a call to Ipswich, where he was assistant to the Agawam Cobbler until he was chosen successor to Mr. Cotton. He then removed to Boston, and took up his new duties in 1653, though it was three years before he was installed. We read that the court formally expressed its congratulations upon his accession to this influential post of duty, which was not a strange thing for the court to do in the days when church and state were intimately connected. Both of these ministers exerted a powerful influence upon the town both politically and in their religious capacity, and were

* The ferry over the Charles River from Brighton was at the foot of Dunster Street. In 1662 a bridge was built at the foot of the present Boylston Street, on account of the increase of travel, especially on lecture days.

complimented by their people with constant expressions of fondness, but they left behind them no posterity equal to them in this respect, to continue their prestige. This the Mathers did, founding a dynasty which continued in uncrowned power for almost a century.

The second person to honor the name Mather was born in the year 1639, and in consequence of the fact that there was "increase of every sort" at the time, he received the name Increase, which in his formal writings he sometimes translated into Latin—"Crescentius." At the time of Winthrop's death he was almost ready for Harvard College, and he actually entered at the age of twelve; though he did not take his first degree until he was seventeen. Two years later he preached in his father's pulpit and then sailed for Ireland, where he became a student at Trinity College, Dublin. After the Restoration he found it best to return to his native land, and in 1644 he became minister of the North Church, Boston, which stood on North Square, then the very centre of the most aristocratic and influential homes. His own dwelling was on North Street, near Clark.

For almost sixty years Increase Mather continued to hold the congregation by the force of his personality, the strength of his logic, the adroitness of his policy, and the sagacity of his devices. No man was so powerful in Boston as he for the first half of that period, and few or none dared to stand up against his known views. Probably his scholarship and his accomplishments have not suffered by the mediums through which their fame has been carried down to

Increase Mather   Jus ad aras
              Crescentius Matherus

posterity; but making all allowances for the favorable prejudices of his biographers, we may conclude that he enjoyed an ability to labor which is almost incomprehensible, that his knowledge had a wonderful sweep, and that his diligence as a writer and speaker, as well as a counsellor to his fellow-townspeople, was so great that one marvels that his physical system did not break under it long before he had reached fourscore years of age.

Increase Mather married a daughter of John Cotton, and thus united two noted families; the eldest child of the couple, who has been called the "literary behemoth of New England," in the colonial era, was named, for his grandfather, Cotton. The historian of our literature calls him "a precocious and decidedly priggish young gentleman," with a well-developed sense of his own importance.* He entered Harvard at the age of eleven, and when he graduated, the president, Urian Oakes, in handing him his diploma, exclaimed, in Latin, "What a name! But, my hearers, I confess I am wrong; I should have said, what names! I shall say nothing of his reverend father, since I dare not praise him to his face; but, should he resemble and represent his venerable grandfathers, John Cotton and Richard Mather, in piety, learning, and elegance of mind, solid judgment, prudence, and wisdom, he will bear away the palm; and I trust that in this youth Cotton and

---

* "A History of American Literature," by Moses Coit Tyler. In this work one may read an entertaining sketch of the "Mather Dynasty," in which the merits and defects of each member of the family are brought out in an agreeable manner.

Mather will be united and flourish again." Certainly this was high praise, and well calculated to make the young student all the self-conscious and self-important personage that he became. Increase Mather returned his share of the fulsome compliment in 1682, when he wrote that Oakes " was one of the greatest lights that ever shone in this part of the world, or that is ever like to arise in this horizon."

Cotton Mather was a strange mixture of strength and weakness, of wisdom and poor judgment; his conceit must have been unbearable, and in his works it is simply ludicrous. Two notable examples of his self-appreciation are connected with Harvard College, for the presidency of which he supposed himself eminently adapted, though the corporation did not agree with him. When President Willard died in 1707, Mather thought that he ought to be chosen in the vacant place, and actually gave himself to fasting and other exercises, in expectation of the appointment; but it did not come. In 1724, on the death of President Leverett, he was certain that he could be " of singular service " to the college, but Dr. Sewall was chosen; whereupon Mather writes: " I am informed that yesterday the six men who call themselves the corporation of the college met, and, contrary to the epidemical expectation of the country, chose a modest young man, Sewall, for whose piety (and little else) every one gives a laudable character." He adds, characteristically : " I always foretold these two things of the corporation : first, that if it were possible for them to steer clear of me, they would do so ; secondly, that if it were possible for them to act foolishly, they will do so. The perpetual envy with which my essays to serve the Kingdom of God are treated among them, and the dread that Satan has of my beating up his quarters at the college, led me into the former sentiment ; the marvellous indiscretion with which the affairs of the college are managed led me into the latter."

The year that Governor Winthrop died was the same in which King Charles the First was beheaded, and that event had an important bearing upon the interests of Boston. It was also the year in which Parliament passed an act for the promotion of the gospel in New England, which led to the formation of the Society for the Propagation of the Gospel among the Indians, the learned experimental philosopher, Robert Boyle, being appointed the first president, by King Charles the Second, after his restoration, in 1662. This society was useful in supplying funds for the encouragement of the "Apostle" Eliot, in the labors that he had already begun, though it had been anticipated by the general court of the Massachusetts colony two years before Winthrop died.

It is said that at about this time the "scrupulosity" of the good people of Boston was at its height, and in proof of it Hutchinson remarks that Governor Endicott, one of the most rigid of the magistrates, joined in an association pledged to use its influence against the wearing of long hair, as "a thing uncivil and unmanly ; fit only for Russians and barbarous Indians." It was established as good form not to permit the hair to grow below the ears, though governor Hutchinson wonders why some good soul did not retort the text in Leviticus, " Ye shall not round the corners of your heads." There had been much legislation and discussion regarding matters of this kind from the beginning of the settlement. As early as the year after his arrival in Boston, Mr. Cotton was moved to preach at Salem on the subject of veils; the court had passed a law against tobacco,* the use of which Mr. Winthrop had given up before coming to America; and there were laws concerning the wearing of gold and silver laces, girdles and hatbands, embroidered caps, and too great sleeves; concerning all of which, the citizens of the little hamlet in the wilderness had been guilty. It was permitted to those who had such vanities to wear them out, but not to have new ones made. There had previously been a regulation mulcting smokers in the sum of one penny sterling for every time of taking tobacco in any place, but apparently it did not suffice. In 1635 a law was passed fining persons twelve pence for falling into " private conference " in public meetings—that is, for talking in meeting,—and the court was constantly giving its attention to small matters of this sort.

The Agawam Cobbler thought to influence his countrywomen by satire; and though he asserted

* The law reads: " It is ordered that no person shall take tobacco publicly, under penalty of two shillings and sixpence, nor privately, in his own house or in the house of another, before strangers, and that two or more shall not take it together anywhere, under the aforesaid penalty for each offence."

that he was "neither nigard nor cinick to the true bravery of the true gentry," he declared that "it is a more common than convenient saying that nine taylors make a man: it were well if nineteen could make a woman to her mind." "Methinks it would break the hearts of Englishmen to see so many goodly English women imprisoned in French cages, peering out of their hood-holes for some men of mercy to help them with a little wit, and nobody relieves them. We have about five or six of them in our colony: if I see any of them accidentally I cannot cleanse my fancy of them for a month after. . . . It is a most unworthy thing for men that have bones in them to spend their lives in making fiddle-cases for futulous women's fancies; which are the very pettitoes of infirmity, the giblets of perquisquillian toys. . . . When I hear a nugiperous gentledame inquire what dress the queen is in this week, —what the nudiustertian fashion of the court,—with egge to be in it in all haste; I look at her as the very gizzard of a trifle, the product of a quarter of a cipher, the epitome of nothing, fitter to be kickt, if she were of a kickable substance, than either honored or humored." It is doubtful if the "nugiperous gentledames" knew enough Latin to understand the "loose-tongued liberty" with which they were addressed by this ferocious crusader.

During the time of Cromwell the people of Boston kept on their independent way with less difficulty than before; they increased their trade and improved their town; they went so far in the way of independence that in 1652 they began to coin the bullion that flowed to them from the West Indies and elsewhere, putting on the money, not the arms of the king or the name of the mother-country, but simply the words "New England" and "Massachusetts." Parliament was too much occupied to interfere, and it seems that Charles the Second, after his restoration, allowed the process to continue. The town was alarmed by news of the war between England and Holland, which, it was supposed, would make complications with the New Netherlands, and by a rising of the Narragansett Indians in Connecticut, which came about in consequence of the relations between the Indians and the Dutch. Boston did not approve of war in this instance, and it was not prosecuted.

At the Restoration, the struggle over the charter was renewed. Goffe and Whalley, two of the judges who had condemned Charles the First, fled to America at that time, and were received in Boston, as might have been expected, with cordiality. The king was not "proclaimed," and no "address" was sent to him. It was not long before the colonists were called upon to meet more charges made against them by Quakers and others, and then an address was sent to Charles the Second, abounding in protestations of loyalty. To this the king replied in language that seemed kindly, but was not very satisfactory to the colonists. He demanded, at last, that the freedom of conscience, which they emphasized, should be extended to those who used the Book of Common Prayer; that the elective franchise should be given to others than merely the members of the orthodox churches;

and that the fugitive judges should be arrested and returned. The judges probably obtained early information of the king's demands, and when Governor Endicott sent officers for them they were not to be found.

At about the same time the busy industry that commerce had developed was interfered with by an Act of Navigation, under the terms of which every thing imported into Boston, except in English ships manned by English sailors, was liable to forfeiture. The court now thought it necessary to make a declaration of rights under the charter, and at a meeting held in Boston, June 10, 1661, it asserted that the governor and company formed a body politic, competent to make freemen, to set up all sorts of officers, to make laws, and to repel invaders, but in all things to be loyal to the king. The king was proclaimed in Boston in the following August, fifteen months after his accession, by order of this "loyal" court. No wonder the tardy colonists never stood well with his Majesty King Charles the Second. Their real feelings were too apparent. They sent two agents to London in 1662, to look out for the colonial interests, who brought back a letter from the king, which the court proceeded to consider at its meeting August 3, 1664, after a delay of two years. Meantime there had been rumors that men-of-war were coming from England with troops and commissioners charged with the duty of determining all matters of complaint. Eleven days before the August meeting the commissioners had actually arrived. There had been a solemn fast in anticipation of this event, and "in view of the many distractions and troubles under which the country" labored; the train-bands had been put in order and the Castle prepared to give speedy notice of the expected arrivals. The commissioners came, but were not able to remain long enough to attend the August meeting. They went to New Amsterdam, with which also they had business.

After two months of solemn discussion (and we may be sure that the affair was looked upon as a serious one), a letter was ready for the "Dread Soveraigne." In it the poor subjects "prostrated" themselves before the royal feet, and with some eloquence in a now antiquated style, begged favor. They made fervent pleas for themselves, stiffly asserted the rights that they conceived were theirs by the sacred charter, pathetically presented the story of the burdens of a new plantation, referred to "the great labors, hazards, costs, and difficulties" of "wrestling with the wants of a wilderness," and to the royal promise of encouragement and protection conveyed in the king's letter of February, 1660; and asserted that they were grievously afflicted by the plan of sending to them rulers that they had no hand in choosing; who were to proceed, not by established law, but by their own discretions; that it pained them to see His Majesty put to great expense in a business that would never reimburse one-half the amount that was to be laid out on it. They reiterate the assertion that they did not come to the wilderness to seek great things for themselves; that they meddled not with any business but their own; that they were carefully studious of all due subjection to His Majesty, not only for wrath, but for conscience sake; and in conclusion they exclaim, "Royal Sir; it is in your power to say of your poor people of New England, they shall not die . . . Let our government live, let our patent live, our magistrates live, our laws and liberties live, our religious enjoyments live, so shall we all yet have further cause to say from our hearts, let the king live forever! . . . And the blessing of them that were ready to perish shall come upon your majesty, . . . and we and ours shall have lasting cause to rejoice that we have been numbered among your majesties most humble servants and suppliants."

The king's commissioners met in Boston in the following February, and attempted to sit as a court to hear complaints against the governor and company; but the general court disapproved of such action, as inconsistent with the duty to God and the king which every colonist owed, and by sound of trumpet prohibited all persons from sustaining the commissioners, who were, therefore, unable to accomplish any thing, and gave up the contest, telling the Boston people that they would refer the matter to His Majesty, who, they expressively added, "is of power enough to make himself to be obeyed in all his dominions." The king wrote, in reply to the letter of the court of October, that he would recall the commissioners, since it was evident that the colonists thought that the charter had been violated by their appointment; but he directed that four or five persons should be sent to him that he might hear what was to be said on that side. The court acknowledged this demand, but declined to send any one to the king, saying that all had been said that there was to say, and that they preferred to commit themselves to God. Boston and other commercial towns opposed this cavalier action, and the commissioners also protested, but in vain. The colonists endeavored to appease the king, however, by sending him a present of some shiploads of masts and other timber for the royal navy. The contest was for a time closed, and during the following ten years there were few communications between the parties at odds.

John Evelyn tells us in his Diary that when the Board of Trade* met to organize and take the official oaths, May 26, 1671, and "to counsel his majesty to the best of our abilities for the well-governing of his foreign plantations," what was "most insisted on was to know the condition of New England." To the board the people of that colony appeared "to be very independent as to their regard to Old England or his majesty, rich and strong as they now were," and there was "great debate" as to how such colonists should be addressed, "for the condition of that colony was such that they were able to contest with all other plantations about them, and there was

* This important body comprised the Duke of Buckingham, the Earl of Sandwich, Sir George Carteret, and others. Its sessions were held in the house of the Earl of Bristol, in Lincoln's Inn Fields, which had been taken for the purpose. There were seven rooms on a floor, with long gallery, gardens, etc., and the meeting-room was appropriately furnished with atlases, maps, charts, globes, etc.

fear of their breaking from all dependence" on England. Some members were in favor of sending "a menacing letter, which those who better understood the peevish and touchy humor of that colony were utterly against." On the sixth of June there was another debate on the same subject, and it was decided that any action towards New England should be "civil and conciliating," because it was understood that the people were certainly "almost upon the very brink of renouncing any dependence on the crown." One would almost think that this was written in 1771, instead of 1671. It shows that however the Boston people might protest their loyalty, their acts appeared to observers at a distance to be those of men bound to maintain their independency,—to govern themselves under their charter, it is true, but to stretch its provisions to the utmost in their own favor.

The king did not acknowledge the gift of masts until 1669, though his clerk of the navy, the garrulous Samuel Pepys, wrote in his private diary that it was "a blessing mighty unexpected," without which the efforts of the navy might have failed the following year, and he praised God "for thus much good fortune." Eight years later, the same "poor subjects" in the "remote corner of the earth," sent his majesty "ten barrels of cranberries, two hogsheads of special good samp, and three thousand codfish," with their compliments.

XII.

THE CHARTER IS LOST.

Boston was happily situated in many respects, but in one particular it was especially fortunate. Its remoteness from the great body of Indians gave it immunity from those attacks which devastated many towns in Connecticut and others in Massachusetts, as well as those in the more northerly eastern region. We read of intercourse between the immigrants and the natives from time to time: how they came to town to complain of ill-treatment on the part of whites who were supposed to be under Massachusetts jurisdiction; how they asked protection tribe from tribe; how they at one time took advantage of the Sunday gathering to break into an unprotected dwelling; how they were convicted of assaulting Englishmen, and were set in the bilboes for their pains; and how the Pequod tribe had been fought to the fearful death; but these were as nothing to the terrible experiences that were suffered at Haverhill, at Dover, at Deerfield.

There was an Indian called Philip, who made his squalid home at Mount Hope or Montaup, and seemed to have little respect for the whites, and to care nothing whether he offended or pleased them.

Trouble was to come from him, not because Boston had any grievance with him, but because Plymouth complained of his actions, and by the articles of confederation the Massachusetts colony was obliged to give aid to her sister. Philip was accused of hatching a general conspiracy among the Indians for the slaughter of all the Europeans around.

Massachusetts was at peace, her men were busy at their trades, her matrons were caring for their families, her children were going to the schools and the college, her dwellings were growing in elegance and comfort, her fishermen were bringing in the spoil of the mackerel and the whale; those of the inhabitants who stood for men of letters were producing works treating serious subjects that were thought worthy of notice in the mother-country, and there was promise of still greater progress in all that refines and exalts a people. Quaker and Baptist no longer gave solicitude, and no menace came from England. Under such peaceful circumstances Boston, and all New England, were terrified by the most threatening Indian disturbance that had yet been known.

In June, 1675, there came news to Plymouth that Philip and his men were constantly in arms; that they had sent their wives to places of safety; that many strange Indians flocked to them; that the young Indians were "earnest for a war"; and, finally, that the town of Swanzey, the nearest to the Indian country, had been attacked; that two houses had been burned, a dozen more rifled, and several whites killed, upon whose bodies the savages had "exercised more than brutish barbarities, beheading, dismembering, and mangling them, and exposing them in a most inhuman manner." The frightful news was sent post to Boston, and there were hurried arrangements, not for defence only, but for the pursuit, capture, and destruction of the Indians.

John Leverett was governor at the time. He was an old soldier of Cromwell's wars, and knew the demands of the moment. The council was immediately called together, and Captain Edward Hutchinson was directed to proceed to the Narragansetts and order them to break off correspondence with Philip, and to give the English all possible information of his designs. Leverett concentrated what forces he could at Boston and sent messengers to Philip. They found war actually begun, and returned with the news, spreading the alarm as they went. On their arrival drums were beat up for volunteers, and in the short space of three hours one hundred and ten men were ready to set out. It seems that a Dutchman under sentence of death for piracy, with others in like condition, was allowed to volunteer.

Thus Boston made its hurried preparations, and a war which lasted more than a year was begun. It was marked by all the proverbial atrocities of Indian warfare. Massachusetts had six settlements on the Connecticut River, all of which suffered. Northfield, Deerfield, and Springfield were burned; but Northampton, Hadley, and Hatfield, though attacked, were not destroyed. An incident that occurred near

Boston shows the dangers of the times and the spirit of the people. On a Sunday in July, when the members of the houshold, excepting a maid-servant and children, were at meeting, an Indian came to the house of John Minot, in Dorchester, about five miles from Boston, and tried to gain admission. The door was shut, and he attempted a window. The maid, with presence of mind, quickly hid the children who had been left in her charge under two brass kettles, ran upstairs, and fired a musket at the intruder. The Indian also fired, but missed his aim, upon which the maid shot him in the shoulder, but the wound was not severe enough to make him give up his attempt. He was actually entering the window when the maid threw a shovelful of live coals in his face and forced him to retreat in pain, at the same time placing a mark upon him by which he was identified when he was afterwards found dead in the woods. Both the intensity of feeling and the quickness of the Boston men to rally when required are shown by the fact that, on a day in September, when a guard at Mendon, thirty miles away, fired his gun in a drunken excess, the alarm spread until it reached the town at about ten in the morning, and twelve hundred men were under arms in an hour. In consequence of the trials of this war there was a solemn fast in October.

While it was summer the savages had the better of their enemies, but, as winter came on, their prospect darkened. In December a company of foot and horse marched from Boston and fell upon the enemy in the Narragansett country. The Indians were in a fort; snow covered the ground, and there was no shelter for the English for miles.

The fort was stormed, seven hundred fighting Indians were slain, three hundred more were wounded and died afterwards, besides large numbers that perished by fire and cold. The English loss was probably but one hundred, and has been estimated at a smaller number. There was determination on both sides: the natives were fighting for their homes against a people that they felt to be superior to them, and the whites were convinced that their very preservation depended upon striking a heavy blow at an insidious and treacherous opponent. It was a bloody and frightful bravery.

During the winter there were other raids by horse and foot against the Indians in various directions; Philip himself once ventured within twenty-two miles of Boston and destroyed much property, and elsewhere the colonists were shot down by unseen foes, their cattle were killed, and their houses burned. The decisive struggle occurred at Great Falls, on the Connecticut, in May, 1676, and then the cause of the redskins went down apace: their haunts were broken up, and Philip was hunted from place to place until August, when he was surprised, near Mount Hope, and killed by an Indian bullet, fourteen months after he had begun the war at that very spot.

The colonies most distressed were Massachusetts and Plymouth, though Connecticut had done its share of the fighting, and had suffered the penalties of war. Plymouth was almost ruined, but Massachusetts was able to recover from its great loss.

The towns were drained of men; six hundred of the colonists had perished; thousands found themselves suffering from the losses and sorrows that followed; six hundred dwellings had been burned, some towns totally destroyed, and expenses incurred that were enormous in comparison with the resources of the colonists; but not a plea was sent to England for help. The Americans were " poor and yet proud," as Lord Anglesey, " not altogether groundlessly," wrote from London. They were not willing to place themselves under any obligation to the crown, and yet they did not disdain to accept thankfully a gift of a thousand pounds contributed " by divers Christians in Ireland," to those who were, as it was expressed, " impoverished, distressed, and in necessity by the late war." *   Hutchinson is authority for the statement that all the sums bestowed upon the colony from abroad were equalled by remittances sent thence after the fire in London, and at other times, for the relief of sufferers, so that it is evident that even in these cases the colonists kept the generous accounts balanced.

The war with Philip caused the court to enact more rigid laws against Indians, and it was ordered " that a guard be set against the entrance of the town of Boston [on the Neck], and that no Indian be suffered to enter upon any pretext, and without a guard and two musketeers, and not to lodge in

* This charitable gift was returned to Ireland by Boston, in 1847, on the occasion of the potato famine of that and the previous years. Interesting details regarding the facts mentioned are to be found in a contribution to the N. E. Hist. Gen. Register, by Dr. Charles Deane, vol. ii., pages 245, 398.

town." Indians even approaching by land or water were liable to arrest. Most of those who had previously given themselves up to the government were sent to Deer Island, where they remained during the winter, enduring some suffering. Many of the women and children who had been made prisoners were sold into West Indian slavery, in spite of pathetic protests from their friend, John Eliot, who wrote, in a formal letter to the council, that such treatment was worse than death, and contrary to the teachings of the Saviour. He said: "To sell souls for money seems to me a dangerous merchandize." Ever after this terrible war there was a horror connected with the mention of an Indian.

In writing to Governor Leverett, Lord Anglesey took occasion to chide him, and "the whole people of New England," for acting as if they were independent of the crown, and needed not the protection of the king, and he assured them that His Majesty had a tender and compassionate heart for all his subjects who were industrious and orderly. Nevertheless, whatever King Charles may have been desirous of doing for his subjects who were "industrious and orderly," he was not unwilling to take advantage of the distress occasioned by this war to make another move towards the abrogation of their charter. At the very height of the Indian troubles he sent a letter to the Massachusetts court by the hands of Edward Randolph, "the evil genius of New England," as he has been called, authorizing him to institute inquiries which struck at the very foundations of the government.

Randolph, who subsequently crossed the ocean at least fifteen times, reached Boston a few weeks before Philip's death, when the public sorrow and distress were great, and proceeded to stir up all possible dissatisfaction with the magistrates. He learned, and very soon reported, that "the corporation of Boston is the most flourishing and powerful, and at the present gives laws to a great part of this country, by a pretended charter from His late Majesty." He found that there were two parties, the patriots and prerogative men, whigs and tories, one of which was ready to acquiesce in the orders of the king, while the other held by the principles of the fathers, who wished, as they had told their sovereign, to govern themselves after their own manner. Among the members of these parties Randolph sowed the seeds of bitter strife, and as a special measure recommended the appointment of a general governor through whom King Charles might have direct control of the colonies. This done, Randolph returned to England, in July, 1676. The colonists followed him with agents charged with the presentation of their cause to the king. When these agents arrived in London they found, of course, that the minds of those in influence had been prejudiced against them and their cause. They remained until the end of 1679, when they were ordered back, the colonists being directed to send others in their stead.

The first agents had accomplished nothing; and meantime Randolph had been crossing and recrossing the ocean, exciting the Americans on the one hand and the king on the other. Matters thus constantly grew worse ; the king is represented to have been "greatly provoked, and the colonists were almost hopeless. Finally the second agents concluded that the case was too desperate for them, and called upon the general court to decide whether it was best for them to remain any longer. The court met in March, 1683, and voted to allow them to " accept of and consent unto such proposals and demands as might consist with the main end of their predecessors in their removing hither with their charter."

A few weeks after this vote had been taken, Randolph sailed for home, and in June, 1683, made thirteen formal charges against the colonists. He accused them of assuming powers that the charter did not give ; of carrying on the government in another place than that which was intended ; of imposing an oath of fidelity that included no promise of allegiance to the king ; of opposing the acts of navigation ; of levying customs ; of discountenancing the Church of England ; of coining money, and of other misdemeanors. The agents, unable to effect any thing, returned to Boston, in October, 1683, and Randolph followed immediately with a *quo warranto*, or writ requiring the Massachusetts colony to answer by what right certain powers had been exercised. Joseph Dudley, a degenerate son of Winthrop's old friend, was one of the " assistants," and it seems that on a visit to England he had made friends with the "mammon of unrighteousness," and was ready to take an open stand against the colonists, a fact which Randolph had surmised before this time. Dudley saw that the charter was doomed, and wished to gain for himself favor from the king. The colonists at last discovered his true character, and he was dropped from the list of magistrates in May, 1684.

The governor and a majority of the assistants, influenced by Dudley, had by this time become hopeless, and voted an address to the king, in which they declared that they laid themselves at his majesty's feet and would not contend; but from this the deputies dissented, and the freemen of Boston, under the lead of Increase Mather, at a meeting lawfully warned for the purpose of considering the matter, voted unanimously that they would not resign their charter and privileges and make submission to His Majesty. Mather said: " I verily believe that we shall sin against the God of heaven if we vote an affirmative. The Scripture teacheth us otherwise: 'That which the Lord our God hath given us, shall we not possess it?'" It was not the first time that Mather had raised his powerful voice in similar strains. Three years previously he had preached a sermon ostensibly in reference to comets and earthquakes, but really having political lessons, in which Scripture was aptly quoted to prove that God would interfere to protect his New England children.

The records of this notable town-meeting are not preserved, but we have a paper, apparently from the hand of Increase Mather, in which the subject before it is discussed with as much regularity as the charges of Randolph were made in his application for the *quo warranto*. It argues that the sacred document ought not to be given up, because it would be "destructive to the interests of religion"; nothing would be gained by it (those corporations that had already submitted to the pleasure of the court had gained nothing)*; it would be a departure from the ancient principles and policy of the colony, for in 1638, though under a *quo warranto*, which had been issued in 1635, judgment had been given against the charter, the fathers did not and durst not make submission, and in 1664 they would not have commissioners over them; there was fear of "popish counsels" at court; it would be contrary to the advice of the ministers, given only three years before, after "a solemn day of prayer"; and it ought not to be done in any event without the consent of the whole body of the freemen and church-members. Then, there is the sixth commandment, for commonwealth-killing is as bad as man-killing; suicide is forbidden.—Judges, xi., 24, 27: I Kings, xxi., 3, etc.

This was no sudden impulse on the part of the deputies, nor of the town of Boston; the deputies debated the question two weeks, and then voted that they would not consent, but adhered to their former view. It made no difference, however, what the town of Boston thought, what the whole body of freemen and church-members thought; every thing had been arranged by Randolph and the king, and

---

* The allusion is to the *quo warranto* against the city of London, over which there had been great discussion not long before this (June 12, 1683).

the people of England interested in trade stood behind them. Randolph, who now returned to London, took the votes to his royal master, and confidently looked for news that Dudley had prevailed upon the deputies to change their minds; but he was disappointed. Dudley wrote, instead, that all who tried to lead the deputies to cast themselves humbly at the feet of the king were regarded as enemies to public peace and liberty. Worse than all, it was reported that the governor and magistrates at Boston had been very busy repairing fortifications.

The general court again addressed the king, reiterating the appeal, as from his "poor subjects," reminding him that they were the children of those who, under security of a charter granted them by his father, had left "all that was dear to them," etc., etc., as in former addresses. Among themselves they avowed their intention to "spin out the case to the uttermost"; but they were staggered in September, 1684, by the intelligence that a decree had been entered in the court of chancery in June, vacating the charter. A session of the general court was held, and the information presented; but nothing more was done. Five weeks later another session was held, and a last plea prepared to be sent to the king. It sufficed nothing; the sons had lost what the fathers had gained, and it seemed as though the hearty struggles of half a century had availed nothing. King Charles, in his gracious love for the New England colonists, selected as their new governor the notoriously bloody Col. Piercy Kirke of the Second

Foot, whose subsequent atrocities have made him infamous. The colony awaited his coming with dread.* Meantime His Majesty was called to account to a higher power for his share in the transaction of the past years. The people of Massachusetts still treasured the charter; its parchment and its seals were intact, and the sign-manual of the minister of King Charles the First was as distinct as ever; but possession did not give validity. It was dead sheepskin, and dead wax, and conveyed no rights to its holders.

* This was before the Bloody Assize, when Jeffries condemned more than three hundred at once to the gallows; and when Kirke and his officers sat carousing at the White Hart at Taunton, ordering a prisoner hanged for their merriment at every toast, causing drums to give music for the drunken crew the meanwhile. It was at the time when the captured rebels were sold to be sent to Jamaica as slaves, by request of the queen and her maids of honor, to furnish them money to bedeck their bodies. We cannot imagine the terrible forebodings of the colonists.

XIII.

AN AMERICAN DESPOTISM.

To understand the feelings of the Bostonians at this juncture, it must be remembered that the death of Charles the Second, just at the time when the charter was lost, placed on the throne of England a sovereign from whom they could expect only worse treatment, for James the Second was looked upon as surely a papist, and that the colony should have fallen into the hands of such an one was of all things the most to be dreaded. Not only this, but the events that occurred in the rebellion of Monmouth were calculated to throw the colonists into a state of consternation. They expected that Col. Kirke would be their governor; sent over with absolute authority, responsible to the king only; and as the stories of his doings after the battle of Sedgemoor came to them, they doubtless all shuddered with Secretary Rawson as he said: "Our condition is awful!" Accustomed to the atrocities of the savages, the Americans could appreciate keenly the situation that they would find themselves in if their ruler were one trained in African warfare, for Kirke had been governor of Tangiers. Increase Mather said of him: "That cruel, and horrid, and hideous tiger, whose barbarous cruelties have rendered him famous to all succeeding ages, was coming over with a regiment of myrmidons, in quality of governor." It matters not that the character of this threatened governor was blackened by report far beyond truth; we are concerned only to remind ourselves of the consternation into which the people of Boston were thrown by the news that Kirke had been appointed by one king and confirmed by his successor. It presented to them scenes which cannot be described,—real, as they then appeared in the correspondence with their agent and others in the mother-country: pictures of a coarse and brutal soldiery, led by an equally coarse and brutal captain, quartered upon the community, and making themselves free with all that was held sacred. It was a picture of pandemonium, as if the "promiscuous crew" described by the Puritan poet were to be turned loose upon the land that the Lord had reserved for better things.

The suffering in anticipation must have been intense throughout New England; but it was not destined to be real, for James found that the services of Kirke were more needed at home than abroad, and he was never sent to America. In his place the king chose Joseph Dudley, of whom Randolph said, "no man better understands the constitution of your country and hath more loyalty and respect to his majesty's affairs." The old form of government had been continued after the abrogation of the charter simply because there was nothing else to be done, and the court was too much occupied after the death of King Charles to give attention to any thing so remote as the colonies, especially when the rebellion called for prompt action. It was not until the middle of May, 1686, that a commission reached Boston under which Mr. Dudley was elevated to the office of president, a position in which he thought that no American was his equal. Certainly his domain was sufficiently extensive, for his commission made him supreme over the colony of the Massachusetts Bay, Maine, New Hampshire, and the Narragansett Country, and he was also vice-admiral of the seas around New England. A deputy-president and sixteen councillors were to exercise authority with him, but there was no plan for a house of representatives of the people.

Randolph was already registrar of the same region, and he and Dudley now laid their commissions before the general court, addressing them, however, as "some of the principal gentlemen and chief inhabitants of the several towns of the Massachusetts," in order that their official capacity might not be acknowledged. The court gave up under protest, saying that the rule for the administration of justice seemed indeterminate and too arbitrary, and that they were to be abridged of their liberties as Englishmen, which, they significantly added, may not "be safe for you or for us." The court adjourned until a day in the autumn, throwing upon the new officers all responsibility for the government of the people, and hoping, as Randolph said, that by some unhappy accident in England, or by raising dissensions among the new rulers, they might succeed in dissolving the constitution and thus reassume the direction of affairs themselves. The book of the records of the Massachusetts colony was now closed.

A week or so later the new government, which had been duly proclaimed, was convened; twenty-one pounds' worth of wine was drunk in its honor, and there was some affectation of general festivity; but it was factitious, the people were simply acquiescent. Differences soon arose between Dudley and Randolph. Dudley was not sufficiently favorable to the Church of England. He wrote a letter to Increase Mather the very day that he made his demand upon the general court, in which he said that he was exceedingly anxious for the prosperity of his "dear mother at Cambridge," and that he desired to act in civil matters in such a way as to receive the approval of one to whom he had so long looked for ghostly counsel. Mather was at the time president of Harvard College, and also the minister of greatest influence in the colony, and doubtless Dudley was sincere in desiring to retain his favor. Dudley was also not sufficiently active in encouraging the Episcopalians to suit Randolph; and when the minister, Mr. Robert Radcliffe, whom Randolph thought "a sober man," petitioned for the privilege of using one of the three meeting-houses for his service, neither of them was allowed him, but he was "granted the east end of the Town-House, where the deputies use to meet, until those who desire his ministry shall provide a fitter place." After this Randolph discovered that Dudley was "a man of base, servile, and anti-monarchical principles." He complained that his own life was made very uneasy, that "Independent ministers flourish and expect to be advised with in public affairs"; and that but one member of the government besides himself was a member of the Established Church.

On the first Sunday after the inauguration of the royal government, Mr. Radcliffe worshipped according to the rites of the Church of England in the Town-House. Sewall records in his diary that as he sat at home he listened to the reading "in course," by his son of two passages "exceedingly suited to the day." They were the twenty-sixth chapter of Isaiah, and the one hundred and forty-first Psalm. We can imagine the twain sitting that day in the house near the water, on the present Washington Street, near Summer, which had been occupied by his father-in-law, John Hull, the first man to coin money for the colonists.* There sat Samuel Sewall the typical Puritan; the man who would not sell a slice of his grounds to the Episcopalians for a church lot; the rich, sagacious, garrulous scholar, listening to the words as they fell from the lips of his son, and making his inward comments. Both noticed the interesting fact that the passages they read came "in course." Let us listen:

"Lord, I cry unto thee: make haste unto me. . . .

* John Hull owned a house near Pemberton Square (which had been occupied by John Cotton and Harry Vane), described as being "considerably distant from other buildings and very bleak," but Sewall still occupied the old home. The investigations of the late Estes Howe, communicated to the Massachusetts Historical Society in November, 1884, in a letter to Charles Deane, LL.D., settled the matter.

Let the wicked fall into their own nets, whilst that I withal escape. . . . When their judges are overthrown in stony places, they shall hear my words: for they are sweet. . . Our bones are scattered at the grave's mouth. . . . Trust ye in the Lord forever. . . . For he bringeth down them that dwell on high. . . . Lord, wilt thou ordain peace for us . . . Thou hast increased the nation, O Lord, thou hast increased the nation: thou art glorified: thou hadst removed it far unto all the ends of the earth. Lord in trouble have they visited thee; they poured out a prayer when thy chastening was upon them. . . . Come, my people, enter thou into thy chambers, and shut thy doors about thee; hide thyself as it were for a little moment, until the indignation be overpast."

The meeting that Mr. Radcliffe was to have held was deferred until the sixth of June, "at which time the pulpit is provided." "The pulpit is movable," Mr. Sewall says, "carried up and down stairs, as occasion serves; it seems many crowded thither, and the ministers preached forenoon and afternoon"; but it mattered not, the words of David and of Isaiah were comforting to the Puritan, who looked upon the minister of the Established Church as one whose insidious influence would upturn all that was sacred, and fasten upon the colonists the burden of bishops and every hateful thing that they had left their mother-country to free themselves from. To Randolph, acting under directions of his royal master, the establishment of Episcopal services in Boston is due. He counted that there were four hundred attendants upon the services by the following

October, though "some were tradesmen and others of mechanical professions, and threatened by the congregational men to be arrested by their creditors or to be turned out of their work if they come to our church." Few persons in Boston had ever attended such a service, and there was much curiosity in regard to it.

Dudley did not long enjoy his greatness, for in December a new governor, Sir Edmund Andros, arrived in a fifty-gun ship the *Kingfisher*. He reached Nantasket on the nineteenth, but it was Sunday, and he did not land until the next day. Mr. Sewall was engaged in reading the Song of Habakkuk, at the time of the Sunday arrival, when he heard a gun, and immediately thought of the new governor; "but none of the family speaking of it," he writes, "I held my peace." He kept on reading the magnificent words before him, and comforting his soul in the midst of the tribulations of the church and state.

"O Lord, I have heard the report of thee, and am afraid. . . . In wrath remember mercy. . . . The eternal mountains were scattered, the everlasting hills did bow. . . . Thou didst march through the land in indignation, thou didst thresh the nations in anger. . . . Thou woundest the head out of the house of the wicked. . . . Thou didst pierce with his own staves the head of his warriors: they came as a whirlwind to scatter me; their rejoicing was as to devour the poor secretly. . . . I heard and my belly trembled, my lips quivered at the voice. . . .

"Though the fig tree shall not blossom,
Neither shall fruit be in the vines;

> The labor of the olive shall fail,
> And the fields shall yield no meat;
> The flock shall be cut off from the fold,
> And there shall be no herd in the stalls:
> Yet will I rejoice in the Lord,
> I will joy in the God of my salvation."

Monday afternoon Andros came up to Governor Leverett's (now Long) wharf, where Dudley and others met him, and a procession was formed that marched the short distance to the Town-House, where the royal commission was read. Standing with his hat on, he took the oath of allegiance, and showed something of the spirit in which he came, by almost immediately speaking to the ministers in the library about accommodations as to a meeting-house for the Episcopalians, suggesting that one house might serve for two assemblies in the same day. The ministers did not give him a definite reply; but on Wednesday evening, after having taken time to confer with others, Mr. Mather and Mr. Samuel Willard, of the South Church, called upon the new governor at his lodgings, at Madame Taylor's, on Hanover Street, at the corner of Elm Street, and told him "with great plainness" that they could consent to no such arrangement as he proposed. The following day the governor did not attend the "lecture," but on Saturday, which was Christmas, and a very fair and pleasant day, he walked forenoon and afternoon to the Town-House, to hear service. Andros was not able to restrain himself long, and when Good-Friday approached he determined to find better accommodations than a corner of the Town-House. He therefore examined the three meeting-houses, and demanded the use of the South on the Wednesday before. It was refused by those who had control over it, but he prevailed upon "goodman Needham" to ring the

THE FIRST KING'S CHAPEL (1685), SHOWING THE BEACON.

bell and open the door on Friday morning, and the service was held. The governor continued to use the building until the first King's Chapel was built in 1686. On the first Sunday of this use of the Old South, the exercises were very long, and the regular congregation was obliged to stand in the street, probably in a very undevout frame of mind, moving to and fro, until after two o'clock; but an effort was made to harmonize the hours of the two sets of worshippers afterwards.

According to the principles that controlled the governor's action, every privilege and right that had been founded upon the charter now fell to the ground, for the king of England was possessor of the soil of New England by virtue of the discovery of the Cabots. Massachusetts had no legislative nor executive power; the struggles of the past had won nothing for the Americans; every thing was at the mercy of the sovereign as extended through his representative, the governor. The Americans had no interest in the Magna Charta; the governor and council could regulate trade, constitute courts of justice, direct the militia, and plan and execute naval operations; the governor was ordered to protect liberty of conscience, but that valued little, for he was to countenance and encourage the Church of England; he could impose taxes and collect them. The men of Boston felt that they were bound hand and foot.

Andros and Randolph now went to work with a will to carry out the principles which have just been outlined; they called for the public records, and directed that all of them should be deposited at Boston; they demanded fees "extraordinary and oppressive" for registering wills, deeds, and mortgages; they caused jurors and witnesses to kiss the Bible when taking oaths, instead of holding up the right hand, as had been the custom (this was thought idolatrous); they imposed arbitrary taxes, and demanded that new patents should be taken out by all landholders, for which fees were charged. Such dealings as these could not be permitted, and even if the public officers who undertook to perform them had been popular, the people would soon have rebelled. They thought that the taxes should not be levied except by their representatives, and they hoped that even so arbitrary a prince as King James would permit his remote subjects to have a house of representatives; but he was certain to be arbitrary both at home and abroad, and there was no prospect of relief. In 1688, internal trade was obstructed by a law confining the business of every dealer to his own town, and prohibiting the sales of goods by peddlers or travelling merchants; heavy taxes also were laid upon trade; and finally the spring meetings of the towns were estopped.

Matters had reached such a pass by the spring of 1688 that the citizens of Boston determined to send a representative to plead in person for them with the king. They chose the Reverend Increase Mather, then at the age of forty-eight, and at the height of his reputation. He set sail April 17th, and to escape the enmity of Randolph, was obliged to disguise himself and reach his ship by night. The voyage was a short one, and Mather soon had the interview that he sought with King James at Whitehall. The king happened at that time to be desirous to cultivate friendship with dissenters, and listened with courtesy to the Puritan preacher as he asked for checks upon the progress of Episcopacy in New

England; he also vaguely promised a satisfactory settlement of the matter of titles to lands. Mather seems to have had hopes aroused that the king would even recall his favorite Andros. While these delusive negotiations were slowly progressing, on the fifth of November William of Orange landed on English soil, and William and Mary were soon proclaimed. The news did not reach Boston until the following April. It arrived just after Andros had returned from an expedition to the eastward, where he had been with a thousand men to pacify the Indian tribes.

The political movements in England were well known in Boston as they occurred, and it seems that an insurrection was imminent before the final news arrived there. In the middle of April there was a "buzzing among the people, great with expectation" of something, apparently they knew not what. Andros knew before he returned from Maine that William had landed, and he was on the alert to guard against the entrance of any fleet into the harbor; but he was not prepared for what actually happened. On Thursday, the eighteenth of April, it was reported at the South End that there was a sudden rising at the North End, and the same report was spread at the North End regarding the other part of town; by nine o'clock the drums were beating through the streets, an ensign was set up on the Beacon, the people were in arms on all sides; Randolph and the chief supporters of the governor were arrested and lodged in jail, and a number of the principal citizens, including the venerable ex-governor, Simon Bradstreet, convened at the Town-House.

At noon some of these gentlemen appeared on the balcony overlooking King Street (now State), and read to the crowd a "Declaration of the Gentlemen, Merchants, and Inhabitants of Boston, and the Country Adjacent," in which they gave a brief account of the oppression under which the colony had suffered, referred to the "noble undertaking of the Prince of Orange," and declared that the persons of the few of the grand authors of the public miseries had been seized to secure them for such justice as the prince and parliament should decree. It closed by advising all the neighbors, for whom they had endangered themselves, to join in prayer and action for the defence of the land. A message was sent to Andros, in which the signers said: "Ourselves and many others, the inhabitants of the town and places adjacent, being surprized with the people's sudden taking arms, in the first motion whereof we were wholly ignorant, are necessitated to acquaint your excellency" that, to quiet the people and for your own safety, it is best that you give up yourself and the government and fortifications to be disposed of according to orders that are expected to arrive at any moment. Andros was confined for one night in Mr. John Usher's house, and was then taken to the Fort. Dudley, who was absent on official duty, was captured and confined in his house at Roxbury, for his safety, as the people euphemistically expressed themselves. The following day the Castle was surrendered, and the *Rose* frigate struck her topmasts.

Mr. Bradstreet, and the others who had taken the charge of these affairs, formed themselves into "A

Council for the Safety of the People and the Conservation of the Peace," and called a meeting of deputies for the ninth of May. As a matter of prudence the old charter was not resumed, and news was anxiously awaited from England. It came in a few weeks, and William and Mary were proclaimed in Boston with greater ceremony than had ever been known on such an occasion before. Andros and Dudley were kept in confinement about twenty weeks, and then sent to England by royal order in February, 1690.

Meantime Mather was in England, laboring earnestly for the restoration of the charter. He easily obtained promises that religious liberty should be ensured; but the restoration of the charter in its original terms was vigorously opposed, and there was an old-time war of pamphlets. After many delays, after an interview with the queen, at which she promised her influence in behalf of the Americans, and much correspondence, a new charter was signed on the seventh of October, 1691. Sir William Phips was nominated governor by the representatives of New England, and duly appointed by the king. In company with Mather he left London in March, and arrived at Boston May 14, 1692.

XIV.

THE KING'S GOVERNORS BEGIN TO RULE.

THE period that we now close was one of the greatest importance, not only in the history of Boston and New England, but also in the history of the American people. Two generations of emigrants had been carefully building up a republican form of government on strange shores. They had been educating themselves in the independent management of public affairs, and they were the most notable community of men who up to that time had been going through a similar process. At no point on the American continent was there a settlement of Englishmen who had come to the New World for a purpose so explicit and pronounced; nowhere was there one that attracted so much attention in England; nowhere was there one that exerted so great an influence upon the future of the whole nation that afterwards grew up. Whatever Winthrop, and those who came and acted with him designed or thought, they laid the foundation of independence; they stood up boldly against any interference with their management of affairs; and they handed down to their children the spirit that animated their own hearts. The children in the second generation, though inferior to their fathers,* likewise stood manfully for their heritage, but they were overpowered, as we have seen; still they did not intend to allow the English government one particle of authority among them that they could hinder it from obtaining. We shall see their children in turn wrenching from the sovereign every thing that he had gained in 1684.

The era of the biblical commonwealth that the fathers of Boston had endeavored to establish, forever closed with the abrogation of the charter of King Charles the First. The change in every thing that concerns the management of public affairs was complete. The Puritans, in their protest against the "corruptions" of the church to which they belonged, had laid down a hard and fast line of conduct, and all who overstepped it were liable to censure. Every member of the Boston community who tried to be just to the royalists was looked upon askance by those who could see nothing good in men whose theological opinions did not agree with their own. Thus moderate men were naturally kept in the background, and our impressions of the real condition of affairs are in many respects necessarily somewhat one-sided. We see that many acts in themselves indifferent were thought then to be of the greatest moment. In his determination not to

* The officers of government in the second generation were, Hutchinson says, some of them *Dii minorum gentium*; and one of the New England divines is reported to have said that "they were in danger of being undone by creeping statesmen." In the first generation they "confined themselves to the principal gentlemen of family, estate, understanding, and integrity."

overstep the rigid line that had been laid down, the early Bostonian, like his partisans in England, went to extremes of intolerance and bigotry. It is difficult to find fault with earnest men who in times of excitement and strife err in this way; but the facts regarding them must be known or the men themselves can but partially be understood.

It strikes us as a little odd that, when (in 1687) "brother Wing," of Boston, arranged seats in a convenient room in his private house, and gave permission for "a man to shew tricks in it," certain other brethren, including Judge Sewall, should have found it necessary to go and "deal" with him, showing him from "what Dr. Ames saith of callings," that this "man's practice was unlawful, and therefore Capt. Wing could not lawfully give him accommodation." There was a solemn time when, as Sewall says, they "sung the ninetieth Psalm from the twelfth verse" before they "broke up." We can hardly appreciate the feelings of men who were so severely "exercised" as these were because the cross appeared in the national colors; but it was to them the symbol of all that they protested against in papacy and in the Church of England. As late as 1686, fifty-two years after Endicott cut the cross out of his flag at Salem, we find Sewall writing in his diary:

"I was and am in great exercise about the cross to be put in the colors, and afraid, if I should have a hand in it, whether it may not hinder my entrance into the holy land. . . . Went and discoursed with Mr. Mather. He judged it sin to have it put in, but the Captain not in fault; but I could hardly understand how the command of others could wholly excuse them, at least me, who had spoken so much against in April, 1681, and that summer and forward, upon occasion of Capt. Walley's putting the cross into his colors."

The change in affairs was shown by the fact that though the cross had been kept out of the colors for half a century, Sewall says that he "fetcht home the silk Elizur Holyoke had of me, to make the cross," though he faithfully read Cotton's arguments to the contrary. He was obliged sadly to record: "The cross much set by in England and here." Degenerate times, he thought them.

The Bostonians began to keep Sunday on Saturday afternoon at sunset, and it disturbed them very much when the royalists, who came with the king's governors, did not think it necessary to do the same. When the queen's birthday came, on Saturday, in 1686, it was duly proclaimed through the town by drum-beats; but bonfires were forbidden. In consequence of the strict regulations in town, the persons who wished to have a celebration went to the royal ships in the harbor, where flags were raised, and guns fired in the evening, and there were many huzzas, which were very offensive to the Puritans. The following day the Reverend Mr. Willard, of the South meeting-house, expressed great grief (in his prayer) for the "profanation of the Sabbath." The day of the Thursday lecture was not so sacred; but when a man came to Boston towards the end of the year 1685 and sought to set up dances, and especially mixed dances, and to hold his meetings on lecture-day, boldly proclaiming that he could teach more divinity by one play than Mr. Willard could, or than would be found in the Old Testament, the Boston ministers came to court and complained of him. Mr. Moodey said that it was not a time for New England to dance; and Mr. Mather, as one hearer reported, struck at the root in an argument against mixed dances at any time. Just fifty years later the selectmen allowed a school for dancing to be opened; but the application warily set forth that it was a school for "reading, writing, cyphering, dancing, and the use of the needle"; which shows that in all probability it was thought necessary to cover up the iniquitous feature of the proposed school under the other harmless subjects that were to be taught. Previous applications to open a dancing-school had, in fact, been denied.

On Sunday, which was called the Sabbath Day, Bostonians were exceedingly strict in their observance. Not only did the law direct that there should be no work on that day, but every person was obliged to apply himself to the duties of religion and piety, public and private; there was to be no unreasonable walking in the streets or the fields, no digging of graves or making of coffins, no funerals; two or three persons who might meet on the street by accident were not permitted to stop to talk; they might not walk down to the water-side on hot summer days, nor take the air on the Common; nor could they be entertained in taverns except in emergencies. Justices were ordered to walk about for the purpose of observing the people, to make sure that the Sunday laws were obeyed. Marriages were, in the early times, solemnized not by the minister, but by a magistrate, and once, when it was proposed to have a wedding in Boston, with a minister from Hingham to preach a sermon, the magistrates sent word to him to forbear, because they were not willing that "the English custom of ministers performing the solemnity of marriage, which sermons at such a time might induce," should come into vogue. At a funeral there was at first no service; but the company came together at the tolling of a bell, and carried the body solemnly to the grave, standing by until it was covered with earth, and that not in a consecrated ground, but in some such enclosure by the roadside as one sees now frequently in America.

It is hardly necessary to say that in many respects the habits of the royalists who came with the king's governors were quite the reverse of all this, for the customs of the emigrants had been modelled for the express purpose of avoiding resemblance to those they left behind them. The religious customs of the Boston churches did not continue in the form at first established, however, as we learn from a detailed account of them printed by Cotton Mather in 1726. The Sunday laws remained strict, and it was said that the body of the people were a sober, honest, industrious, and well-disposed sort of men, "unexceptionally loyal to the British sceptre," and "better acquainted with religion than in any other country on the face of the earth," some whole towns having no household that did not maintain religious worship.

In conducting funerals a change had come before the time of Cotton Mather's death, and we find that there were prayers at the house, and sometimes a speech at the grave. Weddings were then generally conducted by the ministers, though the justices had still the legal right to marry people. Before marriage the parties to be united were " published," and at the time of the ceremony a certificate that this had been done was presented to the minister, bearing the signature of the town-clerk. Sometimes there was a " Contraction " a little while before the actual wedding, on which occasion the pastor preached a sermon; but that custom fell into desuetude. The ceremony began with the presentation of the certificate of publishment, after which the minister offered a prayer. He then said to the couple: " You are now to attend unto a covenant of God: the covenant of your marriage before him. Give therefore your hands with your hearts unto one another." The hands being joined, the minister called upon the man to promise to love, honor, and support the woman, and upon her to love, honor, and obey the man. The consent to these covenants being " in some way signified," the minister pronounced the couple " married, according to the laws of God and of this province." The wedding-ring was especially omitted; and the exercises were concluded by a comprehensive prayer. In due time a return of the marriage was made by the minister to the secular authorities.

The men of the Boston " State-Church," as Cotton Mather calls it, protested mightily against imposed holy-days, as " the first weapon wherewith the bishop of Rome played his prizes against other churches"; but they thought fit that the governor should proclaim a fast-day in the spring season and a thanksgiving-day in the autumn, the proclamation to be read by the ministers before their congregations on a Sunday. Other such days were allowed

THE FIRST CHURCH, OR "OLD BRICK."
Built on the site of the present Joy's Building in 1713, and occupied until 1808. Its bell sounded the alarm at the time of the "Massacre," March 5, 1770.

to be appointed by the churches also from time to time.

Every Sunday the congregations met twice, the intermission between the services being shortened in cases where the people lived at considerable distance from the meeting-house. When the people were assembled, the pastor began the services by reading any "bills" which might have been handed him, asking for special prayers or praises by any of the neighbors. There was no liturgy—pagans had a form, but the Saviour did not provide any prayer-book,—and the minister was allowed "liberty" to make such supplications as seemed to him appropriate in the opening, or "larger prayer." A psalm was next sung, it being read line by line by some person appointed by the minister, and sung to some grave tune, "disorderly clamors" being especially inhibited. The way was now clear for the sermon, which was a well-studied treatise, based upon a text from the Bible, longer or shorter, as the minister pleased, and the example of St. Paul was pleaded in case the minister felt disposed to continue an hour or two, for the Apostle is said to have preached till midnight, on one occasion at least. Preaching "with notes" was "extremely fashionable" in 1726, Mr. Mather says, and he approved it, provided the minister could still speak with vigor and vivacity, and not lose his fervor. The sermon was followed by a short prayer and another psalm, and in the afternoon there was often a "collection" for church expenses. It had formerly been thought improper to read the Bible in the meeting-houses without explanations, but Mather approves the custom, and says that it was practised with profit in many of the churches, a fact that shows that there was a gradual change in the habits and customs of the people in some respects. Private prayers on coming into church were especially disapproved, it being deemed a "vanity that a Christian cannot have his devout ejaculations without signalizing them unto the notice of his neighbors."

It was a part of Randolph's work to overturn all these Puritan customs, and bring the people back to their allegiance to the Church of England, as well as to loyalty to the king. He began by asking that some able ministers should be appointed to perform the duties of the church, and that no marriages should be lawful except those solemnized by a minister of the Church of England. He thought that there would be some who would contribute largely to the maintenance of such, and that something might be raised from the estates of those persons who should prove treasonable to his majesty. He wrote that Boston was the chief place in the seven colonies; that it was managed by "men of weak and inconsiderable parts"; that it had become great by reason of the continual concourse of people from all parts; that it drove a large trade, and gave laws to all the other colonies, but that it was itself controlled by the ministers, without whom the magistrates dare not act. To supply a new clergy, and a new form of service, would, Mr. Randolph thought, very much help in changing all this. He therefore arranged to have a supply of prayer-books, tables of marriage, homilies of the church, etc., ready to be sent over with Mr. Dudley's commission as president, and in the same ship with the Reverend Robert Radcliffe, who, as we have seen, was the first Episcopal clergyman to hold service in Boston. Radcliffe had been in town but three or four days when he solemnized the first marriage in the Town-House, according to the service-book, though it was found necessary on the occasion to " borrow a ring."

If the Puritan ministers were objectionable, so much more was Harvard College, of which Governor Cranfield wrote to Sir Leoline Jenkins, Secretary of State:

"There can no greater evil attend his majesty's affairs here than those pernicious and rebellious principles which flow from their college at Cambridge, which they call their University, from whence all the towns both in this and in the other colonies are supplied with factious and seditious preachers, who stir up the people to a dislike of his majesty and his government, and the religion of the Church of England, terming the liturgy of our church a precedent of superstition, picked out of the popish dunghill ;' so that I am humbly of opinion that this country can never be well-settled, or the people become good subjects, till their preachers be reformed, and that college suppressed, and the several churches supplied with learned and orthodox ministers."

Mr. Randolph ventured to suggest that the funds of the society for converting the Indians might well be used in setting up good schools and providing for the Church minister ; but, as he had already given the people offence, he was afraid to attempt

FURNITURE OF THE WEALTHIER TOWNSMEN IN PROVINCIAL TIMES.

to seize it lest he should too greatly increase their hatred for him. The royalists might well speak as they did about Harvard College, for it was at the moment presided over by Increase Mather, whom Randolph, venting his vain spleen, called "Mather, their Mahomet," "the bellows of sedition and treason."

A French refugee, who described Boston in 1687, said that at this time very handsome dwellings of brick were going up; that the citizens were served, to a considerable extent, by negroes and negresses, no family being too poor to have less than one or two, and many having five or six, and that savages were employed to work in the fields. These negro slaves cost from two hundred to four hundred francs, and there was no danger that they would run away, there being no well-defined roads except those that led to the English towns and villages. the citizens of which would immediately return the runaways; and, if they took to the woods, the savages would find them for small compensation. Workmen were scarce and wages high, but materials for building were cheap. All sorts of cattle were said to thrive well, and horses and cows were plenty. The woods were full of strawberries, and there were chestnuts and hazel-nuts of "wonderful flavor," while the grape throve and produced good fruit. No account was made of the fish, for the sea and the fresh waters were full of them. Beef, mutton, and pork were plenty at two or three pence per pound, and flour and vegetables were provided in ample quantities. The trade was great with the

American islands and with Spain. To the islands the ships carried salted beef, pork, codfish, salmon, oysters, and mackerel, and brought back sugar, molasses, indigo, and sago; while with Spain dried fish was exchanged for oils, wine and brandy, all of which, however, was taken by way of London, where the duty demanded by the navigation laws was paid. Bears and wolves abounded and committed ravages among the sheep, and there were many rattlesnakes. There was perfect liberty for travellers, though those who wished to carry on business were obliged to be naturalized in London. As for the inhabitants, this Frenchman found good and bad, "as elsewhere," though the good preponderated; and there were all kinds of life and manners. Some practised no formality of marriage, except joining hands and then living together. There were not more than twenty French families, and the number was daily diminishing, for they were going to settle elsewhere, probably with a view to bettering their condition.

The first of the king's governors arrived at Boston at an inopportune moment. The witchcraft delusion broke out at Salem that year, and two weeks after Sir William landed a son of John Alden, the Plymouth hero, was accused of witchcraft and taken to Salem for examination. It was not at all strange that the settlers of New England should have brought over to their new home the belief in witches that had been fully accepted in Europe for centuries, nor that they should have felt it necessary to visit condign punishment upon them, since they read in the Bible, upon which their commonwealth was founded, the command, "Thou shalt not suffer a witch to live." Witches had been executed by the hundred in England in the reign of Charles the First, and in comparison with that butchery the score of executions in Salem in 1692 counts as scarcely nothing, while the three poor sufferers who expiated their supposed crime in Boston prove that the citizens of that town must have been much more merciful and rational than their English and other European contemporaries.

The disagreeable literature of this subject is extensive, and in it we find the names of Increase and Cotton Mather frequently repeated. That they shared the weakness of their age, in company with the wisest and the best, not only in Boston but elsewhere in Christendom, is no indication that they were worse than other men, but simply that they possessed the failings of human nature. Sir William Phips was also involved in the persecution of witches; he instituted a court for the trial of such cases, of which Samuel Sewall was one of the judges,* It sat at Salem and Boston, but the governor was absent during most of the proceedings, prosecuting a campaign against the Indians and building a fort at Pemaquid. On his return he found to his dismay that his own wife was an object of suspicion, and he put a stop at once to the horrid proceedings. The fourteenth of January, 1697, was observed as a day

---

* We have already read, in Michael Wigglesworth's verses, the preconceived notions which the New Englanders entertained regarding the "hellish fiends" to be found in the howling American wildernesses. Perhaps some who at this period read his lines regarded him as a seer.

of general fasting and prayer throughout the province, and " the late tragedy was referred to as having been " raised up by Satan and his instruments." On that day Judge Sewall sent up a " bill " in the Old South, in which he confessed that he had offended in the matter of the witchcraft condemnations, and asked the prayers of the congregation that the divine displeasure " might be stayed against the country, his family, and himself," and he humbly remained standing while the minister read the paper. This childlike man annually made his mourning, and humiliated himself on this account during the remainder of his long life.

The first royal governor was son of a blacksmith, who, if Cotton Mather's love for the marvellous did not lead him to make an extravagant statement, had twenty-five other children. He was born in the woods of Maine, near the mouth of the Kennebec, in 1651. His opportunities for education were but small, for his mother, who was left a widow when he was a child, probably had no easy task to provide for her phenomenal family. He naturally engaged in building ships at first, but visions of something better rose in his mind, and at the age of twenty he went to Boston. There he worked at a trade, tried to learn to read and write, and married a widow much his senior who had some property, which he lost for her. At last he found a fortune beneath the ocean, for he searched for a Spanish treasure-ship that had gone to the bottom half a century before, found it, and received as his share of the enterprise one hundred thousand dollars, a knighthood, and a goblet valued at five thousand dollars for his wife. After serving as high sheriff under Andros, he built a "fair brick house," as he described it, in Boston, and went to England, where he was ready to be selected to be first governor when Mather was asked to nominate a fit person. Sir William found it difficult to make up for the lack of early advantages; he never could write with ease, and spelling was an accomplishment that, in common with many of his day, he either despised or thought beyond his capacity. He did not become proud, either on account of riches or honors, and never forgot that he had been a ship-carpenter; perhaps he wished sometimes that he had never been any thing else, especially when he was involved in strife with men who understood far better than he the ins and outs of political life. He was a communicant in the church of the Mathers, but grace did not entirely overcome nature in his case, and when Captain Short, of the *Nonesuch* frigate, crossed his path, he coolly knocked him down; likewise, when the collector of customs offended him, he gave him pugilistic arguments. Probably the lieutenant-governor, William Stoughton, was in danger from his brawny arm, for there was very "warm discourse between them" when Phips rescued Captain Dobbins from a sheriff, and told the sheriff that if he touched the captain he should himself be sent to prison. Sir William's style of argumentation did not suit his Boston subjects, and they sent complaints to London, which caused him to be summoned to England in 1694, and thither he went in November. He died early the following year.

William Stoughton, who had been chief of the judges in the court formed by Phips for the trial of witches, performed the duties of governor after the departure of Sir William until his successor, Richard Coote, Earl of Bellomont, appeared in Boston with a commission from his Majesty, May 26, 1699. England and France were at war, and the Indians on the American frontier were incited by their French neighbors to make bloody raids upon the unprotected settlements of their enemies. The war continued until 1697, in which year the Peace of Ryswick was celebrated in Boston with an earnestness which only the relief from such distresses as accompany an Indian war can give. The struggle had lingered for ten years, and many inhabitants of Boston had been killed by the savages or lost on the weary marches through the woods. The Indians had escaped almost with impunity, and it was estimated that every one of them that was killed cost the country a thousand pounds. For several years a noted chief from the Kennebec region named Bomazeen, who had incited many of the enormities that his tribe had committed, was imprisoned in Boston in a jail that Hutchinson confesses was "a very bad one." He was exchanged in December, 1698.

XV.

THE GOVERNORS AND THE BOSTON PEOPLE.

THE period during which Boston was governed by rulers of the king's appointment was one of perpetual strife and friction, and we find several questions coming up with constancy, all being connected with the paramount topic, the independence of the colonists of all interference from England. The Americans had opposed the change of government for so long a time and with such persistence that they could not very easily fall into the ways that the king and his agents pointed out for them.

The colonists protested in the first place against the appointment of rulers for them by any authority but their own votes, and Boston was always the most active in protesting. They naturally fortified themselves with the pertinent words of Jeremiah—

"Their nobles shall be of themselves,
And their governors shall proceed from the midst of them."

This privilege had been exercised from the day when John Winthrop was first chosen to office, and it did not appear to the colonists that any right to change the custom existed, nor that there was any need for such a departure from old usage. If the royal governor were a representative of the king, his presence was an impertinence; and he certainly did not represent the Americans. The presence therefore of such an officer gave them a not unnatural feeling that they were looked upon as citizens of a conquered province. This sensation was deepened when Massachusetts lost its separate and distinct existence, and became but a fraction of a satrapy that stretched from the Gulf of St. Lawrence to Delaware Bay; when her governor was acting under a roving commission,—was at one time attending to their concerns in their own Town-House, and at another holding court at Hartford or New Amsterdam; when the laws that their representatives made (sitting with deputies from Plymouth colony and appointees of the king) were suspended from their full force for three years, in order that his Majesty might have that unreasonable length of time in which to consider their bearing upon current politics.

Under such conditions there was, of necessity, a perpetual jealousy and a constant fretting, for the governors were sure to be on the look-out for every assertion of an independent spirit, and the colonists were equally alive to all suspected usurpations of authority based upon kingly prerogative. If the colony had been begun with an organization of this sort there might have been peace between the parties; a spirit of loyalty might have been developed, such as Virginia showed, for example, in its earlier history, but in Massachusetts, where quite different principles had obtained at the beginning, nothing but conflict was to be anticipated,—and nothing but conflict was, as a matter of fact, the rule, from the abrogation of the charter until the time when the Revolutionary war ensured to the entire body of colonists, from Maine to Georgia, complete and acknowledged independence of the mother-country.

When a governor was sent to Boston from England an early question presented itself in regard to his support, and the people were always quite certain that, as he was not their servant, he should not be in their pay. They therefore usually declined to vote a regular salary for him, and there was generally an unseemly struggle on the subject. If, on the other hand, the king undertook to pay his servant, the unlogical colonists protested that he had no right to keep an officer among them in his pay for the purpose of acting the spy over their affairs. Thus, for example, when Joseph Dudley demanded a salary, the court speciously argued that "the circumstances of this province as to our ability to support the government are at times so different that we fear the settling of fixed salaries will be of no service to her majesty's interest," and further, that, as it was the privilege and right of English subjects from time to time to raise and appropriate such sums of money as the immediate exigencies may require, they hoped that they might continue to enjoy the privilege under her most gracious Majesty. On the other hand, when Thomas Hutchinson (in 1772, seventy years later) received a grant from the crown for his salary, a committee of the Assembly reported that it was " a dangerous innovation, which renders him, as a governor, not dependent on the people, as the charter has prescribed, and consequently not, in that respect, such a governor as the people consented to * at the granting thereof"; and the house most solemnly protested that the innovation was an important change of the constitution, which exposed the province to a despotic administration of government. It happened that each of the governors thus opposed was a native of the colony, but that fact made no difference to the people; they were just as much on the alert in watching the movements of the other governors, and not a whit more.

Most of the New England provinces had no foreign commerce, but received all their imported goods through traders at Boston, who dealt directly with London, and therefore any laws made by parliament which affected trade were of the greatest interest to Boston, and the merchants there were watchful of all legislation in the mother-country on this subject. When, therefore, Parliament secured, in 1651, the monopoly of trade with the colonies to the English merchant by making active a principle that had been established in the reign of Richard the Second, and when, in 1660, it avowed its design of sacrificing the natural rights of the colonists to home interests, ruling that "no merchandise shall be imported into the plantations but in English vessels, navigated by Englishmen," and thus excluded the merchants of

* Governor Hutchinson was prompt to point out that the charter was not of the nature of a treaty between the king and his New England subjects, but was a grant of defined privileges of the sovereign's good pleasure.

Boston from a profitable trade, it aroused indignant opposition. Governor Bellomont said, in 1698, that Boston had one hundred and ninety-four ships of different sizes engaged in its trade, and ventured to assert that there were more good vessels belonging of her than all Scotland and Ireland owned. The commerce increased so rapidly that the Board of Trade reported, in 1717, that the trade of the country employed continually no less than three thousand four hundred and ninety-three sailors, and four hundred and ninety-two ships, making twenty-five thousand four hundred and six tons. These figures were derived from the accounts of the naval officers of the ports of Boston and Salem. The activity of Boston commerce had excited the envy of the English, and the measures in antagonism to it were made by degrees more strict.

In 1663, a law was enacted prohibiting the colonists from obtaining supplies from Europe except by way of England and in English vessels. Later still Parliament took away even the liberty of free traffic between the colonies themselves; and, growing more grasping as time went on, it was ordered, at last, that America should not even manufacture those articles which might possibly compete with English goods in foreign markets. What England would not buy the colonists were entirely at liberty to sell to other nations, for otherwise they might find it difficult to pay their London bills. By unintended irony, for the protection of Virginia, the cultivation of tobacco was prohibited in England and Wales, where it would have been difficult to have brought a crop to maturity!

If Parliament had paid attention to its Shakespeare, it might have derived a lesson from Shylock. Forsooth, England hindered Boston of more than Shylock's "half a million"; she laughed at her losses, mocked at her gains, scorned her nation, thwarted her bargains, cooled her friends, heated her enemies; "and what 's her reason?" Boston was in far-away America, and was supposed to be weak. Boston might well have retorted: "Hath not an American eyes? hath not an American hands, organs, dimensions, senses, affections, passions? fed with the same food, hurt with the same weapons, subject to the same diseases, healed by the same means, warmed and cooled by the same winter and summer, as an Englishman is? If you prick us do we not bleed? if you poison us do we not die? and if you wrong us, shall we not revenge? If we are like you in the rest, we will resemble you in that. The villainy you teach us we shall execute, and it shall go hard but we shall better the instruction!"

There were ten governors sent over during the period we are now considering. Let us see how they managed their uneasy subjects. The time of suspense during which Stoughton was at the head of affairs was pretty well filled up by Indian strife; but there were also fears of attacks upon Boston by some fleet from France; commerce was always in danger from buccaneers or pirates; and there was an epidemic of small-pox, which carried off a thousand persons in a twelvemonth, a great proportion in a town which counted but about seven thousand inhabitants in all. There were some one thousand houses in Boston at this time.

Cotton Mather bewailed the increase of vice, the great number of drinking-houses, and the advent of fortune-tellers, "consulted by the sinful inhabitants," and warned his fellow-citizens that Port Royal in Jamaica was "swallowed up the other day in a stupendous earthquake," and that just before that catastrophe "the people were violently and scandalously set upon going to fortune-tellers upon all occasions." The town was full of widows, in consequence of the Indian butcheries; and there were multitudes of helpless orphans. Mather estimated that one sixth of the communicants in his church were widows and that the proportion was not far from that through the town.

Phips was followed by Richard Coote, Earl of Bellomont, who was appointed governor of both New York and Massachusetts in 1697. He did not reach Boston until May, 1699, when he was received with the cordiality that a nobleman of fine person, elegant manners, conciliatory actions, and respectable years might have expected. He took occasion to make himself popular with the religious portion of Boston citizens by attending the Thursday lecture, for which the court usually adjourned, and by professing a high esteem for the ministers, though he did not find the precisians the most agreeable private company, nor the most entertaining intimate acquaintances, much as he professed to respect them in public.*

* In his efforts to achieve popularity Governor Bellomont avoided all unnecessary contests with private persons or with the representatives of the people, and knowing the general detestation in which

History records the fact that on returning from lecture one day surrounded by a crowd of curious citizens, Bellomont passed one Dr. Bullivant, who did not attend the service; upon which he remarked in an audible tone, probably for the benefit of his attendants, "Doctor, you have lost a precious sermon to-day," in reply to which the doctor said in a whisper to a companion, "If I could have got as much by being there as his lordship will, I should have been there too." On another occasion when the governor was dining in his own house with a number of deputies from the country towns, he said to his wife: "We must treat these gentlemen well, for they give us our bread." The feeling towards the royal governors is shown by another anecdote. It is related that on an occasion when a deputy objected to voting money to defray the funeral expenses of a governor's wife, he said that if it were for the purpose of burying the governor, he should have voted it gladly.

Lord Bellomont was particularly directed to take orders for the extirpation of piracy and the establishment of the authority of the acts of trade, which were very little regarded in any of the colonies. In

the Stuart dynasty was held, he ventured to make *ad captandum* remarks about the reigning sovereign, whom he characterized as " the glorious instrument of our deliverance from the odious fetters and chains of popery and tyranny." He saw something godlike in King William, though, speaking after the familiar manner of the Puritans, he added : " I would not be misunderstood so as to be thought to rob God of the glory of that stupendous act of his providence, in bringing to pass the late happy and wonderful revolution in England. His blessed work it was, without doubt, and he was pleased to make King William immediately the author and instrument of it."

endeavoring to destroy piracy, he entered into an agreement with one William Kidd, who was to range the oceans capturing pirates, and on his return to divide the profits of his expeditions with Bellomont and others who were associated with him. Whether rightly or wrongly, history has recorded that Kidd turned pirate himself, and he was tried, and, in due course, hanged for the crime,—an offence, be it remembered, of which many persons who would have scorned not to be rated as respectable in New York society had been for a generation guilty without having penalties meted out to them, and for which Bellomont's predecessor in office in that city had issued formal commissions.

Bellomont remained at his post in Boston but about fourteen months. By his suavity and conciliatory measures he led the court to vote to him "presents" (in lieu of a salary, which they would not grant even to him), amounting in the aggregate to a larger sum than he had expressly desired as a formal stipend. This was far more than any of the other royal governors was able to accomplish. He found it entirely impossible to cajole the "Bostoneers," as Randolph had called them, into any habit of dependence upon the crown; nor could he lead them to give up a single privilege that they considered theirs by right. He went to New York in 1700, and died there in the following March.

Stoughton became the chief executive upon the death of Bellomont, but he died himself in the following July, and then the council carried out the laws until a successor could be sent from England.

The times were thought to be very bad, and Increase Mather preached two sermons that he entitled "Ichabod; or, the Glory Departing from New England," in which he showed that both church and State were fast declining. "O New England! New England!" he exclaimed, "look to it that the glory be not removed from thee! It has come to the threshold of the house, if not to the East Gate!" "If the fountain should fail; I mean the college, which has been one of the glories of New England, or (which is worse) become a nursery, not of plants of renown, but of degenerate plants, . . . the glory is like to be gone from these churches in less than one generation." On the death of Stoughton, Mr. Willard preached another sermon, entitled: "Prognosticks of Impending Calamities."

Looking from the Puritan stand-point, there appeared to be reason for these forebodings. The crops had been poor for several years, the French and Indian wars had filled the land with mourning, and besides there were efforts to give a new, and in the opinion of the old ministers, a dangerous, turn to the teachings of the college. It was in 1699 that Brattle Street Church was begun, and it was one of the indications of change, for it departed from the "Cambridge Platform," and broke in upon the Order of the Churches, for which reasons it was made the object of a protest by the existing ministers. The church bore the name of the "Manifesto" Church, among those opposed to it, because it issued a manifesto defending its course. It had for its first minister, Benjamin Colman, and he was followed by

William and Samuel Cooper, Joseph Stevens Buckminster, Edward Everett, John Gorham Palfrey, and the late Samuel K. Lothrop, all of them eminent as scholars and preachers. In this church the Psalms were no longer read and sung line by line, as had been the custom, a society for practising music was established, and singing by note was first introduced.*

The choice of the sovereign for governor was made in 1702, and Joseph Dudley, who had been in England since he was sent there with Andros, some ten years previously, was appointed. He had often expressed a desire to lay his bones in America, and had long been an active aspirant for the office that he now obtained. Colman was a friend of the new governor, but the Mathers were his bitter opponents. Dudley was determined to rule the colony with a firm hand, and, remembering his former experience, he immediately objected to every member of the existing council who had taken part in his condemnation, and also entered upon the usual struggle for salary. The court offered him less than one half the sum that had been given Bellomont (as a present, of

---

* Instrumental music was apparently not relished or not approved, especially in churches ; and at about the time of the Restoration of the Stuarts, we find an uncle writing to a student in Harvard College, in regard to his studies : " Music I had almost forgotten. I suspect you seek it both too soon and too much. This be assured of, that if you be not excellent in it, it is nothing at all ; and if you be excellent, it will take up so much of your time and mind that you will be worth little else ; and when all that excellence is attained, your acquest will prove little or nothing of real profit to you, unless you intend to take up the trade of fiddling." See Palfrey's " New England," ii., 67 ; iii., 134.

course), and he refused it until he was advised to take it rather than nothing.*

The war known as Queen Anne's began in 1702, and did not close until the peace of Utrecht in 1713. During that period New England was again devastated by the savages, and the French, and armed bands were sent out from Boston by sea and land to attack and to repulse the enemies. Bounties were offered for Indian scalps, as high as forty pounds, in one case at least, and the men of the colony were debased by this new incentive to blood-shedding. In the midst of this war a vessel was sent to Nova Scotia with a flag of truce, the owner of which remained absent a long time, and on his return he was accused of having engaged in trade with the enemy. A number of persons were thought to have been implicated in the venture, and, after a trial by the court, several of the persons were heavily fined. Dudley was accused of conniving in the crime, if not of sharing its profits, and a bitter petition was sent to the queen asking for his punishment.

It was at about this time that the Mathers burst out with their virulent letters against Dudley. They charged him with most of the political crimes that a statesman can be guilty of, among which were bad faith, cruelty, corruption, bribery, and hypocrisy. Three days after these letters were written, as Judge Sewall was returning from the funeral of Mrs. Anne Needham (Jan. 23, 1708), in company with the

* In 1708, about the first of July, the deputies voted a present to the governor of two hundred pounds, and two hundred and twenty-five to the treasurer, " at which the governor was very angry, and said he would pass none of them [the votes], they would starve together."

younger Mather, engaged in very devout conversation, they turned aside to go to Madam Usher's, where Mather showed the Judge a copy of his letter, and Sewall expressed much interest to learn what the result of such plain-dealing would be.

These matters seem to have been fought out at funerals, and in prayers and sermons. We are told that Mr. Colman shortly after "lashed" the Mathers in a sermon, for what they had "written, and preached, and prayed about the present contest with the governor." On January 25th, Mr. Mather made a prayer about certain faithful ones, in which Judge Sewall thought that he intended to animadvert upon his own vote against the virulent petition sent to England for the governor's removal; and on the 26th of May Mr. John Norton, minister of the church at Hingham (nephew of the former minister of the First Church in Boston), took up the matter and preached a "flattering sermon as to the governor." The newspaper in Boston[*] in those good old days seems not to have been familiar enough to be used for such personal matters as these. Mr. Norton was formally thanked by the court for his discourse, and a copy of it was desired for publication. Mr. Sewall was in close quarters at this time, for his son had married a daughter of Governor Dudley.

[*] The first American newspaper, *Publick Occurrences*, appeared in Boston, September 25, 1690, but its editor, Benjamin Harris, a "brisk asserter of English Liberties," possessing too great a share of colonial independence, uttered "reflections of a very high nature," and the authorities stopped his venture at its first number. *The Boston News-Letter*, which followed, April 4, 1704, was for fifteen years the only newspaper in America.—Hudson, "Journalism in the United States," ch. i.

INTERIOR OF CHRIST CHURCH AT PRESENT (BUILT 1723).

Judge Sewall relates an amusing occurrence of this sort that happened in 1710. It seems that the judge had failed to invite the testy pastor of the South Church, the Reverend Ebenezer Pemberton, who was some twenty years his junior, to court on a certain November day in that year. Mr. Pemberton resented the omission as an injury, "with extraordinary vehemency" and passion, "capering with his feet," the judge relates. Sewall replied that his "carriage was neither becoming a scholar nor minister," and he tells the readers of his Diary that he was surprised to see himself insulted with such extraordinary fierceness by his pastor. He was destined to be surprised again, for at the afternoon service at the South Church on the following Sunday, Mr. Pemberton asked the congregation to sing the first five verses of the fifty-eighth Psalm, and when the judge turned to the place he saw that that particular Psalm was directed against unjust judges, that it described their inveterate wickedness, and prayed for their speedy punishment. As the congregation sang:

"Speak, O ye judges of the earth
 if just your sentence be :
Or must not innocence appeal
 to heaven from your decree?

"Your wicked hearts and judgments are
 alike by malice swayed ;
Your griping hands, by weighty bribes,
 to violence betrayed.

"No serpent of parched Afric's breed
 doth ranker poison bear ;
The drowsy adder will as soon
 unlock his sullen ear.

> Unmoved by good advice, and deaf
>   as adders they remain ;
> From whom the skilful charmer's voice
>   can no attention gain."

It is not surprising that Sewall wrote of this act :

"I think if I had been in his place, and had been kindly and tenderly affectioned, I should not have done it at this time. Another Psalm might have suited his subject as well as the fifth verse of this. 'T is certain one may make libels of David's Psalms ; and if a person be abused, there is no remedy. I desire to leave it to God, who can and will judge righteously."

In 1714, Boston received the news that Queen Anne had died, and that a new dynasty was upon the British throne. George the First became king August 1st of that year, but the news did not reach this side of the ocean until September 15th. Dudley occupied his office, with a brief intermission, until November 9, 1715, when he retired from public office to his estate at West Roxbury, where he died in 1720. On the occasion of his death laudatory notices were printed, and the Rev. Mr. Colman, of the Manifesto Church, preached from a pulpit hung with black, from the text, selected by Dudley, " By faith, Joseph, when he died." The clergy set the fashion of this affected use of Scripture. When Sewall's second wife died suddenly in the middle of the night, Thomas Prince, of the South Church, preached from the words : " At midnight, behold a cry was made "; and when the judge himself died the same minister based his funeral discourse upon the words in I. Samuel vii., 15: "And Samuel judged Israel all the days of his life." This custom was long continued. The father of Mrs. John Adams, the Rev. William Smith, of Weymouth, is said to have preached in reference to her marriage in 1764, from Luke vii., 33: "John came neither eating bread nor drinking wine, and ye say, 'He hath a devil.'" John Adams was a lawyer, and there had been an ancient prejudice against his calling, which was thought hardly honest. Mr. Smith's eldest daughter had married Richard Cranch, on which occasion he is reported to have preached from Luke x., 42, "Mary hath chosen that good part, which shall not be taken away from her."

The colony was not in a prosperous condition between 1675, when the war with Philip began, and 1713, when the struggle called Queen Anne's war closed. Five or six thousand of the best young men of the country had lost their lives, either in actual service or by disease contracted in it. This had retarded the growth of population, and the wars themselves had directly increased taxation, and this sent many persons to other colonies, thus adding to the burdens of those who were left. The strife of war had quieted party disputes during the last few years of Dudley's official life, but it cannot be said that the experiment of governing Boston and the colony by rulers of the king's choosing had been remarkably successful thus far.

XVI.

STRAINED RELATIONS.

COMMUNITIES, like private persons, are often free to overlook matters in their times of prosperity that would be considered very annoying in periods of penury or pain. The same contrast exists between times when the mind is occupied by the effort to accomplish a much desired purpose, and the season after the design has been effected. It was not surprising that while the New England communities were occupied in war with the Indians they allowed their party strifes to lapse, nor that at those periods they had no wish to engage with the governor in quarrels about his salary. During the war that was closed by the treaty of Utrecht, public expenses, which were of course heavy, had been defrayed by issuing bills of credit; and at the end of the struggle it was found that gold and silver had been banished from circulation, that exchange had risen, and that prices of commodities had followed it. There was financial distress, and various suggestions were made by those who wished to alleviate it.

The first party thought best to draw in all paper currency, and return to the use of gold and silver; a second, and very numerous one, was in favor of the establishment of a private bank, which should issue notes to be received as money; and the third party wished to arrange for loans from the government to such citizens as would mortgage their estates for the purpose of providing security for principal and interest. The hard-money scheme had but few supporters, and the colony was divided between the two other plans; but as Boston favored the public loans, that method of relief was adopted, after a long struggle, and fifty thousand pounds in bills of credit were placed in the hands of trustees to be loaned to any of the inhabitants at five per cent. interest for five years.

The choice of the sovereign for governor at this juncture fell upon Colonel Samuel Shute, whose brother, afterwards Lord Barrington, was leader of the dissenting interest in Parliament. The family of Shute were generally dissenters, and he himself sustained a good character as a friend of liberty, but not long after his arrival in Boston he professed that he was a member of the Church of England, and he was certainly very positive in efforts to bring the Bostoneers into a state of proper dependence upon the crown. He sustained the king's prerogative, and was determined to repress every token of popular government. Such a governor was destined to be in continual conflict with the inhabitants, except in measures against the still troublesome savages.

The policy of controlling trade in such a manner as to militate against the interests of America, which had so long been popular in England, was now maintained with oppressive force. The "Board of

Trade" was a department of government which seems to have been developed from an arrangement made by Cromwell in 1655, who then directed his son Richard, and others, to meet and consider means to promote the national commerce. In 1660, Charles the Second erected two councils of Trade and Plantations, which were soon made one, and that, after various fortunes, was given a new life in 1695. John Locke, one of its wisest and most influential members, advised the appointment of a dictator to control the colonies; and in 1701 the entire board urged the abrogation of all the charters and the establishment of such a government as should make the colonists duly subservient to England. Though this policy was not determined upon in form, it was the constant aim of the governors to bring about such a dependence as it proposed. The Board of Trade* asserted, in 1728, that the inhabitants of Boston did not make suitable returns to his majesty for the extraordinary privileges they enjoyed, and were "daily endeavoring to wrest the small remains of power out of the hands of the Crown, and to become independent of the mother kingdom."

Governor Shute joined the opponents of the banking scheme, and while he was incompetent to devise any plan to give effectual financial relief, he permitted another emission of bills of one hundred thousand pounds to run ten years, which merely

---

* Hutchinson says that Col. Martin Bladen, for many years one of the Board of Trade, often expressed to the colonial agents and others his apprehension that the Bostoneers intended to "set up for themselves."

added to the difficulties. He took sides with the royal surveyor of the forests of Maine, who claimed certain white-pine trees for the king's navy, and caused the formation of parties which continued to give him trouble as long as he remained in Boston. On his arrival in America he gave consent to the levying of an impost duty upon goods from the West Indies and England brought to New England. This was considered to conflict with the interests of English traders, and notice was received from London that the action must be reversed. This the court declined to do, and a long conflict followed.

The people were, as usual, ill-disposed in the matter of salary, and refused to make this governor the customary "present," reducing the sum offered until, in the depreciated currency, it amounted to but three hundred and sixty pounds. The governor attempted to take from the house of deputies the privilege of choosing its own speaker, and this still further aroused their jealousies. The strife on this point was long and bitter. In the midst of it the house attempted to retaliate by taking into its own hands the appointment of the annual fast; and, in consequence of the prevalence of the small-pox in Boston, it ventured to assert itself by adjourning to Cambridge, which brought about another controversy. The resentment of the house was finally extended to the governor's friends, and at last Shute left for England somewhat abruptly at the beginning of the year 1723, for the purpose of laying his grievances before the king.

The year 1721 was notable for the scourge of

small-pox, which has been mentioned. It attacked some six thousand persons, of whom one thousand died. Inoculation had just been introduced in England by Lady Mary Wortley Montague, who began, in the face of intense opposition, by practising upon her little daughter, afterwards Lady Bute; and now Dr. Zabdiel Boylston did the same thing in Boston, in the face of similar opposition, which caused him much suffering in business and repute. Dr. Boylston likewise submitted one of his own children to the ordeal. The selectmen investigated the matter and pronounced against it; it was thought little better than murder, but Cotton Mather came out in its favor, and gave his powerful encouragement to Dr. Boylston. Mather invited the physicians to meet and consult about undertaking inoculation, in order, he said, "that whoever first begins this practice may have the concurrence of his worthy brethren to fortify him." The conservative physicians did not accept the invitation, but Dr. Boylston was not deterred; he inoculated two hundred and eighty-six persons, of whom but six died, and it was shown that the recovery of those who died would have been little short of a miracle. Of five thousand seven hundred and fifty-nine who were not inoculated eight hundred and forty-four died.

This scourge was a serious detriment to the progress of the town; but in the midst of the infliction (in spite of the ill-success of the second newspaper, the *News-Letter*), James Franklin, brother of the more celebrated Benjamin, began the third paper in Boston. The Franklins had no reverence for the Mathers, being more influenced probably by the puerile pomposity and vanity of Cotton Mather, for example, than by his piety and learning. The venerable Increase, then eighty-four years of age, discerned "the inspiration of the devil" in the third number of the *Courant*, in consequence of which he denounced it in the columns of the *News-Letter*. He said that though it had been reported that he was one of the supporters of the *Courant*, he was, on the contrary, "extremely offended with it," because in one of its numbers it insinuated "that if the ministers of God approve of a thing, it is a sign it is of the devil; which is a horrid thing to be related." "I, that have known what New England was from the beginning," he continued, "cannot but be troubled to see the degeneracy of this place. I can well remember when the civil government would have taken an effectual course to suppress such a cursed libel, which if it be not done, I am afraid that some awful judgment will come upon this land, and the wrath of God will arise and there will be no remedy. I cannot but pity poor Franklin." The court did take the matter in hand, and the publisher was obliged to give bonds not to print any thing that had not passed an appointed censor.

Governor Shute did not return to Boston, and for several years the lieutenant-governor, William Dummer, occupied the post. He was largely employed by the ever-active Indians to the eastward. Being a native, it might have been expected that he would accomplish something towards mediating between the crown and the colonists, but he did not affect any thing in that direction. During the time that he was performing the duties of chief executive, the efforts of Shute resulted in the granting of an " Explanatory Charter" (in 1725), which ensured to the governor a veto power upon the nomination for speaker of the house, and took from that body the right of adjourning for longer periods than two days; but left the vexed subject of salary open, to remain a matter of constant dispute.

During this interval, also, both Increase and Cotton Mather died, the one in 1723, and the other five years later, and with them closed the paramount influence of the dynasty upon the affairs of the town and the colony. The father had preached sixty-six years, and had presided over Harvard College for twenty; the son was in the pulpit forty-seven years, and was one of the overseers of the college. In spite of his lack of ordinary judgment and his great credulity, he must be acknowledged to have been a person of merit, and his ability to acquire all sorts of recondite information has, perhaps, never been equalled in America. Six of the first ministers of Boston bore Cotton Mather to the tomb, and the body was followed by all the principal officials, ministers, scholars, and men of affairs, while the streets were thronged and the " windows were filled with sorrowful spectators all the way to the burying-place," which was on Copp's Hill.

Judge Sewall lets us into many an intimate view of character in the days of the Mathers, and some of his pictures are by no means adapted to hold up the good old times to our admiration. In many particulars the men of those days acted in a way that would be thought quite unworthy of persons in the same stations now, and the way in which they used language, especially opprobrious language, is astonishing to those not familiar with the vigor of some of the contemporary worthies in the mother-country. There was in those days a bookseller named Richard Wilkins, whose shop was a favorite resort, and we are told that one day Mr. Cotton Mather went there and talked very sharply against Sewall, who was then captain of the "Ancient and Honorable" Artillery Company. He said that Sewall had used his father, Increase, worse than a nigger; and he spoke so loud that he was audible in the street.* The humble and guileless captain says that he had read that morning Mr. Dod's saying "Sanctified afflictions are good promotions," which he now found was a cordial; but he thought it well to expostulate with Mr. Mather a little in the same shop two days later, "from I. Timothy v., 1," in company with witnesses. Mather said he had considered the passage mentioned; whereupon Sewall turned upon him his own book upon the "Law of Kindness for the Tongue," and asked whether Mather considered that his acts corresponded with his precepts, and whether they corresponded with Christ's rule. Mather only justified his "reviling me behind my back," says Sewall,

* When Cotton Mather was excited in debate he found, as he said to Governor Dudley, in 1708, with his usual pompous verbiage, that "the schemes of speaking and modes of addressing used among persons of the most polite education" did not prove equal to the demands made upon them. He, therefore, adopted the "schemes of speaking" used among less polished persons, as in the present instance.

and charged the council with "lying, hypocrisy, tricks, and I know not what all." Sewall asked if this were done with meekness; and Mather replied, confidently, "Yes!" retorting a speech made by Sewall in the council, to the effect that if Mather should go to Cambridge, his example would do more hurt than his going would do good. Sewall owned his words, and asked if Mather would like to have him exclaim against him in the street, if he supposed him to have done amiss as a church officer, and added, very appropriately, it seems to us, that he conceived that Mather had done much that was unbecoming a minister of the Gospel. The discussion became so loud and unseemly that Wilkins was fain to have Mather go into a private room; but Mather would not, and soon Sewall was called to a meeting of the council, where, he says, we "hammered out an order for a Day of Thanksgiving." The next day Mr. Increase Mather went to the shop, and declared that, as he was a servant of Jesus Christ, "some great judgment would fall on Captain Sewall or his family." Two days later still, Sewall gave a copy of his speech in council to Wilkins, to show, in order that all might see the grounds of Mr. Mather's anger.

While we are with this unreserved diarist, let us see something of the customs of the time, as he exhibits them in his bland and childlike style. One June day in the year 1701, Sewall heard that Josiah Willard, son of the minister of the Old South Church, had cut off his hair, and put on a wig,—and he had a full head of hair,—so he felt it his duty to call upon the young gentleman. He found his mother, and announced his errand, upon which Josiah was sent for. Sewall began the conversation by enquiring what " extremity had forced him to put off his natural hair," and Josiah was obliged to reply that there was none at all; but said that his hair was straight and parted behind, and seemed to argue that men might as well shave their heads as their faces. Sewall responded that half of mankind never have any hair on the face, which was an unexpected admission that women belonged to " mankind." He continued to the effect that God seems to have given men hair as a test, to see if they would be content to remain as he made them, or whether they would be their own " carvers and lords." He said that such conduct as this of Willard's would be displeasing to good men, and " they that care not what men think of them, care not what God thinks of them." Sewall was prepared for this interview, for he had that morning read the " tenth chapter of the third book of Calvin's Institutions," " in course," (*Comment il faut user de la vie présent et ses aides*) and he commended the same to Willard. He told him that such cutting of the hair was condemned at a meeting of ministers at Mr. Stoddard's house in Northampton, " when the said Josiah was there," upon which the young man wavered, " and seemed to say that he would leave off his wig when his hair was grown." Willard's father afterwards thanked Sewall for this plain-dealing, and promised that when the son's hair was long enough to cover his ears, the wig should be put off; that the cutting should never have been accomplished had he known it; and that Mrs. Willard heard her son talk of doing it, but seemed to fear to forbid it, lest the son should do it in spite of her, and "so be more faulty."

In June, 1701, the aged lieutenant-governor wished to go to commencement at Cambridge, his special desire being to make a present of a "grace cup to the corporation." He proved too feeble to go, and Sewall made the presentation in a vein of solemn pleasantry. After the dinner, Sewall took the cup, had it filled up, and drank to the President (Increase Mather), saying that by reason of the absence of "him who was the firmament and ornament of the province and of that society," he presented the Grace Cup, adding, "The providence of our Sovereign Lord is very investigable in that our Grace Cups, brim-full, are passing round, when our brethren in France * are petitioning for their *coup de grace.*" It was not only on such occasions as this that Mr. Sewall and those of his strictly religious views partook of the brimming cup; they appreciated highly the virtues of "canary wine" and good beer, and we find that it was a not infrequent custom to step into a place where such creature comforts were legally supplied, for the purpose of obtaining them and of using them "on the premises."

They were exceedingly careful about many things that are yet considered important, as well as about such indifferent matters as cutting the hair, and the

---

* This was at the time of suspense between the death of Charles the Second, of Spain, and the formation of the Grand Alliance against Louis the Fourteenth.

style of dress. The world has overtaken them in the matter of dress, and any man who should now array himself in the ribbons and gold that were affected by the Cavaliers, and against which the Puritans protested would be deemed little better than a coxcomb, if he were not supposed to have lost his wits. The simple black of the Puritans is now the color of all well-dressed gentlemen in American society. On the other hand we have not followed them in their views about the garments of women, nor in their appreciation of the moderate amount of education that the fair sex may be permitted to obtain. We can well sympathize with Sewall, however, when he writes: " Having been long and much dissatisfied with the trade of fetching Negroes from Guinea, at last I had a strong inclination to write something about it; but it wore off. At last reading Bayne about servants, who mentions Blackamoors, I began to be uneasy that I had so long neglected doing any thing. . . . Mr. C. Mather resolves to publish a sheet to exhort masters to labor for their conversion, which makes me hope that I was called of God to write this apology for them." Judge Sewall was decidedly in advance of " C. Mather," for he wrote a tract entitled " The Selling of Joseph," in which he amplified an expression of his own that we have already quoted regarding the slave trade. He said there was no " proportion between twenty pieces of silver and LIBERTY " (which he spelled large); that Joseph's brethren had no right to sell him, and that (bringing the argument down to a low basis) it " may be a question whether all the benefit received by Negro slaves will balance the account of cash laid out upon them." Finally, rising in the argument, he says: "Methinks when we are bemoaning the barbarous usage of our friends and kinfolk in Africa, it might not be unseasonable to enquire whether we are not culpable in forcing the Africans to become slaves among ourselves." Sewall was out of sympathy with his time, but we find that six months after this tract was published, some had come to see the weight of his reasoning, for one of the officers of the crown, at the time of taking his official oath, thanked him for " The Selling of Joseph," saying " 't was an ingenious discourse."

The correspondence and diaries of the time are full of evidences of that conscientiousness which is apparent in those of the earlier day. Sewall tells us, for example, that in August, 1701, he went down the harbor to the Castle, now Fort William, where Colonel Romer, a famous engineer, more noted for his ability in the line of his profession than for his Puritanic character, was rebuilding the works. The object of the visit was to "tell the young men that if any intemperate language proceeded from Col. Romer," it was not the intention of the authorities in employing him to " countenance that, or to encourage their imitation," but that they should obey his directions only in so far as he was exercising his professional skill in the work, " lest it should be thought," he carefully adds, " that the Council had too much winked at his cursing and swearing, which was complained of."

We find that the tables at this time were exceedingly well provided. Mrs. Sewall feasted some of her women one day with a dinner that her husband called "good," comprising "boiled pork, beef, fowls, very good roast-beef, turkey pie and tarts." On other occasions there were provided "roast beef, venison pastry, cake and cheese," and there was not uncommonly "cider, apples, and a glass of wine," sack and posset, or similar provisions, even when they "sung several Psalms," or when there were exhortations and prayers.

XVII.

IS IT LAWFUL TO RESIST?

In the last days of the Mathers there stood in the North End, on the corner of an alley that ran from North Street eastward to Ship Street, an inn sometimes known as the *Two Palaverers*, because it bore on its sign a representation of two old gentlemen in wigs, cocked hats, and knee-breeches, ceremoniously saluting each other. It was better known as *Salutation Inn*, and from this fact the alley was called Salutation Alley. It was in the vicinity of the ship-yards, and the hospitable apartments of this inn, at about the year 1724, a score of men, most of whom lived in that region of Boston, were accustomed to meet from time to time as a club, or "caucus," to lay plans "for introducing certain persons into places of trust and power."* The most prominent member of this club was Samuel Adams, a man born to be a leader, then thirty-five years of age, a justice of the peace, and deacon in the Old South Church, not far from which he occupied a pleasant home on Purchase Street. He was a wise man, a good man, and

---

* "The History of the Rise, Progress, and Establishment of the Independence of the United States of America," by Wm. Gordon, D.D., vol. i., p. 252, note.

was entrusted by his fellow townsmen with the important offices of selectman and member of assembly.* Samuel Adams was of Celtic blood, descended from an immigrant reputed to have come to Quincy from Devonshire, England, who became ancestor of a long line of men who made the name of Adams famous in the annals of America for a century and a half. The "Caulker's Club," as the organization just referred to was called, is an indication that the Bostoneers were uniting for the purpose of strengthening their hold on public affairs, and we shall find that it proved an educating influence that was influential not on the membership alone, but also through them upon the whole Boston community.

At the time of the departure of Governor Shute, and during the interval that Dummer was acting in his stead, a son of the famous Bishop Burnet was governing New York and New Jersey, and he was doing it so judiciously that when George the Second wished that position for a favorite, he transferred William Burnet to Boston, and made him governor of Massachusetts. Burnet did not look upon this change as a reward, but as a calamity; for he had come to America to retrieve his fortune, and he foresaw that the new post was not a favorable one for that purpose, as, indeed, it was not. He complained that his fate was a hard one, and it was evident that his spirits were depressed.

* Mr. Adams was one of the most influential among those persons who formed the New South Church in 1715, and built a meeting-house on land granted them by the town. The site was apparently intended by the early settlers for such a use, and was known as Church Green. It was on Summer Street, in the "South End" of those days. The building was completed in 1717.

SAMUEL ADAMS—AT THE AGE OF 45 YEARS.
After the portrait by Copley in the Art Museum (1772).

When he came to Boston, which was not until July, 1728, he was welcomed with wondrous pomp; many gentlemen went as far as Narragansett Bay to meet him as he disembarked from the schooner in which he arrived from New York, and such a multitude of horses and carriages waited upon him as he approached Boston that he passed along the Neck accompanied by a cavalcade greater than had ever been seen on such an occasion, and none equalled it for many years afterwards.* The town expended eleven hundred pounds upon the pomp and parade; there was a thunder of artillery, from the ships in the harbor and the cannon in the forts, and loud huzzas from a multitude that was described as almost numberless; there were addresses and there was a poetical welcome written by that uncontrollable punster, the bombastical Mather Byles, afterwards minister of the Hollis Street Church. In this effusion the young theologian gave free wing to his fancy and patriotism, crying out in his enthusiasm,

> " Welcome, great man, to our desiring eyes ;
> Thou earth proclaim it, and resound ye skies !

---

* At the time of these joyous proceedings, Sir William Keith, once Governor of Pennsylvania, proposed to the king that duties of stamps on parchment and paper should by act of Parliament be extended to the American colonies. Sir Robert Walpole, it is said, remarked that he would leave the taxing of the colonies to some successor possessing more courage and less desire to increase commerce. Walpole wished to enlarge American trade; but eleven years later the proposal was renewed by some British merchants, and received consideration. Later still (1765) the suggestion was adopted, much to the disadvantage of English commerce, as Samuel Adams shall show us.

> Voice answering voice in joyful consort meet,
>   The hills all echo, and the rocks repeat :
> And thou, O Boston, mistress of the towns,
> Whom the pleased bay with amorous arms surrounds,
>   Let thy warm transports blaze in numerous fires,
>   And beaming glories glitter on thy spires ;
> Let rockets streaming up the ether glare,
> And flaming serpents hiss along the air !"
> " While rising shouts a general joy proclaim,
>   And every tongue, O Burnet, lisps thy name !"

Burnet's commission was opened at the courthouse, and received with uncommon joy. He was himself conducted to the *Bunch of Grapes* tavern, a few doors from the town-house, for what reason the anti-temperance principles of the people may allow us to guess. It is not strange that in the face of such exuberance as this Burnet should think that his path was to be smoother than he had been led to expect. In addressing the citizens he disssimulated his disappointment and said that it was not easy for him to express the pleasure he had in coming to Boston, that his commission had been received " in so respectful and noble a manner," and the " glory and wealth of this great province had appeared in so strong a light " that he had no doubt that they would settle the matter of salary in a suitable manner.

This began a contest, for the people were then just as determined as they had been before, that all taxes should be laid of their own free will, and not by dictation of king or parliament. They were just as determined then as they were fifty years later ; in fact, their stand was not changed from the beginning,—they were independent at all times. The house was willing to meet the expenses of the governor's coming to them, and to support him; but they would not vote a "salary"; and the governor was true to his instructions; he would receive nothing less than an established stipend. The colonists were somewhat encouraged in their course by the fact that the inhabitants of Barbadoes were at the same time engaged in a contest with their governor against a fixed salary, especially as the islanders could not sustain their cause by an appeal to a charter. The people of the Barbadoes had given their governor a large salary, but he had oppressed them, and they retaliated in this way. They gave up the struggle at last, but compromised by decreasing the amount of the stipend. Governor Burnet thought to gain his point by refusing consent to all acts of the legislature until the salary should be voted, and thus the members of the house were unable to obtain their own pay; but the merchants of Boston stepped to their relief and advanced the necessary funds, the people voting them at the spring town-meeting.* The governor said that the house was too much influenced by the inhabitants of the town; for in voting the money to the representatives the Bostonians had unanimously declared their opposition to the salary. This Burnet, in great wrath, pronounced "an unnecessary forwardness, an attempt to give law to the country," and accordingly he adjourned the legislature to Salem, "where

---

* In all of these discussions the town of Boston was stiff in its independence, though the deputies from the country places sometimes favored the royal prerogative.

prejudice had not taken root." The change of place did not effect any change of temper, and the unhappy dispute continued. Nothing was done after several unsuccessful sessions, and the governor adjourned the house to Cambridge. Meantime he was in straits for money, himself, but no town offered to give *him* help, and he was much distressed; but ever true to his royal master, he would not compromise the matter. The discussion grew warmer, the breach wider, and messages flew faster and faster between the house and the governor, until, at last, the governor being overthrown in his chaise on the Cambridge causeway, caught a cold, which, with his official perplexities, so wore upon him, that his death followed, of a fever (after an illness of about five days), at Boston, September 7, 1729. He had held his office but fourteen months.

Governor Burnet was an amiable and estimable man in many respects, and the people of Massachusetts found no fault with him; they objected to a principle only. When he died they appropriated eleven hundred pounds for the expenses of his funeral, which was conducted after the English fashion. Gloves and rings were given to the mourning members of the general court, and the ministers of King's chapel, to three physicians, the bearers, the president of Harvard College, and the women who laid out the body; while gloves only were given to the under-bearers, the justices, the captains of the castle and of the man-of-war in the harbor, to officers of the customs, professors and fellows of the college, and the ministers of Boston who happened to attend the funeral. Wine was furnished to the Boston regiment as much as was thought needful.* Several years later a grant of three thousand pounds was made to the governor's children, who were orphans.

George the Second now commissioned as governor Jonathan Belcher, son of a prosperous Boston merchant, and a graduate of Harvard College, who had previously been in office in the colony. He was a polished and sociable gentleman, had travelled extensively, and in the course of his European wanderings had been more than once at the court at Hanover, where he had been noticed with distinguished politeness. As governor he lived elegantly, entertained much, made great show in equipage and dress, and might have been popular had he not been indiscreet in his personal remarks about those whom he disapproved. He was a supporter of the royal prerogative, and the people found very soon that in changing governors they had gained nothing; but had simply changed the person with whom they were fighting.

* The distribution of rings was common at New England funerals, and gloves and scarfs were also given away at such times, until 1721 when the general court decreed that scarfs must not longer be distributed, because a burdensome custom. In 1741, wine and rum were forbidden to be distributed. In the English funerals of the olden time vast quantities of eatables and drinkables were given away, and we read that on the occasion of burying a lord in the time of Charles the Second, while an oration was delivered, "a large pot of wine stood upon the coffin, out of which every on drank to the health of the deceased." One Boston clergyman, in 1748, left a record of two thousand nine hundred and forty pairs of gloves that he had received. He sold as many of the rings and gloves as he could.

Governor Belcher landed from a war-ship, August 10, 1730, and was received with much parade. He soon began his efforts to obtain a salary, and it was found that his instructions were couched in much stronger terms than those of Burnet, the sovereign threatening that in case of obstinacy the previous unwarrantable practices of the colonists would be brought to the attention of Parliament. Belcher was directed to return immediately to England if the salary were not voted. Session after session passed; the house voting as usual that to grant a salary would deprive themselves of their rights as Englishmen, and the governor threatening that he would go back to London if a salary were not provided. At last, in 1735, orders came from England to Belcher, first to accept certain particular grants, and then to take whatever he could get. Robert Walpole, who did not care to meddle with the affairs of the colony when he could with decency let them alone, probably had enough to occupy his attention in his efforts to keep England out of a continental war, and did not enjoy the constant stories of bickerings that came to him from the distant colonies of New England, the importance of which he could not so clearly estimate as he could that of those nearer home. The victory seems to us to have been clearly on the side of the Americans.

At this time (1740) the currency was paper, and it had so greatly depreciated that five hundred and fifty pounds of it were worth but one hundred pounds of sterling exchange. The balance of trade was against Boston, and the good coins that Hull had made in 1650 and 1660 had all gone out of circulation. The projector of the bank of 1714, who had seen his plan ignored, now proposed it anew, and the people were pleased to establish what was known as the " Land Bank " scheme, a private enterprise by which it was hoped to put farther off the day when financial affairs should be brought to a specie basis. This action was opposed to an act of Parliament passed twenty years before, which had, however, no bearing upon the plantations; and now Parliament suppressed the new bank, by simply declaring that its former act should extend to the colonies from its passage; a singular retroactive assertion, the propriety of which may well be doubted. Its effect was not only to stop the operations of the land bank, but to give every bill-holder a right to sue every partner or director for the sum which he might have lost. This threw the directors into consternation. The stockholders of this bank were men of character, and among them we find the names of Samuel Adams, of Purchase Street, Robert Hale, of Beverly, and others of equally high repute.

During this time there had been a dispute between Massachusetts and New Hampshire regarding their respective jurisdictions, and it was settled by Belcher in such a way that Massachusetts lost a considerable territory that she had claimed. The same process had been pursued in the region of Plymouth and Rhode Island, and Massachusetts had also lost in those directions. There had always been a party in the colony disaffected with the governor, and his opposition to the bank strengthened it and increased the number of his enemies to such an extent that they were able to undermine him in England and finally to effect his recall. He was removed in 1741. England had accomplished nothing in the way of breaking down the spirit of independence in New England by his instrumentality.

The year that Governor Belcher came to Boston was the close of the first century of its existence, and "centennial sermons" were preached in which the occasion was made the most of, not by way of historical edification so much as for the purpose of impressing proper moral and religious lessons. It happened that Judge Samuel Sewall died on the first day of January in that year, and at his funeral his pastor, Thomas Prince, the chronologist, who was minister of the South Church, being colleague of Joseph Sewall, son of the judge, preached a sermon which was of the nature of a centennial discourse. At the opening of the general court in May, Mr. Thomas Prince again was preacher, and he made fitting reference to the events of 1630, and probably repeated to his hearers many facts that he had received from his old parishioner Judge Sewall, who had been familiar with the history of Boston to within thirty years of the landing of Winthrop. In August Mr. Thomas Foxcroft of the First Church followed with a discourse entitled "Observations Historical and Practical on the Rise and Primitive State of New England"; and during the sessions of the court Mr. John Webb, of the North Church, preached a Thursday lecture "On the Great Concern of New England," in which he brought before his congregation the "awful signs of God's withdrawing from us," mentioning especially the "flood of irreligion and profaneness," the "terrible cursing and swearing, pernicious lying, slandering and backbiting, cruel injustice and oppression, rioting and drunkenness," etc.

In 1740 Boston had a visit from the celebrated young evangelist, George Whitefield, who had gone to Georgia the year before and now stopped in New England on his way home. He preached for Dr. Colman and Mr. Cooper in the Brattle Street Church first, September 19th, and at the South Church the following day, to vast crowds on each occasion; and he spoke several times on the Common to audiences estimated at from eight thousand to twenty thousand persons. A very acrimonious warfare of pamphlets was waged over him afterwards, but it is unquestioned that his audiences were deeply impressed by discourses which are said to have been delivered in "such a tender, earnest, and moving manner as melted the assembly into tears."

When Mr. Whitefield visited Cambridge, he was rather sharp in his criticism of the college. In his diary, published afterwards, he wrote, under date September 24, 1740:

"Went this morning to see and preach at Cambridge, the chief college for training up the sons of the prophets in all New England. It has one president, four tutors, upwards of one hundred students. It is scarce as big as one of our least colleges in Oxford, and as far as I could gather from some who well knew the state of it, not far superior to our universities in piety and true godliness.

Tutors neglect to pray with and examine the hearts of their pupils. Discipline is at too low an ebb. Bad books are becoming fashionable among them."

A few weeks later he added: "As for the universities, I believe it may be said their light is now become darkness,—darkness that may be felt; and is complained of by the most godly ministers."

President Holyoke was inclined to think well of Whitefield, though he deprecated his extravagance, and thought that his "godly jealousy for the churches of Christ" had caused him to bear false witness against the college, and he united with the professors in publishing a pamphlet in which the evangelist's "arrogance, rashness, and censoriosness" were exposed, and he himself boldly pronounced an "uncharitable person and a deluder of the people." Tutor Flynt thought that Whitefield was a "composition of a great deal of good and some bad," as "very apt to judge harshly, and censure in the severest terms those who differ from his scheme." Doubtless there was truth in what Tutor Flynt said. It must be remembered that Whitefield was at the time only twenty-five years of age, had been flattered and caressed in a remarkable manner, and that he might well have been led into extravagances by persons not friendly to the college.

The last years of the official life of Governor Belcher are to be remembered as connected with the foundation of one of Boston's most noted public buildings. For many years the subject of markets had been discussed in one form and another. In 1717 it was represented that the inhabitants were imposed upon by hucksters, and a committee of the town-meeting reported in favor of establishing a market-house, but the town, after debating the subject, disallowed it. It 1733 it was voted to put up three such buildings in different parts of town, and money was appropriated for the purpose. They were erected; but that at the North End was taken down and the timber used for building a work-house; one at the South End was changed into shops; and the third, which was at Dock Square, was demolished by a mob that carried off the timber for private use.

Now the matter was brought up again, and many favored the erection of such a structure, but a majority could not be obtained at town-meeting until Mr. Peter Faneuil, a wealthy member of a Huguenot family from Rochelle, offered to build a market-house on the site of the one destroyed at Dock Square, provided the town would legally authorize it and make proper regulations for its care. So great was the opposition to the project even in this form that three hundred and sixty persons voted against accepting the gift, and but seven more in favor of it. The majority of seven votes carried the day, however, and Faneuil Hall was given to the town. It was finished and formally accepted in 1742; but so few people resorted to it that it was almost entirely abandoned, and in 1747 the town voted to close it. It was opened again in March, 1748, for three days in the week, but in 1752, after a sharp contest, it was indefinitely closed. It was destroyed by fire in 1761, but rebuilt in 1763, with some alterations, but of the original size, a lottery being authorized for the purpose of supplying the funds. The first building was of brick, one hundred feet by forty; in 1806 it was enlarged to eighty feet in width and one story was added to its height. Faneuil Hall became the favorite place for public meetings, and it is not a little notable

THE SECOND FANEUIL HALL. (1764).

that the first formal oration pronounced in it was delivered March 14, 1743, on the occasion of the founder's death. The Reverend Charles Chauncy, of the First Church, began the exercises with prayer, after which Mr. John Lovell, master of the South Grammar School, advanced to the moderator's seat, and pronounced his eulogy, in the course of which with prophetic forecast he exclaimed: "May Liberty always spread its joyful wings over this place!"

The year 1740 is memorable because it was the one in which a son of Samuel Adams of the Caulkers' Club graduated at Cambridge. Of all the orators who ever opened their lips in Faneuil Hall this son, who was, like his father, named Samuel, was the one who gave it the right to be called the "Cradle of Liberty," and may be said to have begun the fulfilment of the somewhat rhetorical prophesy of Master Lovell. "Sam" Adams, as his contemporaries called him, probably in affectionate distinction from his father, was a Puritan of the Puritans; educated in the atmosphere of strict fidelity to the religious faith of the fathers, familiar with the independent conversation of the members of the Caulkers' Club, some of whom were doubtless among the throng of welcome visitors at the Purchase Street dwelling, an intelligent pupil at the wooden school-house that then stood back of King's Chapel, and gave its name to the street; stirred in his soul by the preaching of Whitefield, which quickened all Boston, he was ready after his college course was completed to exemplify in his life the principles upon which the generations before him had founded the commonwealth. Three years after graduation Sam Adams began to show that he was to be a thoughtful and daring speaker for the liberties of the people, for he took for his subject when candidate for the degree of Master of Arts the question, "Whether it Be Lawful to Resist the Supreme Magistrate, if the Commonwealth Cannot Otherwise be Preserved?"

Whatever Adams said on this occasion, standing in the presence of the President, Edward Holyoke, the dignified professors, and his excellency the governor, representing His most gracious Majesty, King George the Second, besides the other officials of the Crown, he showed in what direction events were tending. The people had now been for a hundred years standing up for what they considered their rights, in the employment of measures of a peaceful kind; they had placed every obstacle in the way of the king when he attempted to take from them their charter; and when it had been snatched away, they had made the path of the governors sent to them as full of thorns as they could, interposing obstacles almost insurmountable to the peaceful performance of the duties demanded of them; now they stood at a place where Samuel Adams could ask them whether it was lawful to take up arms in case the liberties of the people could not otherwise be preserved. It was a bold step on the part of a young man, and it was taken at a moment when its influence must have been great, and on a spot to be remembered.

Public occasions at Harvard College were important in those days, and they are still considered times when high themes are to be presented and discussed in a rational manner. In one of his least objectionable "poems," Mather Byles describes a festal occasion at Harvard College in glowing terms. It was a day when all the neighboring towns emptied themselves into Cambridge, when those who followed the throng hastened

> "To that admired solemnity, whose date,
> Tho' late begun, will last as long as fate!"

Mr. Byles describes the passage of the Charles River by ferry in a way that is quite amusing. He shows us the crowd from Boston waiting for the slow-approaching boat, into which

> "With impetuous haste they clustering pour ;
> The men the head, the stern the ladies grace,
> And neighing horses fill the middle space.
> Sunk deep, the boat floats slow the waves along,
> And scarce contains the thickly crowded throng ;
> A general horror seizes on the fair, . . .
> Till rowed with care, they reach the opposing side,
> Leap on the shore and leave the threatening tide.
> And now the time approaches when the bell
> With dull continuance tolls a solemn knell.
> Numbers of blooming youth in black array
> Adorn the yard and gladden all the day."

In the rugged and monotonous verse we see the procession formed, the president at the head, followed by the senate, the clergy, the undergraduates, and the populace, until they enter the church, where

> "The work begun with prayer, with modest pace
> A youth advancing mounts the desk with grace,
> To all the audience sweeps a circling bow,
> Then from his lips ten thousand graces flow.
> The next that comes a learned thesis reads."

We can readily imagine Adams "sweeping the circling bow" to the crowded audience at Cambridge, and dropping into their minds seeds that he desired to have spring up in the future. No man knew better how to time his utterances, and we may be sure that it was not chance, nor the prescription of any tutor, that led him to take the particular subject that he discussed on this notable occasion. He knew that Cambridge would be crowded, that the audience would come from all the country around, that Boston would be well represented, that the learned clergy would be present, that the hearers would be in a frame of mind adapted to receive what was told them without specially questioning it, and, above all, he knew that he was to address the young men upon whom the answer to the question was to depend a few years later. Perhaps James Otis, who was a member of the class, graduated that morning, heard the weighty words, and did not forget them.

XVIII.

TESTED AND NOT FOUND WANTING.

MORE than a hundred years before this time, after the war with the Pequods, it seemed to some of the inhabitants of Boston that a military organization would be a good thing, and accordingly, in 1637, certain men formed themselves into a company, which continues to this day, the oldest band of citizen soldiery in America. The organization was very informal at first. John Winthrop says, in his journal:

"Divers gentlemen and others being joined in a military company desired to be made a corporation, but the council, considering from the example of the Prætorian Band among the Romans and the Templars in Europe, how dangerous it might be to erect a standing authority of military men, which might easily in time overtop the civil power, thought fit to stop it betimes; yet they were allowed to be a company, but subordinate to all authority."

Accordingly, the "Military Company of the Massachusetts" was formed, and Robert Keayne (who afterwards had the trouble with Mrs. Sherman and her pig) was captain. These persons had a formal charter authorizing them to choose officers, to assemble and drill wherever they pleased, and to make laws for their own government; it being specially stipulated that no officers should be put upon them but those of their own choice. One thousand acres of land were given them for the payment of any charges they should be put to, and the first Monday of every month was set apart for their drill-day, no other training, or even town-meetings, being permitted on that day. Captain Keayne had been connected with the "Honourable Artillery Company" of London, and, in course of time, this new organization was called the "Honourable" Artillery Company. In 1738, it was styled the "Honourable and Ancient Company;" since that time it has been known as the "Ancient and Honorable Artillery Company," and the last name has been confirmed by the Legislature. In 1770, this body stood forth in gold-laced hats, blue coats, buff underclothes, silk stockings, and white-linen spatterdashes; its days of parade were signalized by a drummer, who passed through the principal streets vigorously beating the rappel, and the company was assembled by the same martial sounds.* The election of its officers is a notable ceremony, and on the occasion there is still, as there was in the days of the fathers, an "Election Sermon."

All men in Boston between the ages of sixteen and sixty were, in early times, required to belong to the militia, and the privates were provided with pikes, muskets, swords, bandoleers (pouches for powder and bullets), and a rest for use in taking aim; while

* "History of the Ancient and Honorable Artillery Company," by Zacariah G. Whitman, Boston, 1842, p. 456.

their bodies were sometimes protected by little cuirasses, and by coats quilted with cotton. These men were formed into train-bands, each of which counted not less than sixty-four, nor more than two hundred, members, and these, in turn, were distributed into regiments, the governor being commander-in-chief. At stated times, the train-bands met for exercise, and there were prayers before and after the drill; the whole business being entered upon and performed with the same religious earnestness that characterized all the doings of the Bostoneers of the olden time. Officers, when chosen, considered their elections cause for thanksgiving to God, and entered upon the discharge of their duties after solemn prayer. The people believed and said that "piety could not be maintained without church ordinances and officers, nor justice without laws and magistracy, no more can our safety and peace be preserved without military orders and officers," and that it was an equally solemn duty to support them all. Doubtless the trained soldiers of the regular armies of France and England, when they came in contact with these American militiamen in times of peace, felt some disdain for them; but, when they met in war, they found to their dismay that the New Englanders, trained from early life to the use of the musket, and accustomed to desperate encounters with savage foes, were not wanting in courage nor in effectiveness, though they did not wear the gorgeous uniforms nor understand the intricate manœuvres of older peoples. Probably the Boston company that did escort duty to the soldiers of La Tour, on that training-day in 1643 when the Frenchmen were permitted to come ashore for purposes of exercise, were as much interested as the governor and magistrates were in the "variety of military movements" that the strangers went through; and at other times, when English veterans came among the Bostonians, similar feelings must have been excited.

The next royal governor, William Shirley, though a native of London, was practising law in Boston at the time of his appointment, May 16, 1741. He was well acquainted with the distracted condition of the colonial currency, and he knew also what difficulties his predecessor had encountered in managing His Majesty's affairs among an unsympathetic people. He served until 1756; but was absent from Boston four years of that time. He was much occupied by important movements in King George's War, which lasted from 1744 to 1748, and in the French and Indian War, so-called, which began two years before he left, the treaty of Aix-la-Chapelle having proved only a truce in the contest that was at the same period exciting Europe. Governor Shirley was a bustling and spirited military man, and took his share in actual warfare, besides giving his counsel to those who fought when he did not; though he left the colony in a state of great depression, probably greater than that in which he found it.

Three points demand notice in the career of Governor Shirley: first, the struggle for a salary; next, the capture of Louisburg; and lastly, the Albany Convention of 1754, called by the American governors, by advice of the English Board of Trade.

The governor opened the dispute about the salary very promptly, and it ran through the usual stages, until, at last, both he and the ministry at home concluded that the colonists were only aggravated by pressing the matter and that it had better be dropped, especially since the coöperation of the colony was needed in war at the time.

King George's War was declared in the early spring of 1744. By means of fast sailing vessels the news had reached the French at their strong fortress at Louisburg some time before it was known at Boston or by the English in America anywhere. Immediate advantage was taken of this early information, and an expedition was sent out which captured an English garrison at Canso. It was an unfortunate advantage, for it alarmed Boston and the rest of New England, and put them in the way of valuable information that might not otherwise have come into their possession. Some of the prisoners from Louisburg found their way to Boston and told the authorities just what they wished to know about the strength, but especially the weakness, of that celebrated garrison.

The French had occupied themselves for thirty years in building fortifications around Louisburg, and it was thought at this time that every point that an enemy could possibly approach was protected by the wall, which was of stone, from thirty to thirty-six feet high, guarded by a ditch eighty feet wide outside of it. Two batteries commanded the entrance to the harbor. The position of Louisburg was very important to the French, for it was not only convenient to protect the St. Lawrence, but it was also a good place from which to send out expeditions to operate on the New England coast. There was at the time living at Damariscotta, Maine, a graduate of Harvard College, who was engaged in the fishing business, and therefore interested in whatever the French might do affecting the safety of vessels in that part of the Atlantic. He collected all the information that he could about Louisburg, and then went to Boston to tell Governor Shirley what he had learned. The governor was also informed that in the winter the snow was piled up against the great walls in such a way that soldiers could easily climb over into the fortress, and that the garrison was badly provisioned and insubordinate.

The court of Massachusetts had already been warned by the governor that it was necessary to prepare for a war, and the fact was well adapted to carry dismay among the members as they contemplated the condition of the colonial finances; but he amazed them now by bringing before them, under the seal of secrecy, a scheme for the capture of the "Gibraltar of America," as Louisburg was called. He told them all that he had learned from Vaughan and the escaped prisoners, and added that he had asked for a fleet from England to "defend Annapolis," and had written to Commodore Warren, then commanding the forces in the West Indies, asking him to take some of his vessels thither. The court was naturally astonished; the proposition that Massachusetts should send out an expedition against a place so well fortified was preposterous. The matter was submitted to a committee, which reported that the undertaking was altogether beyond the power of the province, and that, if it were possible, there was not enough money in the treasury to permit of entering upon the project. The matter was dropped; but one of the members, who referred to it in his domestic worship, in a moment of inadvertency, was the means of bringing it again to public notice, upon which the people became excited about it. The governor, we may be sure, took no pains to allay the interest; in fact, it is thought that he encouraged it, and in consequence a petition was presented to the court from merchants in Boston and elsewhere urging the undertaking of the enterprise. A committee now reported in favor of it, and the court approved the report by a single vote; though even this majority would have been wiped out had one of the delegates not fallen and broken his leg when on his way to the meeting, where he intended to oppose the scheme.

When the plan was once adopted it was entered upon with enthusiasm, and the citizens of Boston and the towns about vied with one another in making preparations. Business was dull; seamen were unemployed; provisions were abundant, thanks to a good harvest; and when it was known that William Pepperell, of Kittery, had taken the position of commander of the expedition, grave deacons and justices of the peace presented themselves ready to officer the regiments; while rich farmers, mechanics, and enthusiastic Protestants, desirous of wiping away the popish French from the northern region, volunteered to take places in the ranks. After a day of fasting and prayer the fleet started for its foolhardy enterprise in March, 1745. On the seventeenth of June the garrison surrendered, the victorious New Englanders marched in, and the Catholic chapel was occupied for religious worship by Protestants. The colonists were much elated by this success, which, however, was more creditable to their daring than to their judgment or their military skill.

Governor Shirley had given directions that the fleet should sail through wintry seas, to a harbor that its pilots had not explored; should meet after dark, effect a landing in spite of the surf, march three miles through woods and bogs, and then simply scale the stone walls and take the place! When the fortunes of war placed him inside of the fortress, Pepperell saw, of course, the futility of such wild plans as these. The joyful news reached Boston on the morning of the third of July, and the exultant populace kept holiday with earnestness that night did not repress. England showed the same jubilant symptoms, and Pepperell was made a baronet, being the first native American to receive that distinction. The colonists were lost to reason, and visionary plans were made for the capture of all Canada, plans which the British ministry deemed too grand, fearing that the conquest of a country so vast might give rise to too strong a sentiment of independence in the Americans.

The colony paid the price of victory in a greatly increased public debt, and all institutions and persons that depended upon incomes found themselves in a condition of distress, for the currency depreciated anew to an alarming extent. Clergymen and officers employed by government felt the depreciation keenly, and the governor informed the court that many of the ministers would probably be forced to betake themselves to secular occupations for a livelihood.* Trade degenerated into barter, and sharp practices, which many felt necessary in order that they should increase their incomes to the utmost, threatened to make the whole body of the people corrupt. Parliament at last came to the rescue and British gold was seen in Boston streets, sent over in settlement of an equitable claim which the ministry recognized on account of the efforts of the Americans in a common cause. The war had, indeed, been brought upon them rather by European complications than by any reason touching the needs of the colonies. It was four years, however, before the distress was alleviated. Then the financial troubles which had so long perplexed legislators and people were settled. In September, 1749, the money for this purpose arrived at the Boston wharves in hundreds of casks and chests, containing Spanish dollars and coins of copper. It is much to the credit of Thomas Hutchinson, then Speaker of the House, that through his efforts this coin was, with the ap-

* The ministers were probably not all in this danger. Some may have had the foresight of the Rev. Nicholas Gilman (H. C. 1724), who, when he was settled over a parish at Durham, N. H., made out "A Carnal Scheme," in which he put down in detail the supplies that were to be furnished him, especially stipulating that in case the currency should depreciate his nominal income should increase in the same ratio. "The Gilman Family," by Arthur Gilman, page 59.

proval of the governor, set apart for the payment of the provincial bills, and that thus the embarrassments of fifty years of paper money were done away, and for a quarter of a century afterwards Massachusetts was blessed with a solid medium of exchange. Rhode Island and Connecticut, which did not at this time reform their currency, felt a shock in their trade from which it took long to recover.

We have now to notice the influence of Boston in the direction of self-government in the colonies in general. In the year 1690, when the news of the massacre at Schenectady reached the Bay, Governor Bradstreet urged upon the other colonies the necessity of providing immediately for common defense, and the general court of Massachusetts caused letters to be written to the governors inviting them to send delegates to a meeting to be held at New York. William Stoughton and Samuel Sewall of Boston were commissioned from Massachusetts, and in accordance with the plan laid down by their governor they there met the others. On the first of May an agreement was signed to raise a force for the purpose, "by the help of Almighty God, of subduing the French and Indian enemies." This was the first time that the colonists had held a congress. The seed thus dropped (it was during the interval just after Andros had been banished from Boston) was destined to bear fruit nearly two generations after; though there were to be important intermediate steps before a union could actually be formed. In 1698 William Penn presented a plan for united action; and from time to time the different governors met or sent delegates to meetings for consultation upon occasions of common danger. The people generally were slowly learning lessons of self-government: but, singularly enough, it was not from themselves but from the British ministry that the motion for a general congress next came. The Board of Trade invited a meeting, that was held at Albany, June 19, 1754, at which the delegates of most note were Thomas Hutchinson, of Massachusetts, and Benjamin Franklin, then of Philadelphia. Franklin and Shirley had discussed the subject of colonial union at Boston earlier in the year without coming to common ground, and Franklin had published in his paper* a rough picture of a snake cut into thirteen pieces, accompanied by the motto: "Unite or die!" No plan presented at Albany found general acceptance, the delegates being too positively divided between prerogative men and independents,† and the subject was dropped for the time.

In 1755, Governor Shirley, the most prominent political character in the colonies, met a number of royal governors at Alexandria, and with General

---

* The press was now becoming very important in American history. It dropped its fresh intelligence and its stirring appeals into a thousand minds at the same moment, and gave the same impulse to each of the thousand. We shall see with what eminent skill it was used by Samuel Adams and those who knew its power in the preliminary stages of the Revolution.

† The origin of the two parties, patriots and prerogative men, is dated from 1683, and the controversy between them did not end until America was free from Britain. There had been the same difference in earlier times between those who stood for all the privileges of the charter and those who sided with the king and Parliament.

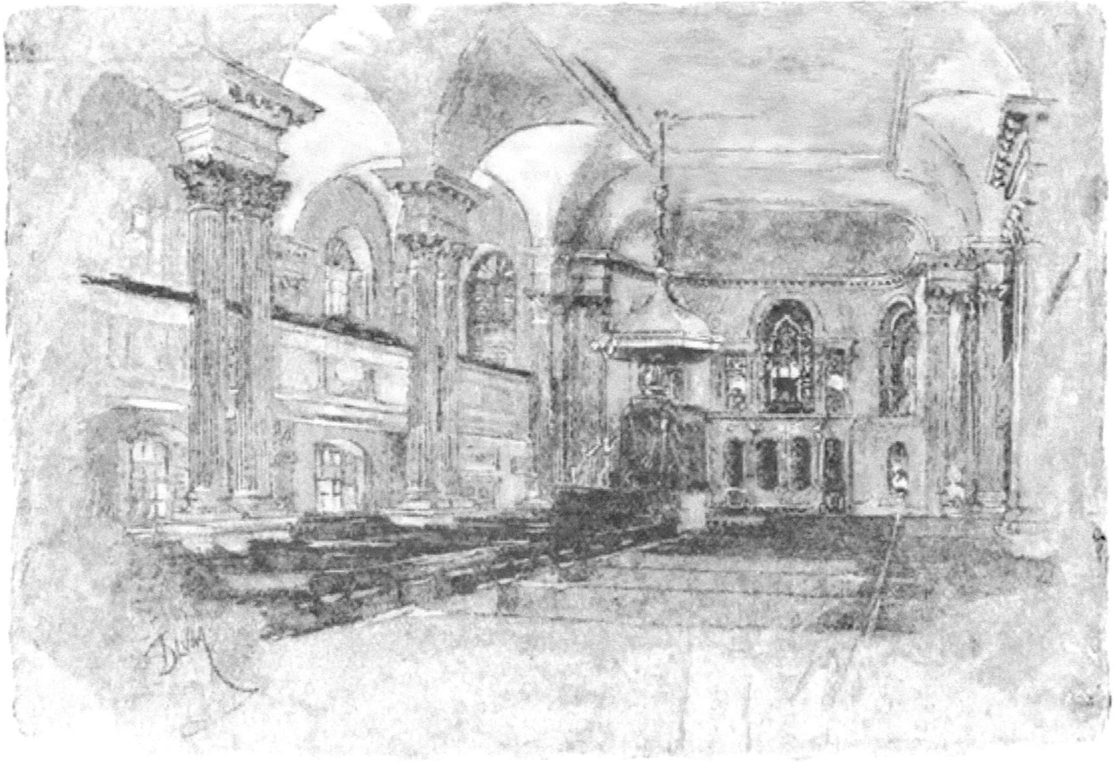

INTERIOR OF THE PRESENT KING'S CHAPEL (CORNER-STONE LAID 1749).

Braddock, then commander-in-chief of His Majesty's forces, planned the quadruple scheme for the conquest of the French by campaigns respectively against Ohio and the Northwest, Crown Point, Fort Niagara, and Nova Scotia,—for Louisburg and the region about had been restored to France by the treaty of Aix-la-Chapelle. In putting this great scheme into practice, Braddock was defeated and killed; Shirley failed at Niagara; John Winslow, of Boston, effected the pitiful carrying away of the poor Acadians; and Sir William Johnson accomplished nothing at Crown Point. Shirley, who had become commander-in-chief upon the death of Braddock, was superseded after his disastrous campaign, and was recalled to England in the autumn of 1756. When Louisburg had been acquired, it was necessary to protect it, and as a very large number of soldiers had died there, in consequence of a severe winter, Governor Shirley "impressed" such seamen as he could find on the Boston wharves, and sent them, much against their will, down to the dreary land of colds and disease. This simply irritated the people; but when the testy Commodore Knowles, who had co-operated with Pepperell, arrived in the harbor and proceeded to fill the places of some deserters by carrying away mariners from the vessels moored at the wharves and men peacefully at work building ships, he threw the citizens into a flame of anger. Boston was not familiar, as London was, with this hard and arbitrary custom, and the bereaved families of the impressed men cried to the court, which convened that day, for revenge. The mob armed themselves with sticks and clubs and pitch-mops, and, in their rage, caught an innocent lieutenant, who happened to be ashore, and threatened him with vengeance. They surrounded Governor Shirley's dwelling, where it was said that some officers were; they filled the yard; they seized a sheriff who tried to calm them, and carried him off to the stocks, where he furnished them a little merriment, and put them in a frame of mind more ready for dinner than for blood. When dusk fell upon the town, another crowd of several thousand persons gathered about the town-house; bricks and stones were thrown through the windows into the apartment in which the council was sitting, and quiet was not restored until the governor appeared at a balcony and expressed his disapproval of the impressment, and his intention to obtain the freedom of the men that had been arrested. The mob demanded the seizure and restraint of the officers in town, and the governor was so much alarmed that he retired to his house, where the mob soon appeared with a boat, supposed to belong to one of the ships, and proposed to burn it on the spot. On consideration of the danger to the town, this boat, which proved to belong to quite a different vessel, was burned elsewhere. The governor retreated to the Castle for safety; Commodore Knowles, in his blunt and reckless fashion, threatened to bombard the town; and Captain Erskine, of the *Canterbury*, and other officers were arrested by the authorities. The military was aroused by Shirley, and Boston was thronged with men from Cambridge, Roxbury, and other towns, many of whom had never carried a gun. The governor was escorted by them to his house with great parade, the people having expressed in town-meeting at once their sense of their insults and injuries, and their desire that tumultuous and riotous acts should be stopped. The House also indicated its determination to stand by the governor, and to make exertions to have the wrongs redressed. The upshot of the tempest, which was indeed very threatening, was that the irascible Knowles released most of those whom he had impressed, and sailed out to sea, greatly to the relief of Boston.

Governor Shirley is to be remembered for another reason. At the beginning of the year 1752, one Charles Paxton, a native of America, was commissioned as Surveyor of the Port of Boston. He was a man of energy, who had obtained his office by purchase, for the purpose of making his fortune. The officers of the crown at the time openly allowed smuggling, and a large trade had grown up, in contravention of the Molasses Law, or Sugar Law, as it was indifferently called, which (1733) laid a duty on molasses, sugar, rum, etc. This law was felt to be so unnatural, that scarcely any attempts had been made to carry it into execution,* and officers of His Majesty's customs service accumulated fortunes by conniving at the importation of contraband goods, dividing the ill-gotten gain with their English patrons, to whom they were indebted for the opportunity of wrenching it from the merchants. The

* See "The Rise of the Republic," by Richard Frothingham, page 163.

independent people were indignant at the thought that England, supposed to be bankrupted by its late heavy war with France, was determined to make America pay a part of her indebtedness. The customs officers aroused them still more by demanding of Governor Shirley general warrants, authorizing them to enter any house, shop, cellar, warehouse, room, or other place in which they might suspect prohibited goods would be found, and, in case of resistance, to break open doors, chests, trunks, or other packages, and take the goods to His Majesty's warehouse for examination. Hutchinson considered it extraordinary that Shirley, who was a lawyer by education and a man of sense, should have given such authority, and expressed the belief that the writs had no legal value. When Shirley learned (in 1752) that his warrants were pronounced illegal, he discontinued them; but they were issued by the Superior Court, on application of the revenue officers. This, Judge Sewall thought, was also illegal, though it was not disputed that the court might issue a warrant authorizing search of a particular place mentioned, in which there was ground to suppose contraband goods were to be found. The "general" character was objected to. These warrants were similar to the writs of assistance issued by the English Court of Exchequer, and their legality was accepted in the mother-country. Much more irritation was caused by them a little later in Boston.

XIX.

A MALTSTER ENTERS POLITICS.

WHEN Samuel Adams left college he began to prepare himself to practise law; but he soon turned to commerce and entered the counting-room of a prominent merchant, though he had no taste for trade. Leaving this pursuit in turn, he began business for himself upon money given him by his father, all of which he managed to lose, and then he joined his father in carrying on a malt-house on Purchase Street. He was a young man of twenty-three when the triumphant soldiers from Louisburg brought home the iron cross[*] which they wrenched from the chapel in that stronghold, and when the tumultuous crowds in Boston's streets celebrated the victory probably no one rejoiced more heartily than he. His father was prominent in all public affairs, and was a member of the military committees of the legislature, while the son, though looked upon as a thriftless person, was making himself felt in the clubs and the newspapers. Three years after the victory the father died, and the following year the

[*] This cross, freshly gilded, now stands over the principal entrance to the Library of Harvard University.

JOHN HANCOCK,
After the Portrait by Copley in the Museum of Fine Arts (1737-1793).

son married and settled down in Purchase Street, nominally to attend to the malt-house.

At the time of the Louisburg rejoicings a younger man, James Otis, who had graduated at Harvard the year that Adams took his second degree, began also to study law, and he did not, like Adams, give it up. He began to practise at Plymouth in due time, and he was laboring there in his vocation at the time that Adams married. Younger than either of these men— fifteen years younger than Adams—there was John Hancock, just ready to enter Harvard College, in 1749, whose home was in Quincy. He was destined, a little later, to be identified with the contest in which both Adams and Otis were soon to be engaged, and by his considerable inherited wealth to serve it effectively.

Thomas Pownall, the next royal governor, reached Boston in August, 1757, while the last French and Indian War was in progress, at a time when Boston was stirred by news of the capture of Fort William Henry under circumstances of barbarity which spread dismay throughout all the northern provinces, and especially gave pain to Boston, because many of the troops had been sent from that place. There was a general feeling of despair, and this was intensified when the governor received a letter from Captain Christie, in command at Albany, dated August 10th and 11th, couched in these frantic terms: " For God's sake exert yourselves to save a province; New York itself may fall, save a country; prevent the downfall of the British government upon this continent!" This letter was well calculated to spread alarm, and, in fact, all Massachusetts was aroused, for it was thought that there would be a prompt advance upon both New York and the Bay State. Twenty thousand militiamen were soon under arms under command of Pepperell. The fortunes of the war are not the subject of these pages; suffice it to say that Louisburg, Ticonderoga, Crown Point, Quebec, and Montreal were all taken by 1760, and that there was great rejoicing in Boston. In celebrating the fall of Quebec forty-five tar barrels, two cords of wood, and fifty pounds of powder, besides other combustibles, were burned on Copp's Hill. The Peace of Paris, in 1763, marked the close of the French and Indian wars, which, for nearly fourscore years, had filled the land with horror, and made the settlers on the frontiers and in many a New England hamlet familiar with savage butchery.

It was the good-fortune of Governor Pownall to arrive in Boston at the time of distress, when all minor matters were forgotten in thoughts of the necessities of self-preservation, and to leave when the successes at the close of the long struggle with France made it certain that the colonists were no longer to be menaced by that enemy, and that her dominion was soon to be extinguished on the continent. The people were, however, uneasy, and ready to magnify every act that could possibly be construed as antagonistic to their interests, and to withstand the execution of any scheme that could be made to appear as a contravention of their rights and privileges as British subjects living under a charter government.

When Shirley had been relieved of the command of His Majesty's forces in America, the commission was given to Lord Loudoun, and soon after Governor Pownall came to his office there arose a conflict between this officer and the Massachusetts legislature. Lord Loudoun sent soldiers to Boston, and the officers called upon the justices to allow them to be quartered on the inhabitants, according to the terms of an act of parliament. The justices refused; Lord Loudoun became furious, and threatened; but all to no purpose, the general court insisted that the act of Parliament did not affect the colonies, and, after a short but fierce quarrel, the court came off victorious. The troops were quartered at the Castle, and not long afterwards Lord Loudoun was relieved of his command, though not until another angry quarrel seemed imminent between him and the court.

It was evident that the strong sentiment of loyalty, which Cotton Mather said was felt in Boston in 1726, had become much weakened by August, 1760, when Francis Bernard arrived, though as the commissioned governor he was received with respectful parade and due ceremony. Governor Pownall, who was a man of intelligence and cultivation, had, during his short administration, made himself very pleasing to most of the inhabitants of Boston and of the colony, and, when he went away he carried with him a mass of information in regard to the province, which he used in writing works on the subject. From 1768 to 1780 he was a member of parliament, and in that position he uttered warnings against the measures opposed to the interests of the Americans, and foretold the fact that our country was destined to take its place among the nations, a prophecy which, as he lived until 1805, he saw fulfilled. Of all the Englishmen who held that the Americans had rights that ought to be respected, Pownall was the most clear and definite in his views and in his expressions. He was the first person to call American citizens "sovereigns," and though Governor Shirley thought that centuries would pass before the Americans would "grow restive, and disposed to throw off their dependency upon their mother-country," Pownall saw the great possibilities of the New World, and prophesied that the Americans were soon to be an independent sovereign people, with which it would be well for England to make sure of friendly relations. He expressed high hopes for the "liberties of America," and for the country itself, which he thought would be "an asylum one day or another to a remnant of mankind who wish and deserve to live with political liberty."

Governor Hutchinson says in his history that speculative men had figured in their minds "an American empire," but that they placed it at such a distant age that, like Governor Shirley, they did not think that any one then living could expect to see it. In this respect Governor Pownall was far in advance of his English contemporaries, and comparatively few in America even were, up to this time, able to discern with like distinctness the trend of affairs. It soon became apparent, however. The antagonism that had long been strengthening between the Bostonians and the officers of the crown began to show itself in the language of the town, for those who were attached to the principles of the house of Hanover, who approved the views of the ancient whigs, and felt that the revolution which brought William and Mary to the throne was a benefit to the people of England and America, were called whigs, while the small number, comprising the officers of the king and those who supported them and the royal prerogative against the " rights of the people," were branded as tories. The mass of the inhabitants of Boston, and of the entire colony in fact, looked upon the English whigs as right, and considered a tory to be a sympathizer with despotism and wrong.

While this feeling was rising in Boston, Mr. Adams was by no means a silent observer of the progress of events. He saw that a storm was coming, and felt that a responsibility rested upon every American to stand for the right as he saw it. His speech, on taking his second degree at Cambridge, has already been referred to ; it was but a part of a methodical scheme of action that he had marked out for himself. He plainly saw that the state must look to her educated young men for direction and support in the coming emergency, and he took every favorable opportunity to lay his views before such youth of parts as he could find. Among the young men whom Adams thus brought out to help his cause, were Otis and Hancock, who have been already mentioned, besides John Adams, of Quincy, afterwards President of the United States; Dr. Joseph Warren, afterwards major-general of the colonial militia, and martyr at

Bunker Hill; Josiah Quincy, called by John Adams "the Boston Cicero," a man of marked moral courage, who wrote vigorous essays against the British ministry, and stirred the Bostonians by his powerful eloquence; and Benjamin Church, who, though he proved recreant to the American cause afterwards, was perhaps as active and popular before his defection as either Hancock or Warren, or even as Adams himself. Adams did not make himself unduly prominent, but put forward one or another of those upon whom he trusted, as from time to time he saw that their peculiar qualifications made their services useful.

It was not only in this way that Adams urged his cause. He became a constant and vigorous contributor to the newspapers of the day, and for fifty years *Principiis Obsta, A Religious Politician, Valerius Poplicola, Vindex, Candidus, An American, A Son of Liberty, Alfred, Sincerus, Cedant Arma Togæ, A Layman, Determinatus, Populus, A Bostonian,* even *A Chatterer,* or *A Tory,* were the ostensible authors of the sarcastic, sharp, forcible, patriotic, argumentative, indignant papers that his hand wrote, often by the light of the candle that passers-by found burning in his library window late in the night. Nor did Mr. Adams stop with this wonderfully prolific public correspondence. As early as 1747, during the time of Governor Shirley, he formed a club with some of his political friends, ("ardent young rebels," Hudson, the historian of American journalism, calls them,) the object of which was to present to the people essays on public affairs, every one of which should, of course, strengthen the cause that they had at heart. The *Independent Advertiser*, printed by Rogers & Fowle, became the medium through which these essays saw the light. It began its career January 4, 1748. For some time this pioneer revolutionary paper managed to avoid collision with the authorities, but it was not at the expense of consistency, or by holding back one whit of the truth about the nature of loyalty or the rights of freemen, as its supporters held them. Isaiah Thomas, who was a well-known printer in Boston a few years later, said that the club which supported the *Independent Advertiser* was composed of whigs who "advocated the rights of the people against those measures of government which were supposed to infringe upon the privileges of the province secured by charter."

We can scarcely imagine with what avidity this little sheet was welcomed as it presented itself each week with its roughly engraved embellishment at the head of columns that contained a few items of foreign and domestic news, accompanied by a strong dose of argument for loyalty and against sedition, in favor of "liberty," and against any form of government that did not provide for the representation of the people. The readers were assured that, as no man ought to be abridged of his liberty, so also no one had the "right to give up or even part with any portion of it"; that multitudes of persons have not even the vestige of such liberty, "but hold their property and even their lives by no other tenure than the sovereign will of a tyrant, and he often the worst and most detestable of men"; and that "our invaluable charter secures to us all the English liberties, besides which we have some additional privileges which the common people there [in England] have not." True loyalty, the club informs its readers, cannot subsist in an arbitrary government, its object being a "good legal constitution," which condemns oppression and lawless power, and allows the sufferer to "remonstrate his grievances," and points out "methods of relief *when the gentle arts of persuasion have lost their efficacy.*" Finally the *Advertiser* included *ad captandum* arguments, as, for example, when it said that he who "despises his neighbor's happiness because he wears a worsted cap or leathern apron, he that struts immeasurably above the lower size of people and pretends to adjust the rights of men by the distinctions of fortune, is not over loyal." No doubt that Adams at least was at this time meditating a separation of the colonies from England, and the suggestion that other arguments than the "gentle arts of persuasion" might be used seems to indicate that he was ready to apply them in case of necessity, and that he was intentionally preparing men's minds to agree with him when the time for action should arrive.

Opposed to this little band of Bostonians stood the governor, Bernard, and his lieutenant, Thomas Hutchinson, both dependent upon the crown, and not representatives of the people whom they governed, though Hutchinson was probably attached to the land of his birth. He was a descendant of Anne Hutchinson, who had been so severely dealt with by the Bostonians in the time of Winthrop, was polite and intelligent, and, at a previous period, quite popular with the people. He wrote a history of the province, in three volumes, which is remarkable for the self-restraint that it shows, for Hutchinson was called upon to bear much treatment that must have appeared extremely harsh to him. Both the governor and his lieutenant were greedy of office for the wealth that they expected to derive from it, and this was not adapted to beget in them traits that would commend them to the colonists. Besides being lieutenant-governor, Hutchinson held the office of governor of the Castle, was a member of the Council, and judge of Probate, and finally took the office of chief-justice, thus combining legislative, executive, and judicial functions in a way that was considered incongruous and monstrous. Mr. Otis severely criticised Hutchinson for this, and said that it was a fundamental maxim that the legislative and judicial powers should be kept separate; asserting that when they are combined in one person the government is hastening fast to ruin, and its mischief and miseries are apt to be "as bad as those felt in the most absolute monarchy."

It happened that James Otis, of the group that sympathized with Adams, was the one first to come into conflict with Bernard and Hutchinson. He was a person of fiery temper, sensitive nature, and fitful passions; he lacked the caution and cool calculation of Adams, and he was so poorly balanced that his mind soon gave way under the strain of the exciting times. Incapable of malice, his sympathetic nature caught the enthusiasm of the circle in which he

(1725-1783.) AT THE AGE OF THIRTY.
After a portrait by Blackburn.

happened to be ; and he sometimes took up a cause of which he repented, which made his course appear at times irresolute and contradictory. In 1761 Mr. Otis was employed by some Boston merchants, who had been affected by forfeitures under the Molasses Act, to which reference has been made in a former chapter, to appear for them in a trial brought for the purpose of settling the question whether the provincial treasurer might not demand the money that had accrued to the colony from fines collected under that act. The effort of Mr. Otis was successful, and he was soon after engaged in a much more important cause. The legality of the writs of assistance had been called in question, and the matter was now to come before the court for decision. James Otis then held the profitable office of advocate-general, and it was his duty to support the cause of the customs officers ; but he believed the writs to be illegal and "tyrannical," and promptly resigned, to argue the cause of the suffering merchants, though it must be confessed that these merchants had themselves been doubtless guilty of infringing the letter of the law in their illicit importations.

The now famous trial came on in February, 1761, in the council-chamber of the old town-house of Boston. This was an imposing and elegant apartment at the east end of the building, ornamented with fine full-length portraits of Charles the Second and James the Second. Hutchinson, who had just been made chief-justice, presided, and there were four associate-judges, in great wigs, their persons adorned with scarlet robes and broad bands ; while about them were the chief citizens and the officers of the crown, all of whom were very anxious to hear the arguments on the subject, for everybody felt the importance of the occasion. The case was opened by Jeremiah Gridley, who was king's attorney. He had been the instructor of Otis in his younger days, and the pupil now treated him with respect and esteem, almost with affection, while, as John Adams says, with some exaggeration, he "confounded all his authorities, confuted all his arguments, and reduced him to silence."

Otis began by saying that he had been asked to examine the subject of writs of assistance; that he had done so; and that the result was that he had determined to oppose, with all the powers and faculties that God had given him, every such instrument "of slavery on the one hand and villainy on the other." He explained his resignation of public office because he could not conscientiously uphold the cause that his official oath would have obliged him to support, and added that "the only principles of public conduct that are worthy of a gentleman or a man are to sacrifice ease, health, and applause, and even life, to the sacred calls of his country." After this preamble he went on to consider the rights of man in a state of nature, the rights of British subjects to representation, external and internal taxes, the acts of trade, the navigation act, and the writs of assistance, as designed to enforce the acts of trade. He described the tyranny of taxation without representation, and in treating this branch of his theme gave full scope to his powerful talent for declamation and invective. He emphasized the maxim that every Englishman's house is his castle, and showed how the writs made it possible for custom-house officers and their menials to destroy this most essential branch of British liberty—the freedom of one's home ; and at last he argued that the writs were not consistent with the colonial charter. He closed his speech of five hours with a reproach of the nation, the parliament, and the king for their "injustice, illiberality, ingratitude, and oppression" of the Americans, in a style of oratory that John Adams, who was an attentive listener, declares he never heard equalled in this or any other country.

At the end of the term, Hutchinson declared that the court was not satisfied of the legality of the writs, but that, in order to learn the practice in England, it was thought best to continue the question until the next term. The next term came in November, 1761, and the legality of the writs was sustained, whereupon the general court reduced the annual appropriation for the judges, of whom Hutchinson was the chief. Upon the opening of the legislature, Governor Bernard recommended the members to "give no attention to declamations tending to promote a suspicion of the civil rights of the people being in danger." Mr. Otis had just been elected a member, and it was thought that these words were aimed at him ; the representatives therefore replied that they would give due weight to the words of the governor, but that it was their intention to see for themselves, and that in fact they did not observe any cause for suspicion. They considered the governor's communication highly indecent and improper; but they restrained their feelings and replied in words of calm good judgment. Otis had now put himself forward, and was recognized as, "the great incendiary of New England," though Samuel Adams was standing by pouring oil on the flames that it may be said he himself had kindled.

In the summer of 1762, Governor Bernard, with the approval of the council, took the liberty, during a recess in the sessions of the legislature, to expend a comparatively trifling sum in fitting out a vessel to quiet the fears of the Boston merchants, who were alarmed lest the French should make advances upon the fisheries. The jealousy of the opponents of the administration led to a remonstrance against the governor's unwarranted outlay, by a committee of the legislature, of which Otis was chairman. In this it was said that "no necessity can be sufficient to justify the House of Representatives in giving up such a privilege; for it would be of little consequence to the people whether they were subject to George or Lewis, the king of Great Britain or the French king, if both were arbitrary, as both would be, if both could levy taxes without a parliament." When this passage was read, a member cried out, "Treason! treason!" and there was an excitement similar to that which occurred in the Virginia House of Burgesses three years later, when Patrick Henry uttered his memorable words of similar import. The representatives were unreasonably sensitive, and the governor was clearly injudicious in stickling for the royal prerogative. The times demanded calm consideration of the proprieties and necessities of the case, and this neither Bernard nor Otis was prepared to offer. Otis, indeed, at the request of the court, but without waiting for its approval, published "A Vindication of the House," in which he argued with quaint extravagance that the punctiliousness of the representatives was warranted, and laid down a series of political maxims in some respects similar to the arguments used by Franklin against Governor Shirley in 1754. "This production," according to Dr. Snow, "has been considered the original source from which all subsequent arguments against taxation were derived."* Otis asserted that God had made all men naturally equal; that kings were made for the good of the people, and not the people for them; that no government had the right to make "hobby-horses, asses, and slaves" of its subjects, nature having made enough of the two former, and none of the latter, which proves them unnecessary; and he ridiculed the governor's sensitiveness, while he applauded warmly all outspoken and bold resistance to "every sort and degree of usurped power." At the same time he declared that plain English when used in complaints of grievances was not dangerous to the province.

* "History of Boston," p. 253.

XX.

BOSTON OPPOSES A TAX.

THE plantations now engaged almost the whole thoughts of men in power in England, and of the places that were carefully watched Boston stood first. It was looked upon with truth as a centre of discussion, and as a community that would not fail to act when the time came for action. The people of Boston were watchful, too, and among those who were jealously marked by the "friends of freedom," the members of the Church of England were prominent; for every officer of the king, from the highest down, was presumably a member of that body, and suspected of intriguing for its establishment in the New World. The discussion of taxation was mingled with more or less violent debates on the subject of the Establishment, and in 1763 these grew more exciting than ever. Then the Reverend Mr. East Apthorp, rector of Christ Church, Cambridge, who was said to be "hot from Oxford," discussed the purposes of the Society for the Propagation of the Gospel in Foreign Parts, arguing that a portion of its duty was to give the "British subjects on this vast continent the means of public religion," whereas the conversion of the Indians seemed to be the sole object aimed at by its conductors. The mere suggestion that there was a society, a part of the object of which was to supplant the form of religion established by the founders of the colony, and to bring in a sort of worship that the fathers had opposed, aroused an active spirit of discussion, which before it ended involved all denominations in America, and brought forward the then aged Dr. Samuel Johnson, and others in Europe. It was thought that if parliament could tax the colonies, it had power to establish the Episcopal form of worship, and thus the question became one of religion as well as of politics. The two subjects were united also by Dr. Jonathan Mayhew of the West Church, one of the most outspoken preachers of civil liberty, who denied that parliament had any control over religion in Massachusetts, arguing that the charter conferred absolute authority in such matters upon the colonists. Dr. Mayhew, then a young man, had in 1750 delivered a discourse on the Sunday following the anniversary of the execution of " King Charles, the Martyr," as he was still called in the Prayer-Book, in which he discussed " unlimited submission and non-resistance to the higher powers, with some reflections on the resistance made to King Charles the First," in much the same spirit that Samuel Adams had shown seven years before on the platform at Cambridge, boldly and eloquently declaring the principle of free civil government. It has been called " the morning gun of the Revolution."

All Boston was soon engaged in a fervent discussion of topics of this sort, and opinions were formed and principles established, which afterwards united the citizens firmly upon the basis of entire independence of the mother-country. It is often said that the colonists did not desire this political independence; that they loved England and rejoiced in her prosperity; and that they submitted with docility to gross abuses and high-handed political measures in a way that proves this statement. One cannot read the history of Boston from the time of Winthrop to the days of Samuel Adams without seeing that the same spirit filled the hearts and controlled the actions of her citizens from first to last. Doubtless they all had the interest in England's past that is still felt by enlightened Americans; doubtless they were long-suffering, and wished to keep the peace; but there can be no mistake in asserting that their actions were exasperating to the kings and their ministers, and that they asserted themselves and claimed their assumed rights under the charters in a way which made it unmistakable that nothing less than practical independence would ever give them satisfaction. The only wonder is that the supreme contest was not precipitated sooner than it was; and the only explanation of the anomaly is found in the fact that the sovereigns were so much occupied at one time and another with matters of deep significance at home that it was impracticable for them to deal with their rampant Boston subjects in the strong manner that their case required. The "causes" of the American Revolution generally given would not have been sufficient to produce that great upturning, had they not been preceded by years and years of struggle, which had finally brought the contestants to a point at which each was unyielding.

In spite of these facts, it required all the unrivalled skill of Samuel Adams in managing men to keep the freemen of Boston up to the pitch of daring indignation and rebellion that he thought necessary for his purposes; and it may be reasonably doubted if there would have ever been any independence if he had not labored in season and out of season, openly and in secret, by himself and through others, in the town and the colony, and in the other colonies, for the attainment of an end that he had determined in the councils of his own tenacious will should be accomplished. It was he who years before dropped the seed into the minds of educated youth; he harangued the populace; he counselled the clubs in secret; he faced the king's officers in their strength; he mocked them and taunted them; he elevated a street riot into a "Massacre," and caused it to be celebrated year after year; he devoted himself without reserve to the accomplishment of his purpose, indifferent alike to poverty and pleasure, daring proscription and death; he succeeded, and his name will always remain on the tablets of history as the Father of the American Revolution.

In arguing against the writs of assistance, Otis had declared that taxation without representation is tyranny; not that any Bostonian desired representation in the British parliament, for that was wellnigh impracticable; but no one was willing to bear taxation for the purpose of replenishing an exhausted treasury on the other side of the ocean. Adams argued at length at another time against the propriety of levying taxes for the government and defence of the regions that had been acquired in America from France. He urged that the colonists had already incurred debts in the war, which was rather for the increase of British trade than for the sake of affording stability and security to the American governments, and that England had the whole advantage of the new commerce. The national debt had increased to one hundred and forty million pounds, or more than sixty million pounds in one year—the last of the war, and it was to make the home burdens easier that the American tax was laid. This was the feature that galled the colonists.* When, therefore, in 1764, it was known in Boston that a stamp tax was to be laid upon the colonies, that stamps were to be obligatory upon all legal and business documents, that offenders against the new law under which it was laid were not to have the privilege of trial by jury, and that the policy was to be enforced as asserting the right of England to obedience. Boston, as well as other centres, was disturbed by heated discussions of the relations between the mother-country and the colonies. In May Bos-

* It was all the more galling because the taxes were already extravagant. Dr. Gordon relates that some time before this date a Boston gentleman of fortune sent his tax bills to London for comparison with such rates there. His correspondent replied that he did not believe there was a man in all England who paid so much in proportion to the support of the government. A man was actually obliged to pay in taxes two thirds of his income, beside the excise on tea, coffee, rum and wine.—" American Revolution," vol. i., page 110.

ton instructed her representatives in the general court to maintain the rights of the province under the charter and the rights of the citizens as free-born subjects of Great Britain, by preventing the proposed proceedings against the colonies. The important paper in which these instructions were conveyed, drawn up by Samuel Adams, contains the first public denial of the right of parliament to tax America, and the first suggestion of a union of all the colonies for mutual protection, and an intimation that if the burdens were not removed, the Americans would retaliate upon English manufacturers by entering into agreements to import none of their goods. It would be difficult to mention any paper in the history of our country that proved so momentous in its consequences as this, the first public document that remains in the handwriting of its author. It was immediately published, and accepted as expressing the sentiments of Boston, and of Massachusetts, and it became the basis of the public policy of the province. A year later Patrick Henry wrote on the blank leaf of a law book the now celebrated "Virginia Resolves," as they are called, in which he took the same ground, asserting that obedience was not due to a law imposing a tax unless it had been sanctioned by the representatives of the people, and the principle was accepted by the colonies in general. The idea struck off by the sagacious Boston patriot became the keynote of the Revolution.

In all of the acts of these stirring times Adams was supported by James Otis with his impetuous and unrestrained eloquence; and by Oxenbridge Thacher, the calm and business-like defender of colonial rights, who stood in the confidence of the men of Boston as high as any other of her patriotic citizens. When the legislature met in June, it was Otis who prepared a memorial to be sent to the Massachusetts agent in England, following almost the very words of Samuel Adams, and it was he who published a treatise on the rights of the colonies, though he made the usual assertion that independence was not the aim of the Americans. It is difficult to follow the line of argument by which the patriots discriminated between their determination not to submit to certain acts of parliament, and their reservation of sovereign rights to themselves, and their disclaimers of all desire to free themselves from the authority of the king. That they were honest, we must allow; but we must also think that they imperfectly comprehended the meaning of their acts, and the real desire for complete independence that they harbored in their hearts. Doubtless they thought that they would "choose subjection to Great Britain upon any terms above absolute slavery," rather than "independency"; but when the time for action came they resented every act on the part of the king and parliament which involved subjection, or seemed to limit colonial liberty in the remotest degree.

The legislature took up another idea of Mr. Adams by appointing a committee to correspond with the similar bodies in the other colonies, and thus take advantage of union as a means of strength. The Bostonians were familiar with this idea, for upon it the New England Confederation of 1643 was founded ; but its revival at this juncture is none the less creditable to Adams. Out of it grew the congress at New York in 1765, the continental congress at Philadelphia in 1774, and finally the union of the colonies, and independence.

None of the resolves, instructions, protests, or prayers of Boston had any effect in warding off the hated tax, and on the twenty-second of March, 1765, the stamp act received the king's sanction. The news arrived at Boston on the twenty-sixth of May, and then the people found that they were doomed to pay a duty of from half a penny to twenty shillings on every skin of vellum or parchment, or sheet or piece of paper on which any document should be written or printed, if it was to have legal validity. They learned also that parliament had passed a " Mutiny Act," which required the colonies to provide quarters for the king's troops (even in private houses) when on service in their limits. Three days later, Patrick Henry made his celebrated speech in the Virginia House of Burgesses ; and the Massachusetts legislature almost immediately proposed a congress, to be held in New York on the first Tuesday of October, since the act was to begin its operation on the first of November.

People were everywhere excited to watchfulness ; it was whispered about that some provinces were resolved not to use the stamps, though business could not legally go on without them ; though vessels could not enter nor go out of a harbor without stamped papers ; though colleges could not grant their degrees, and marriages could not be made legal without them; though newspapers and almanacs should be stamped; though "this mark of slavery" was necessary in every line of activity. There was more than a spirit of watchfulness abroad; Mayhew wrote: "I am clear on this point, that no people are under a religious obligation to be slaves if they are able to set themselves at liberty"; and the Boston papers declared that, though Liberty was dead, happily she had "left one son, the child of her bosom, prophetically named Independence," and that all looked for the day when he should come of age. It is too late for us to be dragooned out of our rights, the people declared, when there are two million inhabitants in America, and two hundred thousand in the province of Massachusetts alone. It was determined that the officers appointed by the king to distribute the stamps should be forced to resign, and it was evident that the act would not execute itself.

Andrew Oliver, secretary of Massachusetts, accepted with temerity the office of distributer of stamps in Boston. When the sun rose on the fourteenth of August, a few days later, passers by "the Great Tree," which was one of a group of majestic elms that stood at the head of Essex Street, near the entrance to the town and opposite Boylston Market, saw hanging from its branches an effigy of Mr. Oliver, with a boot (representing Lord Bute) from which the devil peeped out, bearing a copy of the stamp act in his hands. No one was permitted to take the image down, though Lieutenant-Governor Hutchinson demanded that it should be done. "We will take them down in the evening," said the crowd. From the streets about, and from adjoining towns, men gathered to look at the sight, and business was quite laid aside. Governor Bernard and Mr. Hutchinson conferred with their council, but all the satisfaction they obtained was the statement: "The country will never submit to the execution of the stamp act!" As the day wore on, the numbers about the tree grew to a multitude. Then the effigy was taken down, according to promise, and, with huzzas and cries of defiance, it was carried in orderly procession towards the town-house, where the governor heard his subjects shouting at the top of their voices: "Liberty, property, and no stamps!" "Death to the man who offers a piece of stamped paper to sell!" "All the power of Britain shall not oblige us to submit!" "We will die upon the place first!" A building on Kilby Street, that was supposed to be intended as a stamp office, was demolished, and the men, taking sticks from the ruins, carried them to Fort Hill, where a bonfire was made, in which the effigy was burned in view of Mr. Oliver's house. The residence itself was afterwards attacked, its windows broken, and its fences torn down. The lieutenant-governor and the sheriff, who attempted to disperse the crowd, were set upon with sticks and stones, and escaped with bruises by favor of the darkness. The next day, Oliver was forced to resign his office.

In the midst of these excitements, Dr. Mayhew preached a sermon, on the twenty-fifth of August, from the words: "I would they were even cut off

which trouble you, for, brethren, ye have been called
unto liberty." (Galatians v., 12, 13.) He spoke
against the stamp act as a heavy grievance, and expressed himself strongly in favor of civil and religious
liberty; but, at the same time, protested against
abuses of liberty, and cautioned his hearers against
riotous proceedings. The following day was marked
by an occurrence of the character against which Dr.
Mayhew had protested. A mob, inflamed by strong
drink, attacked Hutchinson's house with savage fury,
scarcely allowing him to escape with his life; they
carried off his family plate, his specie, and other
valuables, and destroyed his unique collection of
manuscripts that it had required a lifetime to bring
together. The next morning the house was found
with its roof partially uncovered, its cupola thrown
down, its ornaments destroyed, and the streets about
scattered with money, plate, gold rings, etc., which
had been dropped in the darkness. The frenzied
spirits had also destroyed the records of the vice-admiralty court, and ravaged the house of the
comptroller of customs. The day after this disgraceful riot, the enemies of Dr. Mayhew circulated
reports of his sermon, declaring that he had encouraged the resistance to the government, and had thus
been the cause of the public disgrace. The doctor wrote directly to the governor, expressing his
horror at the riot, and said that he would rather lose
his hand than encourage such outrages. The circumstance shows that in times of such excitement
the better class, while limiting themselves to lawful
methods of action, cannot put such restrictions upon

those whose unbridled passions find opportunity for bursting out,—who cannot distinguish liberty from license.

Such proceedings were, of course, abhorred by Adams also, and the soberer inhabitants generally, and on the following day at a town-meeting held in Faneuil Hall, which was as full as had ever been known, a unanimous vote was passed, declaring an utter detestation of the violent doings of the mob, and calling upon the selectmen to suppress such disorders in the future. Hutchinson states that many of the immediate actors in the orgies of the night before were present at this meeting; and he shows that he appreciated the situation of affairs, for he says also that England had placed herself in a serious dilemma, for if "parliament should make concessions, their authority would be lost, while if they should use external force, affection would be forever alienated." Governor Bernard had already fled for safety to the Castle, and now Hutchinson followed him, while the attorney-general dared not to sleep in his house, nor for two consecutive nights in the same place elsewhere, and all the other officers of the crown were terror-stricken.

John Adams expressed the fears of many persons in Boston when he said: "There seems to be a direct and formal design on foot in Great Britain to enslave all America," and he announced her determination also when he added that liberty was to be defended at all hazards. He called upon the pulpit to declare the truth that consenting to slavery is a sacrilegious breach of trust; upon the bar, to proclaim the rights of man delivered from remote antiquity, having their foundations in the constitution of the intellectual and moral world, in truth, liberty, justice, and benevolence; upon the colleges, to impress upon the tender mind of youth the beauty of liberty, the true ideas of right, and the sensation of freedom; and finally on all, to impress upon their souls the aims of the forefathers in exchanging their native country for a wilderness. Under direction of Samuel Adams the town of Boston denounced the stamp act and the courts of admiralty, as contrary to the constitution of Great Britain, the province charter, and human rights, and expressed a lively interest in the result of the congress to be held in New York in October. This body met in accordance with the call, and remained in session a single week. It accomplished its most important labor in bringing together representative men from the different colonies, and in making them familiar with their mutual views as a basis for concerted action in the future; but it also prepared and issued addresses to the king, the lords, and the commons of England, all of which were consistent with the already familiar expressions of Samuel Adams.

Meantime preparations were making in Boston and elsewhere for the first of November. Everywhere it was the universal determination that the stamp act should not go into operation. Merchants countermanded their orders for British goods, domestic manufactures were encouraged, engagements were made to eat no lamb in order that the supply of wool for cloth might increase, and men and women vied with one another in admiration of clothing that was entirely of American manufacture. Otis declared that one act of parliament had "set the people a-thinking more in six months than they had done in their whole lives before." The papers abounded in songs intended to rouse the citizens to action. The *Massachusetts Gazette* contained a Boston Song, of which the following is a stanza:

> "With us of the woods
> Lay aside your fine goods,
> Contentment depends not on fine clothes;
> We hear, smell, and see,
> Taste and feel with high glee,
> And in winter have huts for repose."

Efforts of this kind were long continued, and the *Boston Evening Post* of February, 1766, contained instructions for the children of America, in which we read:

> "With nervous arm strike deep the whale,
> pluck codfish tugging at your line;
> Take the broiled mackerel by her tail,
> let fops among tea-trinkets shine.
> Let oxen spread my valleys over,
> drinking at the crystal rills;
> While fleecy flocks do nibble clover,
> growing on my verdant hills.
> Rise up, my daughters, light your tapers,
> take the spinning-wheel in hand,
> Your babes shall prattle how your labors
> helped to save a sinking land!"

Notwithstanding the fact that many of the best citizens feared that the day on which the stamp act was to go into effect might be marked by the same excesses that had made the twenty-sixth of August notorious, the liberty party determined to make a demonstration, probably with a hope that the authorities might be overawed and caused to give up all expectation that the act would either execute itself, as some had thought it would, or be submitted to, as most of the partisans of the crown expected. The spot selected for the purpose was the vicinity of Essex and Newbury (now Washington) streets, already mentioned. In September the largest of the famous elms that stood at that place had been adorned with a copper plate on which was stamped in letters of gold: "The Tree of Liberty, August 14, 1765."

The fateful first of November was a Friday; it was ushered in by the tolling of bells; and the vessels in the harbor displayed their colors at half-mast in token of mourning; the Liberty Tree was ornamented by two effigies of British statesmen who supported the tax, which remained hanging until three in the afternoon, the subject of ridicule by thousands of spectators who gathered from town and country. Amid the shouts of the crowd the images were finally cut down and carried in solemn procession to the court-house, where the assembly was in session, and then to the gallows on the Neck, where they were suspended again, and afterwards cut down and subjected to indignities thought to be merited by the persons they represented. After loud cheers the multitude dispersed quietly to their homes, and the detestation of the Bostonians was supposed to have been duly expressed. The town was more than ordinarily quiet that night, as though the citizens desired to bear witness to their disapproval of the riotous proceedings of the twenty-sixth of August.

There was by no means unity on the other side of the sea in regard to the propriety of enforcing the stamp tax, and intimations of this fact were received from time to time in Boston, before and after the first of November. This encouraged the resistance that had been determined upon. Parliament became the arena upon which one of the most memorable debates in the annals of England occurred. The subject of managing America was uppermost in all minds. Adams and Otis on the one side, and Bernard and Hutchinson on the other, stood for the two phases of the question in Boston. Benjamin Franklin, the Boston boy, was brought before the House of Commons, and examined, in order that light might be cast upon the debate by one well acquainted with both sides of the question. When asked if he thought that America ought to be protected without paying any portion of the cost, he replied that the colonies had during the late war raised, clothed, and paid twenty-five thousand men, and spent many million pounds. He assured his questioners that the stamp tax would never be paid; that if an armed force were sent to carry out the act, no one would be found in arms, and that it would be impossible to force the citizens to buy stamps, if they chose to go without them.

In March, of the year 1776, the act was repealed; the king gave his consent very much against his wishes; the bells were set to ringing in London; flags were generously displayed from all the ships on the Thames; there were bonfires and illuminations. On the sixteenth of May the news was known in Boston, brought by a vessel owned by John Hancock; and similar scenes were repeated. The Liberty Tree was covered with flags by day and illuminated at night three days later; money was raised to release poor debtors from jail; Hancock gave a grand dinner, and treated the populace in the street to a pipe of Madeira wine.

Boston rejoiced that America had resisted, and that England had been forced to give up her darling project; but sober men reflected with solicitude that parliament still declared itself supreme over all colonies, in all cases whatsoever. There was cause for congratulation that the courts of law, which had for some time been closed, were open, and that business, which had been embarrassed, was able to run on in its usual channels, but the future was not clear to those who reflected.

XXI.

IN THE GRIP OF THE ARMY.

THE time at which we have now arrived in our story is one of continually increasing excitement in Boston, and the skill and sagacity of Samuel Adams, and of the company of men of which he formed the centre, become more and more impressive at every step. They were men of positive views, who suffered no doubts of the righteousness of their cause to shake the firmness of their actions. The influence of the chief town in the colony grew day by day; the jealousy that had from time to time been felt by other towns, and their delegates in the court, had now, according to Hutchinson's History, disappeared, and all were more than willing that Boston should exert the power that it seemed to them her patriots had the ability and the wisdom to use aright for the common good. In bringing about this result no one had been more influential than James Otis, since his entrance upon the duties of legislator. There were constant meetings of the general court in which his voice was effectively heard; and in the intervals there were more frequent gatherings of the freemen of Boston, at which action was taken without reluctance that affected the interest of Boston no more than that of the entire province. The leaders in both legislature and town-meeting were the same, and the chief among them held private evening meetings, at least once a week, at which arrangements were made for concerted action in the public gatherings. Thus measures were projected and settled by the few that were ratified by the many, and at the same time it was determined how the public should be influenced through the press, for, as has been observed, Adams knew the power of printing-ink, and it is certain that those who labored with him agreed with him almost unanimously.

In a speech delivered in parliament by Colonel Barré, one of the staunch friends of Massachusetts, he called the Bostonians "Sons of Liberty," and the name was adopted by a society comprising about three hundred active patriots, many of whom were mechanics and laboring men, organized under sagacious leaders. This influential body was successful in arranging secret caucuses, preliminary to elections and celebrations, and in the "Life of Samuel Adams," by W. V. Wells (vol. i., p. 64), it is said that it went so far as even to issue warrants for the arrest of suspected persons. The public gatherings of the society were held in "Hanover Square," as it was then called, which was the open space in the highway around "Liberty Tree," at the junction of Newbury, Orange, and Essex streets, which was re-named "Liberty Hall," and afforded room sufficient for several thousand persons to come together. More private meetings were held, it is said, in a counting-room on the same square. Through this organization the leaders directed the popular movement against the government. As early as 1766 the Sons of Liberty, whose organization was quickly imitated in other towns, had every thing in their hands, and just before the news of the repeal of the stamp act reached Boston, they put Adams, Hancock, Otis, and other tried men into the legislature. Adams was chosen clerk, a position that enabled him to keep a watch of all action, and made it possible for him to give form to much of the legislation, while it did not at all interfere with his freedom as a debater whenever he wished to utter his sentiments.

In spite of the repeal of the stamp act, England had in no degree renounced her intention of deriving a revenue from America, and parliament now felt new incentives to this plan in consequence of wounded pride and mortified ambition over the "fatal compliance," as the king called the repeal. Accordingly, in June, 1767, through the influence of Charles Townshend, Chancellor of the Exchequer, a tax was laid upon glass, paper, paints, and tea, a board of commissioners of customs was established at Boston, and writs of assistance were formally made legal. Such acts as these gave the leaders of the Sons of Liberty the opportunity they wished, for they represented that liberty was to be snatched from the helpless colonists, that ships and troops would soon come, that military rule would be established, and that the officers who were to carry out the acts of oppression would be paid out of the moneys wrenched from the Bostonians.

One of the means of keeping the people interested in the movement against the government, that Adams and Otis knew would be efficacious, was the celebration of appropriate anniversaries. When the anniversary of the repeal of the stamp act came around, March 18, 1768, the occasion was celebrated with enthusiasm, but without any exhibitions of violence, though Hutchinson says that "fresh disturbances" were threatened, and Bernard in his timidity recorded that "many hundreds paraded the streets with yells and outcrys which were quite terrible,"—quite terrible, indeed, the shouts of the people may have seemed to his Excellency, conscious of his own deserts, remembering how he had hectored the people's representatives, encouraged all movements that they feared and opposed, and how he was then constantly trying to influence the home government to send him troops that he might intimidate and not be intimidated. There was, it is true, a feast at Faneuil Hall, and toasts had been drunk to "martyrs of liberty," but the company separated early, and a crowd that assembled in the evening desisted from lighting bonfires, at the earnest request of influential gentlemen. Two effigies were suspended on Liberty Tree in the morning, but they were cut down without excitement. In like spirit the outbreak of the fourteenth of August against the stamp act was celebrated the same year. The British flag was flung to the breeze from the Liberty Tree at dawn (August 15th, for the 14th was Sunday); the principal gentlemen and chief inhabitants met under its shade; the populace crowded around; there was music; "the universally admired American Song of Liberty" was sung; cannon were discharged; "the fair daughters of liberty" adorned the windows of the neighboring houses, from which they "testified their approbation by smiles of satisfaction." After all, the gentlemen repaired to the Greyhound Tavern at Roxbury, the cavalcade being allowed to be the finest that had ever been seen in America, and there were salutes, toasts, and a frugal entertainment. In 1769 there was another celebration on the fourteenth of August, at which there were present besides Otis, Adams and Hancock, John Adams, and visitors from Philadelphia with whom the Bostonians had sympathetic converse. Two tables were laid in the open field by the barn near Robinson's Liberty-Tree Tavern at Dorchester, and there were three or four hundred plates. Three large pigs were "barbecued," there were toasts and thunders of cannon, Francis Bernard and the commissioners—" infamous calumniators of North America"—were denounced as worthy of condign punishment, "strong halters, firm blocks, and sharp axes" were spoken of as appropriate for the "taskmasters" of America, and all was life, patriotism, and jollity. John Adams remarks that such celebrations tend to "tinge the minds of the people, they impregnate them with the sentiments of liberty, they render the people fond of their leaders in the cause, and adverse and bitter against all opposition." Hancock led the procession in his chariot on this occasion, and the line extended a mile and a half behind him. Before the day came around again the chiefs had found another day fit for celebration, and one that they thought it would be even more profitable to impress on the popular mind.

Troops were now constantly expected in real earnest. Adams gave himself up to the cause of liberty without reserve, laboring day and night, and not making a single personal scheme, or looking forward to laying up any thing for himself or his descendants; in fact, it is certain that with his devotion to the public good he could have succeeded in no business of a private nature. He owned his modest Purchase Street home, over which his thrifty wife presided with care, and for income he had a pittance as clerk of the assembly; but it is evident that it must have required all the skill of the most skilful New England housewife to keep the children and herself fed and clothed. Adams was not afraid of honest poverty; his "wife and children understood him and idolized him as their protector, adviser and companion, whose genial, courageous disposition knew not despondency and preserved a warm sunshine in the hearts of all who shared his society." *

At the motion of James Otis, June 3, 1766, the debates of the assembly were thrown open to the people, a gallery was provided for their accommodation, and "for the first time in the history of legislative associations it was made the right of the plain citizen to hear and see—a usage which has modified in important ways the proceedings and very character of deliberative bodies." † This politic step is

---

* "The Life and Public Services of Samuel Adams," by William Vincent Wells, vol. i., page 273.
† "Samuel Adams," by James K. Hosmer, page 94.

another mark of the sagacity of the leaders of Boston at this juncture. It was a means of educating and inspiring the people at once, and at the same time it increased the importance of the legislative proceedings. *

In June, 1768, another of the irritating occurrences of the day aroused the citizens. Some men were impressed by the captain of the frigate *Romney*, which lay in the harbor, lately arrived from Halifax. The captain made peace with a committee of gentlemen who called upon him to remonstrate, but the people, from among whom the men had been taken, cherished their resentments, while the merchants believed that the frigate had been sent to enforce the revenue laws. A few days after these impressments customs officers seized a vessel named the *Liberty*, belonging to John Hancock, declaring that she had violated the revenue laws. † She was carried off and placed under cover of the guns of the *Romney*. A furious mob collected at the wharf from which the *Liberty* had been taken, and swore vengeance against the "oppressors," as most of the

---

* "Life of James Otis," by Professor Francis Bowen, page 143. Tudor, "Life of Otis," page 253.

† There is little doubt that the revenue laws had really been violated, and yet it would be a harsh use of language to call John Hancock a "smuggler." The new commissioners enforced laws that had long been in a state of desuetude, and the *Liberty* was made an example of quite unexpectedly. In popular fancy laws lapse through desuetude, and it seems as though the burdensome customs laws had so lapsed at this time, not only in popular fancy, but by the law of long custom and with the connivance of English officers in America, perhaps influenced by intimations from their superiors on the other side of the Atlantic.

representatives of the royal government were habitually called, for it was supposed that more impressments had been made. When it was known that a vessel belonging to so popular a man as Hancock had been seized, the mob set upon the officers; Joseph Harrison, the collector, was severely wounded by a stone; his son, who held no official position, was thrown down and barbarously used; other officers were similarly treated; the house of the inspector-general was broken into and damaged, while a pleasure boat belonging to the collector was dragged to the Common and burned. There was no further violence that night, and Saturday and Sunday, which followed, were quiet, but the feelings of the people were rising, and there were threatening gatherings in different parts of the town. The commissioners began to feel insecure and took refuge on board the *Romney*, asking the governor to admit them to the Castle for protection. The governor gave them permission to go to the Castle, but at the same time informed them that he could not guarantee them protection.

On Monday, June 13th, notices were posted by the leaders, calling a meeting at " Liberty Hall " on the following day; but when the day arrived it was rainy, and the gathering, which was composed of several thousand persons, adjourned to Faneuil Hall. A town-meeting was called for three o'clock, at the same place, but the room was found too small, and there was another adjournment to the Old South meeting-house, where James Otis was moderator. Otis directed the meeting with great good judgment, and put aside all extravagant motions without offending the movers. A committee was appointed to address Governor Bernard at his seat in Roxbury. The governor, knowing that he was completely at the mercy of the people, treated the committee with great consideration, gave them wine before they left, and led them to think that he was really a well-wisher of the town. Bernard's fears were well founded. The town of Boston had said, in instructing its representatives: "It is our unalterable resolution at all times to assert and vindicate our dear and invaluable rights and liberties, at the utmost hazard of our lives and fortunes," and the people meant what they said, as the governor well knew.

There had been expectations before this that troops would be brought to Boston to overawe the citizens, and these anticipations were now intensified, for it was evident to both governor and people that unless an armed force should support the royal officers they would be powerless. Still, Bernard was too timid to ask for troops; he wished to be able to say that he had not gone so far as that. He therefore continued to satisfy himself by making complaints intended to show that troops were needed. In July he received information from Gage, who was commander-in-chief, that troops had been ordered from Halifax to Boston, "if they are wanted"; and he replied that he could not apply for troops, but wrote home that he felt it improper to prevent their coming, if they were ordered by others.

Early in September an officer arrived from Halifax, whose mission was suspected to be to look for quarters for soldiers. On the thirteenth a town-meeting was held, and it was voted that "as there is at this time a prevailing apprehension of approaching war with France, every inhabitant is requested to provide himself with a well-fixed firelock musket, accoutrements, and ammunition," though in reality such a war was as much a legal fiction as ever was John Doe or Richard Roe. A committee, comprising Adams, Otis, Hancock, Warren, and others, had already been formed to take the state of public affairs into consideration; and now a fast was appointed, and the town was in consternation. A convention of deputies from all the towns in the province was called to meet in Faneuil Hall, September 22d, and, at the time set, more than ninety towns sent delegates. This body declared its allegiance to the king, as usual, and its abhorrence of violence and riot, though, at the same time, it asserted the natural and chartered rights of the people, and expressed confidence that the wrongs under which the colony felt that it was suffering would be redressed by their "gracious sovereign." The convention adjourned September 29th, and the next day, Friday, six of His Majesty's ships-of-war came up the harbor and anchored around the town with loaded cannon, as if intending a regular siege. On the following day two regiments, a train of artillery, and two pieces of cannon were landed at Long Wharf, and the soldiers marched up King Street, "with insolent parade," the citizens thought, their drums beating, their fifes playing, and their colors flying, each one supplied with sixteen rounds of shot. Then there was a dispute about quarters, and finally some of the troops were lodged at Faneuil Hall, others in the town-house, and the remainder in store-houses. The people of Boston went to bed that night feeling that they lived in a garrisoned town, and that his "gracious Majesty" was a cruel father.

There was a period of quiet after the arrival of the troops, though it was the calm before a storm; the people were not accustomed to the sight of soldiers, and were in fear; day by day their discontent became more manifest. Very little matters irritated the citizens; they were accustomed to the night-watch of the town, but they did not like to be stopped and called upon to answer for themselves by an armed sentinel; they objected to the noise of drum and fife and the sight of marching men on Sunday. The general and the other military officers were desirous of avoiding unnecessary irritation of the people, and the rules of the army were relaxed, as far as consistent with discipline; but it was not at all the desire of certain citizens that the army should appear inoffensive. Every occasion of disturbance was taken up and magnified by the papers, and the intruders were made as odious as possible.

At the same time, patriotism was stimulated in every way. Students of Harvard College, "with a spirit becoming Americans," bound themselves to use no more tea, which was stigmatized as "that despised article," the "pernicious herb," and by the sixth of October two hundred families in Boston had also agreed to give up its use. The agreement extended to other towns, as also to other provinces.

Congenial and innocent amusements were renounced, one reason being that they would necessarily have to be shared with men who were the "instruments of despotism"; and when the British officers, thinking that the prevailing gloom was disloyal, endeavored to engage the fashionable classes in assemblies, no ladies outside of their own limits favored the occasions with their presence. "Elegant manners, gay uniforms, animating bands of musick, the natural impulse of youth,—all were resisted; the women of Boston refused to join in ostentatious gayety while their country was in mourning," as the contemporary journals tell us.

During the closing weeks of 1768, Boston was disturbed in many ways by the presence of the soldiery; outrages were complained of every day; there were drunken brawls in the streets; men were knocked down at night; women were insulted by day; one Captain Wilson was accused of exciting the slaves against their masters; a tradesman was thrust at by a soldier with a bayonet as he was going under the rails of the Common on his way home; a merchant was struck down by an officer; and finally John Hancock was arrested by the commissioners for some matter connected with the seizure of his sloop *Liberty*.[*] The Superior Court convened on the eighth of November, in the townhouse, where troops were quartered, and Mr. Otis moved to have the session in Faneuil Hall, for, as he said, "not only might the stench occasioned by

---

[*] The charges, Mr. Bancroft says, were "confidently made, but never established." "History of the U. S.," vol. vi., page 213.

the troops in the representative's chamber prove infectious," but because it was derogatory to the court to administer justice at the mouths of cannon and the points of bayonets. In May, 1769, the general court came together, and, finding the building surrounded by troops, Otis rose, and in a short speech declared that it was unworthy of a free legislature to deliberate in the presence of the military, and moved that the governor be called upon to order the immediate removal of the soldiery, by sea and land, out of the port and gates of the city during the sessions.* The governor replied that he had no control over the troops; and the legislature thereupon declined to attend to business, upon which Bernard adjourned the body to Cambridge. It assembled in the chapel of Harvard College, and the students naturally came to hear the discussions. Otis, following the example set by Samuel Adams twenty-six years before, took advantage of the occasion to excite the young men with the enthusiasm that he was controlled by. He expatiated on the darkness of the times, spoke of the "persecution" under which the colony was suffering,

---

* It has been remarked that the leaders in the colonial legislature were also the leaders in the councils of the town of Boston. It is natural, therefore, to find that this action had been taken by the selectmen, before the town-meeting at which the Boston delegates were chosen. They waited upon General Gage, and informed him that an election was to occur on May 5th, and that the presence of the troops was not in accordance with the rights of British subjects. Gage replied that though he could not march the soldiers out of town, he would confine them to their barracks; but even that was not considered sufficient, and the town protested that, though the election should be held, the act should not be esteemed a precedent at any future time.

made rapid and glowing allusions to the classic models of patriotism that then formed the study of the young men, which they might soon be called upon to emulate, and assured them that they might erelong have an opportunity to perform the noblest of all duties,—to serve their country, even, perhaps, to give up to her their lives. The students were roused to a high pitch of excitement, for they already held the principles that Otis recommended, and were prepared to be affected by such an eloquent harangue.

The legislature resolved to petition the king to remove Governor Bernard, who had lost all the little popularity that he ever possessed by writing letters to the British ministers, in which he urged measures that were considered prejudicial to American interests. Probably this petition had no more to do with the recall of the governor than similar less public prayers had had; but the following day he announced that he was called to London to give a report to the king of the state of affairs in the colony. The legislature asserted that it was owing to his misrepresentations to the ministers that the military force was, at the time, quartered in the town of Boston; that he was an avowed enemy of the colony and of the nation in general; that he was wanton and precipitate in his official actions, and acted against the spirit of a free constitution.

Perhaps the ministers thought that there might be some truth in the statement that the troubles in Boston were owing to the injudicious actions of Bernard. He did not again assume the duties of governor of Massachusetts. The day of his departure was made a time of rejoicing; flags were raised, bells pealed forth their liveliest notes, cannons roared, Fort Hill was crowned with a huge bonfire that night, and Liberty Tree was exultantly adorned. This governor's character has been blackened by writers since his day, as it was at the time; but he was apparently an honest supporter of prerogative, and not an unprincipled trickster as he has been represented. He had education, refinement, and good taste; but he did not know how to govern Massachusetts in a way that would please its citizens. It is not easy to say, even now, how any man could have filled the place that he held to the satisfaction of Samuel Adams and King George at once. He is credited with having brought about the Revolution by his injudicious management of affairs; but it is probable that the Revolution would not have been greatly retarded by the most judicious governor that England could have sent to Massachusetts.

XXII.

BLOOD IS SPILLED.

AT the time that Governor Bernard left Boston, the public life of James Otis, long one of the popular idols of the town, and one of the most influential of the group of patriots, practically came to an end. Otis had labored with all his might, and his mind began to show the effects of overwork; he grew garrulous and reckless in his utterances, he was irritable and curiously eccentric. The abuse and false charges that were made against the popular party, and largely against him, specially aroused his indignation, and by means of an ill-advised advertisement, inserted in the *Boston Gazette* of September 4, 1769, he took occasion to give vent to his disordered fancies in very plain words, addressed to the four commissioners of customs, whom he mentioned by name. The following evening he encountered one of these commissioners at the British Coffee-House, and there was an altercation, from which Mr. Otis came out bearing severe wounds that had been given with a sword in the hands of the commissioner. The occurrence excited the public mind, already in a feverish state, and intensified the opposition to the government. Otis took legal measures against the commissioner, and recovered two thousand pounds damages, not a penny of which would his proud spirit allow him to accept above the doctor's bill and the actual expenses of the trial, as the records of the Supreme Judicial Court of Massachusetts still testify. Mr. Otis was from this time seen little in the councils of Boston and of the colony, the leadership devolving more exclusively upon Samuel Adams; but the cause did not suffer, as the friends of the king supposed it would, if only "Otis and two or three more factious leaders could be removed."

The place occupied by Bernard was taken now by Thomas Hutchinson, lieutenant-governor, whose history we are already somewhat familiar with. Descended from worthy Puritan ancestors, a graduate of Harvard College, possessing ample wealth, and agreeable manners, he had been at this time in public life for more than thirty years. He had been selectman of the town, a member of the colonial legislature, and its agent in London, and latterly he had, as has been stated, held a number of almost incompatible offices,—offices possessing both legislative and judicial functions,—that the leaders in Boston, at least, thought incompatible, however judiciously their duties may have been performed. He had been opposed by Adams in the past, and now that patriot becomes the one among the opponents that he had to meet whom he deemed of any importance. Hutchinson called Adams "the master of the puppets," a title that is not just to the strong men who were about him, though the ability with which Adams directed legislation and popular movements forces us to allow that it had a remarkable significance.

The breach between the Bostonians and the king widened in a very natural way. When Governor Bernard returned to London he was looked upon as one who must be acquainted with the sentiments of the Americans, and his counsel was accepted accordingly, as based upon thorough information. When, therefore he assured the Londoners that the most respectable of the Boston merchants would not adhere to their non-importation agreements, merchants in England were encouraged to renew their exportations. In the autumn of 1769 Samuel Adams received intimations that large importations might soon be expected " under ministerial favor." This information was correct. On September 4th an agent arrived, charged with a considerable consignment of goods. The merchants who had agreed not to receive such importations held a meeting the next day, at which they directed that the goods should be returned to England. The town of Boston, which Hutchinson said was the "chief seat of the opposition," held a meeting likewise, and began a list of those who had made themselves "infamous" by violating the non-importation agreement,* in order "that posterity might know who those per-

* Josiah Quincy, Jr., was most ardent in urging retaliation on Great Britain, and insisted upon breaking off not only business relations, but also "all social intercourse with those whose commerce contaminates, whose luxuries poison, whose avarice is unsatiable, and whose unnatural oppressions are not to be borne." (*Boston Gazette*, Feb. 12, 1770.) "Memoirs of the Life of Josiah Quincy, Jr.," by Josiah Quincy, page 23.

sons were that preferred their little advantage to the common interest of all the colonies in a point of the greatest importance." At the same meeting a strong committee was appointed to vindicate the town from the false imputations put upon it by Bernard, Gage, and others, in their letters, and after a delay of but two weeks an "Appeal to the World," appeared, from the pen of Samuel Adams. In this the town calmly placed itself on record as determined never to consider its wrongs redressed until the whole assumed right of taxation was renounced by England, whose ministers were thus boldly warned against the consequences of persistence in the action urged by the governor and others like-minded.

Considerable forbearance was shown by the troops at this time, for the people often goaded them almost beyond endurance; and though Hutchinson thought that matters ought to have gone to extremities, he doubted his authority to order the soldiers to fire upon the populace. In October an informer who had given evidence regarding some wine that had been smuggled from Rhode Island, was tarred and feathered and carried in a cart accompanied by a large concourse of people, and at last was brought to the Liberty Tree, where he was obliged to swear never to be guilty "of a like crime in the future." An intelligent Scotch bookseller, who published a newspaper which found its interest in supporting the government, was threatened with the like treatment, but escaped. In many other ways the soldiers were offered opportunities to interfere, but they were restrained until the following spring. Meantime the first blood was spilled.

On the twenty-second of February, 1770, some boys set up a board before the shop of an importer* named Lillie, who had been denounced for breaking the non-importation agreement, on which were carved the faces of four similar offenders. One Richardson, an informer, endeavored to persuade some country teamsters to drive their carts against the board and to throw it down, and this incensed the crowd that stood around. Insulting language was used on both sides; boys threw stones at Richardson; he withdrew to his house, shut himself in, and at last fired upon the crowd. Two boys were wounded, one of whom, Christopher Schneider, aged eleven, died the next day. The bells of the New Brick were set ringing, a vast concourse collected, Richardson was arrested and held for trial.† Schneider died at his father's house on Frog Lane, now Boylston Street, and was announced as the "first martyr to the noble cause," the "first victim to the cruelty and rage of oppressors." Opportunity was taken to have an impressive funeral. The little corpse was brought to the Liberty Tree on Monday, the twenty sixth, in a coffin that bore Latin inscriptions adapted to excite the lookers-on. Six of the boy's playfellows acted as pall-bearers; a procession of four hundred or more schoolboys marched in couples before the body; thirteen hundred citizens followed

* This shop was near the Second Church or New Brick, which then stood on Hanover Street. The church was surmounted by the large gilded cock shown in Revere's picture of Boston, which now stands on the spire of the Shepard Memorial Church in Cambridge.

† Richardson was found guilty of murder, but was finally pardoned by the king, Hutchinson having refused to sign a warrant for his execution.

on foot, and many chariots and chaises closed the procession, which made a lasting impression on the beholders; and indeed the whole of the citizens shared the sadness, or reflected upon the consequences that might flow from the circumstance that "the son of a poor German," as Hutchinson expressed it, had been killed.

Doubtless the funeral was exasperating to Hutchinson and to the soldiers, who were cordially hated by the populace, as the constant bruising affrays between them amply testify. The troops were some of them quartered in "Murray's Barracks," near the former site of the Brattle Street church, and most of the remainder just south of King Street, the main guard being directly opposite the south door of the town-house. A sentinel was placed in a tunnel or covered passage between Cornhill and Brattle Street, then known as Draper's or Boylston's alley. The position of the soldiers became more and more difficult, and within a week after the funeral a notable affray occurred between the twenty-ninth regiment and some men employed in one of the rope-walks * near the present Post-office Square, which was not far from the home of Samuel Adams. It is impossible to determine on which side the fault

* Rope making was one of the most important industries in early Boston. It dates from 1641 or 1642, when John Harrison set up his establishment on ground at the foot of Summer Street, afterwards "purchased" by the town, whence the name of the street on which Samuel Adams lived,—Purchase Street. In 1712 Edward Gray began his business on a tract near Pearl Street, and soon the family were the most celebrated of all in their line of business. Harrison Gray, grandfather of Harrison Gray Otis, was a son of the first Edward.

should be placed in this case, for the accounts differ widely; it is enough for our purposes to know that the strained relations between the soldiery and the townspeople, especially the less intelligent of them, resulted in a serious street affray, and that in the desperate encounter several of the soldiers were severely wounded, while the rope-makers fared equally badly. The soldiers were constantly followed in the streets by hooting and hissing crowds, and it required all the skill of the officers to restrain them from showing natural resentment.

On the third of March the commanding officer of of the twenty-ninth made formal complaint to Lieutenant-Governor Hutchinson of the insults that his men had received, especially from some of the men of the rope-walk, and on Monday, the fifth, the matter was brought to the attention of the council. Some of the council assured Hutchinson that the people would be satisfied with nothing short of the removal of the troops, and another said that he knew that some of the principal citizens had several times met for the purpose of consulting about a plan for their removal. Nothing was done, however, and soon after nine o'clock that evening, which was moonlight, the danger from the presence of the soldiers was proved again. Hutchinson relates that early in the evening parties of soldiers had been observed driving about the streets as though there was something more than ordinary on their minds, and that the citizens had been noticed clustering together; that at eight o'clock a bell was rung as if for fire, and that this brought a crowd to the market-place, not far from King Street, armed with bludgeons. Whether there was really any extraordinary stir at that time or not, it is certain that the streets were soon thronged by excited men and boys who pelted the sentinels with bits of ice, and when a body of nine soldiers was brought out and stood before them with loaded pieces, they still shouted coarse insults and dared the men to fire. It is not unlikely that some of the threats were thought by the soldiers to be a command from their own officer, Captain John Preston, for there was such a din that words could with difficulty be distinguished. However it happened, the mass of confused and contradictory testimony does not make clear, but the results we know. There lay on the icy snow the bodies of Crispus Attucks, a mulatto, and Samuel Gray, one of the rope-makers who had had previous quarrels with the soldiers, both of whom were active in this affray, and James Caldwell, a sailor. Several other persons were more or less wounded, and two of them died. The wildest confusion followed; Preston restrained his men from a second discharge; but the bells were rung, the drums beat to arms, and soon King Street was crowded by a throng said to comprise four or five thousand men. Hutchinson appeared and reprimanded Captain Preston for his share in the affair, while he called upon the people to retire to their homes. Being informed that the crowd would not disperse until Preston had been placed under arrest, Hutchinson had the captain brought before him and an investigation was begun which lasted until three o'clock the next morning.

As soon as daylight came the town was again filled with buzzing crowds, that gathered from the country around to learn every detail of the thrilling events. An informal town-meeting was held in Faneuil Hall at eleven o'clock, at which witnesses of the affray gave their accounts of what had occurred, and Samuel Adams made an address. A committee was sent to the governor, to tell him again that the peace could not be preserved while the troops remained, and a more formal town-meeting was appointed for three in the afternoon, so urgent was the emergency considered. At the appointed hour the people came to the hall, but it was found too contracted for the throng, and an adjournment was had to the Old South, where the result of the interview with Hutchinson was awaited with breathless interest. The crowd, as it passed from the hall to the meeting-house, went over the ground still stained by the blood shed the evening before, and under the windows of the town-house in which Adams and the others were engaged in their important argument with Hutchinson. "This multitude are not such as pulled down your house," said one of the council to the lieutenant-governor, as the people passed beneath their eyes; "but they are men of the best characters, men of estates, and men of religion; men who pray over what they do."

Into this determined crowd Samuel Adams soon issued at the head of the committee, with the report that the regiments could not both be removed; that only one was to go; and as he passed along with bowed head, he whispered to those near him: "Both regiments or none! Both regiments or none!" Once inside of the crowded building, the report was formally announced that the twenty-ninth, because of the part it had played in the affray, was to be removed to the Castle, but that the fourteenth would remain in town. Then the shout of the people, who remembered their cue, burst forth in deafening power: "Both regiments or none! Both regiments or none!" A new committee was carefully selected, and Hancock and Adams were counted in it, with Joseph Warren, the eloquent physician. These gentlemen returned to the council-chamber and reported to the lieutenant-governor the determination of the people. Adams spoke in his usual manner, arguing, as he had so often argued, against the legality of quartering troops on the people in time of peace without the consent of the legislature, and insisting upon the necessity of the removal of them all. To this Hutchinson replied that the presence of the soldiers was both legal and necessary, and that they were, however, not under his command. Adams replied that if he had power to remove one, he had power to remove both regiments. "A multitude," said he, "highly incensed, now wait the result of this application. The voice of ten thousand freemen demands that both regiments be forthwith removed. Their voice must be respected, their demand obeyed. Fail not, then, at your peril, to comply with this requisition. On you alone rests the responsibility of this decision; and if the just expectations of the people are disappointed, you must be answerable to God and your country for the fatal consequences that

THE OLD STATE-HOUSE IN 1801. THE STATE-STREET END, SHOWING THE OLD BRICK CHURCH (ON WASHINGTON STREET) BEHIND IT. BUILT IN 1748.

must ensue." Hutchinson declares that he indignantly resented the menace and absolutely refused to dismiss the troops. However, after a long debate, the commander of the forces, Lieutenant-Colonel Dalrymple, gave his word of honor as a soldier that the removal should take place at once, and the committee returned to the waiting crowd at the church to announce the news. The report was received with tokens of great satisfaction, but the cautious citizens did not feel like adjourning until they had appointed the gentlemen who had just waited on the authorities a Committee of Safety, and had made arrangements for a strong night-watch in which the most important citizens were afterwards called upon to carry their muskets and cartridge-boxes. This guard was continued until every soldier had left town.

Before the troops could be removed, on the following Thursday, March 8th, the funerals of the slain were celebrated with all the pomp that Boston was capable of displaying at the time. The assemblage was the "largest ever known"[*]; the bells were tolled in Boston, Cambridge, Roxbury, Charlestown; the bodies of Caldwell and Attucks, the friendless ones among the victims, were taken to Faneuil Hall, Maverick's was borne from his mother's home on Union Street, and that of Gray from his brother's on Royal Exchange Lane. The four hearses formed a junction on the fatal King Street,

---

[*] This estimate of the numbers in public gatherings is often repeated by enthusiastic narrators, and probably means that the crowd was great.

and thence the procession continued six deep to the Middle or Granary Burying-ground, where the bodies were solemnly laid in a single grave. Thus the last view that the retreating soldiers had of King Street was marked by the passage of thousands of Bostonians doing honor to the men whose taunts and insults had goaded them beyond endurance, and they felt the humiliation of their situation as they gave way before the successful "bullies" of the little town who had put them to ignominious flight. It was not "ignominious" in Dalrymple, however, to take his men away from an infuriated populace; there were then thousands of sturdy New Englanders in the towns about, ready to crowd into Boston at the proper signal; and what were two single regiments to do if they had come? It was foolhardy in Hutchinson to resist the demand of the determined gathering at the Old South. He had been wise the evening before, but on that day his sagacity deserted him. When Lord North, the unwise minister of King George, heard of the circumstances, he was interested in every detail, and the picture of Adams before Hutchinson impressed him so deeply that he afterwards called the fourteenth and twenty-ninth "the Sam Adams regiments."

The Boston leaders showed their practical knowledge of human nature by making notable the funerals of the men killed on the fifth of March; they showed it again when they put forth John Adams and Josiah Quincy, Jr., patriots whose loyalty could not be aspersed, to defend Preston and the soldiers when they came to their trial. It was real courage that these men exhibited when they appeared in court for this purpose, at a time when the public mind was exasperated by what the people considered the "murder" of their fellow-citizens by a brutal soldiery.* It is an instance of the desire of Samuel Adams and the other leaders to have their motives proved above suspicion. John Adams said, that he and Mr. Quincy heard their "names execrated in the most opprobrious terms" whenever they appeared in the streets of Boston, by men who could not restrain their passions long enough to let justice be heard. The trials came off in October and November, and Preston was acquitted. Of the eight men, two were found "not guilty," and two were sentenced to be slightly branded in the hand in open court, for manslaughter, after which all were discharged and sent to the Castle.

Magnified into a patriotic "struggle for liberty" against an oppressive military power, the King

* Mr. Quincy's father wrote from Braintree: "Good God! Is it possible? I will not believe it. . . . I have been told that you have actually engaged for Captain Preston; and I have heard the severest reflections made upon the occasion, by men who had just before manifested the highest esteem for you as one destined to be a savior of your country. I must own to you, it has filled the bosom of your aged and infirm parent with anxiety and distress. . . . I will not believe it unless it be confirmed by your own mouth, or under your own hand." To this the son replied that the criminals, though charged with murder, were entitled to all legal counsel and aid, and that he at first declined to be engaged until urged by an Adams, a Hancock, a Molineux, a Cushing, a Henshaw, a Pemberton, a Warren, a Cooper, and a Phillips," and added: "I dare affirm that you and this whole people will one day rejoice that I became an advocate for the aforesaid 'criminals,' *charged* with the murder of our fellow-citizens."—"Life of Quincy," page 26.

Street affray had an immense influence in strengthening the sentiment, then rapidly growing, in favor of the independence that Adams had been laboring for. "From that moment," said Daniel Webster, "we may date the severance of the British empire." When the fifth of March came around, in 1771, some citizens gathered in "the Manufactory House," a building then standing on the present site of Hamilton Place (selected because the first opposition to the soldiers had been made there in 1769, when it had been refused to Governor Bernard as a barracks for the troops), and listened to a patriotic address by Dr. Thomas Young. The same evening, Paul Revere had his house in North Square illuminated, exhibiting in one window a representation of the ghost of young Schneider, in another a view of the "Massacre," and in a third the Genius of America in tears. Several thousand persons thronged about the house, and a melancholy gloom and solemn silence subdued them as they looked, which were intensified by the dismal tolling of the bells on the meeting-houses from nine to ten o'clock. This was a private celebration, but in accordance with their policy of emphasizing any event that might increase the differences between the people and the government, the leaders dignified the King Street encounter by calling it "the Boston Massacre," and then celebrating its anniversary. The fourteenth of August was no longer honored, as it had been, for the stamp-act riot; and, until 1783, when the Fourth of July became the day for stirring up the patriotism of the people, the fifth of March was taken advantage of by the delivery of an annual oration, and by a commemoration of the "martyrs" of the day. The following lines, which were circulated at the time of the funeral of the victims, show the spirit in which the affair was regarded.

> " Well-fated shades! let no unmanly tear
> From Pity's eye disdain your honored bier ;
> Lost to their view, surviving friends may mourn,
> Yet o'er thy pile shall flames celestial burn ;
> Long as in Freedom's cause the wise contend,
> Dear to your country shall your fame extend,
> While to the world the lettered stone shall tell
> How Caldwell, Attucks, Gray, and Maverick fell."

XXIII.

STIRRING UP A CONTINENT.

The day of the Boston "Massacre" was that on which parliament removed all of its odious duties except that upon tea, which was retained in order to insist that England still had the right to impose such taxes on her colonists. The "Massacre" itself had the influence of making the opponents of Boston in England still more determined that the spirit of the Americans should be broken, and it made the Bostoneers more firm in their opposition to all encroachments upon their "liberties." Hutchinson was now more than ever jealous and afraid of the influence of Boston in the councils of the colony, and in calling the legislature together he mentioned Cambridge as the place of meeting. He had thought of Salem,— "the further from Boston the better," he said. This fear on the part of colonial governors was no new thing; we have seen the legislature meet before this at Cambridge, and we shall yet see it meet at Salem. Hutchinson thought the legislature as a whole "sour and troublesome enough," but all the other delegates were comparatively easy to manage, and he said: "I am very sure, if the members of Boston were out of the house, I should find a majority in favor of the government." All that the other towns can do," he exclaimed, " will be a perfect trifle compared with the trouble the town of Boston gives me. . . . I would give up all, if the town could be separated from the rest of the province. . . . It is the common language of Adams and the rest that they are not to be intimidated by acts of parliament, for they will not be executed here." This he wrote in a letter to England, and he cautiously said to his correspondent: " I am sure you will not suffer what I write to come back again, even by rumours." Hutchinson was to have occasion not long after this to mourn that some of the things that he had written came back again, but in a more powerful form than mere rumors.

One of the results of the doings of March 5th, was that the king made Boston harbor the rendezvous for all his ships stationed in North America, and directed that the Castle should be garrisoned by his troops, instead of by those of the province. Hutchinson lost no time in giving up the keys of the fortress to Colonel Dalrymple, though the act was a direct contravention of the charter, and while the lieutenant-governor looked upon his prompt action as a means of giving him favor at home, and of furthering his design to get the appointment as successor of Bernard, as well as a sure step towards armed coercion, Adams saw in it a stab at the public liberties and an opportunity for stirring up the town and the province against the government. Both obtained what they expected. It was but a few months before Hutchinson received a commission as governor, with the promise of a salary directly from the sovereign. This provision for the salary did not quiet the Bostonians; they looked upon it as making the governor an instrument of the king in establishing "a perfect despotism," as Adams expressed it.

Governor Hutchinson draws a rose-colored picture of the condition of affairs in Massachusetts at this time. There was certainly "a pause in politics," as Dr. Cooper wrote; but Hutchinson said that "in no independent state in the world could the people have been more happy than they were in the government of Massachusetts Bay." The province, he asserted, was free from real evils, and felt so lightly the ordinary burdens that all people in a state of civilization must feel, that in order to keep up a spirit of discontent it was necessary to excite them by merely imaginary evils. Molasses and tea were the only articles that paid any tax of account; more tea was annually imported into Massachusetts legally, in spite of the opposition to its use, than into all the other colonies, and the tax was so small that " the poor people in America drank the same tea in quality, at three shillings the pound, which the people in England drank at six shillings." The governor verily seemed to think that if the men and women of Boston only had enough to eat and drink, they ought to be contented: he had no sympathy with the feelings of men who did not relish the sight of ships-of-war in their harbor, and of red-coated soldiers in their streets, commanded and paid by other authorities than their own legislature, and apparently menacing the freedom of their actions. He did not realize that a small tax laid upon an unwilling people bears harder than a heavy one that the same people assume of their own free-will. He had so long trained his perceptions to sympathize with a king, that he was unable to enter into the feelings of the people among whom he had been born and bred, and whose aspirations ought to have been his own.

In pursuance of the order making Boston harbor a place of rendezvous for the English fleet, twelve war vessels arrived in August, 1771, and another opportunity was afforded Samuel Adams for warning his fellow townsmen of the danger, that was rapidly approaching, of the " slavery " with which they were threatened. He told them that it was useless to endeavor to console themselves because the duty was removed from all articles excepting tea, because, that remaining, it was plain that parliament proved its power to levy taxes, and if it was allowed that it had the right to take three pence because it pleased, the sovereign control of the purses was given up to it ; it was no better to have the charter taken away in parts than in the whole. " The liberties of our country," he exclaimed, " the freedom of our civil constitution, are worth defending at all hazards ; and it is our duty to defend them against all attacks. We have received them as a fair inheritance from our worthy ancestors. They purchased them for us with toil and danger, and expense of treasure and blood, and transmitted them to us with care and diligence. It will bring an everlasting mark of infamy on the present generation, enlightened as it is, if we should suffer them to be wrested from us by violence without a struggle, or be cheated out of them by the artifices of false and designing men." Mr. Adams did not confine himself, as some others did, to denunciations of governmental measures, and appeals to patriotic motives; he went much farther, and denied all right on the part of parliament to tax the colonies, to control their legislatures, or in any way to exercise authority over them.

In January, 1772, Hutchinson wrote: "Except in this town, there is now a general appearance of contentment throughout the province"; for Boston always had to be excepted in such statements, though there were many of her citizens who did not burn with the ardor of Samuel Adams.* Otis would not follow him in denying all parliamentary authority; Dr. Church, the subsequent traitor, was, as Hutchinson said, "now a writer on the side of government"; even John Adams, who had removed back to Braintree, had devoted himself anew to his law practice, avoided politics, political clubs, and town-meetings, even refused to deliver the address on the second recurrence of the day of the "Massacre," and thought that there was not spirit enough to bring the ques-

* The king and his ministers preferred to believe Bernard and Hutchinson rather than Pownall, and thus they were quite deceived in regard to the true state of public opinion. Hutchinson, for example, "repeatedly assured the ministry that a union of the colonies was utterly impracticable; that the people were greatly divided among themselves in every colony; and that there could be no doubt that all America would submit, and that they must, and, moreover, would soon" (1774). Governor Pownall insisted that all the measures against America were planned and pushed on by Bernard and Hutchinson. See the "Memoir of Josiah Quincy, Jr.," pages 197, 205, 211, 215.

tion to a decision, that there would never be a redress of American grievances, but a "trimming." There was Joseph Warren, however, who could hold an audience spellbound, as he did when he stood up in the South meeting-house, March 5th, of this year, and uttered patriotic words on the subject of the connexion between England and the colonies; and there were others like him ready to unite for the protection of right. Samuel Adams had, as we know, long held in abeyance a plan for concentrating the influence of all who were like-minded with him,* and he thought this a proper time to take a step in that direction. His plans were far-reaching, but at this time he proposed to make an humble beginning, to avoid opposition. As long ago as 1766, he had written to Gadsden, of South Carolina, that he longed for a union and a correspondence between the merchants throughout the continent; and, in 1771, he wrote again that when the liberty of one is invaded the liberty of all is in danger, and that he thought it would be wisdom for the colonists to correspond with one another in the times of distress. All the time, from 1764 to 1774, he was using his influence in favor of concert of action between the provinces.

The king had established a salary for the governor, and it was known that the judges were likewise to be made independent of the people. Boston thought it proper to hold a town-meeting to censure the governor for accepting a salary, and to ask him if it was true that the judges were to be paid in the same

* See chapter xx. for reference to the stamp-act Congress.

manner. John Hancock was moderator of the meeting, which was held October 28th. The governor gave unsatisfactory replies to the question propounded to him, and the freemen became restless. Then Adams rose, and moved that "A committee of correspondence be appointed, to consist of twenty-one persons, to state the rights of the colonists, and of this province in particular, as men and Christians and as subjects ; and to communicate and publish the same to the several towns and to the world, as the sense of this town, with the infringements and violations thereof that have been, or from time to time may be made." The discussion on this resolution was prolonged into the evening, and it is said that it was not agreed to until ten o'clock, though then almost every voter gave his assent. A committee was appointed, consisting, as Hutchinson wrote to Pownall, of deacons, atheists, and black-hearted fellows whom one would not choose to meet in the dark, though other historians consider them reputable Boston citizens. Whatever was the character of the members of the committee, it gave life to the Revolution, and enabled the colonists soon to act with order and system, instead of irregularly and inharmoniously.

The committee reported at a meeting held in Faneuil Hall, November 20th, presenting a statement of rights, a statement of grievances, and a letter to the other towns. The letter asked for a free expression of sentiment from each town, and rhetorically expressed the confidence that the people were not prepared to " doze, or sit supinely indifferent on the brink of destruction, while the iron hand of oppression was daily tearing the choicest fruit from the fair tree of liberty, planted by their worthy predecessors, at the expense of their treasure, and abundantly watered with their blood." Six hundred copies of the report were printed and sent out, according to the plan. Many persons thought it was a trifling and unnecessary scheme; but the towns appointed similar committees, and through them reechoed the sentiments of Samuel Adams, that the report comprised. The tories ridiculed the affair, because some of the meetings of the interior towns were slightly attended; but when it was found that almost all of them had adopted the measures proposed, they ceased to think that there was any thing "ludicrous" about the scheme, and one of the ablest of them declared that it was "the foulest, subtlest, and most venomous serpent ever issued from the egg of sedition." John Adams wrote of the feeling elsewhere: "They are still quiet at the south, and at New York they laugh at us." In the south there was, indeed, much jealous fear of Boston. Josiah Quincy, Jr., met at Charleston in March, 1773, an expression of this feeling in the words of Mr. Thomas Shirley, "a well-bred and learned but very warm and irascible" gentleman, who said to him: "Boston aims at nothing less than the sovereignty of this whole continent.—I know it. . . . Take away the power and superintendence of Britain, and the colonies must submit to the next power. Boston would soon have that."

Thus, said Hutchinson, "all of a sudden, from a

state of peace, order, and general contentment, as some expressed themselves, the province more or less from one end to the other was brought into a state of contention, disorder, and general dissatisfaction; or, as others would have it, was roused from stupor and inaction to sensibility and activity." The town of Gorham wrote: "It is better to risk our lives and fortunes in the defence of our rights, civil and religious, than to die by piecemeal in slavery." The selectmen of Petersham declared that "The late appointment of salaries to be paid to our superior court judges, whose creation, pay, and commission depend upon mere will and pleasure, completes a system of bondage equal to any ever before fabricated by the combined efforts of the ingenuity, malice, fraud, and wickedness of man; that it is the first and highest social duty of this people to consider of, and seek ways and means for a speedy redress of these mighty grievances and intolerable wrongs, and that for the obtaining this end this people are warranted by the laws of God and nature in the use of every rightful art and energy of policy, stratagem, and force."

These meetings, says the biographer of Samuel Adams, "constitute the highest mark the town-meeting has ever touched. Never before and never since, have Anglo-Saxon men, in lawful folk-mote assembled, given utterance to thoughts and feelings so fine in themselves and so pregnant with great events. To each letter stand affixed the names of the committee in autograph. This awkward scrawl was made by the fist of a Cape Ann fisherman, on

shore for the day to do at town-meeting the duty
his fellows had laid upon him; the hand that wrote
this other was cramped from the scythe-handle, as
its possessor mowed an intervale on the Connecticut;
this blotted signature, where smutted fingers
have left a black stain, was written by a blacksmith
of Middlesex, turning aside a moment from forging
a barrel that was to do duty at Lexington." *

The result of the committee's first effort was unexpected,
and completely astonished loyalist and
whig. Hutchinson, who had written to Pownall
that the scheme was "foolish," and that the committee
must necessarily make itself ridiculous,† now
became "greatly alarmed with so sudden and unexpected
a change in the state of affairs"; and, as he
records in his history, "was greatly perplexed with
doubts concerning his own conduct on the occasion."
He said that the measure, if pursued to its end,
must cause "not a return of the colonies to their
former submission, but a total separation from the
kingdom, by their independency." He alleged, at
about this time, that no line could be drawn between
an acknowledgment of the authority of parliament
and absolute independence, and it is difficult to controvert
his assertion, though this is what the people
of Massachusetts had been endeavoring to do from
the year 1630, when they first began to establish on

---

* "Samuel Adams," by James K. Hosmer, page 202.

† In his fatuity Hutchinson wrote, February 23, 1773. "I have
stopped the progress of the towns for the present; and I think I
have stopped the prosecution of another part of the scheme, which
was for the assembly to invite every other assembly upon the Continent
to assent to the same principles."

American soil a government that professed to depend upon the charter and not upon parliament for its authority.

In his doubt as to what steps he ought to pursue, Hutchinson saw that he was in danger of being abused both at home and in Boston, but it was plain that unless he should act in some way, he would be properly accused in England of conniving at the proceedings which he confessed were unwarrantable and threatening.' He knew that if he were to bring the matter before the general court he would precipitate a discussion that would tax his abilities, and raise a flame that it would be difficult to suppress. He decided, however, to call the court together, and in January, 1773, he opened its sessions with a speech in which he argued for parliamentary supremacy in a cool and able manner, reviewing past history, with which he was fully acquainted, and assuming successfully an air of candor and moderation that gave a profound effect to his words. The speech was published in the papers and spread throughout the colony and in England, the tories thinking it unanswerable, and the patriots being in some cases staggered by its arguments. It was followed, after a sufficient delay, by a paper, probably prepared by Samuel Adams,—handed to the governor by that gentleman, at least,—which caused Hutchinson to fear that he had made a mistake in admitting that the authority of parliament was a matter about which it was possible to raise a doubt, or around which a discussion could be created. The governor replied, and the court retorted, but neither party was able to produce conviction in the mind of the other; Adams, however, succeeded in placing Hutchinson in the wrong, by making him sensible that it was he who had raised the unfruitful controversy. The court was prorogued on the sixth of March, one day after another celebration of the "Massacre" had occurred in the South meeting-house. At that time Dr. Benjamin Church delivered an eloquent and logical oration to a crowded audience. In this address the speaker said that he rejoiced that Massachusetts had been alarmed by the committees of correspondence, that the people had been led to esteem their rights under the charter to be the "ark of God to New England." He prophesied that some future congress was to be the "glorious source of the salvation of America," and declared that the Amphictyons of Greece, who formed the diet or great council of the states, were "an excellent model for the rising Americans."

It was just at this time that Hutchinson wrote the words about the influence of Boston, and the corporate powers of the Massachusetts towns, to which reference has been made,* in which he exposed the strength of the opposition that he had to face. The governor had the sagacity to see the great influence of the towns, and he reiterated his views of the subject to his different correspondents. He much wished that some change could be made in the charter that would deprive the town-meetings of their powers, and thus keep from the people the constant mindfulness of their rights. The town of Boston

* Letter of March 7th, 1772 to Gage, see page 91.

now proceeded to take the part in the discussion of provincial matters that the governor asserted that it was accustomed to take, by assembling almost immediately after the adjournment of the general

GOVERNOR THOMAS HUTCHINSON.
After a portrait in possession of the Massachusetts Historical Society, once the property of Jonathan Mayhew.

court, for the purpose of considering the misrepresentations of the governor in his late messages, which related to the meeting of the town at which the committees of correspondence had been appointed.

While Adams was thus engaged in local affairs, so deeply that he could give no attention to the plan that he had so long hoped to see realized, for a committee of correspondence uniting the different colonies, the House of Burgesses of Virginia, under the lead of such patriots as Patrick Henry and Richard Henry Lee, adopted resolutions providing for a system of intercolonial correspondence. The resolutions reached Boston in time for action at the town-meeting called for the purpose of choosing delegates to the general court, and a vote was passed recommending the resolutions to the serious consideration of the court. One of the arguments mentioned by the town for the restoration of harmony with Great Britain must have made some of the delegates smile, for it was gravely stated that if England were cut off from her connexion with the American continent, she "must eventually fall a prey to her numerous and jealous neighbors."

The general court adopted the Virginia plan almost unanimously, towards the end of May, and thus there were two committees of correspondence, the one uniting each little hamlet and every large town in the province of the Massachusetts Bay, and the other extending its insidious influence to every legislature of the thirteen colonies, and through them stirring up every patriotic citizen on the continent. Of this action of Massachusetts and Virginia, Hutchinson said that it "ought to have been considered as an avowal of independency, because it could be justified only on the principle of independency." It was, he asserts, a most glaring attempt to alter the constitution of the colonies, against which England ought to have made a stand; but an opinion still prevailed that independency was not the object, and that reasonable concession would lead to due submission, " though advances were every day making to render reconciliation more difficult."

Among the advances that were making reconciliation more difficult may be included an " exposure" made at this time of some of the private correspondence of the governor, which had by some means fallen into the hands of Benjamin Franklin, then agent of Massachusetts in London, and by him had been sent to Boston. Hancock, who was apparently or really indignant at the contents of these letters, determined to make them public. He took occasion one day to announce mysteriously that an important disclosure was to be made within forty-eight hours; well knowing that the spectators in the gallery, that had been set apart for the public by the suggestion of Otis, would spread the information everywhere. The press took up the matter, and reported that dark things were to be brought to light which would " make tyrannical rulers tremble, and give occasion for the whole people to bless the providence of God, who causeth the wicked man to fall into the pit that he hath digged for another." When the due time arrived, Samuel Adams asked to have the galleries cleared, which, of course, made the public more than ever anxious to know what the great matter was that would cause so deep a convulsion. The letters were then read, the injunction being given that they were not to be copied or printed in whole or in part.

They were given to a committee, which reported that they tended and were designed to overthrow the constitution of the government and to introduce arbitrary power into the province. The deductions thus made from the governor's confidential communications to his friends in England are scarcely such as calm readers think legitimate, and they can only be accounted for by supposing that there was a deliberate plan to render the governor odious; or that the patriots had become so deeply filled with the belief that all representatives of the crown were plotters against the liberties of America, that they allowed themselves to be led captive by their too vivid imaginings. Whatever the cause, and whatever the motives which actuated Adams, Hancock, and the rest, the effort to base accusations on the letters thus theatrically brought to the public notice proved successful. It was voted that the governor had lost the confidence of the people, and was an unsuitable instrument for promoting the interests of the king and the colonists, and that it would be promotive of good will, and of the good of His Majesty's loyal and affectionate people, if he were removed from office. This vote, as well as the letters themselves, was afterwards printed and distributed for the purpose of exciting the colonists against Hutchinson.

News reached Boston in the spring of this year that the East India Company, which was embarrassed by the accumulation of tea in England, owing to the refusal of the Americans to buy it, had induced parliament to permit its exportation to

America without the payment of the usual duty. This was intended to bribe the colonists to buy; for there had been a duty both in England and in America. That in England was six pence a pound, that in America, three pence. Ships were laden and sent to Boston, New York, Philadelphia, and Charleston, and they were now expected to arrive in a short time. Samuel Adams felt that the hour had arrived for his Continental Congress, and he proposed that one should be called, for the purpose of drawing up and publishing to the world a Bill of Rights, of providing for an annual congress, and of choosing an ambassador to reside at the British court; for he thought that there was no scheme for preserving the liberties of the people, except by forming "an American Commonwealth." Though Adams labored earnestly to lead others to see as he saw, his longing for a general congress was not to be satisfied yet.

As late as the end of July, 1773, George Clymer, of Philadelphia, wrote to Josiah Quincy, Jr., that the idea of American liberty seemed "to have taken but shallow root in some places, particularly at New York, where all political principles are truly as unfixed as the wind. One year sees the New Yorkers," he adds, "champions for Liberty, and the next hugging their chains. Our Pennsylvanians I take to be in the mean betwixt both. I cannot call it the *golden mean*." This state of affairs was soon to change.

Though the Congress was not held, all Boston, and finally all America, was excited intensely by the expectation of the arrival of the tea-ships. Arthur

Lee wrote to Adams that in his opinion the introduction of the tea ought to be opposed; but said that he was ready to be overruled by his correspondent. Adams had no intention of opposing such a plan. He influenced the Bostonians to adopt it. The agents who had been appointed to receive the tea were called upon to resign; and as they refused, a town-meeting was appointed for November 5th, at which the demand was renewed; it was again refused. Again the town came together, and again the demand was renewed, but the commissioners still refused to resign. The reply was at last voted "not satisfactory," and the meeting immediately broke up. This sudden action, which appeared preconcerted, struck terror into the commissioners. There was nothing more for the town to do, and the committee of correspondence, in connexion with those of Cambridge and of other towns near by, took the management of affairs.

On the twenty-eighth of November, 1773, which was Sunday, the first tea-ship (the *Dartmouth*) entered the harbor. The following morning the citizens were informed by placard that the "worst of plagues, the detested tea," had actually arrived, and that a meeting was to be held at nine in the morning, at Faneuil Hall, for the purpose of making "a united and successful resistance to this last, worst, and most destructive measure of administration." The Cradle of Liberty was not large enough to contain the crowd that was called together. Adams rose and made a stirring motion expressing determination that the tea should not be landed, and it was unanimously agreed to. The meeting then adjourned to the Old South meeting-house, where the motion was repeated, and again adopted without an opposing voice. The owner of the ship protested in vain that the proceedings were illegal ; a watch of twenty-five persons was set, to see that the intentions of the citizens were not evaded, and the meeting adjourned to the following morning. The throng at that time was as great as usual, and while the deliberations were going on, a message was received from the governor, through the sheriff, ordering them to cease their proceedings. It was voted not to follow the advice, and the sheriff was hissed and obliged to retreat discomfited. It was formally resolved that any person importing tea from England should be deemed an enemy to his country, and it was declared that at the risk of their lives and properties the landing of the tea should be prevented, and its return effected.

It was necessary that some positive action should be taken in regard to the tea within twenty days from its arrival, or the collector of customs would confiscate ships and cargoes. The time for this was fast approaching, and all parties concerned appreciated the importance of every moment. The governor felt that he was entirely impotent ; his council could not be depended upon ; and Hancock, who was in command of the cadets, declined to act, because of the danger to which he would be subject. No justice of the peace even was ready to do the governor's bidding ; he stood firmly for prerogative, but still argued and pleaded, though he was told that he was "officious," and his acts useless. The twenty days would expire on the sixteenth of December. On the fourteenth a crowded meeting was held at the Old South, and the importer was enjoined to apply for a clearance to allow his vessel to return with its cargo. He applied, but the collector refused to give an answer until the following day. The meeting therefore adjourned to the sixteenth, the last day before confiscation would be legal, and before the tea would be placed under protection of the ships of war in the harbor.

There was another early morning meeting, and seven thousand people thronged about the meeting-house, all filled with a sense of the fact that something notable was to occur. The importer appeared and reported that the collector refused a clearance. He was then directed to ask the governor for a pass to enable him to sail by the Castle. Hutchinson had retreated to his mansion at Milton, and it would take some time to make the demand. The importer started out in the cold of a New England winter, apologized to his Excellency for his visit, but assured him that it was involuntary. He received a reply that no pass could be given him. By three o'clock the people gathered again at the meeting-house, but the importer had not arrived. The time was filled up by speeches; "Who knows," asked one, "how tea will mingle with salt water?" Josiah Quincy, Jr.,[*] spoke vigorously from the gallery against the

[*] There were three persons of note bearing the colonial name Josiah in the Quincy family, viz.: Josiah, son of Judge Edmund, born in 1709; Josiah, junior, born in 1744; and Josiah, afterwards mayor of Boston, and president of Harvard College, born in 1772.

341 THE OLD SOUTH CHURCH IN ITS PRESENT CONDITION (BUILT IN 1729).

British government, and Harrison Gray responded from the floor, warning "the young gentleman in the gallery" against the consequences of intemperate language. Quincy replied: "If the old gentleman on the floor intends by his warning to 'the young gentleman in the gallery,' to utter only a friendly voice in the spirit of paternal advice, I thank him. If his object be to terrify and intimidate, I despise him!" As he spoke some men disguised as Indians entered, and he added: "I see the clouds which now rise thick and fast upon our horizon; the thunders roll, and the lightnings play, and to the God who rides on the whirlwind and directs the storm I commit my country!"

It was six o'clock before the importer returned, and a few candles were brought in to relieve the fast-increasing darkness. He reported the governor's reply, and Samuel Adams rose and exclaimed: "This meeting can do nothing more to save the country!" In an instant there was a shout on the porch; there was a war-whoop in response, and forty or fifty of the men disguised as Indians rushed out of the doors, down Milk Street towards Griffin's (afterwards Liverpool) Wharf, where the vessels lay. The meeting was declared dissolved, and the throng followed their leaders, forming a determined guard about the wharf. The "Mohawks" entered the vessel; there was tugging at the ropes; there was breaking of light boxes; there was pouring of precious tea into the waters of the harbor. For two or three hours the work went on, and three hundred and forty-two chests were emptied. Then, under the light of the moon, the Indians marched to the sound of fife and drum to their homes, and the vast throng melted away, until not a man remained to tell of the deed. The committee of correspondence held a meeting the next day, and Samuel Adams and four others were appointed to prepare an account of the affair to be posted to other places. Paul Revere, who is said to have been one of the " Mohawks," was sent express to Philadelphia with the news, which was received at that place on the twenty-sixth. It was announced by ringing of bells, and there was every sign of joy. A meeting of citizens was held, and the action was endorsed with claps and huzzas. One prominent gentleman wrote to Boston: " We all allow you have had greater trials than any of the colonies, and we wonder much of your great patience." The continent was universally stirred, at last.

XXIV.

WAR.

"OUR western brother had a dispute with his nurse about a cup of tea. She wanted to force the boy to drink it according to her own receipt. He said that he did not like it, and that it absolutely made him ill. After a good deal of sparring, she took up the birch rod and began to whip him with uncommon severity. He turned upon her in self-defence, showed her to the outside of the nursery door, and never more allowed her to meddle with his affairs." Such are the words of an English traveller who visited America a generation after the Boston Tea-Party.* The nurse and the western brother had now had the dispute about the cup of tea, but it remains to see how the birch rod was applied, and how the nursery door was shut upon the nurse.

We may be sure that when the news of the doings of the evening of December 16th reached England there was considerable excitement. Parliament was in session, and there was no need of losing time in applying the rod to the rebellious boy across the

* Charles Waterton, quoted in Winsor's "Memorial History," vol. iii., page 51.

sea. It was declared that the unruly and defiant spirit of Boston must be checked at all hazards, or there would be an end to the rule of Britain in America. This sentiment was far from universal in England. Private interest led many to be fast friends of America, but they were unable to make their influence felt. Many sensible Englishmen besides those whose voices were heard in parliament justified and even applauded the action of Boston, and denounced the desperate measures of the ministry. "The merchants are alarmed," wrote Josiah Quincy, Jr., in January, 1775, from London, "the manufacturers are in motion, the artificers and handicraftsmen are in amaze, and the lower ranks of the community are suffering"; and they were petitioning parliament to the advantage of America, prodded by self-interest and misery.*

The king sent a message to parliament, in which he denounced the outbreak at Boston as an interference with British trade and an outrage on the English constitution, and a bill was presented for the punishment of the town. In the debate that followed it was said: "The town of Boston ought to be knocked about their ears and destroyed. *Delenda est Carthago!* You will never meet with proper obedience to the laws of this country until you have destroyed that nest of locusts." Lord George Germaine, in introducing the bill, said: "Nor can I think he will do a better thing than to put an end to their town-meetings. I would not have men of a mercantile cast every day collecting themselves together and

* "Memoir of Josiah Quincy, Jr.," pp. 251, 255, etc.

debating about political matters. I would have them follow their occupations as merchants, and not consider themselves as ministers of that country. . . . The whole are the proceedings of a tumultuous and riotous rabble, who ought, if they had the least prudence, to follow their mercantile employments, and not trouble themselves with politics and government, which they do not understand." Lord North considered these sentiments " worthy of a great mind," and the fact shows how little the real state of affairs in Boston was understood in England at that time, though it also proves that the strength of the Americans stood in their democratic gatherings, in which the average of the wisdom of all still seems to be greater than the wisdom of the wisest among them.

Parliament passed an act closing the port of the doomed city during the pleasure of the king, and giving the army and the fleet directions to see that it was enforced ; it was determined that the councillors, who had before been chosen by the general court, should be appointed by the king ; the superior judges were to hold office during the king's pleasure, and receive their salaries from him ; the inferior judges were to be removable by the governor; no town-meetings were to be permitted except such as might be convoked by the governor for the discussion of such business as he might allow; soldiers, magistrates, and officers of the revenue, charged with capital offences, were to be tried in England or Nova Scotia ; provision was made for the legal quartering of troops upon the towns ; Salem was made the capital of the province, and the port of Boston was closed. It was vainly thought that the power of parliament to make laws for the colonies in all cases whatsoever was now vindicated.

The general court met in January, 1774. Hutchinson made an opening speech, in which he avoided reference to the "tea-party," and to the fact that other shipments of the "detested herb" had been treated to salt-water baths, because he feared the response that he might meet from the deputies in their excited state. The governor contented himself by mentioning "such things only as were least likely to give room for any harsh or unkind return"; that is, he brought up the general business and expressed the king's disapprobation of the sittings of the committees of correspondence during the recess of the court. This gave Adams an opportunity to defend the committees and their action before the public, and to strengthen the faith of any who might be weak. He argued that, during the recesses of the court, the governor and other officers of the king were accustomed to correspond with the ministers and to concert measures grievous to the colonists, and urged that as the court met only at the pleasure of the governors (who therefore had the power to hinder any measures that the colonists might wish to carry for their protection), it could not be thought unreasonable or improper for the colonists to correspond with their agents, as well as with one another, to the end that their grievances might be so explained to his Majesty that, in his justice, he might afford them necessary relief.

The next move looked to the impeachment of the chief-justice, Peter Oliver, for accepting the salary promised by the king; but the governor resolved to prorogue the court before action could be completed. He therefore prepared a message in which he said that he had passed over the illiberal charges and insinuations against himself, but that when they struck "directly at the honor and authority of the king and of the parliament, he was obliged to stop them from proceeding any farther." The house learned that such a message was coming, and barred its doors so effectually that the governor's secretary was unable to obtain admission. Meanwhile they perfected arrangements for their own pay, and passed a resolution to the effect that they had done all that they could do for the removal of the chief justice, and boldly declaring that the refusal of the governor to act with them was probably because he also received his support from the crown. They also directed the committee of correspondence to write to Benjamin Franklin, the colonial agent in London, on the public grievances. This was the last appeal made by Massachusetts for redress.

The governor had previously prepared the court for prorogation, and had informed them that he had obtained the king's permission to go to England, and intended soon to go. The close of the session of the court left the management of affairs in the hands of the committee of correspondence, which had, indeed, directed the action of that body during its sessions. The governor's authority was now gone; the course of law was stopped, because juries would not act while Oliver held his office; and Hutchinson declared that "the danger of revolt was daily increasing." At this juncture the lieutenant-governor, Andrew Oliver, died from a stroke of apoplexy, and Hutchinson postponed his departure, because his absence at the moment would have given up all power to the opponents of the king's government.

The fifth of March arrived three days before the court closed its sessions, and a remarkable arrangement was made for its celebration. The town assembled at Faneuil Hall, but adjourned to the Old South, where the usual oration was delivered by John Hancock. It was the speaker's first public address, and was pronounced with dignity, grace, and oratorical skill, but it was not the composition of the orator. Samuel Adams is reputed to have written it, and he "sat blandly by as moderator, while the people were deceived into the belief that the man who surpassed all in social graces and length of purse could thunder also from the rostrum with the best."[*] John Adams records that "the composition, the pronunciation, the action, all exceeded the expectations of everybody." The oration closed with those impressive words of Habakkuk, from which Judge Sewall derived so much comfort on the dark day that Andros arrived: "Although the fig-tree shall not blossom," etc.[†] As the dignified speaker resumed his seat, a committee, of which Samuel Adams was chairman, was appointed to thank the

---

[*] "Samuel Adams," by J. K. Hosmer, page 263.
[†] See page 164.

orator in the name of the town for "his elegant and spirited oration," and to ask a copy for publication, while thanks were unanimously voted to Adams himself for "his good services as moderator." Hancock thus gained applause that he did not deserve, and (what was most desired by "the mover of the puppets") was more firmly committed to the cause, while the people were impressed by the patriotism of a rich and well-born gentleman; but it was a peculiar transaction.*

The port was to be closed on the first of June. The news reached Boston on the tenth of May; there was a convention of the committees of correspondence of eight neighboring towns, including Lexington and Cambridge, on the twelfth; and a circular-letter, prepared by Samuel Adams, was issued, declaring that the town of Boston was suffering in "the common cause," and that "all should be united in opposition to this violation of the liberties of all."

* This is not the only occasion, if history does not malign him, on which Hancock availed himself of the help of another in literary composition. When the adoption of the federal constitution was under consideration in Boston, in 1788, he was much in doubt as to his course, and, in order to avoid discussion, remained at home, as was usual with him on such occasions, wrapped in flannel, suffering from, or affecting to suffer from, the gout. He was flattered into the belief that "the salvation of the nation" rested upon him, by some persons interested in the adoption of the constitution, and after much urging he appeared in the convention, (which was in session in the Federal Street church, by adjournment from the Town House,) carried in the arms of several young gentlemen, and asked permission to read a speech which he said he was unable to make in any other manner. He then read a speech which had been written for him by Theophilus Parsons, and when he concluded one of his friends hastily took the manuscript from him, that the handwriting might not be observed. (See Wells' "Life of Samuel Adams," vol. iii., page 258.)

Military companies were formed, and everywhere men were assiduous in learning the use of firearms; though, as Hutchinson says, "not under the officers of the regiments to which they belonged," but "under officers of their own choosing." Five hundred barrels of gunpowder were purchased, ostensibly "for His Majesty's safety in the service of the province," and it was plain that a conflict was only to be avoided by the most judicious measures on the part of the royal officers. A town-meeting was held on the thirteenth, so promptly did one act follow another, at which it was voted, against the opposition of the tories who came out to confuse the public counsels, that the salvation of the liberties of America was to be obtained by a joint resolution of all the colonies to stop all importations from and exportations to England, and that, "on the other hand, if they continue their exports and imports, there is high reason to fear that fraud, power, and the most odious oppression will rise triumphant over right, justice, social happiness, and freedom." The day of this town-meeting was made memorable by the arrival of the new governor, General Gage. Paul Revere carried this manifesto of the town to Philadelphia, reaching that place on this occasion in six days, and responses of the most encouraging character began immediately to come to Boston, offering help, assuring her that she was considered as "suffering in the common cause," and calling for a congress of the colonies.*

* John Adams wrote to his wife: "We live, my dear soul, in an age of trial. What will be the consequence, I know not. The town of Boston, for aught I can see, must suffer martyrdom; it must ex-

Gage had been instructed to act with promptness against the leaders; but he was a man of moderation,* and feared the effect of any decided action before he had brought together troops enough to ensure himself against a popular rising, though the impression was general among Englishmen that Americans were all cowards and poltroons. The general court met on the twenty-sixth of May, and on the first of June was adjourned to Salem, by General Gage. Hutchinson left that morning for England. At noon the port of Boston was closed; no ferry-boat could start for Charlestown, no vessel sail for London; the bells were tolled, and there were profuse signs of mourning. Even in Philadelphia business stopped, and in Virginia the day was observed by fasting and prayer. Bancroft paints a graphic picture of the transformation of the busy town into a place of idleness and want: "No anchor could be weighed, no sail unfurled, no vessel so much as launched from the stocks"; the king had changed the " busy workshops into scenes of compulsory idleness, and the most skilful naval artisans in the world, with the keenest eye for forms of beauty and speed," were forced by act of parliament to fold their hands. "Want scowled on the laborer, as he sat with his

pire; and our principal consolation is that it dies in a noble cause,— the cause of truth, of virtue, of liberty, of humanity, and that it will probably have a glorious resurrection to greater wealth, splendor, and power than ever." May 12, 1774.

* Joseph Warren considered Gage "a man of honest, upright principles, and one desirous of accommodating the differences between Great Britain and her colonies in a just and honorable way," though he confessed that he wrote an "ill-judged" answer to the provincial congress.

wife and children at his board. The sailor roamed the streets listlessly without hope of employment."

The law was enforced with a rigor that went beyond the intentions of its authors. It went hard with Boston; but the people of Philadelphia sent her sympathy, and gifts were offered from far and near. South Carolina sent two hundred barrels of rice, and promised to make the gift a thousand; Washington headed a subscription paper in Fairfax County, Virginia, with fifty pounds; Wilmington, N. C., raised two thousand pounds currency in a few days; flour, cattle, sheep, fish, came from New England towns; Quebec sent over a thousand bushels of wheat; and Augusta County, Virginia, offered one hundred and thirty-seven barrels of flour. Salem and other ports were open, and received all that was sent, conveying it overland to the distressed town; while the Bostonians themselves endeavored to smile at the strange fact that they were "seventeen miles from a seaport."

There were a large number of delegates present at the meeting of the court at Salem; and business was begun, after listening to Governor Gage's speech, by protesting against the removal, and then arrangements were made by Adams and those in sympathy with him for the selection of delegates to the congress that was to be held in Philadelphia, for which it was intended that Boston should make the plans. Adams proceeded with secrecy, and on the seventeenth of June, when he thought all was ready, after locking the door and putting the key into his pocket, he submitted resolutions assigning September 1st as the day, and Philadelphia, "or any other place that should be decided upon," as the place for the congress. Five delegates were chosen, and five hundred pounds were provided for their expenses. In the midst of the discussion, which began by an uproar at the bold and, to some, unexpected suggestion, a member, feigning illness, managed to get out of the room and to give Gage information of what was going on. The governor immediately sent his secretary with a brief message dissolving the assembly. The closed door made his entrance impossible, and the messenger stood on the stairway and read the impotent proclamation to a few loungers. When Adams was ready, the door was opened, the prorogation was allowed, and there was no longer a general court in Massachusetts.

While the sleepy town of Salem was agitated by these proceedings there was a town-meeting in Boston (June 17th) over which John Adams presided. It was called for the purpose of providing employment for the poor, and to talk about paying for the tea that had been destroyed.* Though there had been two opinions on the propriety of paying for the tea, and though Franklin thought best to take such a conciliatory step, the meeting was firm and unanimous in asserting that Boston was willing to endure the

* Owing to the fact that the citizens of Boston no longer had the right to hold town-meetings at their pleasure, this one, known as the Port Bill Meeting, was not dissolved, but simply "adjourned," in order that when another meeting should be found serviceable, it would not be necessary to ask Governor Gage's permission to hold it. The "adjourned" meeting was finally held on the day appointed for the celebration of the Massacre, March 6, 1775.

worst rather than surrender any right. A memorable meeting was held at Dr. Joseph Warren's house that evening, and the hearts of those who were present were cheered by the intelligence from Salem, by letters from Baltimore and New York, and by the news found in the public journals.

Congress met at Philadelphia, September 5th, and remained in session until October 26th. After it had adjourned John Dickinson wrote to Josiah Quincy, Jr.: "I now congratulate you on the hearty union of all America from Nova Scotia to Georgia, in the common cause. If it be possible the return of the members into the several colonies will make them still more firm. The most peaceable provinces are now animated." Dr. Charles Chauncy wrote in November: "The colonies are marvellously united, and determined to act as one in the defence of this town and province." In fact "Boston must be regarded as suffering in the common cause!" became the popular expression of colonial sentiment. Mr. Adams considered the Congress to be a collection of the greatest men upon the continent, in point of abilities, virtues, and fortunes. They looked upon tories as the most despicable animals in creation, to be compared only to "spiders, toads, and snakes." While this was occurring, the patriots in Boston convened in a county meeting,* first at Dedham, and then at Milton, where they passed the "Suffolk Resolves," as they are called, in which it was declared that no

---

* This was done on account of the difficulty and danger of holding meetings in Boston. See "A History of Boston," by Caleb H. Snow, M.D., page 298.

officers appointed by parliament were to be acknowledged; that no more moneys were to be paid to the royal treasurer; that friends of the people should be put in command of the militia; and that obedience should be given to the acts of the continental congress. A provincial congress was favored, and threats were made of seizing all crown officers as hostages, in case of any arrest by the governor for political reasons. The gathering expressed a determination to act on the defensive, as long as reason and self-preservation would allow,—" and no longer." A system of couriers was established at the same meeting, to communicate promptly with corresponding committees and with town officers, and the bold resolves were sent to the congress at Philadelphia, by Paul Revere, who had been twice before employed on like errands. They were received with applause and commended to the country.

Gage was not an uninterested spectator of all these acts. He was busily collecting troops and ammunition, and building fortifications and barracks; and he thus stimulated the Americans not only to watchfulness, but to indignant opposition, for the powder that he took was the property of the province, and the men who assisted him were looked upon as base renegades. On the first of September two hundred of his men embarked on a marauding excursion from Long Wharf, and went up the Mystic. They took two hundred and twelve half-barrels of powder from Quarry Hill, and a detachment captured two field-pieces in Cambridge. The next day several thousand people assembled at the latter town armed to repel the force, but as it had disappeared, they laid their pieces aside and visited the houses of certain tories, whom they obliged to forswear all connivance with the royal government in the future.

The acts of Gage were distorted by rumor, and one day the country around was aroused by a story that the fleet and army were firing into the town of Boston. It is said that thirty thousand people collected from a radius of thirty miles about, to take part in the action. The rumor reached Philadelphia as actual news, and had the effect of uniting the delegates and hastening their action. Mr. John Adams wrote from congress September eighth: " We are waiting with the utmost anxiety and impatience for further intelligence. The effect of the news we have both upon the congress and the inhabitants of this city was very great. Great indeed! Every gentleman seems to consider the bombardment of Boston as the bombardment of the capital of his own province. Our deliberations are grave and serious indeed."

Gage had called a meeting of the general court to convene at Salem October 5th, but the tumults that came on led him to issue a proclamation, on the twenty-eighth of September, proroguing the body. The members, however, met at the time appointed, but after a little delay adjourned to Concord and organized themselves into a " provincial congress." The new body held its sessions for three weeks, during which time steps were taken to provide the towns with ammunition and stores, and to organize the militia. The governor in his impotence denounced the congress, but it met again in spite of him in November, at Cambridge, and kept on with its work. It provided at this time for a "committee of safety," which became the real executive of Massachusetts, with power to procure stores, organize the militia, and generally to look out for the welfare of the people. Thus, in various ways, Massachusetts calmly prepared for any aggressive movement, taking every precaution, however, not to be aggressive herself. Minute-men were enrolled by the towns and carefully drilled and equipped. These soldiers were looked upon with disdain by the regulars under Gage, while some of them, who had been with Pepperell at Louisburg, ridiculed the earthworks on the Neck, which they compared disdainfully with the great stone walls that had proved no obstacle to their success in that memorable campaign.

The second provincial congress convened at Cambridge on the first of February, 1775, with John Hancock as president, and proceeded to exercise the functions of the general court. It appropriated moneys for the purchase of warlike stores, selected officers for the command of the minute-men who might be brought into actual service, and appointed Samuel and John Adams, John Hancock, Robert Treat Paine, and Thomas Cushing delegates to the continental congress. Meantime, events crowded upon one another. The fifth of March came around again, and Dr. Warren craved the privilege of delivering the customary address in the Old South. A warrant was issued for a town-meeting on March 6th (the fifth being Sunday), in adjournment of the

Port Bill Meeting of June 17th of the previous year. Gage had now gathered a considerable force in Boston. At the close of 1774 he had eleven regiments of infantry and four companies of artillery, and five hundred men were on duty every day to overawe the citizens. It required considerable nerve to speak in public at the time, for it was known that some attempt was to be made to interrupt the meeting on this hated anniversary. When forty British officers entered the building Adams asked the civilians occupying the front seats to vacate them, and seated the military men in their places. He was determined to put them in the wrong, in case of any disturbance. It was afterwards learned that an attempt was to have been made to seize the persons of Adams, Hancock, and Warren, and that a certain ensign had been appointed to give the signal for the others by throwing an egg at Dr. Warren in the pulpit. The young fellow had a fall on his way to the meeting, which dislocated his knee and broke the egg, on which account the scheme failed.

The oration was delivered by Warren without much interruption. He was obliged to enter the meeting-house through a window behind the high pulpit, and then, taking his handkerchief in his right hand, he began and ended without action. At one point an officer held up a few pistol bullets in his open palm; Warren quietly dropped his handkerchief upon them and went on. It is passing strange that the peace was not disturbed, for some of Warren's words were well adapted to excite the royalists. He spoke of the "ruin" around, and asked:

"Does some fiend, fierce from the depth of hell, with all the rancorous malice that the apostate damned can feel, twang her destructive bow, and hurl her deadly arrows at our breast? No, none of these: but how astonishing! it is the hand of Britain that inflicts the wound. The arms of George, our rightful king, have been employed to shed that blood which freely should have flowed at his command, when justice or the honor of his crown had called his subjects to the field."

The congress that had met in February at Cambridge convened again, March 22d, at Concord, when it resolved anew that for the people to relax their preparations for defence would be attended with the most dreadful consequences, pointed out the danger of "subjugation," and called upon all to be prepared to oppose force to force if any emergency should arise. The movements of the military had been strictly watched during the winter by a body of thirty persons who patrolled the streets by twos at night. At about dark, on the eighteenth of April, eight hundred British troops were taken from their barracks and marched to the foot of the common, where boats had been sent to meet them at a point not far from the present site of the Providence railroad station. Information was taken to Dr. Warren, and he immediately sent one William Dawes to Lexington, to inform Adams and Hancock, who were there. Dawes started across the Neck and went through Roxbury. At a later hour Warren sent for Paul Revere, and begged him to go to Lexington also, to tell Adams and Hancock of the movement. Revere had given certain friends at Charlestown to understand that, in case of such a movement of troops by way of the Neck, he would display a lantern in the steeple of Christ Church (or " the North Church," as it was familiarly called), and if by Charlestown, two. Making hurried arrangements, therefore, to have two lights hung out, he hastened across the Charles River and found his friends, who had seen the lights, waiting for him. A horse was provided, and he hastened on towards Lexington. Meantime most of the inhabitants of Boston slept quietly, little suspecting the momentous interests that were at stake. By daylight Gage was informed that the country had been alarmed in advance of his troops, and he determined to hurry forward reinforcements under young Earl Percy, then about thirty years of age. It was nine o'clock before these were ready to march, and then they went out through Roxbury to the Brighton bridge at Cambridge, and thence up the Menotomy road (through the present Arlington) towards Lexington. It was hot and dusty, and Percy's men were soon fatigued. Boston saw no more of them until eight o'clock that evening, when their bayonets gleamed on Bunker Hill, where they bivouacked for the night. In the interval the " battles " of Lexington and Concord had been fought; the American minute-men had been tried, and had learned that under some circumstances at least it was possible for them to make the redcoats run.

The " siege of Boston " that was then begun lasted for eleven months.

John Adams relates that once on a business journey, in 1774, he arrived at Falmouth (now Portland) late in the afternoon after riding at least thirty-five miles. He said to his hostess: "Madame, is it lawful for a weary traveller to refresh himself with a dish of tea, provided it has been honestly smuggled or paid no duties?" "No, sir," said she; "we have renounced all tea in this place; but I 'll make you coffee." "Accordingly," he added, "I have drank coffee every afternoon since, and have borne it very well."

XXV.

BOSTON BESIEGED.

AFTER the battles at Lexington and Concord, Governor Gage wrote to his friends in England: "Conciliation, moderation, reasoning is over; nothing can be done but by forcible means. Tho' the people are not held in high estimation by the troops, yet they are numerous, worked up to a fury, and not a Boston rabble, but the farmers and the freeholders of the country. A check anywhere will be fatal, and the first stroke will decide a great deal. We should therefore be strong, and proceed on a good foundation before anything decisive is tried." These were true words, and our story will show how true they were. Gage acted upon them. During the summer he fortified the town as carefully as he could, having, after May 25th, the counsel and assistance of General Howe, who, with Burgoyne and Clinton (the "three bow-wows," as they were called), arrived on that day.

The meetings of the selectmen of Boston ceased on the nineteenth of April, 1775, the record being broken off in the midst of a list of the members of the body who were present, and, so far as the records go, martial law then took the place of the usual government of the town. Boston was closely shut up; and Governor Gage was obliged to leave all the rest of the province over which he was appointed by George the Third, to be governed according to the pleasure of those of the colonists who were left outside. From every direction men pressed toward the scene of action as soon as the alarm of the doings at Lexington and Concord reached them, and there was a fair army in Cambridge by the next evening after the battles. It was composed of such men as Gage describes, and it was so firm and so efficient that no force was able to get out of the capital except in one direction,—by water,—and in that direction all the British were forced out in the following spring. Many of those in the vicinity of Boston who sympathized with the British, hastened to find refuge within the town; and large numbers already there made equal haste to get out, and there was mutual fear lest the Americans should march in, or the British march out. There was a town-meeting on the twenty-second, followed by a conference with Gage, which resulted in an agreement to allow citizens who would give up their arms to take their goods and leave the town. Many people actually did this; but the general proved to be like Pharaoh of old, for when he feared that he had made a mistake, he hardened his heart, and refused to let any go whom he was able to hold back. He reasoned that if he could keep the Bostonians in, he would protect himself, for the patriots he thought would hesitate to destroy their friends. For similar reasons he ordered that those who did go out should leave their most valuable possessions behind them. Martial law was formally established on the twelfth of June by a proclamation, in which pardon was offered to all who would accept it, with the important exceptions of Samuel Adams and John Hancock, who were thus placed in the enviable position of leaders *par excellence* of the opposing citizens.

Percy and his troops did not remain at their camp on Bunker Hill. The wounded were taken to Boston by transports as promptly as possible, and soon afterward all the rest followed; for Gage was really not strong enough to do more than protect himself until the reinforcements arrived under the " three bow-wows." The American army, then under command of General Artemas Ward, had reached the total of fifteen thousand men. There had been no general engagement since the battles at Lexington and Concord; but Charlestown had been astonished in May by the marching of an army of two thousand men to the ferry and back under General Putnam; the "rebels" had amused themselves also by burning the houses on Hog Island,—" just under the admiral's nose," Lord Percy indignantly wrote to his father; they had captured a barge belonging to a man-of-war at Noddle's Island, and after carrying it to Cambridge in triumph, had taken it to Roxbury in a cart, with the sails up and three men in it; and there had been other raids, but no actual war. The doings with the barge showed the exuberant spirits of new recruits to whom blood-shedding was unknown.

The region about was alarmed from time to time by reports that the British were intending to march out, and, by the third week in June, rumors of this kind became more definite. It was understood at Cambridge that an effort was to be made to fortify Dorchester Heights (now South Boston) and Charlestown. General Ward determined to be first at Bunker Hill, and despatched a force, under command of Colonel William Prescott, with orders to fortify that eminence. When Prescott reached the point, a consultation was held under the light of the moon, and it was determined to begin the works on Breed's Hill, which was nearer Boston,—less than a mile, indeed, from the fortifications on Copp's Hill, just across the Charles River. It was nine in the evening, of June 16th, before the men left Cambridge; but they worked very rapidly, and by dawn a redoubt had been thrown up about eight rods square. Work was begun on a breastwork, to extend from the east side of the redoubt to the bottom of the hill, but hot and heavy firing by the British interrupted operations. After looking over the ground as well as he could, Gage decided, against the advice of his officers, to attack the works immediately in front; and two thousand men were landed for the purpose under General Howe, near the present site of the Navy Yard. After hard fighting the Americans were overcome by greater numbers and forced to leave their position, having lost one hundred and forty-five killed and missing, and three hundred and four wounded. Two hundred and twenty-four of the attacking force were killed, and eight hundred and thirty wounded. It was a fierce struggle, which showed the colonists their fighting ability, while it taught the British never to lead their troops against the Americans when entrenched; and it proved the decisive battle of the war. The British burned the town, destroying, with the meeting-house, court-house, school-houses, and nearly four hundred other buildings, all the goods and chattels of the inhabitants, as well as much property belonging to citizens of Boston who had hurriedly carried it thither for safety. Among the losses were the books and manuscripts of the Reverend Samuel Mather, comprising those which he had received from his father, his grandfather, and his great-grandfather, many of them being, however, such as the present generation would probably consider of little value, except as showing the sort of books and writings which were in vogue in the colonial days.

This was a desperate battle, and Mrs. John Adams writes that Howe was reported to have said that the fight upon the Plains of Abraham was but a bauble to it. It was thought astonishing that all the Americans were not cut off. The engagement began at three o'clock on Saturday morning, and the firing did not cease until after three o'clock Sunday afternoon. The towns about were excited. They all contained refugees from the city, and everybody feared that an immediate advance would be made over the Neck. There was so much alarm at Braintree, that no service was held in the meeting-house on that Sunday, nor even upon the next. While this was the state of affairs in the country, Boston itself was no less distressed. After the battle, wagons and carts were in active demand to convey the wounded to hospitals and the dead to their graves, and Howe was too much occupied and astonished by the audacity and bravery of the Americans to make plans for any immediate advance.

We must conceive of the town at that time as deprived of all of its usual channels of supplies; of course provisions soon became scarce, and wood for fires was to be obtained only by taking down dwellings and other buildings. Mrs. Adams, in writing to her husband, said :

"The present state of the inhabitants of Boston is that of the most abject slaves, under the most cruel and despotic of tyrants. Among many instances I could mention, let me relate one. Upon the seventeenth of June, printed handbills were posted up at the corners of the streets and upon houses, forbidding any inhabitants to go upon their houses or upon any eminence on pain of death ; the inhabitants dared not to look out of their houses, nor to be heard or seen to ask a question. Our prisoners were brought over to the Long Wharf, and there lay all night, without any care of their wounds, or any resting-place but the pavements, until the next day, when they exchanged it for the jail, since which we hear they are civilly treated. Their living cannot be good, as they can have no fresh provisions ; their beef we hear is all gone, and their wounded men die very fast, so that they have a report that the bullets were poisoned. Fish they cannot have, they have rendered it so difficult to procure ; and the admiral is such a villain, as to oblige every fishing schooner to pay a dollar every time it goes out. The money that has been paid for passes is incredible. Some have given ten, twenty, thirty, and forty dollars to get out with a small proportion of their things. It is reported and believed that they have taken up a number of persons and committed them to jail, we know not for what in particular. Master Lovell is confined in a dungeon; a son of Mr. Edes is in jail; and one Wibert, a ship-carpenter, is on trial for his life. God alone knows to what length these wretches will go. We shall soon have no coffee, nor sugar, nor pepper here; but whortleberries and milk we are not obliged to commerce for."

Words were not strong enough to give expression to the hate and detestation felt for the Howes, and John Adams followed his gentle wife in vigorous denunciation of England. "We have nothing to hope for from our loving mother-country," he wrote, "but cruelties more abominable than those which are practised by the savage Indians." A few days later, Mrs. Adams received news from a man who escaped from Boston in a fishing schooner, and wrote to her husband :

"Their distress increases upon them fast. Their beef is all spent; their malt and cider all gone. All the fresh provisions they can procure they are obliged to give to the sick and wounded. . . . No man dared to be seen talking with his friend in the street. They were obliged to be within every evening at ten o'clock, according to martial law; nor could any inhabitant walk any street in town after that time without a pass from Gage. He has ordered all the molasses to be distilled into rum for the soldiers; taken away all licenses, and given out others; obliging to a forfeiture of ten pounds if any rum is sold without written orders from the general. . . . As to the situation of the camps, our men are in general healthy, much more so at Roxbury than at Cambridge. . . . Every article in the West India way is very scarce and dear. In six weeks we shall not be able to purchase any article of the kind. I wish you would let Bass get me one pound of pepper and two yards of black calamanco for shoes. I cannot wear leather, if I go barefoot. . . . Not one pin to be purchased for love or money."

A writer inside of the town wrote that the fare was "pork and beans one day and beans and pork another, and fish when we can catch it."

The officers of the British occupied the best dwellings they could find. Lord Percy lived a part of the time in the Gardiner Greene mansion,* and a part in a dwelling on the corner of Tremont and Winter streets, which was afterwards the home of Samuel Breck; Burgoyne was in the house of the learned James Bowdoin, who was governor of the State after the war †; General Clinton occupied the house of John Hancock, on Beacon Street, fronting the Common. The South meeting-house was used as a riding-school for the light dragoons; some other meeting-houses were occupied as barracks; the North meeting-house was pulled down for firewood, as were many other buildings of less pretence, including, probably, the house of John Winthrop, that stood near the Old South meeting-house. Cutting

---

* The estate of Gardiner Greene comprised the greater portion of Pemberton Hill, now kept in memory by Pemberton Square, and his dwelling was the finest in Boston.

† This house stood on Beacon Street, near the corner of the street that bears the governor's name. It stood back from the street, and, like the massive building now on the site, was approached by a long flight of stone steps.

down the Liberty Tree afforded the troops amusement one day.

The colonial congress met at Philadelphia May 10th, and George Washington, of Virginia, was appointed to take the lead of the armies of the united colonies. At the same period the citizens of Massachusetts, not being able to get at their rightful capital, formed a new government, organizing the " Territory of Massachusetts Bay," with its capital at Watertown, where the representatives and councillors, without any governor, held their sessions in the village meeting-house. Washington was appointed two days before the battle of Bunker Hill, and left for Cambridge as soon as he could, stopping at Watertown to pay his respects to the new government. On the third of July he took command of the forces, and began to establish discipline among the men, who were entirely unaccustomed to it. He made the blockade of Boston as complete as possible, and laid plans for the capture of the town.

On the other side of the sea, his Majesty George the Third, was fully occupied with considerations touching America. He recalled Gage so soon as the report of the " victory " at Bunker Hill was received, made arrangements with the ruler of Hesse to buy men to send over to fight his once loyal subjects in Boston. On the twenty-third of August, he made a proclamation for suppressing rebellion and sedition, in which he charged the colonists with forgetfulness of their allegiance, with obstructing commerce, with actual rebellion, and commanded all civil and military officers and all loyal subjects to use their utmost efforts to suppress the outbreak, promising " condign punishment" to the rebels themselves,—when caught. His Majesty declared that he was "unalterably determined at every hazard, and at the risk of every consequence, to compel the colonies to absolute submission," and the determination gave him the appearance of ease and composure, even of gayety, while it was said of his minister, Lord North, that neither he nor any one else had ever been seen in higher spirits.

The summer of 1775 was very hot, and it was followed by a winter of more than ordinary mildness. There was inactivity on both sides, and this was, of course, less endurable in the city than outside of it. The British found some enjoyment in a theatre that they improvised at Faneuil Hall, where amateurs took parts in plays selected or written for the occasions. One of these is credited to General Burgoyne. It was called "The Blockade of Boston," and on the eighth of January, 1776, when it was performing, and an actor was ridiculing Washington, the alarm was given that the Yankees were attacking Bunker Hill. The audience thought that this was a part of the play, until there came a sharp command: "Officers, to your posts!" and the performance was brought to a sudden and inglorious end. In the same month, arrangements were made for a masked ball, to be held on the eleventh of the following March. It was thus advertised:

Masquerade.

On Monday, the eleventh of March, will be given at Concert Hall, a Subscription Masked Ball.—By the fifth of March a number of different masks will be prepared and sold by almost all the milliners and mantua-makers in town.

The *News-Letter* referred to the ball in an editorial article, on the twenty-second of February, saying: "We hear ten capital cooks are already employed in preparing supper for the masquerade, which is to be the most brilliant thing ever seen in America."

Among the trusted military men about Washington was one whom he was wont to call the ablest engineer officer of the war, whether American or French. It was General Rufus Putnam, a veteran of the Old French War, who, with a regiment from Worcester County, had joined the camp at Cambridge, just after the battle at Lexington. Washington wished for ice on which he could transfer troops from Cambridge to Roxbury, in order that he might make an attack upon Boston from that side. The season was open, and ice did not form until near spring, and then the cold froze the ground so that it was like solid rock to the pickaxe. One evening during the winter Washington invited Putnam to dine at head-quarters, and detained him after the company had departed in order to discuss the subject on his mind. Putnam was ordered to consider the matter, and report at once if he should find any means of executing the plan. Putnam left in company with another gentleman, and, on the way, passed General Heath's. "I had no thoughts of calling," he relates, "until I came against his door, and then I said: 'Let us call on General Heath,' to which he agreed. I had no other motive but to pay my respects to the general. While there I cast my eye on a book which lay on the table, lettered on the back 'Muller's Field Engineer.' I immediately re-

quested the general to lend it to me. He denied
me. I repeated my request. He again refused, and
told me he never lent his books. I then told him that
he must recollect that he was one who, at Roxbury,
in a measure compelled me to undertake a business
which, at the time, I confessed I had never read a
word about, and that he must let me have the book.
After some more excuses on his part, and close
pressing on mine, I obtained the loan of it." When
Putnam glanced over the table of contents his eye
was attracted by the word "chandelier," which was
new to him. The word was described as applying
to a movable parapet of wood instead of earth, made
of stout timbers ten feet long, into which were
framed posts five feet high and five feet apart.
These were placed on the ground in parallel lines,
and the spaces were filled in with bundles of fascines
strongly picketed together. The problem was solved.

Washington decided to take advantage of the
return of the day of the "Massacre" to open his
fires. Putnam set men at work in apple orchards and
woodlands cutting and bundling up the fascines and
getting them ready for the appointed time. As has
been well said: "When the sun went down on Boston
on the fourth of March Washington was at Cambridge, and Dorchester Heights were as nature or
the husbandmen had left them in the autumn."
During that night troops were transported thither,
the chandeliers were put in position, the ground was
thrown up in the form of earthworks by willing
hands, and in the morning the British, looking through
a fog that had before covered the Americans and

now magnified the size of their works, found themselves overlooked by fortifications that seemed of indefinite magnitude. It took General Howe but twenty-four hours to decide that his position must be evacuated, and after a delay of some days, he acted upon that decision.

By four o'clock on Sunday morning, March 17th, the British began to embark on their ships, and by ten o'clock, so rapid was the movement, the vessels were all under sail, carrying with them such loyalists as had remained in the town to share the discomfiture. As the last passengers went on board, General Washington entered the abandoned town, crossing the Neck by the street which now bears his name in memory of the fact. He was received with acclamations as he passed along, for the citizens were happy to be released from their trials.

On the day that the mantua-makers were to have sold masks for the most brilliant ball ever seen in America, " an officer of distinction " wrote that the Americans had, during the previous night raised redoubts at Dorchester, " with an expedition equal to that of the genii belonging to Aladdin's wonderful lamp "; and the next day he continued : " We are now evacuating the town with the utmost expedition, and are leaving behind us half our worldly goods." Before the day arrived that had been set for the ball, Boston was in utter confusion, in vigorous efforts to complete what the same distinguished officer called " the retreat from the town." If the " ten cooks " prepared the supper of which the editor of the *News-Letter* heard, they lost their labor. At noon of the day of Washington's entry, Mrs. Adams wrote :

"To what a contemptible situation are the troops of Britain reduced ! . . . I hear that General Howe said, upon going on some eminence to view our troops, who had taken Dorchester Hill unperceived by them until sunrise : ' My God ! these fellows have done more work in one night than I could make my army do in three months.' And he might well say so, for in one night two forts and long breastworks were sprung up, besides several barracks. Three hundred and seventy teams were employed, most of which went three loads in the night, besides four thousand men, who worked with good hearts. From Penn's Hill we have a view of the largest fleet ever seen in America. You may count upwards of one hundred and seventy sail. They look like a forest."

The close of the siege of Boston is also the close of a period in the existence of the town. Previously to that event it had been the most important place in the colonies, and the one against which the British ministry aimed their most virulent shafts. The siege reduced the population to about six thousand inhabitants, though there had been more than three times as many before, and during the period of recuperation that followed, it contained but little more than twelve thousand inhabitants, while New York had more than twice as many. The heroic age of Boston ended when Washington took possession of it for America. There was thereafter no more war within its limits ; there was no longer a struggle for a charter ; there was no odious tax to be discussed, denounced, and rebelled against; thenceforth there was only the practice of the arts of peace, of commercial enterprise, varied by exhibitions of patriotism when any other portion of the land was aggrieved, when the life of the nation itself was threatened. Boston was destined to grow in the lines that the fathers laid out for it, to become rich and to be useful; but never again was it to have an heroic age.

XXVI.

INDEPENDENCE DECLARED AND WON.

AFTER the departure of the British, the scene of action for the men of Massachusetts changed, and the more enlarged sphere opened to such men as Samuel and John Adams, Hancock, Cushing, and the others who had made the town-meeting and the provincial legislature their means of influencing public opinion. It has been said that " no other town ever played so conspicuous a part in connexion with important events " as Boston did in the early period. Samuel Adams, said Hutchinson with truth, depended upon the town-meeting, where he originated the measures that were followed by the other towns in the province, and adopted and justified by the legislature, and, he might have added, were considered at Philadelphia, and, by his influence there, made a part of the impulse that stirred the continent. Massachusetts thus, through its representatives, moved the general congress; Boston gave the cue to Massachusetts, and Samuel Adams ruled Boston. Jefferson considered Samuel Adams, " more than any other member of congress, the fountain of the most important measures," and declared that " if there was any Palinurus to the Revolution," he was the man. Adams was constantly holding caucuses in Philadelphia, as he had held them in Boston, that were attended by distinguished men, where "the generality of the measures pursued were previously determined on, and at which the parts were assigned to the different actors who afterwards appeared in them. John Adams had a very little part in these caucuses; but as one of the actors in the measures decided on in them, he was the Colossus." *

At an early period Samuel Adams was called "the Father of America," and certainly no one better deserved the title; after his death he was spoken of as the "Father of the American Revolution," and no one could dispute that honor with him. It is not our province to follow the events that Massachusetts men were engaged in after they called them away from Boston, but some reference to contemporary history is unavoidable.

The British fleet remained in the harbor some time after the evacuation of Boston, and deserters reported that there was much sickness among the men. Efforts were initiated for setting fire to the vessels, but before they were ready the ships sailed away, perhaps informed of the proposed attempt. Washington went away in April, 1776, leaving Artemas Ward in command, and he was followed in succession by Heath and Gates. Efforts were made to fortify Fort Hill; the islands were inspected, and slowly the place was made strong; but there were occasional alarms lest the fleet should return and do damage. When the inhabitants recovered from

* Thomas Jefferson, under date 1825.

their amazement and looked around, they found their homes in many cases devastated, though a few of the occupants at the time of the siege had left sums of money for them in the nature of rent. Goods were held at extravagant prices in the two or three shops open, and it was difficult to obtain men to do necessary work. The fortifications erected by Gage on the Neck were soon levelled, and the two thousand effective men that Washington left, when he went to the southward, were put in the best order possible for the protection of the town.

The Americans watched the movements of the ships that came toward Boston, as well as of those that went from it, and in May a large armed ship, named the *Hope*, appeared, bringing supplies to the town, which was thought to be still occupied by a British garrison. Ward had commissioned a brave captain, named Mugford, to watch for such vessels, and he attacked this one, which proved to have on board among its cargo a supply of powder, which was then much needed. Mugford carried her safely to Boston. There were other similar captures, which relieved the Bostonians and were thankfully acknowledged. Mrs. Adams wrote:

"The remarkable interpositions of Heaven in our behalf cannot be too gratefully acknowledged. He who fed the Israelites in the wilderness, 'who clothes the lilies of the field, and feeds the young ravens when they cry,' will not forsake a people engaged in so righteous a cause, if we remember his loving-kindness. We wanted powder—we have a supply. We wanted arms—we have been favored in that respect. We wanted hard money—

twenty-two thousand dollars and an equal value in plate are delivered into our hands."

Congress was in session at Philadelphia, and on the nineteenth of May, 1776, a vote was passed, recommending each of the colonies to form a local government. The resolution asserted that it was irreconcilable with the conscience and reason of the people to take oaths to support the royal governments, that all such ought to be suppressed, and governments established that depended upon the power of the sovereign people. The tories opposed this, of course, and so did the representatives of the proprietary governments of the middle colonies, and there was an outburst of bitter passion; but all opposition was powerless, and the resolution became the platform of the popular party, the touchstone of fidelity. Massachusetts, we know, had already taken this action; New Hampshire had followed in January, 1776; and South Carolina did the same March 26th that year. A few days before this, the most influential member of the Massachusetts legislature, then in session at Watertown, wrote:

"The tories dread a declaration of independence, and a course of conduct on that plan, worse than death. . . . My hand and heart are full of it. There will be no abiding union without it. . . . Without a real continental government, our army will overrun us; and people will, by and by,—sooner than you may be aware of, —call for their old constitutions, as they did in England, after Cromwell's death, call in Charles the Second. For God's sake, let there be a full revolution, or all has been done in vain. Independency and a well-planned continental government will save us. God bless you! Amen and amen!"

One branch of the Massachusetts legislature passed a vote in favor of a declaration of independence, but the other refused to agree until Congress had legislated on the subject, because it was considered that such action might appear dictatorial, and thus injure the cause. Both branches agreed, however, on an act requiring all citizens to "defend by arms the United Colonies, and every part thereof," against the fleets and armies of Britain, and the towns were called upon to meet and determine whether, in case Congress should declare for independence, they would solemnly engage with their lives and fortunes to support the measure. Accordingly, the towns met in May and June, and voted, that if the American Republic were not established, the age would be recreant to its duty; that there was no alternative but ruin or independence; that they would defend such a measure to the death, as the various phraseology ran.

"In this way, from the battlefields of Lexington and Concord, from the ruins at the base of Bunker Hill, from Faneuil Hall, from a hundred villages aglow with patriotic fires, went forth the pledge of determined and stern men to support such a declaration as Congress might make with their fortunes and their lives." *

Twelve of the thirteen colonies (all, except New York) had, by the end of June, given their voices in favor of a declaration of independence, and had designated Congress as the body to take the final action.

* Frothingham, "The Rise of the Republic," pages 507, 508.

Under these circumstances Congress met at Philadelphia on the first of July, having among its number two members,—Samuel Adams and John Hancock,—who were outlaws, proscribed by the king, and it set itself to the consideration of independency, the only topic that seemed of present importance. John Adams, of Massachusetts, was called upon to present the arguments in favor of the step that seemed to be demanded. He rose reluctantly and somewhat confused, he said, and expressed his views. The debate that followed was not long, and on the following day it was solemnly resolved that "These United Colonies are and of right ought to be free and independent states; that they are absolved from all allegiance to the British crown; and that all political connexion between them and the state of Great Britain is and ought to be totally dissolved." Then John Adams wrote to his wife:

"The greatest question has been decided which ever was debated in America, and a greater perhaps than ever was or will be decided among men. . . . When I look back to the year 1761, and recollect the argument concerning the writs of assistance in the Superior Court, which I have hitherto considered as the commencement of this controversy between Great Britain and America, and run through the whole period from that time to this, and recollect the series of political events, the chain of causes and effects, I am surprised at the suddenness as well as the greatness of this revolution. Britain has been filled with folly and America with wisdom, at least this is my judgment. Time must determine. It is the will of heaven that the two countries should be sundered forever."

John Adams said that the second day of July ought to be celebrated as a great anniversary festival by succeeding generations,—" commemorated as a day of deliverance,—by solemn acts of devotion to God Almighty. It ought to be solemnized with pomp and parade, with shows, games, sports, guns, bells, bonfires, and illuminations from one end of this continent to the other, from this time forward forevermore."

How was the news that Adams sent to his wife with such an outburst of patriotic enthusiasm, received in Boston? The day of the Thursday lecture was set apart for the reading of the Declaration, and after a good sermon the congregation followed the crowd to King Street. The town was thronged by crowds in holiday suits, with joy beaming from every eye. Artillery was drawn up in front of the jail on Court Street, and infantry lined the adjoining streets. Exactly as the clock struck one, Colonel Thomas Crafts appeared on the balcony of the State House, and read the Declaration, the great audience listening with attention to every word. When he sat down a shout, " God save our American States!" was heard in the hall, to which the throng below responded with three hearty cheers; the bells rang, cannon were discharged from the shipping and from the forts and batteries, the infantry followed, and Mr. Bowdoin gave the sentiment, " Stability and Perpetuity to American Independence!" The better class of citizens attended a banquet in the council-chamber; much liquor was distributed to the populace, according to the old custom; and the king's arms were taken down from the town-house, custom-house, court-house, and every other place, and consumed in a general bonfire in front of the Bunch of Grapes tavern at the corner of Kilby and State streets. In the evening there was a general illumination, and as Mrs. Adams wrote: "Thus ends royal authority in this state; and all the people shall say amen!" On the fifteenth of August, by order of the council, Dr. Chauncy read the Declaration from the pulpit of the Brick Church, which stood on the spot now occupied by the Joy Building, on Washington Street, and asked a "blessing upon the United States of America, even until the restitution of all things," in a manner that universally struck his audience. Mrs. Adams thought, however, that Boston was behind the other colonies in joy over the establishment of the new government.

Both John Adams and his wife had high notions of what ought to be expected of Boston, and in many respects they doubtless were right. Mr. Adams wrote from Philadelphia that there was no one thing in which Massachusetts excelled the other colonies so much as in its university, scholars, and preachers. "Particular gentlemen, here," he added, "who have improved upon their education by travel, shine; but in general old Massachusetts outshines her younger sisters. Still, in several particulars they have more wit than we. They have societies, the Philosophical Society, particularly, which excites a scientific emulation, and propagates their fame. . . . My countrymen want art and address. They want knowledge of the world. They want the exterior and superficial accomplishments of gentlemen, upon which the world has set so high a value. In solid abilities and real virtues they vastly excel, in general, any people upon this continent. Our New England people are awkward, and bashful, yet they are pert, ostentatious, and vain; a mixture which excites ridicule and gives disgust. They have not the faculty of showing themselves to the best advantage, nor the art of concealing this faculty; an art and faculty which some people possess in the highest degree. Our deficiencies in these respects are owing wholly to the little intercourse we have had with strangers, and to our inexperience in the world. These imperfections must be remedied, for New England must produce the heroes, the statesmen, the philosophers, or America will make no great figure for some time." *

At this time the cost of living was double what it had been the year previous; the merchant complained of the farmer, and the farmer of the merchant, but both were alike extravagant, in the opinion of the buyer. Mrs. Adams wrote to her husband that she wished a little green tea, for there was none to be had in Boston; but she explained that she merely wished it as a " medicine and as a relief to a nervous pain " in her head, and added, perhaps to show the unreasonableness of human nature: " Were it as plenty as ever, I would not practise the use of it." With the progress of the war there came a gradual change in Boston society, and extravagance of manners and of equipage fol-

* " Familiar Letters of John Adams and his Wife," page 207.

lowed. Mr. Curwen in his diary relates (February 10, 1780) that those who in 1772 were the "meaner people," became a few years later, by a strange revolution, almost the only men of power, riches, and influence, while those who at that time had been leaders in the highest line of life, were happy if by remaining unknown they could escape "insult and plunder." This is the opinion of a loyalist, who had left his country to escape the indignation of the patriotic people; but Mrs. Adams wrote to her husband that a lethargy seemed to have overcome the people, that there was a great rage for privateering as a means of gaining riches; that the town of Boston seemed to be really destitute of the choice spirits that once inhabited it; that though she had not heard that toryism was on the increase, there was a spirit of avarice, a contempt of authority, an inordinate love of gain, and that prices of ordinary necessaries of life were exorbitant, in spite of an ordinance vainly passed for the purpose of restraining speculation. New England rum was, in the spring of 1777, as high as eight shillings a gallon, and molasses the same; coffee, two and sixpence a pound; and mutton, lamb, and pork not to be had at any price. There were those who refused to take paper-money, offered articles for sale at a lower price for silver, and bought up goods for the purpose of speculation, which they would not sell at any price for paper. Five of these were, one Saturday afternoon, in April, 1777, carted through the streets of Boston to Roxbury, followed by a concourse of some five hundred persons, under command of one "Joice junior," who was on horseback, dressed in a white wig, a red coat, and bearing a drawn sword. The drum and fife made music. When Roxbury was reached Joice ordered the cart tipped up, and the men were informed that if they were found in Boston again it would be at the expense of their lives. "Joice junior" was a name given to a man appointed to this duty of terrifying royalists, and it seems that he attended well to his work.

A little later, a number of "females," angry because some merchants held their sugar for a rise in price, went to the store of one of them, Thomas Boylston, a bachelor, called by Mrs. Adams "eminent, wealthy, stingy," and demanded his keys, which he refused to give up. They were provided with carts and trucks, and Mr. Boylston was quickly seized by the neck and tossed into one of them; whereupon he delivered up his keys and was tipped out again. The warehouse was opened, and a hogshead of coffee was hoisted out and carried away. It is related that "a large concourse of men stood amazed, silent spectators of the whole transaction."

Less than a week after this all Boston was in confusion, for there was a rumor that the enemy was about to attack it. People were seen hastily packing up and carting from the town all the household goods, merchandise and military stores that could be gathered together at once, and a thousand teams were employed in taking them into the country. The alarm was, however, found to have been baseless. The progress of the war led the people to seek to cultivate their own resources, and among other expedients it was thought that molasses and even sugar might be obtained from the corn-stalk. Scarcely a town about Boston was without mills for the purpose of crushing the stalks and making molasses, which it was thought might be boiled down into sugar.

The news of the surrender of Burgoyne's army at Saratoga, in October, 1777, was received in Boston with the usual demonstrations of joy. A service of thanksgiving and praise was held on the twenty-sixth of the month, and the "vaporing Burgoyne" was expected in Cambridge soon after. The general himself entered town in a pelting storm, and was quartered at Porter's Hotel, then Bradish's Tavern, which was afterwards exchanged for the large dwelling opposite the college library, often called the "Bishop's Palace." The captured artillery was parked on the Common. General Riedesel and his wife were assigned to the "Jonathan Sewall house," which then stood on the corner of Brattle and Sparks streets, but now, in a considerably altered condition, has found a resting-place on the corner next beyond, the street being named in honor of the baron. The Hessian and English soldiers were strictly guarded by Massachusetts militia. They were sent in detachments to the interior of the State, the last leaving in October, 1778.

Though Mrs. Adams had not heard of the appearance of toryism, it seems that the spirit made itself felt in the spring elections in Boston in 1778, when some of those who had gone to Halifax with Howe returned and asked to be permitted to resume their former rights and residence. Samuel Adams especially was positive against such action. He had wished to see Boston a "Christian Sparta," and he felt that the influence of the tories was always on the side of display and ostentation, of extravagance and luxury, which he thought demoralizing to the community and fatal to liberty. He felt sure that the tories were all watching for an opportunity to return and damage the prospects of the country, and he thought it unwise as well as impolitic to give them any assistance in their evil work.

Samuel Adams had been made Secretary of State in 1775, and though he was much of the time absent at Philadelphia he was continued in office, performing its duties personally when in Boston and through a deputy at other times. In the summer of 1779 he returned to his home, but it was to find Boston society quite different from what it had been when he first began the fight for independence. Otis was gone, Warren was gone, Josiah Quincy junior had died abroad, and Hancock, whom he had brought to the front, had become his bitter opponent. The characters of Samuel Adams and John Hancock were directly opposite to one another. Adams now came back by slow stages on horseback to an humble home destitute of every luxury, which he occupied by the liberality of the legislature, for he had never been able to repair his Purchase Street dwelling after the depredations of the British during the siege. Hancock travelled from Philadelphia accompanied by a guard of cavalry, and housed himself in a mansion adorned with all that money could buy, in which he lavishly entertained the rich and the great. Hancock, who had opposed the scheme for the committees of correspondence, which had been so warmly adopted by Samuel Adams and proved so useful, came again into antagonism with him when he seconded the motion of John Adams that Washington should be commander-in-chief of the colonial forces. The feelings of Hancock against Adams must for some years have been of the worst, but they were changed in 1788, when the twain were candidates together for office in their native state, and their names were printed in letters of gold on the electoral tickets in token of the gratification that the fact gave to their supporters.

In the autumn of 1780 the first election occurred under a new state constitution that had been adopted the previous spring,[*] and Hancock was elected governor. The occasion of the beginning of the new government was made the excuse for a round of balls and entertainments that Samuel Adams thought inconsistent with the sober republican principles in which it was founded. "Why," he wrote to a friend, "should this new era be introduced with entertainments expensive and tending to dissipate the minds of the people? Does it become us to lead the people to such public diversions as promote superfluity of dress and ornament, when it is as much as they can bear to support the expense of clothing the naked army? Will vanity and levity ever be the stability of government, either in state or in cities,

[*] This constitution, which was largely moulded by Adams, was read by him to the people assembled in Faneuil Hall, May 3, 1780.

or, what, let me hint to you, is of the last importance, in families?" Adams struck not only at the abuse, but at his former friend when he thus wrote, for it was the influence of Hancock that led to these glittering assemblages which the patriots thought inconsistent with former professions, as well as with the true spirit of republicanism. There were meetings in Faneuil Hall to protest against extravagance; but though Samuel Adams presided, the meetings were not like those of a few years before.

"The voice that once made George the Third through fear turn cold," was listened to, but the men upon whom it spent itself were not those of other days and the effect was small. Adams wrote:

"It was asked in the reign of Charles the Second of England, How shall we turn the minds of the people from an attention to their liberties? The answer was, By making them extravagant, luxurious, and effeminate, Hutchinson advised the abridgement of what are called English liberties by the same means. We shall never subdue them, said Bernard, but by eradicating their manners and the principles of their education. . . . Pownall, who was, indeed, a mere fribble, ventured to have his riots and his routs at his own house to please a few boys and girls. Sober people were disgusted at it, and his privy-councillors never thought it prudent to venture so far as expensive balls. Our Bradfords, Winslows and Winthrops would have revolted at the idea of opening scenes of dissipation and folly, knowing them to be inconsistent with their great design in transplanting themselves into what they called this 'outside of the world.'"

These were by no means mere words with Adams. While he had been away from Boston his wife had supported his family by the labor of her own hands, and when he was at home he did not suffer a complaint to escape him on account of the hardness of his lot. He gave up his all for his country, and uttered no murmur. He proved the honesty of his words by his works.

John Adams also preached and practised economy and modesty in personal and public expenses. In 1778 he wrote to his wife from Passy, where he was in the capacity of commissioner at the French court:

"My dear countrymen! how shall I pursuade you to avoid the plague of Europe! Luxury has as many and as bewitching charms on your side of the ocean as on this; and luxury, wherever she goes, effaces from human nature the image of the divinity. If I had power I should forever banish and exclude from America all gold, silver, precious stones, alabaster, marble, silk, velvet, and lace. 'Oh, the tyrant!' the American ladies would say. What! Aye, my dear girls, these passions of yours which are so easily alarmed, and others of my own sex which are exactly like them, have done and will do the work of tyrants in all ages. Tyrants different from me, whose power has banished, not gold, indeed, but other things of greater value: wisdom, virtue, and liberty."

John Adams exemplified his personal modesty in the response that he made when some one in France asked him if he were the "famous Adams." He replied that he was only the cousin of that distinguished person. Certainly, however, he was a famous Adams.

While John Adams was in France trying to strengthen the ties that bound the two nations, he was cautious enough to see that the connexion might be a dangerous one, and feared lest French counsels should have too great weight in American affairs. The alliance that he saw was of greatest moment to the united colonies was threatened with rupture after the attack on Newport, in 1778, then, and for two years previously, in the hands of the British. General Sullivan attributed the failure of that expedition to the action of the French fleet under d'Estaing, and there were many ready to reanimate the ancient animosity of the times of the French and Indian wars; the tories, too, were on hand to fan the flame which they saw would tend to weaken the French alliance. There was a serious riot in Boston caused by these ill feelings between the French and American seamen. Samuel Adams and Washington endeavored to promote harmony, and Hancock gave the officers lavish entertainment in his great mansion, where thirty or more were dined daily, with a profuse exhibition of the plate and livery that both the Adamses abhorred. Hancock gave them also a great ball at Concert Hall, on the corner of Court (then Queen Street) and Hanover streets (October 29th). This hall was many years after still the most elegant place of the kind in town, and had then long been the principal headquarters of the friends of liberty. Mrs. Adams reported to her husband, then in France, that she saw much of the officers of the French fleet, that d'Estaing had been very polite to her, and that she had dined on the vessels, being on one occasion "sumptuously entertained with every delicacy that this country produces, and the addition of every foreign article that could render our feast splendid. Music and dancing for the young folks closed the day. The temperance of these gentlemen," she continued, " the peaceable, quiet disposition, both of officers and men, joined to many other virtues which they have exhibited during their continuance with us, are sufficient to make Europeans, and Americans, too, blush at their own degeneracy of manners. Not one officer has been seen the least disguised with liquor since their arrival. Most that I have seen appear to have been gentlemen of family and education. I have been the more desirous to take notice of them, as I cannot help saying that they have been neglected in the town of Boston. Generals Heath and Hancock have done their part, but very few, if any, private families have any acquaintance with them." Mrs. Adams anticipated the wishes of her husband, who was anxious lest the affair at Newport should produce heartburnings, as he wrote to her when the news reached him in November.

The victory of October, 1781, at Yorktown caused great joy in Boston, intensified by the depression of the previous months, and when, in the autumn of of 1782, the French army was in Boston, which had marched from the Hudson to set sail for the West Indies, her citizens, in town-meeting, under the familiar lead of Samuel Adams, finally expressed the sense of gratitude and obligation that was felt by all true Americans for their assistance in the war.

XXVII.

THE OLD ORDER CHANGETH.

WHEN peace came to the country, Boston town entered upon a new stage of existence. A new aristocracy took the lead in its affairs; the men of wealth and station who had formed the court of the royal governors—who had succeeded to the places once filled by Winthrop and those who followed him—were gone, and their estates were confiscated. In their stead there stood forward men who had made solid, but sudden, fortunes during the war. It was of some of these that Samuel Curwen, the royalist refugee, wrote to William Brown, also a refugee from Salem, afterwards governor of Bermuda:

"It is a melancholy truth that whilst some are wallowing in undeserved wealth that plunder and rapine have thrown into their hands, the wisest, most peaceable and most deserving, such as you and I know, are now suffering want, accompanied by indignities that a licentious, lawless people can pour forth upon them. Those who five years ago [that is, before the war] were the 'meaner people," are now, by a strange revolution, become almost the only men of power, riches, and influence; those who, on the contrary, were leaders and in the highest line of life, are glad by this time to be unknown and unnoticed, to escape insult and plunder—the wretched condition of all who are not violent, and adopters of Republican principles."*

There had, indeed, been a "revolution" in politics, commerce, and social life. Old Boston was never to be what it had been, though the seeds sown through the years that had elapsed since the first step was taken by Winthrop and his fellows in England were to bear much fruit, and it remains for us to ask what that fruit was. The war had changed every thing; not only were the most forward people " new," but the very streets themselves began to change, and those regions that before the war had been frequented by the fashion and wealth of the day, were by degrees deserted, and the move toward the south and west ends began. The North End, especially, lost by degrees its precedence, and in process of time was almost completely abandoned by those families which had given it its character.† The population

---

* "The Journal and Letters of Samuel Curwen," page 256.

† Boston was divided into three natural parts. The "North End," containing about seven hundred dwelling-houses and tenements, and six meeting-houses, which was the court end before the Revolution, extending only to Blackstone Street. The " West End," or " New Boston," comprised less than two hundred dwellings and tenements, and one meeting-house. It was somewhat sheltered from the east winds, and was very pleasant. The largest territorial division was the " South End," practically ending at Dover Street, which included all the regions south of Blackstone Street and east of the present Tremont Street. In this part of town were all of the public buildings (except the powder-house), and there were ten meeting-houses and more than twelve hundred dwellings, some of them elegant. It was the seat of business, and contained the principal shops and warehouses. Shurtleff's "Topographical and Historical Description of Boston," page 138.

was much less at the end of the war than it had been at the opening of hostilities, and New York and Philadelphia then took the lead that they have kept. It was ten years before Boston regained its former numerical strength.

Commerce and manufactures had suffered, and, like the confederacy, the town and the state were unable to pay their debts. It was the first duty of the townspeople to make efforts to retrieve their financial losses. Though, as has been said, "the great industries which have built up the Massachusetts of our time, in a material sense, were established on quite a secure footing" during the first generation of the history of Boston, yet shipbuilding, fishing and navigation were the most prominent occupations before the Revolution, while rum was the chief manufacture.* In a statement of the commercial condition of Massachusetts, made in 1750, the importance of the manufacture of rum was distinctly shown.† The course of trade was exhibited thus:

"A great part of the inhabitants of Massachusetts Bay live chiefly by the sea, and are employed in fisheries, navigation, and building and providing materials for ships. They depend on Great Britain for clothes, materials for furnishing their houses, cordage and sail-cloth for equipment of their vessels, their lines, hooks and cables for the fishery. They are dependent on the northern colonies for bread corn. Rum is their chief

---

* Winsor's "Memorial History of Boston," vol. iv., page 69.
† Minot's continuation of Thomas Hutchinson's "History of the Province of Massachusetts Bay," vol. i., page 155.

manufacture, there being upwards of fifteen thousand hogsheads of rum manufactured in the province annually. This, with what they get from the English islands, is the grand support of all their trades and fishery, and without it they can no longer subsist. Rum is a standing article in the Indian trade and the common drink of all the laborers, timber-men, mast-men, loggers and fishermen in the province. These men could not endure the hardships of their employments nor the rigor of the seasons without it. . . . The rum carried from Massachusetts Bay, and other northern colonies, to the coast of Guinea, is exchanged for gold and slaves. The gold is sent to London to help pay for their annual supplies, and the slaves are carried to the English sugar colonies, and exchanged for their commodities."

This extract illustrates the character of the commercial activity of the Bostonians, as well as the freedom with which they used a particular creature comfort, and the dependence of the people upon the mother-country for most of their manufactured articles. When the Revolution began, Boston families expected that the household loom would give them most of their textile fabrics, and it was the good pleasure of England that no provision more systematic and extensive should be introduced, for it would deprive her of a market for her goods if America should supply herself. Of what good, indeed, were colonies, if they did not stimulate the industry and commerce of the land from which their settlers went forth? Such was the narrow policy accepted generally in Europe, and England was only following the fashion in endeavoring to restrict the Americans.

During the war, not only political but also industrial independence had been aimed at, and manufactures were encouraged so effectually that when the struggle ended there was apparent prosperity in business circles. Many fortunes had been accumulated, also, in the dangerous pursuits of the privateersman, and as commerce increased after the peace, an era of extravagance opened, and luxuries and comforts previously unknown were found in Boston homes. Still, in the average household the comforts were few, if compared with the condition of affairs in our day. The house was perhaps unpainted; sand was still strewed over the floors instead of carpets; great caverns yawned at the chimney side, and poured forth apparently but one half of the heat of the burning logs, and more than that proportion of the blinding smoke. Electricity, gas, and even kerosene oil, for purposes of lighting, were not dreamed of, and dimly burning whale oil made the darkness visible and the atmosphere detestable. Dress was thoroughly studied, both in regard to fashion and cost, and carefully preserved, so that many a fair bride's wedding gown has been carried down to a generation which will never preserve its own less costly garments for a granddaughter or great-granddaughter.

The burden of debt left by war to which reference has been made, was so great that commerce soon began to feel its influence. This, united with the extravagance of the times, brought many debtors into the hands of the law, and very soon dissatisfied men, especially in the western part of Massachusetts, began to inveigh against the courts as " engines of

JOHN HANCOCK'S HOUSE, FACING THE COMMON.

destruction," and in a few years the outburst known as the "Shay's Rebellion" disturbed the commonwealth. Demagogues and tories were interested thus to break the public peace in the hopes of making some nefarious gain.

It is evident that quite different public men were needed for these times of building up a commonwealth from those who fought the battle of freedom and won the prize independence. Samuel Adams showed himself unadapted to the times. He was not at home in the extravagant routs and balls and glittering assemblies that are noted in the history of the period, though doubtless they were innocent and even tame in comparison with similar dissipations at the present day. He came into conflict with his ancient ally, Hancock, in this matter, for Hancock was, as we know, of an ostentatious and profuse hospitality, and went to extremes in his efforts to surround himself as governor with consequence and dignity. Mr. Hancock carried his notions of official dignity too far at times. In the autumn of 1789, the year after the adoption of the federal constitution, Washington visited Boston, and was received with every token of reverential delight. In Cambridge, where he stopped an hour to look at his former headquarters, a thousand militia-men in line formally saluted him, and a long procession escorted him to the State House, where an ode in his honor was sung by a choir in a triumphal arch near by. Hancock, who was then governor, chose to expect the president to call and pay his respects to the chief magistrate of the commonwealth, but as Washington did not agree with him, Hancock called in his old friend the gout, and, making that an excuse for more prompt action, appeared at the president's quarters swathed in flannel and carried on the shoulders of attendants. State sovereignty bowed to federal supremacy, and all went well!

Adams was firmly opposed to any treaty of peace with England unless the full rights of the Americans in the Newfoundland fisheries were restored and confirmed, for their value to Boston trade was esteemed then even more than in after-times. Under his influence the reigning toast in the East was, according to Marbois the French agent, " No peace without the fisheries." Adams also resisted all measures designed to reinstate the tories in their previous position of respect or even toleration. He considered them traitors to the American cause, and not entitled to any mercy. Though much in public life, though three times chosen governor of the state, and always possessed of great influence, he did not move the people as in former times. When the question of adopting the constitution of the nation came up in 1788, he was fearful lest the people were founding a federal union which would swiftly and imperceptibly run into a consolidated government, pervading and legislating through all the states; not for federal purposes only, as it professed, but in all cases whatsoever. Such a government, he thought, would soon totally annihilate the sovereignty of the several states, so necessary to the support of the confederated commonwealth, and sink both in despotism.* While op-

* See letter to Richard Henry Lee, quoted in Wells's "Life," vol. iii., page 273.

posing the hasty rejection of the constitution, Adams urged the adoption of an amendment which should give security on this point.

The struggle that preceded the adoption of the constitution in 1788 was long and active, and divided the people of Boston into two parties, that became well defined. The opponents of a strong central government, who had sympathized with the Shays' rebellion, took sides against it; but the conservatives, now called Federalists, firmly supported the constitution, and labored for a strong republican government which could make itself respected at home and abroad. Hancock was brought over to this side, as has already been stated,* and, by means of a meeting of the mechanics at the Green Dragon tavern, under the lead of Paul Revere, Adams was influenced to give it his still influential help. The Federalists won the day, having a majority of nineteen votes, and the decision was solemnly declared in the church on Long Lane, where the sessions had been held. The church and street were thenceforward known by the name Federal Street. There was great joy on this occasion; the citizens went in procession to the houses of the representatives of the town who had sat in the convention, and saluted them; there were appropriate badges on the rejoicing citizens, and there were salutes from cannon, and finally a dinner in Faneuil Hall. In 1797 Mr. Adams finally retired from political life, his last public paper being a proclamation for the annual Fast Day. The Father of the American Revolution

---

* See page 350.

lived until Sunday morning, October 2, 1803, when his long and useful life came to an end.

During the last years of the life of Mr. Adams, slavery, though never formally abolished, came to an end in the state, and in 1783 it was declared from the bench that it no longer existed. Previous to that date the newspapers familiarized the minds of the people with the good points of "prime young slaves from the Windward Coast," or the bad traits of "a pock-broken fellow, a scar on one of his shins," who had "lost one of his fore teeth, and pretended to be a doctor," a fugitive from a perhaps not too indulgent master. "A likely hearty male negro child" is offered to be given away, or a likely negro woman "about thirty-five years of age," recommended for her honesty, is offered for sale cheap for cash. After 1783 such things ceased to be.

The next year Boston was stirred, or rather many patriots were stirred, with apprehensions lest the newly formed society of the Cincinnati should give birth to an aristocracy, should become joint proprietors of vast tracts of land, people their territories with multitudes from Germany, oblige them to live in feudal servitude, and thus raise up something like the mediæval system, dangerous to the state. Such fears seem absurd to us now, when the government has proved its strength for a hundred years, but at that time, when the very existence of the Union was new and experimental, it is not strange that those who, like Adams, had struggled for independence, trembled at the thought of any risk.

Before the tumults of war had yet left the

citizens of Boston to the quiet necessary for the conquests of peace, some of them began to look towards the Great West, and to ask themselves what might be done to extend to those little-known regions the benefits that the war had been fought to obtain. It was a natural fruit of the education through which the town had passed under the guidance of such men as Adams, and it became a marked trait in the character of the Bostonians. They never ceased to endeavor to influence the other portions of the land in the direction of right, as they conceived it.

It was on the first day of March that a seed was dropped in the familiar " Bunch of Grapes " tavern, which bore fruit in the " Northwestern Territory," and gave their permanent character to the states which were formed in that region. Soon after peace General Rufus Putnam, an officer of the Massachusetts line, the same one who had furnished the successful plan for the fortifications on Dorchester Heights, in company with two hundred and eighty-two other officers, petitioned Congress for a grant of lands in this region, and Putnam himself wrote an elaborate letter to Washington requesting his influence in its favor. In this letter the veteran officer, who had practical knowledge of the work of a surveyor, suggested the plan for the districting of the region, and he also urged the setting apart of a portion of each township for the support of schools and the ministry, a plan which was adopted and has ever since been followed. Putnam rightly thought that it was " of great consequence to the American empire," that the vast region south of the lakes should be filled with inhabitants who should be loyal subjects of the United States, and "banish forever the idea of our western territory falling under the dominion of any European power," as well as that the eastern States should thus be "effectually secured from savage alarms." He wrote to Washington again, in 1784, that the settlement of the Ohio country engrossed his thoughts and much of his time, and that he believed that there were thousands who would remove thither as soon as Congress should open the way. Little did he dream of the great immigrations of subsequent years. In June, 1785, Putnam received in Boston notice that Congress had appointed him one of the surveyors of the Ohio lands, but being at the time otherwise occupied, he urged the substitution of General Benjamin Tupper, another Massachusetts soldier, and that gentleman went to the Ohio country. Tupper returned with testimony that increased Putnam's interest in the proposed colonization scheme. The two Massachusetts generals therefore proposed an association for the purpose of buying lands of the government, and once, on the ninth of January, they spent almost the whole of the night in conference on the momentous subject. The result was that the next morning they composed a circular proposing a convention for the purpose of perfecting an association uniting the officers and soldiers who had served in the war, as well as "all other good citizens who wish to become adventurers in that delightful region." So slow were the methods of publication at the time that it was not until the twenty-fifth of January, 1786, that the persons appealed to read in the public prints under the head, "INFORMATION," the call that was put forth by the two generals. The meeting was held at the "Bunch of Grapes," as we have said, and an association formed. It included Manasseh Cutler, who carried the negotiation with Congress to a successful termination, and Winthrop Sargent, who became secretary, and rendered important assistance. Other meetings were held at Bracket's tavern, otherwise known as "Cromwell's Head," on Latin-school Street, but with them we cannot meddle. It is sufficient to record the impulse that Boston gave to western immigration at the important moment when its character was to be formed. It was certainly a Boston notion, that of setting off two full townships for a university, and two particular sections of a mile square in every township for the support of schools and religion.*

Though all New England was interested in the scheme for the settlement of the Ohio region, and though many Boston men were specially attracted to it, it was but one among many movements for the increase of the influence and wealth of the town which had their birth in the years following the close of the war. Probably the building of the bridge to Charlestown is as good an indication as any of the progress in material resources, for it was the greatest undertaking of the kind that had ever been projected in America. There was still but one mode

---

* In order that there might be no doubt about this latter provision the sections numbered sixteen and twenty-nine were specified.

of access to Boston—the Neck. The new bridge was fifteen hundred and three feet long and forty-three feet wide, and it was formally opened on the anniversary of the battle of Bunker Hill, in 1786. There were military salutes at sunrise, and peals from the bells of the church which served as a beacon when Paul Revere wished to warn the people of Charlestown that the British were leaving Boston for Lexington by water. A procession consisting " of almost every respectable character in public and private life " moved from State Street in the afternoon, and, amid salutes from the Castle and from cannon on Breed's Hill and Copp's Hill, and honors from the companies of artillery and artificers, marched over the new structure to the site of the battle, where tables were spread, and the remainder of the day was spent in " sober festivity," as the historian Snow observes. This was the beginning of the work of connecting the promontory with the mainland by means of bridges, the latest of which, the Harvard Bridge, to be completed during the present year, is by far the finest of all. Cambridge was next thus brought into communication with Boston by the West Boston Bridge, completed in 1793. The bridge to Dorchester Neck, a tract which was at the time " annexed " to Boston and called South Boston, was completed in 1805. Four years later, on Commencement Day, 1809, the Craigie Bridge to East Cambridge was opened to the public, and there were then five avenues into the city.* " All these bridges," says Snow, " are well

---

* At the present time the waters about Boston are crowded with bridges, and they are a considerable obstruction to vessels.

lighted by lamps when the evenings are dark, and the lights, placed at regular distances, have a splendid and romantic appearance." It is certainly true that the many lights on the long low bridges that span the waters around Boston still have a very attractive appearance, now that they are produced by gas or electricity.

More important than any of these bridge projects for the future of the town was the Boston and Roxbury Mill Corporation, a scheme projected by Mr. Uriah Cotting, since called the Chief Benefactor of Boston. It was a stupendous project for the time, for it contemplated the building of a dam forty-two feet wide with a roadway upon it twenty-two hundred feet in length, reaching from the foot of Beacon Hill to Brookline, which was at that time accessible only by way of Roxbury over the Neck. This great dam was intended to confine the waters of the Back Bay in such a way that they could be used for mill purposes. The company was chartered in 1814, but it was not until 1821 that the road was opened to passengers. The enterprise was opposed with the vigor that projects for the good of a town are pretty certain to meet, one indignant citizen writing to the *Advertiser*,[*] in the following excited terms:

"Citizens of Boston! Have you ever visited the Mall; have you ever inhaled the western breeze, fragrant with perfume, refreshing every sense, and invigorating every nerve? What think you of converting the beautiful sheet of water which skirts the Common into an empty mud-basin, reeking with filth, abhorrent to the

[*] Quoted in Winsor's "Memorial History," vol. iv., page 33.

CROSSING OF THE RAILROADS IN THE BACK-BAY REGION IN 1840.

smell, and distasteful to the eye? By every god of sea, lake, or fountain, it is incredible!"

The process of improving this portion of Boston was not, it must be confessed, an agreeable one, and in 1849 the Board of Health declared that the region had become a "nuisance, offensive and injurious to the large and increasing population residing upon it," for it was then an open cesspool, receiving the sewage of a large community. Then measures were taken in earnest to overcome the difficulty.

Before the beginning of the present century the territory of Boston remained of the same form that it had in the earliest times. The North End was separated from the rest of the promontory by an inlet which put up from the Bay at the present Blackstone Street and became eventually Mill Creek, affording vessels a passage through to Mill Cove, an enlargement of the Charles River, which also was changed in time to Mill Pond by the formation of a dam or causeway across its mouth. In 1643 this cove was granted to four partners on condition that they would erect one or more corn-mills on or near the premises. One hundred and sixty-one years after this grant (in 1804), the successors of the men to whom it was made were incorporated as the Boston Mill Corporation, and they proceeded to fill up the pond, obtaining the necessary earth by digging away Beacon Hill. By this process fifty acres were added to the area of Boston, and the shore line much altered. The railways running to the northward all start from stations erected on the land thus formed. At a later period both Copp's Hill and Pemberton Hill were made tributary to this filling in of the Mill Pond,* and the topography of the town was thus materially changed.

* The digging down of Copp's Hill was begun in 1806, and was continued for several years. Pemberton (formerly Cotton's) Hill, famed for the elegant estate of Gardiner Greene, fell into the hands of others upon Mr. Greene's death in 1832, and was laid out in lots after the grading had been completed.

XXVIII.

THE TOWN BECOMES A CITY.

BOSTON was deeply interested in the convulsions in Europe preceding and during the wars of Napoleon, for in the earlier period her merchant ships reaped a rich harvest in the carrying-trade, and great fortunes were built up by the enterprising adventurers. This state of affairs was not destined to continue long, for Great Britain was just as desirous after the peace as she had been before to cripple the commercial progress of the Americans. In every way practicable the shipping business was hampered by restrictions laid upon it by the British government, for England was determined not to allow the carrying trade to pass away from her if it could be avoided. Indignation rose so high in Boston, only three years after the war had closed, that a businessmen's meeting was held in Faneuil Hall (April 16, 1785), at which it was voted not to have any commercial relations with the British mercantile agents in America, who were receiving large consignments of goods, "greatly to the hindrance of freight in all American vessels." A call was made upon all other sea-ports to enter into similar agreements, and a memorial to Congress was ordered. In the following July the legislature of Massachusetts doubled the duties on goods brought to the ports of the commonwealth in British vessels, and entirely prohibited the exportation of American products in British ships, until the odious restrictions should be removed. London soon felt the pressure, and some houses there failed; but the government was not to be easily turned aside from its plan. Neither were Boston merchants to be baffled, and they gave their attention to the Eastern trade, sending many vessels to China, and reaping large returns from their intelligent activity. The wars between England and France complicated matters. American shipowners found themselves suffering greatly, and in 1807, when Jefferson enforced his embargo in consequence of the Milan Decrees of Napoleon and the British Orders in Council, the commerce of Boston was almost destroyed, and the party feelings that were engendered ran so high that there were threats of "secession," such as had been uttered in Boston when Louisiana was bought,—such as were to be heard from Josiah Quincy in Congress apropos of the plan to form a state west of the Mississippi River.* John Quincy Adams informed the President that the embargo could not be enforced in New England, that the Federalist leaders were making arrangements to break off from the Union, and had received an offer of aid from the English govern-

---

* The essential portion of the speech referred to (delivered in January, 1811), may be read in Edmund Quincy's "Life of Josiah Quincy," pages 206-213. This has been pronounced the "first announcement" of the doctrine of secession "on the floor of Congress."

ment.* Such representations as these about his political opponents moved the President and members of Congress on the Republican side, and the Non-Intercourse Act took the place of the embargo, March 4, 1809.

The harm had been done, however, and the ships rotted at the Boston wharves or were taken from service and dismantled; shipyards were deserted; the fisheries were given up, and even the farmer felt the pervading distress; ruin stared the merchant in the face, and the laboring man knew not in which direction to look for work. Meanwhile the second war with Great Britain came on, in opposition to the interests and desires of the people of Boston.† Then

---

* The correspondence of Josiah Quincy might have afforded some ground for a statement like this, for Mr. Harrison Gray Otis wrote to him, December 15, 1808, "it would be a great misfortune for us to justify the obloquy of wishing to promote a separation of the states and of being solitary in that pursuit." At the same time Mr. Otis suggested a convention of delegates from the commercial states "at Hartford or elsewhere, for the purpose of providing some mode of relief that may not be inconsistent with the Union of these states." The Federalists did not hold their convention at Hartford until December 15, 1814, just as the war which they had opposed was closing. It was, as President Woolsey has said, a scheme "with an ugly look," and though it declared that "no hostility to the constitution" was intended, its actions called out the statement from the Richmond *Enquirer*, that "no man, no association of men, no State or set of States, has a right to withdraw itself from the Union of its own accord," and it was supposed to have uttered the principles of nullification as clearly as South Carolina ever did.

† Josiah Quincy, then the leader in the Massachusetts senate, showed the feeling of Boston by drawing up an address, protesting against the war as impolitic and unjust, and the action was followed in other states. We read in Mr. Quincy's "Life," that the stagnation of business carried distress and anxiety into every New England house-

there was no use for vessels except as privateers, domestic produce rose greatly in value, and imported goods were held at very high prices; money was scarce, and men were reduced to straits to supply the wants of their households. Peace was declared in February, 1815, and though it did not in explicit terms secure a single one of the objects for which the war had been fought, it was welcomed with rejoicings on all sides. Notwithstanding the fact that the war did not explicitly ensure "free trade and sailor's rights," as the watchword of its supporters demanded that it should, it was evident that the naval supremacy of Great Britain had been worthily challenged, and that England could not longer be said to rule the seas, and there was no further impressment of seamen from American vessels.

When the news of peace reached Boston, an extra number of the *Evening Gazette* was issued, giving the announcement in the barest terms, and on the twenty-fourth of February there was a grand ball in the concert hall on Hanover Street, which had been long before a resort of friends of liberty. A lady who entertained scruples about attending a public ball, fired by the enthusiasm of the occasion, went, and she describes her costume in the following words: "My dress was a sheer dotted muslin skirt, trimmed with three rows of plaited white satin ribbon an inch wide. The boddice of white satin was also trimmed with the same ribbon. I wore white

hold, and the ruin of the commercial states seemed to be settled. The Massachusetts legislature refused to furnish troops at the call of the President.

lace around the neck, a bouquet, gold ornaments, chain, etc. My hair was arranged in braids, bandeau, and curls. The building," continues the same lady, "was illuminated within and without, and was decorated with flags and flowers." The few British officers who were present seem to have been the favorites with the ladies. The floor was arranged for dancing, and had a springing motion, which our lady informant declares she "never saw equalled." So great was the social rebound from the trials of war * that one of the Boston ministers felt called upon to remind his congregation, in a sermon, of the necessity that still remained for the practice of forbearance and self-denial!

During the long period since Governor Winthrop set foot on the peninsula of Shawmut to the time now under consideration, Boston was a simple democracy. It was the duty of every freeman to meet at some appointed place, when called upon, to confer upon the interests of the town. The government was first of the most informal sort; Winthrop and nine others seem to have acted for the whole body during the intervals between the meetings, which occurred at first twice each year. They were known as the "ten men," or the "town's men," until 1643, when they are incidentally mentioned on the records as "selectmen," a name which was fixed upon them after 1647, in which year their election became annual. The semi-annual meetings of the freemen were warned from house to house,—

---

* See Winsor's History, vol. iv., p. 22, for more particulars in regard to the return of peace.

a very slow method one would suppose. Altogether the town system was a bungling one for communities of much size, although in small places it was exceedingly effective under skilful guidance, as a means of bringing the sentiment of all the citizens to bear upon one point.

As early as 1650 the difficulties of the informal government were apparent, and Boston petitioned the general court that it might become a corporation; but there is no evidence that the court took any steps in the premises. The original plan was economical, for, in the earliest times, at least, the "town's men" not only received no pay for their services, but were allowed to liquidate their own incidental expenses. In 1637, it was agreed that the charges for the meetings of the town's men should be borne by the town in general, and the gentlemen soon found it convenient to "refresh" themselves after their arduous duties. Thus in 1647 a charge was made of two pounds eighteen shillings for "a selectmen's dinner," and a custom arose that has been followed until very late times. The "junketings" of the city fathers have sometimes reached such an extent as to spread dismay among the less favored citizens who were permitted to pay the expenses of the government.

Though the general court did not take steps to constitute Boston a corporation in 1650, it allowed it to choose seven commissioners in 1651, who were magistrates authorized to hear and give judgment upon civil actions; but in 1708, the selectmen reported that the government was inefficient because there was no "proper head" through whom the law should be put into execution, and they thought that as the town was growing more populous, good order could not be expected without more strict regulation. They therefore urged that a charter of incorporation be prepared for presentation at the next annual meeting of the town. A committee was appointed, and a scheme drawn up. It was in due time presented to the town, and, though most of the principal inhabitants were in favor of it, the people felt misgivings lest some of their privileges were to be taken away, and it was voted down. One of the popular champions made a conclusive speech, ending with the warning: "It is a whelp now, it will be a lion by-and-by; knock it in the head! Mr. Moderator, put the question!" The "whelp" was killed, and no effort of a similar nature seems to have been made until the March meeting in 1762, when the freemen voted, almost unanimously, that no steps should be taken towards making the town a corporation.

Meantime the difficulties of the situation were increasing. It was found that no public building could possibly hold all of the freemen, if they should all attend a meeting, and even though but a small proportion appeared, it was impracticable for them all to take part in the discussion, or even to hear all that was said by others. The result naturally was that the control of the affairs of Boston, fell into the hands of a small number of persons, and, though at the time these were the persons best qualified to give them proper direction, it was not at all the normal condition of things, nor that likely to continue satisfactory. In case of an exciting subject coming up the hall would be crowded ; but on other occasions the business was carried through by thirty or forty persons besides the town officers. The majority of the citizens took things upon trust, and few gave public affairs careful consideration.

The intervals between the discussions of the subject of a city government were becoming shorter. The matter laid quiet fifty-eight years after the first proposition of 1650; fifty-four years elapsed before the discussion of 1762 ; and in twenty-years it came up again. Upon its presentation in 1784, at a meeting especially called to consider a carefully prepared plan, there was " an unabated roaring," and amid the cries of " No corporation—No Mayor and aldermen—No innovations !" there were incessant calls for the question ; no discussion was allowed, and the vote was recorded against the plan. Similar efforts were made in 1791, 1804, and 1815, all without success, though the need of a more efficient police, as well as one responsible head " to take a general oversight," was generally felt, and the difficulties of transacting public business increased. The plan presented in the year last mentioned approached more nearly the form of a city government than any which had preceded it. It provided for an "intendant," and a "municipality" consisting of two citizens from each ward, and a body of selectmen chosen by the citizens generally. This scheme was defeated by the very small majority of thirty-one.

On the last day of December, 1821, the town was

called to consider and act upon another plan for a city organization.

In his municipal history of Boston, Mr. Quincy shows that in view of the want of safety and responsibility of the loose methods of the town government, the "inherited and inveterate antipathy to a city organization" had now much diminished. The looseness of the financial methods are astonishing, and are only to be explained on the hypothesis that each freeman had entire confidence in every other. The selectmen, overseers of the poor, and board of health were the "committee on finance," which exercised the whole power of taxation. After the money was collected by an officer whom the three boards appointed, it was kept by a treasurer whom they also chose, and spent by them as they pleased, each board taking as much as it deemed requisite for its purposes. The amount to be raised annually was formally voted by the town meeting of which the members of the board were apt to contribute the majority of the freemen present. It is not strange that great interest attached to the subject at this time.

For three days Faneuil Hall was thronged, and earnest but decorous discussions were carried on by some of the most respected citizens. On Monday, January 7, 1822, the final ballots were cast which decided the long-discussed subject. It was voted that there should be a city government, and that the name of the town should be changed to the City of Boston. A charter was granted by the legislature and signed by the governor, February 23d. The charter was accepted by the people at its last town-meeting, held March 4th, and the governor announced the fact by proclamation, three days later. The first day of May was designated as the beginning of the municipal year, and it was necessary that the city should be divided into wards before the second Monday in April, in order that upon that day there should be an election of mayor and aldermen and subordinate officers. The inferior offices gave no trouble, for it was found practicable to divide them among the different political parties in such a way that each was satisfied; but, as Dr. Snow observes, the mayoralty was "an honor that could not be divided," and a spirited contest immediately opened for that office.

Mr. Josiah Quincy had been chairman of the final town-meeting, and it was considered by many prominent citizens that he was the man for the chief magistracy. Mr. Quincy accepted a nomination, not knowing, it is said, that other citizens proposed to raise Mr. Harrison Gray Otis, who had lately resigned his seat in the United States senate, to that office, as a stepping-stone to the higher post of governor. Mr. Otis was a gentleman of "the old school," who had long been prominent in public affairs, though, partly because he had been a member of the Hartford Convention, his popularity was at this time considerably less than it had formerly been.* Mr. Quincy possessed many traits that fitted him for the office to

---

* Mr. Otis was one of the Latin-School boys, who attended Master Lovell's celebrated institution the last time on the morning of April 19, 1775, passing, on his way, by the British troops who occupied Tremont Street from Scollay's Building almost to the bottom of the Mall, and running home as fast as his young legs would carry him, for fear of the soldiers, when he heard the words, *deponite libros*, with which the exercises were indefinitely postponed.

which he was nominated, though he had resisted the effort to make a city of the town, because he believed that the pure democracy of the town-meeting was less liable to abuse and more suited to the New England character than the more compact form.

On the eve of the election another candidate was nominated, and the next day his name was presented at the polls, without his knowledge, and much to his displeasure, with such success as to draw enough votes to prevent an election. Thus the era of city government seemed to fulfil Mr. Quincy's prophetic opinion, by opening with a small political trick. Mr. Quincy and Mr. Otis immediately withdrew from the contest, and Mr. John Phillips, a person who was familiar with public business, and who bore an undisputed character for honesty, discretion, and sound judgment, was, after a few days of great excitement, chosen to the position by a vote almost unanimous.

Great preparation was made for the inauguration of the new government. At the appointed hour, Faneuil Hall was filled to excess; the newly chosen officers occupied positions of prominence on a platform erected for the purpose, and two of the galleries were filled with ladies. After a prayer by the senior minister of the city, the oaths were administered, and the chairman of the retiring board of selectmen delivered an address to the mayor, handing him a silver case containing the town charter and books of records, after which Mayor Phillips made his address. In the course of his remarks, Mr. Phillips said : " Purity of manners, general diffusion of knowledge, and strict attention to the education of the young, and above all a firm practical belief of that divine revelation which has affixed the penalty of unceasing anguish to vice and promised to virtue rewards of interminable duration, will counteract the evils of any form of government." Mr. Phillips' son, the late Wendell Phillips, relates that his father built the first brick dwelling on Beacon street. It stood on the corner of Walnut, next to the stone house of John Hancock, and was thought so remote from the other dwellings that his uncle, Judge Oliver Wendell, was asked what had induced his nephew " to remove out of town."

Mr. Phillips conceived it to be his duty simply to organize the new government, to make the people of Boston familiar with an unaccustomed and somewhat uncongenial form, with as little friction as possible; to make as few innovations as were consistent with effectual work. As Mr. Otis said, he "respected the force of ancient and honest prejudices," and, in making a novel experiment, aimed " to reconcile by gentle reform, not to revolt by startling innovation." He accomplished this with much success. Naturally such a prudent line of conduct was not adapted to give cause for complaint, neither was it likely to excite special admiration; and many felt disappointed that no more energy characterized the new government.

The feelings of the officials, as well as of the citizens generally, are shown in the motto adopted for the municipal seal,—*Sicut patribus, sit Deus nobis,* "As God was with our fathers, so may he be with us,"—an adaptation of the fifty-seventh verse of the eighth chapter of the first book of Kings, as it appears in the Latin vulgate.

XXIX.

THE SECOND MAYOR.

At the time of which we have now to treat Boston is said to have been more purely English than any town of its size in England itself. It was, as the biographer of Josiah Quincy says, singularly homogeneous in its population; "the great Irish and German emigrations had not then set in," and it is probable that no town of fifty or sixty thousand inhabitants could have been kept in peace and safety with so small a body of watchmen as proved equal to the requirements of the Puritan city. There were, we are told, but twenty-four policemen, and at night not more than eighteen watchmen were on duty at a time. This peacefulness is accounted for by the fact just mentioned, that the inhabitants of New England were of pure English descent, with but little mixture of other blood. Their ancestors were the Winthrops, the Quincys, the Saltonstalls, the Endicotts, the Adamses, of other times, and it was a part of their heredity to keep peace themselves without the help of any guardians.

When the time came for another election of chief magistrate, Mr. Josiah Quincy was chosen almost unanimously, and he entered upon his duties in a

JOSIAH QUINCY (1772–1864).
From the portrait by Stuart now in the Museum of Fine Arts.

very different spirit from that which has been remarked in his intimate friend and predecessor. Mr. Quincy did not take the office as a stepping-stone to any greater position of usefulness, but he made it a post of signal service to his native place. He was a Boston man through and through, born of a line that was begun in the town three years after the arrival of Winthrop, by an ancestor who arrived there in company with the Reverend John Cotton. He was son of Josiah Quincy "junior," whose words to his father, when remonstrating with him for defending Captain Preston for firing upon the mob at the time of the "Massacre," seem to have been the motto upon which he acted. Said Josiah Quincy "junior": "I never harbored the expectation, nor any great desire, that all men should speak well of me. To inquire my duty, and to do it, is my aim."*

Mr. Quincy had been long before the Boston public, though he was but fifty-one years of age. His career may be said to have begun in 1798, when he delivered in the Old South church a Fourth-of-July oration marked by youthful enthusiasm, which drew passionate tears from his audience, and attracted so much attention that it was reprinted in Philadelphia, then the seat of government, and called from President Adams the statement that it was "one of the most precious morsels that our country has produced upon such occasions." Mr. Quincy had been a member of the Massachusetts senate and of the Federal Congress (then sitting in Washington), of which he had for a time been Speaker. His chief

---

* See "Memoir of Josiah Quincy Junior," by his son, pp. 34–36.

practical knowledge of the problems with which he was now called to deal was gained while he was a member of the general court (where he was chairman of a committee appointed in 1820 to investigate pauperism), and as judge of the municipal court of Boston, which had jurisdiction in all criminal cases not capital. In March, 1822, in a charge to the grand jury, Mr. Quincy treated the subjects of poverty, vice, and crime in their relations to one another; pointed out the necessity for reform in the methods of dealing with criminals, as well as for the separation of the different classes of convicts; and declared in favor of private executions instead of the ghastly public "occasions" by which the Boston public had been brutalized, since the day when the people went from the "Thursday Lecture," in 1659, to see the three Quakers hanged, and poor Mary Dyer taken down from the gallows-tree by main force.* At the time of his election, Mr. Quincy lived in a house on Tremont Street, at the corner of Hamilton Place, to which he had removed in 1820.

The new mayor was not only determined that the business of the young city should be done well, but he felt it desirable that he should be conversant with every part of it. He therefore decided to make himself chairman of every one of the committees of the board of aldermen, and to take the "laboring oar" into his own hands. He then looked over the ground, sought out the weak places in the government, and the neglected places in the city, and laid

* See "The Puritan Age and Rule in the Colony of the Massachusetts Bay," p. 463.

his energetic plans to strengthen the first and purify the others. He divided the acts that he had to perform into four classes: those relating to morals, comfort, convenience, and ornament, and began his work at the first division. There was in the "West End," so-called, a region of the city where vice was audaciously obtrusive, and where murders were so frequent that he was assured that no man's life would be safe in attempting to enforce order without the support of the military. This was the emergency that suited Mr. Quincy's temperament. He examined the laws and found that, under an antiquated provincial enactment, he had authority, as justice of the peace, to arrest the fiddlers whose strains inspired the orgies of the dance-houses, and they were arrested. He then took away the licenses of the tippling-houses, and the enemy succumbed under stress of thirst and low spirits. Wealth and respectability afterwards took possession of the region thus reclaimed. When, on another occasion, the constabulary proved insufficient to quell a riot among the most disreputable townspeople, Mr. Quincy put himself at the head of the sturdy "draymen" and sent the rioters about their business by force of muscle, directed by proper strategic ability.

Mr. Quincy looked over the lines of his municipal fence and saw that Philadelphia and New York managed their fires and firemen in better style than Boston knew, and he obtained from the legislature, with great difficulty, be it said, the necessary powers to make a reform in this particular. At that time a fire was an event of direst confusion; there were thirty-six officers, all equal in authority, and no guiding head gave unity to the efforts for the preservation of property. At the stroke of the alarm every citizen so disposed rushed to the scene, if he could find it, armed with a water-bucket and a bag. Engines there were, manned by voluntary companies, and directed by officers chosen by the people; their power was small, and for water they depended upon the buckets brought by the citizens, who formed lines to the nearest pond or dock, and passed the supply along with what rapidity they could. The officers might press all passers-by into the service, and many a head is reported to have ached from knocks from the poles that they bore as tokens of their puny power. Mr. Quincy, with a temerity that astonished sober Bostonians at that time, caused cisterns to be provided at convenient points to supply water; he bought two engines and a "hydraulion" in Philadelphia and New York, furnished them with hose, and abolished the ancient confusion. The proposition of a fire department which should "exclude" citizens, instead of demanding their assistance, was indignantly opposed, and it was said that, though such laws might be obeyed in despotic countries, or in cities where the inhabitants lack fellow-feeling, the men of Boston would never be prohibited from helping a fellow-townsman in distress. When engines were bought in other cities it was publicly asked whether the mechanics of Boston were so inferior in skill to those of New York and Philadelphia, that public money had to be expended in patronage of their workmen. Every possible obstacle was placed in the way of the mayor in his efforts. The engines were disabled in the night-time; their hose were cut, even at fires; and the perpetrators of these acts were so thoroughly shielded that large rewards failed to discover them.

Mr. Quincy recognized the relations between morals and cleanliness, and saw that the subject of the removal from the streets of all that offended the senses or endangered the health would at once increase municipal self-respect and add to the public comfort. He therefore collected all the city offal and utilized it upon city property, so that the outlay was largely repaid in the improvements. Streets that were dark and crooked were widened and made straight; drains were laid; a new mall was created on Charles Street; the finances, which were still managed in a loose manner,* were systematized and made effective, while the management was more responsible; measures were initiated looking to obtaining a supply of fresh water; a census was taken, and it was found that the population was fifty-eight thousand two hundred and eighty-one (in 1825); the evils to which Mr. Quincy had before drawn attention, resulting from the mingling of honest poor with rogues in the almshouse, were overcome by the establishment of a house of correction, and a house of reformation for juvenile offenders; and finally the city was provided with a new and commodious market-house.

* The four boards of the city government at this time exercised equal and independent power in disbursing public money, and were responsible to no one else.

The building of the market-house, which familiarly goes by Mr. Quincy's name, though, owing to personal feeling, it did not receive it formally, was the most noteworthy event of the second mayor's term of office. Mr. Quincy was accustomed to say, with more truth than poetry, that no man could do his duty in such an office without finally being rewarded by being turned out. This proved his experience, and after five elections he was, in 1828, relegated to private life by the votes of those whose projects had been disturbed by his honest efforts to advance the public interests.

The market facilities of Boston, at the time that Mr. Quincy took up his office, were the same that they had been nearly one hundred years before, though the population had increased fourfold, and one of the first problems that he undertook to solve was how they might be increased. It was a difficult question, rendered unnecessarily hard of solution by the bitter opposition which the plan the mayor finally made encountered from prominent citizens, less far-seeing than he, from the members of the city council, and from the legislature, though it was acknowledged that Faneuil Hall Market was inadequate for the needs of the city, and though the situation was notoriously unhealthy and inconvenient of access. It is almost past belief that at the time the entire space occupied by stalls in and around Faneuil Hall was not more than fourteen hundred square feet.* The Hall itself was erected on " made " land, and had the town dock, with its festering filth, di-

* Winsor's " History," vol. iii., page 228.

rectly to the north, though now it is separated from the water on all sides by warehouses and streets, and seems to stand on solid earth.

The difficulty of the plan that he had conceived, as well as the eminent desirability of giving Boston the facilities it needed, increased the charms of the undertaking in the eyes of Mr. Quincy, rather than daunted him, and he entered upon the work with persistence, and accomplished success, for which his name has ever since been held in grateful remembrance. He opened six new streets, enlarged a seventh, obtained for the city unincumbered possession of docks, flats, and wharf-rights, to the extent of more than three acres in the centre of the town, without drawing upon its resources, or creating a debt, but by actually adding largely to its productive possessions. The dock was filled in, and besides furnishing land on which the improvements were erected, it gave the city an estate which was sold for enough to pay for the entire outlay, besides adding to the taxable property the value of the warehouses that the buyers erected. The market-house itself is an edifice of granite, five hundred and thirty-five feet in length, by fifty feet in width, covering over half an acre, and costing one hundred and fifty thousand dollars. This building is a permanent monument to the memory of the great mayor of Boston.*

Another subject to which Mr. Quincy gave atten-

* The corner-stone was laid with much ceremony in April, 1825, and the building was formally opened in 1826. The entire outlay for the improvements was more than eleven hundred thousand dollars.

tion was the water supply for the city. At that period the nature of disease originating in contaminated waters was not understood so well as it is at present, and though Mr. Quincy urged the matter with zeal upon the city government, he could only venture to base his action on the claims of health with caution. He mentioned with confidence the need of protection against fire, the culinary and other domestic necessities of the citizens, which made it desirable that water from a stream or pond should be introduced into every house in the city; and then he added that "physicians of the first respectability," had urged upon him that the spring water of Boston was harsh, and impregnated with salts that impaired its excellence as an article of drink, and that they had "been led to the opinion that many complaints of obscure origin owed their existence to the qualities of the common spring water of Boston." The city was at the time supplied from wells and cisterns, and by water brought from Jamaica Pond through pine logs, and though this was, as Mr. Quincy said, insufficient, conservatism and interest proved so strong as to put off the day in which the supply could be increased for twenty-one years longer, when Lake Cochituate (then Long Pond) was tapped.*

* The mayor at that time was "Josiah Quincy," son of the one at present under consideration, though the aged father, then seventy-four years of age, took part in the ceremony (Aug. 26th, 1846), in company with his son and ex-president John Quincy Adams, thus having the opportunity of seeing his former desires realized under the management of his namesake.

When the time for a new choice of mayor arrived, in December, 1828, Mr. Quincy failed of receiving a majority of the votes on the first and second ballots, and immediately announced that he should under no consideration again accept the office to which he had devoted his time unremittingly for so long. He formally laid down the harness after his notable career, with a final address to the other members of the city government, in which he rapidly glanced at the record of the previous six years. He spoke of the improvement in the conduct of the fire department, and of the reduction of insurance premiums; of the steps taken in behalf of general health, and their success; of the advance in provision for public education; of the reformation of certain portions of the city; of the decrease of street-begging; of the value of the public improvements carried through at such great personal labor on his own part; and he refuted the animadversions of those who said: "The Mayor assumes too much. He does not sit solemn and dignified in his chair, and leave the general superintendence to others, but he is everywhere and about every thing, in the street, in the docks, among the common sewers,—no place but what is vexed by his presence." He laid his hand on the city charter and found his vindication by reading the duties laid upon the chief executive officer,—duties to which he was sworn, and showed that as he was made responsible for every thing, it was necessary that he should not shift the performance upon others. Recalling the assurances with which he entered upon his duties, he closed with the noble words of the prophet Samuel, uttered likewise on laying down office : " Behold, here I am. Witness against me. Whom have I defrauded? Whom have I oppressed? At whose hands have I received any bribe ?"

Mr. Quincy lived long after this time, an honored citizen of his loved town,* and when partisan feeling had subsided, it was acknowledged that he had not only laid the foundations of the present system of city government in Boston, but had established its permanent form, for the changes that have been made since that time have been chiefly those that have been rendered necessary by the increasing population.

* As soon as it was known that Mr. Quincy was to be no longer mayor of Boston, a movement was made to place him at the head of Harvard College, that position having been vacated by the death of Dr. Kirkland. The relations between Boston and the college were at that time even more intimate than at present. Commencement day was a legal holiday, and the road to Cambridge was on that day crowded with eager throngs on horseback, on foot, and in carriages of all sorts. The election of Mr. Quincy was notable, because he was the first person not a minister who had been thought worthy of the office, and because, as is said, it was the last occasion on which at the inauguration the Latin language was used by the president-elect and the governor of the State in their addresses to each other and to the public. Mr. Quincy removed to Cambridge with his family, and after his remarkable career of sixteen years there (having made such changes in the institution that he has been called "the great organizer of the University)," he retired to private life, and took up his abode in a dwelling which he had bought in anticipation of the event, on the top of Beacon Hill. After a dozen years he removed to a house fronting on the Common, where he remained until his ninety-second year, when he was taken to Quincy. He died on the first of July, 1864.

XXX.

THE NEW ORDER ESTABLISHED.

THE government of Boston city was now established. There had been two mayors; there have been twenty-eight on the list in all, counting the one who entered upon his duties in 1889. The first one prepared the citizens for the change in the mode of carrying the public business on; and the second set an example for all who were to follow, of devotion to duty, of high aims, of determination to perform what was necessary, even at the risk of life and popularity, and his work as a public officer has never been surpassed. Still Boston was a rural city; her citizens pastured their cows upon their Common until after the time of Mayor Quincy, for they were not excluded from its precincts until 1828, and most of the streets were unpaved.

Boston has developed greatly in every direction since the time of Mayor Quincy, but there is scarcely a tendency that may not be traced to that period, or further back. It is notable that the early mayors laid much stress upon the need of popular education, and that the great progress that has since been made in that direction may be traced to early times. Still it must be recollected that, much as the early

Bostonian esteemed education, he had for a long time no conception of free, unsectarian public schools and higher institutions of learning as they are known now.

The education provided by the town was for boys only; it was intended only to fit them for Harvard College, through which they were to enter upon the only career open to the learned, that of the ministry in the Congregational Church, and it was strictly a religious and a sectarian education. According to the laws of Harvard College, framed by the first president and long in vogue, much more attention was given to the moral and religious training of the students than to the other branches of their education; and it was specially ordered that "every one shall consider the main end of his life and studies to know God and Jesus Christ, which is eternal life"; all very appropriate for the theological seminary that it was.* President Increase Mather (in 1698) characterized the students as "forty or fifty children, few of them capable of edification by such exercises" of Bible exposition as he was obliged to give them. President Quincy thought that for the students not destined to be ministers, the college exercises must have been irksome, if not, in their opinion, unprofitable.

Mr. Quincy found, when he came into office, that girls were permitted to go to school, but that they were not allowed to attend more than one half of the time. Down to 1789, indeed, girls had never been permitted to attend the town schools at all.

* See Quincy's "History of Harvard University," pp. 190, 515.

During his term of office the experiment was tried of giving to girls a high-school education, but it was abandoned as too costly, and it was thirty years before the same opportunity was given to girls again. This first girls' high-school had a curriculum occupying three years, which did not include Greek or Latin. There were one hundred and forty-six boys in the Latin school, and it was expected that the number of girls would be smaller. The committee was astonished to find that they had twice as many applicants, when they called for them. Mayor Quincy opposed the girls' high-school on the ground that it was expensive, and that "schools requiring high qualifications as the condition of admission are essentially schools for the benefit comparatively of a very few"; and that "the higher the qualification the greater the exclusion"; a principle which would cut down all the high-schools at a blow. Mayor Quincy professed to wish to raise the standard of public education "by raising the standard of the common schools," apparently not perceiving that the higher the standard is carried the smaller the number of pupils must be, whatever the plan employed.

Mayor Quincy said that the "great interest of society is identified with her common schools," and it has been supposed that in this utterance he embodied the convictions of the inhabitants of Boston from the earliest period. This is not exactly correct, for there was no school supported by public funds that corresponded to our present common schools for more than half a century after the settlement of Shawmut. Four years after the landing of Winthrop, indeed, a Latin school was set up as a training-school for college and the ministry, and for boys only. The common English branches were not taught, and it did not occur to our ancestors before the Revolution that their daughters had any need of the education that boys required.

It was in 1634 that it was determined to have a boys' Latin school, and accordingly one was established on a street which still bears its name. It did a great work; but it was the only school of the town until 1684, and at that time the population had increased to four thousand or more. One Latin school and no common school would not be considered very ample for a town of that size in our day *; and yet, when we consider the history of the forefathers, and remember the trials under which they built up their community, we are apt to exclaim in surprise at the enterprise that founded so good a school, and one which had such vitality as to endure through the vicissitudes of centuries, at so early a period.

In 1713 there were five town schools in Boston, and there were no more until after the Revolution, though the population had increased to some eighteen thousand. On the twenty-third day of June, 1741, when a count was made, it was found that five hundred and thirty-five pupils (all boys, of course) were in attendance at the schools. Another count was made in 1772, and eight hundred and twenty-three boys were found in their places. By 1800 the

* For comparison we may take the town of Lee, in Berkshire County. In 1784 four schools were thought necessary; and twenty years ago, when its population had increased to nearly four thousand, it had twelve common and two high-schools.

number of schools had increased to seven, and there were nine hundred pupils in attendance. It was in 1789, under the influence of Samuel Adams, that the school system was reorganized, and the girls were permitted, for the first time, to pick up the few crumbs that they could in the warmer months, from April to October. Up to this time there was but one text-book, Dilworth's Spelling-Book, and the Bible furnished all the reading necessary; in fact, even the requirements of the day — reading, writing, grammar, and ciphering—were thought by many to be excessive. It seems a ridiculously small curriculum to our eyes, accustomed to the long lists of 'ologies, which our youth are taught to apply themselves to.

It is impossible here to trace the history of public education in Boston through its later and more rapid stages. It was broadened by adding schools for children from four to seven years of age, in 1818, and by bringing in women to teach. Up to that time it was not known that women were " equal to men as teachers, and superior to them in training the tastes and manners of their pupils." [*] Under the influence of Horace Mann, normal schools were founded for the training of women who wanted to teach, and this led to the revival in 1855 of the girls' high-school, and in 1877 to the establishment of the girls' Latin school. The latter movement was attended by a great public excitement. The women of Boston awoke to a sense of their disabilities, owing to the long exclusion from the Latin school, and

[*] Winsor's "Memorial History," vol. iv., p. 246.

there was an excited discussion in the newspapers and in the halls of legislature. It was found that though the statutes had always declared that "all" children should be taught in public schools, that "youth" were to be instructed, and that instruction in Latin and Greek was to be for the "benefit of all the inhabitants," the laws were always construed to refer to boys only. It is curious to note that when the Latin school was established in 1635, it was for the "teaching and nurturing of children," and that the law knew no "children" but boys for a century and a half and more.

At about the same time, an arrangement had been made at Cambridge by which women might take the examinations for admission to Harvard College, and enter upon courses of study under the professors of the college similar to those conducted for the young men, though not under the direct auspices of the college corporation, and there were other opportunities for their classical instruction, for Boston University accepted them as students on the same footing as that on which men were admitted to its classes. Great progress has been made in the instruction of women since the days of Horace Mann, and his influence still continues.

Meantime the education of boys was vastly improved. An English high-school was established in 1821, just as the town was developing into the city, because it was found that there were young men who wished to "complete a good English education," though they did not intend to go to college. In 1868, elementary evening schools were begun, in which newsboys, bootblacks, and others were taught, and the following year there was an evening high-school, for those who could not attend day-schools. There followed schools for deaf-mutes, evening industrial schools, kindergartens, etc. Among the latest buildings for schools, Boston boasts the largest structure in the world used for a free public school. It is the High and Latin School, built at an expense of three quarters of a million dollars, and dedicated to its beneficent uses in 1881.

The school system has reached vast proportions, especially since great additions to the territory of the city have been made by annexation. The outlays amount to hundreds of thousands of dollars yearly; the teachers form a small army of educated men and women. These are all trained for their work. It is no longer the custom, as once it was, to make sure that the candidate possessed sufficient book learning, and then trust to Providence for his ability to convey his knowledge to his young charge. Boston, as well as Massachusetts, has her normal school, in which the technical skill is obtained by candidates, and the entire establishment works like a great machine, into which the raw boy or girl is put at the age of five, and turned out at the proper time from the English High, or the Latin school, fit for business or college. Doubtless the machine is one that does not always accomplish perfect work; but it is watched over by a committee of men and women with hearts, who wish to fit the instruction to the wants of the ever varying throng that is before them. In the beginning, the teacher of the Latin school did his work without much interference that history takes account of, and evidently did it well. In time, when the number of schools grew, the selectmen took upon them the duty of watching and directing the schools. They were not chosen because they knew what schools should be, and it was a change for the better, in 1792, when the town chose twelve good men to attend to this particular work, for it is to be presumed that the twelve were selected with a view to the work they had to do. Their number was increased first to twenty-four, then to seventy-four, and afterwards to one hundred and sixteen, until it became apparent that unity of action could not be attained by so great a "committee," and, in 1876, the legislature reduced the number to the mayor and twenty-four others. A superintendent had been provided for in 1851, and he was continued; but a board of supervisors with salaries was added, to be appointed by the committee. Methods and schemes for use by teachers will improve still further, doubtless, but the present system of supervision by a small committee, with technical experts employed under them, will probably continue the plan under which the schools will be carried on. The course in the primary schools is three years; that of the grammar school, six years; of the high-school, three; but provision is made for advanced instruction. Boys and girls attend the same schools in the first years, but the tendency is to separate them above the primary grade.

In the year 1839 there was established, under provisions in the will of John Lowell (son of Francis C.

Lowell, for whom the city of Lowell received its name), one of the characteristic educational institutions of Boston. One half of Mr. Lowell's property, amounting to more than a quarter of a million dollars, was set aside for the purpose of providing free lectures for the general public, and free instruction in drawing for mechanics and artisans, and every year since valuable courses of lectures have been given by specialists of the highest renown, while many have been instructed in drawing in the school.

It would demand a volume to give, even in outline, an account of the religious life of Boston in the last century, and the subject must be passed with but a reference. There, and in Cambridge, many a theological battle has been fought, and many are the wounds that time only has been able to heal. After the quiet of the generation after the revolutionary war, there arose a controversy when the Rev. Henry Ware, Sr., was chosen to the Hollis professorship at Harvard College, in 1808. Then there followed, some ten years later, the era when Dr. William Ellery Channing, of whom Coleridge said that he had "the love of wisdom and the wisdom of love," gained his position as leader of the Unitarians and the most eloquent preacher among the clergy of that body. Avoiding controversy as much as possible and endeavoring never to force any one to violate the sacredness of conscience, he won to himself a large following, and gave to the Federal Street church a commanding influence. He was followed by Everett, and Palfrey and Gannett and many others who gave strength and increase to the same denomination. Meantime the Trinitarian Congregationalists, who professed to hold to the orthodox theology of the fathers, did not lack stalwart and eloquent as well as learned champions of their own, and the names of Griffin and Jenks and Adams and Beecher, as well as those of later preachers, will never be forgotten. The Episcopal Church also grew and strengthened itself; and other religious bodies rose in "the paradise of ministers," as Boston was called of old. The mental activity of the people was no less apparent in their discussions of every form of belief and every doctrine of every creed, than it was in the early days when there was an established church and all dissent was frowned upon and kept, as far as possible, at a distance.

XXXI.

CHANGING BOUNDARY LINES.

WHEN Mr. Quincy declined to be a candidate for the office he had so admirably filled, the Hon. Harrison Gray Otis was chosen almost unanimously. He had long been a public man, and his popularity had once been immense, but at the time he had lost somewhat of his prestige. He had been active in the Hartford Convention, all the members of which were looked upon with suspicion, and in his first inaugural address he attempted to vindicate himself from criticism.

An era of great commercial progress was opening. The Erie Canal had been finished in 1825; but twenty-two years before that another had been constructed in Massachusetts which established water communication with Concord in New Hampshire, seventy-five miles. When the great waterway of New York was finished, steps were taken in Massachusetts to see if it were possible to build one from Boston to the Connecticut River and thence to some point on the Hudson near the junction of the Erie Canal. A report was made in favor of a route by way of Fitchburg and through a tunnel in the Hoosac Mountain, at an estimated cost of some six million dollars. The tunnel alone was expected to cost a million dollars.* It is not necessary to say that the canal was not built.

Meantime, news of the proposed railway in England between Manchester and Liverpool † reached this country, and interested the builder of the Bunker Hill monument, which was begun in 1825. He had bought a granite quarry at Quincy, and now proposed to construct a railway four miles to tidewater to facilitate his work. Great opposition was made, of course, but finally a charter was obtained and the road built. In October, 1826, a train of cars drawn by horses passed over the whole length of the road. Horses continued to draw the cars for forty years.

There arose immediately a railroad party in Boston and the commonwealth, opposed to the canal party, and long were the debates that followed. A committee was appointed in the legislature to consider the feasibility of constructing a railway to the Hudson. The committee made its report in 1827, through its chairman, an enthusiast in favor of the project, and it encountered the usual fate of schemes for progress. It was ridiculed, one very sensible editor writing that it was impracticable, the cost being "little less than the market value of the whole territory of Massachusetts," and of as little use when completed as "a railroad from Boston to the

---

* The State found that it had expended some thirteen million dollars on the tunnel and the tracks necessary for the railway, when, many years after this, the work was accomplished.
† This road was not opened until September 15, 1830; but it used steam instead of horse-power.

moon." The agitation was continued, however, and finally roads were built to Providence, to Lowell, and to Worcester. After that they were extended in every direction, and Boston men were not satisfied with what they could do in their own State; they contributed capital towards making roads in all portions of the country. Under their management long lines have been successfully built and operated

ADVERTISEMENT OF THE WORCESTER RAILROAD FROM THE PAPERS OF THE DAY.

in the South and West, as well as in the North. The road towards Worcester was opened as far as Newton, May 16, 1834, and on the Fourth of July, 1835, it was formally opened to Worcester itself. The roads to Providence and Lowell, were opened in June, 1835. It was not until 1841 that the road to Albany, then known as the Western

Railroad, was opened its entire length. Then it was announced that "the magnificent system of roads extending from a common centre at Boston" and reaching to four adjoining States was nearly completed.

While these great industrial movements were in progress, Boston passed her two hundredth birthday, and celebrated it with vigor and great ceremony. On the morning of the seventeenth of September, 1830, the city government took possession of the apartments that had just been provided for the purpose in the Old State House at the head of State Street, and after an address by Mayor Otis, went in procession under escort of the Ancient and Honorable Artillery Company to the Old South church, where ex-Mayor Quincy, then president of Harvard College, delivered an oration, and Charles Sprague read a poem. The address of Mr. Quincy is noteworthy on account of the details which it gives concerning the motives of the Fathers in coming to the New World. We have already seen that, as Mr. Quincy now said, " civil independence was as truly their object as religious liberty," but doubtless the statement fell upon wondering ears, for it had been understood that " religious liberty" was their sole purpose in seeking American shores. Mr. Quincy rightly traced the desire for independence directly to Winthrop and his companions, who " by the magic of their daring" transmuted "a private act of incorporation into a civil constitution of a state," though from the circumstances of the case they could not announce their full purpose at the time.

The impetus given to manufactures during the mayoralty of Mr. Quincy is seen in the establishment of two societies for the encouragement of science and the arts. The New England Society for the Promotion of Manufactures and the Mechanic Arts dates from 1826, and in 1827 the Boston Mechanics' Institute was founded, for the promotion of science and the useful arts by means of lectures and other instrumentalities.

The interests of the people became more and more extensive; they began to make lithographs, chain cables, pianos, ships, ferry-boats, printing-presses, locomotives, watches, sewing-machines, boots and shoes, organs, seamless bags, and almost every other article that nineteenth-century civilization requires. They widened out in every direction; they went to Rhode Island and wove woollen goods on power-looms; they built factory towns on the Merrimac, and called them after prominent citizens, Lowell and Lawrence, and then they made broadcloths, doeskins, cambric and flannels, calicoes and alpacas, paper, and steam-engines, railway cars, and carriages, and clothing, employing men and women by the thousand. Time would fail us to tell of the places to which the Boston men went in their enterprise, and the articles that they laid their hands to to make. They did not confine themselves to the continent, nor to the hemisphere, but went everywhere, impelled by their inherited enterprise, and brought home the products of every clime and every tribe.

At the time that the present State House was

begun on John Hancock's pasture in 1795, the appearance of the promontory was not very different from what it was when Blaxton built his small house on the southwestern slope of Beacon Hill; but it was destined soon to lose most of the traits that characterized it then. The State House was at first over-

THE REAR OF THE STATE-HOUSE, AND THE MONUMENT, SHOWING THE REMOVAL OF THE HILL (1811-12).

topped by the sugar-loaf summit of the hill which was crowned by a doric column erected five years before, after designs of Charles Bulfinch, on the site of the ancient beacon. The base of this monument (which was of brick and stucco) rested on the summit, which was some seventy feet higher than at present. The ascent from the north was so steep that wooden steps were necessary, but they did not reach very far, and the rest of the ascent was made by means of footholds worn in the grassy surface. We have already seen that this hill was cast into the sea to fill up Mill Cove, and add to the territory available for building. The other hills followed in turn, and last of all Fort Hill was ordered to be levelled in 1869, and after three years of digging it was no more.

It was not the levelling of its hills however, which made the greatest change in the appearance of Boston. The " Back Bay " improvement has given the city nearly seven hundred acres of additional space for expansion. The cry against the " Back Bay Nuisance," to which we have referred,* that began to go up in 1849, caused the legislature to take possession of the region, and to make arrangements for reclaiming and purifying it. The late Arthur Gilman, one of the architects of Boston, prepared a plan for laying out and filling in the territory, and in 1857 operations were begun in earnest. The most elegant homes in the city have since been erected on the " made " land, and the parks and thoroughfares which have been constructed give Boston preëminence above the cities of America for beauty and taste.

The eleventh person to fill the office of mayor was a son of the second mayor, Josiah Quincy, Jr. His term of office is rendered notable from the fact that he was able to furnish to the city that supply of water

* See pp. 408, 409.

which his father had pleaded for in vain. On the twenty-fifth of October, 1848, the water from Cochituate Lake was turned into the Frog Pond on the Common, rushing to the height of eighty feet amid the triumphant plaudits of the people. An ode by

THE MONUMENT FROM TEMPLE AND DERNE STREETS (1811-12).

the poet Lowell was written for the occasion. Mr. Quincy had some of the traits of his father, and the business of his office was conducted with energy and success. He was in 1847 authorized to make contracts for filling in the flats at the south side of the

"Neck," and in consequence the outline of the city was considerably changed in that direction, and its finances improved by the sales that followed. The police force was reorganized and put upon a more effective footing, and progress was made in school management under the lead of suggestions made by Horace Mann and George B. Emerson.

The following list gives the names of all of the mayors, with the dates at which they took up the duties of office: 1822, John Phillips; 1823, Josiah Quincy; 1829, Harrison Gray Otis; 1832, Charles Wells; 1834, Theodore Lyman, Jr.; 1836, Samuel T. Armstrong; 1837, Samuel Atkins Eliot; 1840, Jonathan Chapman; 1843, Martin Brimmer; 1845, Thomas A. Davis; 1846, Josiah Quincy, Jr.; 1849, John P. Bigelow; 1852, Benjamin Seaver; 1854, Jerome V. C. Smith; 1856, Alexander H. Rice; 1858, Frederick W. Lincoln, Jr.; 1861, Joseph M. Wightman; 1863, Frederick W. Lincoln; 1867, Otis Norcross; 1868, Nathaniel B. Shurtleff; 1871, William Gaston; 1873, Henry L. Pierce; 1874, Samuel C. Cobb; 1877, Frederick O. Prince; 1878, Henry L. Pierce; 1879, Frederick O. Prince; 1882, Samuel A. Greene; 1883, Albert Palmer; 1884, Augustus P. Martin; 1885, Hugh O'Brien; 1889, Thomas N. Hart.

XXXII.

INDIVIDUALISM AND OTHER ISMS.

"It is a wonderful property of the human mind," said Coleridge, the seer, "that when once a momentum has been given to it in a fresh direction, it pursues the new path with obstinate perseverance, in all conceivable bearings, to its utmost extremes." The religion of New England was individual; "the church existed independent of its pastor"; "each one of the brethren possessed equal rights with the elders"; every individual carried in his breast a monitor who interpreted for him the will of God, and he felt himself a judge of the orthodoxy of his companions, as well as of the elders whom he elected to be over the church that he united to constitute.*

Mohammed was wont to assert that the multiplicity of sects in Islam attested its truth. If we accept this statement, we need go no further to prove the truth of the religion of Puritanism and Separatism. They contained in themselves the seeds of schism. There were always in Boston men and women looking for some new light, and ever and anon congratulating themselves that they had put themselves under its direction. Boston was the

* See Bancroft's "History of the United States," vol. i., chap. x.

proper sphere for a woman like Mrs. Hutchinson; Roger Williams found followers, though he did not find enough to enable him to fight with success against others who felt that their light was better than his. The Separatists established a tendency when they left the Church of England; the Puritans followed when they gave up the usages of the old country on the soil of a new world. The tendency was carried wherever the Puritan and the Separatist went, but Boston became the peculiar home of isms of every sort.

The isms that have made themselves most prominent during the past century in Boston are Transcendentalism, Abolitionism, and Woman Suffragism. It is not needful to enumerate others, for the daily newspapers give full notices of the gatherings at which their leaders attempt to make disciples and to enlighten the world in regard to their peculiarities. The historian of Transcendentalism says that New England "furnished the only plot of ground on the planet" where that form of philosophy had a chance to show what it was and what it proposed.* Of all New England, Boston was the focus about which the interests of the new philosophy centred.

The intellectual revival in New England, which marks the beginning of our century, was contemporary with a forward movement in literature and philosophy that began, so far as the beginning of such a movement can be marked, at about the accession of President Kirkland to the head of Harvard

* "Transcendentalism in New England," a history, by Octavius Brooks Frothingham, p. 104.

College. Though the scholars with which he surrounded himself gave a strong impulse to the young men under their care, they did not begin at that early period to study the German writers. It was Coleridge who introduced German philosophy to England. In 1829 President Marsh, of the University of Vermont, published the "Aids to Reflection," with a masterly essay upon it, which was the first fully elaborated estimate of the philosophical opinions of the English seer. At an early period Ralph Waldo Emerson took an interest in the speculations of Coleridge, whom he declared to be "a citizen of the universe," who took a post at the centre and sent sovereign glances to the circumference of things. He was, Emerson thought, "one more human soul bursting the narrow boundaries of antique speculation, and mad to know the secrets of the unknown world on whose brink it is sure it is standing." It was not long after this, in 1832, that Mr. Emerson found it necessary to resign his position as a Unitarian preacher, in which he followed the example of Coleridge, though he did not, like Coleridge, enter the Episcopal Church.

The influence of Transcendentalism is apparent in George Ripley, Mr. Olcott, Miss Margaret Fuller, and Theodore Parker, each of whom had an individual character. All of these, like many a writer of less note, were filled with the same "enthusiasm of humanity," and longed to exert an influence for good in the world, but not through the channels that had been usual for such efforts. They became the radicals, the "come-outers," the ardent laborers for liberty, for freedom, for the abolition of slavery, for humanity everywhere and in every manner. "Earnest men and women no doubt they were; better educated men and women did not live in America: they were well born, well nurtured, well endowed." So speaks the historian of the movement, and he adds: "Their philosophy may be unsound, but it produced noble characters and humane lives." *

To trace the history of the men and women who felt the influence of this movement in Boston would be to give an account of the contemporaries of Emerson who became eminent in philosophy, in politics, in letters, with but few exceptions. It would be necessary, also, to describe the movement that is recognized by the name of its habitation at "Brook Farm." The men and women who, in 1841, went to that rural retreat,† and tried, by leaving a world of institutions, and returning to first principles, to reconstruct the social order under the inspiration and direction of Mr. and Mrs. George Ripley, fully expected "to promote the great purpose of human culture," to "apply the principle of justice and love to the social organization in accordance with the laws of Divine Providence," to "substitute a system of brotherly coöperation for one of selfish competition," and to secure the rights of the individual. They had no doubt that they had laid a foundation for a social structure that would approach more

---

* Frothingham's "Transcendentalism," p. 383.
† It was on the borders of Newton and Dedham, within the present limits of the city of Boston.

nearly the ideal than any that had ever existed. They felt certain that they were "men of common-sense," holding in their hands the means of escape from the evils of society, then suffering from the effects of "civilization," as well as "from the more frightful state to which in all countries it is hurrying." The first stage of the experiment, though it was not looked upon as an "experiment," so fully were its votaries convinced of its success, was enthusiastic; the second systematic; but success did not attend it, and after a few years it dissolved, the last to leave being Mr. Ripley, who made honorable and self-denying arrangements to cancel all obligations to the rest of the world, and then entered upon his notable career as a critic in New York.

The members of the Brook Farm association found that whether it was necessary to get themselves out of the world in order to set it right, or was not, it was impracticable to carry on a reform at that period of history in that particular way. They had not given themselves very much to the next ism to be mentioned. The friends of abolitionism called in vain for a positive utterance from them in favor of the cause to which William Lloyd Garrison had begun to devote his energies in 1829. They asserted that they stood upon broader ground: it was the ground of the Golden Rule, which would do away with every form of slavery and wrong. On the first of January, 1831, Mr. Garrison issued the first number of his journal, *The Liberator*, and from that time until emancipation was declared he gave his thoughts unreservedly to the abolition of slavery. He was an "obscure individual" at first, and seemed destined to have little success, but he kept at his work undaunted by threats and indignities, and lived to see the reform that he had labored for a reality. He sent his paper to the South, and the Mayor of Baltimore wrote to Mayor Otis, asking him to suspend its publication. Mr. Otis replied that his officers "had ferreted out the paper and its editor; whose office was an obscure hole; his only visible auxiliary a negro boy; his supporters a few ignorant persons of all colors." This was a pretty true description of Mr. Garrison's editorial office. One of his life-long friends afterwards said that it bore "an aspect of slovenly decay." He describes "the dingy walls, the small windows, bespattered with printer's-ink; the press standing in one corner, the composing-stands opposite; the long editorial and mailing table covered with newspapers; the bed of the editor and publisher on the floor." Such was the place from which the paper went out in support of this ism.

Mr. Garrison was not accustomed to prophesy smooth things, though personally he was one of the calmest, the kindliest and most courteous of gentlemen. He was inspired by a single thought. He asked, "Is slavery right or wrong?" and satisfied himself that it was wrong. He then fell back upon the belief that it was the particular wrong that he was to fight, and that, being wrong, no compromise was possible. Immediate emancipation, leaving the results to Providence, was his conviction, and upon it he acted with vigor. He said: "I *will* be heard!"

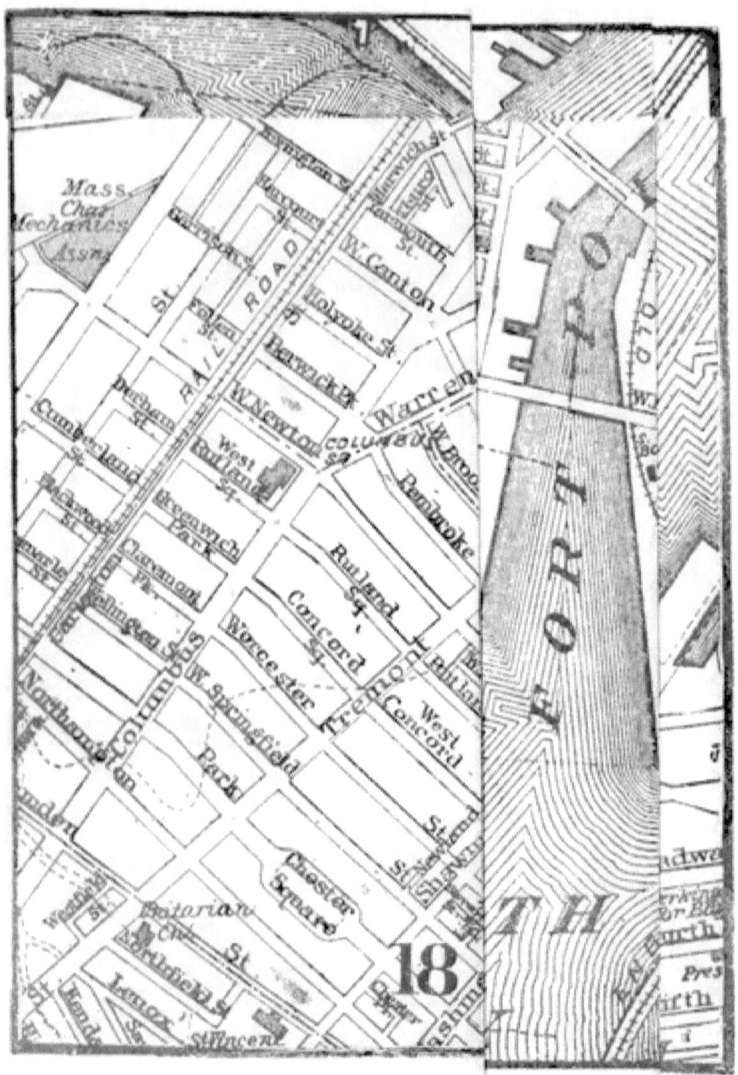

LATEST AUTH

Before the year 1831 closed, on the thirteenth of November, a meeting was held in the office of Samuel E. Sewall,* a descendant of the judge who wrote "The Selling of Joseph," for the purpose of forming an Anti-Slavery Society. Other meetings were held, the society was formed, and the movement which had begun in "an obscure hole" was taken up by some of the most promising men and women of Boston. It was something tangible, and swept many into it who could not be touched by the deep generalizations of transcendentalism; it touched a subject that every man was able to appreciate.

Still, everybody in Boston did not sympathize with Garrison at this time or at any other. In 1835, indeed, a meeting of wealthy and intelligent citizens was held in Faneuil Hall to protest against any interference with slavery, and to condemn the methods of the Abolitionists; and finally, in October of that year, a great stir was raised by a statement that George Thompson, an active English Abolitionist, had declared that "every slaveholder ought to have his throat cut." In the midst of this excitement a meeting of the Boston Female Anti-Slavery Society was held in the building in which *The Liberator* was printed, and a mob of "well-dressed gentlemen" determined that Mr. Thompson, who was falsely announced to address the gathering, should be punished. When it was found that Mr. Thompson was not present, the mob clamored for Mr. Garrison, and dragged him through the streets until he was rescued by the officers of the law and placed in jail for

* Mr. Sewall died in December, 1888.

security. The outrage brought Mr. Garrison into greater prominence. The inhabitants generally were not sorry that the meeting had been broken up. Mr. Garrison himself was made even more fixed than before in his firm determination. Other citizens rose and took his part, and the cause that he had at heart progressed.

Boston was now thoroughly aroused. Edward Everett, who was then governor, took up the subject, and in his message to the legislature in January, 1836, expressed the opinion that the good of the slave and the stability of the Union were endangered by the anti-slavery movement. The legislatures of slave States had desired that it might be made a penal offence to speak or write against slavery anywhere in the Union, and Mr. Everett thought that the Abolitionists were committing misdemeanors by such efforts as they made, for they tended to excite the slaves to insurrection. There was a legislative "hearing," and a report was made against the Abolitionists; but it was laid on the table and never acted upon. It was on the occasion of this hearing that the Rev. Wm. Ellery Channing, the eloquent and renowned pastor of the Federal Street church, took pains to show his warm sympathy with the opponents of slavery. Congress took the matter up, and the discussion passed far beyond the limits of Boston.

In 1837, after the killing of Mr. Lovejoy at Alton, there was an exciting meeting in Faneuil Hall, at which one person placed the "murderers of Alton side by side with Otis and Hancock and Quincy and Adams." This stirred the young heart of Wendell Phillips, who rose and made his first speech, which gave him rank among the orators of the land. There was over-excitement on both sides; the church was denounced as a "brotherhood of thieves," the constitution of the United States was cursed as a "covenant with death," and in 1844 Garrison and those who followed him declared for "No union with slaveholders," thus taking up the cry of secession, which had been a favorite with the dissatisfied whenever union became irksome. Parties were formed in national politics: the "Liberty Party," in 1839; the "Free-Soil Party," in 1848; and finally, in 1856, the "Republican Party," said to have been proposed the previous year by William H. Seward, of New York. In 1848, Charles Sumner took his place among the Free-Soilers.

Like Theodore Parker, John G. Palfrey, and John Albion Andrew, the "war governor" of Massachusetts, Mr. Sumner did not agree with Garrison in opposition to the Union and the constitution, and the event shows that his calmer judgment was correct.* Mr. Sumner was a native of Boston, born January 6, 1811, and had shown his anti-slavery principles before this time, though he was not a member of the Abolition society.

There were constant meetings; the papers were filled with incendiary articles; fugitive slaves were

* Mr. Palfrey, who was a member of Congress when Robert C. Winthrop, of Boston, was Speaker of the House, said in one of his speeches : "If the slaveholders insist that the Union and slavery cannot live together, they may be taken at their own word ; but it is the Union that must stand !"

brought upon the platforms and into the churches to tell their thrilling tales of suffering and escape; and, as in earlier days Samuel Adams sought to keep the citizens up to the point of indignation necessary for carrying out his scheme of revolution, so now Mr. Garrison left no means unemployed that would help bring them to the position that he had taken of antagonism to what he considered a national wrong and a deep disgrace.

In 1854 the Fugitive-Slave act was denounced at a convention of members of the Free-Soil party in Boston; and at about the same time "The Massachusetts Emigrant Aid Association" was chartered with a nominal capital of five million dollars, to send free-State emigrants to the territories, and especially to Kansas. This association gave way to another and more practicable one, which under the guidance and with the support of the late Amos A. Lawrence and his associates began to send out men, August 17, 1854. Other parties followed, singing the words of Mr. Whittier:

> "We cross the prairie, as of old
> The Pilgrims crossed the sea,
> To make the West, as they the East,
> The homestead of the free."

The history of the Kansas struggle belongs to other pages; it brought to Boston at one time and another all the men who were interested in that region. Hither John Brown, of Ossawattomie, formerly a Massachusetts wool-dealer, came to get support and comfort, though his method of making Kansas free, by exterminating slavery " with gun, pike, and sword," was quite opposite to the peaceful mode of the company that Mr. Lawrence directed. Boston never became a convert to all of the views of the Abolitionists, but it never ceased to respect Mr. Garrison, their leader, for his personal character, and it honored him for the manner of his public life in seeking peace and good-will after his great fight was accomplished. A colossal statue in bronze was erected to his memory in the " court end " of the city.

Woman suffragism is the only other ism that we can touch. The women of Boston have since 1854 been moving with some vigor to obtain political rights. We have seen that in the matter of education they had been almost utterly neglected during the earlier periods. In spite of this fact they managed to show considerable literary ability and mental strength, if not power of the highest kind. They have after long effort succeeded in obtaining the right of suffrage so far as it relates to education, and at the latest election, that of December, 1888, they exercised a great influence. The occasion was one that called forth all of their feelings. A certain text-book in history had been dropped from those in use in the schools, and a teacher transferred from one post to another, through the too great influence, as was said, of the Catholic clergy. Women by the thousand qualified themselves to vote, and the day was carried for the Protestant candidates.

The campaign that preceded this election was characterized by much of the violent oratory that had been heard when slavery had been the object of attack. It recalled the excitement of 1834, when it was averred that the Ursuline Convent, which stood in the present limits of Somerville, was injurious to the best interests of the community, and when the story went abroad that a convert from Protestantism had been obliged to fly from the institution, and that one of the Sisters had also gone for refuge to the house of a Protestant neighbor. The worst stories about the convent were believed, and a Boston mob surrounded the building, and "vindicated republican institutions" by battering down the doors, breaking the windows, and leaving the edifice in much the condition in which the house of Governor Hutchinson had been left by the indignant patriots who in his day thought that breaking and burning were the only methods by which American principles were to be sustained. The rioting in Somerville was cool, and, until the men became inflamed by strong drink, unattended by violence. It was properly condemned in Faneuil Hall by Harrison Gray Otis, Josiah Quincy, Jr., and other citizens of the same high character. Still, it left a blot on the fame of the city.

The *Woman's Journal*, which was established at about 1870, has been the channel through which it was hoped to direct legislation and public opinion in favor of woman suffrage and all the civil rights that women claim, and it has exerted much influence. In 1874 it was established that women might become members of the school committee, and in 1879 their right to vote for school officers was confirmed. The New England Woman's Club is another means of concentrating action and of bringing their thoughts to a focus on every subject upon which women think it desirable to make their influence felt.

XXXIII.

MODERN BOSTON.

THE rough promontory to which John Winthrop was invited by the hospitable Blaxton has become the site of a modern city; its hills have been taken down; its borders have been gradually advanced into the surrounding sea; its crooked lanes have become streets and avenues; its territory has been covered with palaces of brick and stone. The business men of the present time store their goods in warehouses of grand proportions, and meet their associates in offices of such elegance that, could the citizens of an earlier day reappear, they would not recognize their former haunts; and if they could be convinced that they were actually in the limits of what they once knew as Boston, they would be certain that the place had entered upon a career of extravagance which could end only in speedy ruin. Gradually a new Boston has been evolved from the old. The children have grown rich, and the city is now perhaps the most wealthy in the land in proportion to its population. While Boston has changed in its external appearance and increased in material wealth, it still draws men to it, in a greater degree than most other American cities, by virtue of its excellent schools and libraries, and by the general intelligence of its citizens. These are inherited traits, and they are strong.

The territorial growth of the city is a noteworthy feature in its later history. Three years are remembered for the annexation of adjoining territory. In 1868 Roxbury, which as a town was as old as Boston itself, and as a city dated from 1846, became a portion of the city. In 1870 Dorchester, which had retained its town organization from 1630, was also absorbed. In 1874 Charlestown, West Roxbury, and Brighton were added, and the enlarged city reached its present extent—twenty-three thousand seven hundred acres. Chelsea, Cambridge, and Brookline still retain their independent existence, though they are as much parts of the suburbs as those sections that have been merged in the corporation. Brighton, indeed, can scarcely be reached from the city proper except by crossing some portion not included in the city limits, or going by water. The " Neck," which was originally hardly broad enough to permit the building of the only street which crossed it, has been expanded to a width of more than a mile and a half; and upon the land thus taken from the sea some of the handsomest and costliest of the public and private edifices of the city have been built, including the Art Museum, Trinity Church, the " New " Old South Church, the building erected for the " Manifesto Church," now owned by the First Baptist Society, and, finally, the High and Latin School building, and the new home of the Public Library.

THE PRESENT STATE-HOUSE (BUILT IN 1795).

In hastily glancing over the Boston of to-day we are attracted by the great growth shown in church buildings, the vast proportions assumed by the organizations for charity and social enjoyment ; the increase of libraries, the creation of a literature, and the development of the business of publishing books, newspapers, and magazines ; the improvement in architecture, the adornment of the streets and squares, the cultivated taste shown in music, the drama, and in the fine arts ; and the growth of manufactures and commerce. From the first Latin School and Harvard College a vast system of educational influences has grown. Colleges and schools, public and private, are many, in which both women and men may obtain the most complete education known to Americans in the different branches of human knowledge. It seems, indeed, as though every line of thought had been followed to its utmost extent in the effort to make complete the development of the faculties, the preservation of mental and physical health, the relief of distress, the protection of the weak and forlorn, the recovery of physical and moral health when lost, and the enlargement of opportunities for study and enjoyment.

The men and women of Boston to-day are not confined in their interests, as their fathers and mothers were, to the discussion of politics and religion, but can carry their thoughts into the realms of space and into worlds of which no one dreamed a century ago. The result is modern civilization. The men know more, they enjoy more, they are broader and larger, but they suffer more also. With the extension of the faculties in one direction comes growth in every other direction. There are, however, no happier homes in Boston to-day than there were when John Winthrop expressed in formal speech his attachment for his Margaret; when Mrs. John Adams wrote her delightful epistles to her absent lord; when young ladies were less distinguished for the charms of their minds than for the elegance of their persons. With the growth of good taste has come a greater sensibility to suffering from those things that offend propriety; with the increase of wealth has come an increased list of wants to be supplied; every convenience of modern civilization has brought with it new cares and new classes of trials.

The memory of the present generation emphasizes certain epochs especially, which are indeed worthy of note. From 1861 to 1865 the hearts of all citizens were stirred by the uprising of the nation and the bloody struggle that settled the government firmly upon its present basis. Then the war governor of Massachusetts, John Albion Andrew, came forth, and placed the state in the fore-front of the movement for the support of the Federal Government, and carried out determined plans with vigor like that displayed by the Father of the American Revolution. The men of Boston supported the governor and the president, and went with alacrity to danger and to death at their call.

When, in 1876, the "Centennial" period of the nation arrived, Boston sympathized to the full with all who rejoiced, and there was a revival of ancient memories as each notable date passed. The impetus to patriotism has not yet ceased to be felt, and it is remembered that we are now in the midst of a series of centennial anniversaries of the stirring times when the constitution of the United States was ratified by Massachusetts, by the convention that adjourned from the Old State House and held its memorable and protracted sessions in the meeting-house on Long Lane, afterwards called Federal Street.

> "The 'vention did in Boston meet,
> But State House could not hold 'em;
> So then they went to Federal Street,
> And there the truth was told 'em."

The revival of historical study is shown by the repeated courses of lectures on American topics in the venerable building of the Old South church, and by the establishment of societies for the special purpose of keeping the memories of the Fathers fresh. The first of these in order of time was the Antiquarian Club, organized in 1879 for the purpose of preserving historical records. The Boston Memorial Association was next formed, in 1880, for the purpose of caring for the memorials of the city, for the preservation and improvement of its public grounds, and the erection of works of art. The Bostonian Society, incorporated at the close of the year 1881, has for its object not the erection of memorials, but the preservation of them from reckless destruction by those champions of progress who would make new every thing old if it happened not to bear upon it the marks of the fashion of the day. Into this society the Antiquarian Club was merged.

The same purposes, to a certain extent, are subserved by the Massachusetts Historical Society. It was founded in 1791, and incorporated in 1794, for the "collecting, preserving, and communicating the antiquities of America," "especially in the historical way," as Jeremy Belknap, its founder, wrote. Eight of its ten original members were Bostonians, as each of its seven presidents have been. The New England Historic-Genealogical Society, which dates from the autumn of 1844, also gave impetus to the investigation of early American history in the Eastern States, and became a centre of antiquarian study.

Reference has been made to the increase of libraries. Boston has long been specially rich in both public and private collections of books, and at the present time affords the student in all branches of history, but especially American history, unequalled opportunities for the study of originals. A catalogue of these collections would be so long as to be tedious, but a few of them must be mentioned. The library of the University at Cambridge, which under its hospitable management is a boon to all students, needs but a passing mention. The great Boston collection in the Public Library, which bears on its outer walls the legend, "FREE TO ALL," now numbers more than half a million volumes, and is as free as its motto promises. This collection was begun in 1848, in consequence of an offer of money made by the younger Mayor Quincy. Prominent citizens at once took an earnest interest in making the collection of books worthy of their city; they gave it money in generous sums; they hastened to put on its shelves the books that had been left to them from their fathers, and made provision in their wills that their own books should follow. In this way it is no wonder that the favorite library grew in numbers. Edward Everett laid down his valuable collection of public documents for the public good; Joshua Bates sent from London fifty thousand dollars; George Ticknor, historian of Spanish literature, gave his time, his money, and finally his unrivalled collection of books in Spanish and Portuguese; the deacons of the Old South Church deposited within its walls the curious and valuable collection made by the Rev. Dr. Thomas Prince, which had long been precariously preserved in the ancient lofts in the steeple of the old meeting-house. Eleven thousand volumes were received by bequest of the Rev. Theodore Parker. The best collection of Shakespearian works known in America came from the library of Thomas Pennant Barton, of New York, which was bought in 1873, and comprised twelve thousand volumes. The result is the largest collection of books for free circulation in the world.

The library of the Boston Athenæum grew out of a literary club called into being by the Rev. William Emerson, father of the more distinguished son, when he took editorial charge of the *Monthly Anthology*, six months after its inception. This was the chief literary enterprise of his life, and the magazine was the longest-lived of those that followed the *American Magazine*, which began its fitful career in 1740. The notable collection of men of literary tastes that Mr. Emerson grouped around him was known as the

THE PRIVATE LIBRARY OF GEORGE TICKNOR, UNTIL LATELY IN THE HOUSE ON THE CORNER OF PARK AND BEACON STREETS, IN WHICH LAFAYETTE WAS ENTERTAINED. (*Cir.* 1870.)

477

Anthology Club. Once a week they met to discuss letters, with especial reference to their magazine, and a dinner of modest character, with reference to their own social life. The club kept its magazine up for some six years, and also formed a collection of books, to which were added some that Mr. Emerson had gotten together when he had taught at Harvard, though he wrote in his journal of himself and his wife at the time: " We are poor and cold, and have little meal, and little wood, and little meat, but, thank God, courage enough." From the collection thus formed grew the Athenæum Library, one of the best in the land, which occupies a prominent building on Beacon Street, and has been in the care of a number of the most noted librarians of America.

No inconsiderable part of the gradual improvement in the appearance of Boston has been made possible by the fires which have destroyed buildings that in the ordinary process of events would have cumbered the ground many years longer than they were permitted to. There have been, as in many other towns, " great " fires from time to time, and each one has startled the inhabitants into new and more rigid provisions against a recurrence of the like disaster. The series began with the fire of 1653. After it householders were directed to provide themselves with ladders of sufficient length to reach to the ridge-poles of their dwellings, and long poles with swabs on the end adapted to "quench fire," and six long ladders were hung on the outside of the meeting-house. By 1670 these simple means had proved inadequate, and householders were ordered to provide at or near the doors of their buildings, hogsheads of water ready filled, with the heads out, and to keep their chimneys well swept. The vision of a hogshead standing at each door throughout the city is an amusing one!

The second great fire, which occurred in 1676, began "an hour before day," and burned forty-six dwellings, besides other buildings, and Increase Mather's church, the "Old North." It led directly to straightening the streets, and all persons were enjoined against building upon the burnt district until the selectmen had staked out the streets anew and given permission. Those who recollect the district burned at the time can but wonder how the streets could have ever been more crooked than they were even within the second half of the present century. The year 1679 witnessed another and even more disastrous conflagration, which began near the Dock, and, as Cotton Mather says, burned fourscore dwellings and seventy warehouses. The fire of 1711 is described as more "sweeping and disastrous" than any of its predecessors. It burned the First Church, the Town House, all the buildings on both sides of Cornhill (present Washington Street) from School Street to Dock Square, and turned a hundred or more families into the streets, besides resulting in the death of several men who were engaged in efforts to arrest the conflagration. In Bonner's map this is called the eighth great fire. Another occurred in 1760, and others in 1787, 1793, 1824, 1825, and 1835 [*]; but all of these were eclipsed

[*] See Winsor's "Memorial History," vol., iv., page 48.

in greatness and destructiveness by the one which fortunately remains *the* great fire of Boston.

It was not remarkable that in the provincial period the town was frequently visited by fire. Indeed Cotton Mather said that "never was any town under the cope of heaven more liable to be laid in ashes," and that "such a combustible heap of contiguous houses" continued to stand he considered a "standing miracle." It was Saturday evening, November 9, 1872 that the greatest Boston fire began. It did not attack such a combustible heap of contiguous houses as Cotton Mather was familiar with, but began and worked its rapid way through buildings built of solid brick and granite that had been supposed to be proof against such ravages. Beginning on Saturday evening at the corner of Summer and Kingston streets, the fire was not stopped until Sunday afternoon, when it had burned over sixty-five of the densest acres of the city, and had destroyed seventy-five million dollars' worth of property, including many public buildings, and most of the newspaper offices. It left the view unobstructed from Washington Street at the ends of Winter, Bromfield, and Milk streets quite out to the islands in the harbor. Insurance companies were made bankrupt, private citizens and corporations found themselves crippled by their sudden losses, and the people were for a time almost in a state of panic. Common-sense took the place of these feelings, however.

Expressions of sympathy came from all quarters. Even as the flames were burning, Henry Ward

Beecher, son of one of the former pastors of the church on Bowdoin Street, speaking from his Brooklyn pulpit exclaimed : " Upon no other place could a calamity have fallen which would have touched so universally the national life and the national feeling as upon the city of Boston—this city from which sprung the earliest American ideas. Her history is written in the best things that have befallen this land, and shame on the man who in the day of her disaster has no tears for her!" The city was glad of the good feeling, but it accepted no other help in the process of recuperation. The streets were straightened and widened; new squares were laid out ; new water-pipes were laid ; and the whole district that had been devastated was rebuilt in much finer style than before.

The one hundredth anniversary of the founding of Boston occurred September 17, 1730, and the two hundredth was celebrated in 1830. Fifty years later, in 1880, there was another hearty celebration, marked by one of the greatest processions that had ever been known. There was likewise an address intended to arouse local pride, as on the former occasions, in the Old South Church. This time the orator took for his theme the character and services of the first governor, who was the first citizen of the town at its beginning. The day was appropriately marked also by the unveiling of a statue of Mr. Winthrop, which stands in the very middle of the rush of modern life, in Scollay Square. It is clothed in the striking garments of the period, and brings back to our eyes the governor as he landed from his ship.

One hand bears to the New World the king's charter and the other the Bible, both of which were held sacred by Winthrop and honored by all true sons of Boston in the early days. The vessel that brought over the precious freight is suggested by a rope attached to a forest tree that bears fresh marks of the settler's axe.

Thus the Story of Boston may stop with this new reference to the man who guided its first steps, whose memory can never fade from the city's records. The city's growth in elegance and perhaps in public and private magnificence may be dated from the late period of the last great fire and of the erection of this statue of Winthrop. The streets and squares are adorned by many monuments, and with other statues, commemorating heroes from Aristides to Lincoln, and events from the "Massacre" to the uprising of the people in 1775, and the establishment of the Nation in 1865.

INDEX.

A

Abolitionism and its energetic prophet, 461
Acadians, the carrying away of the, 252
Acadie, relations with the French in, 99
Adams family, the, origin of, 222
Adams, John, appointed delegate to Congress, 358; asks a question about tea, 362; bravely appears for Preston, 317; brought into prominence, 262; commends an oration by Hancock, 349; inveighs against luxury, 393; on the American congress, 355; points out the excellences and defects of Bostonians, 385, 386; presents his sentiments about independency, 383; recommends a celebration, 384; removes from Boston to Braintree, 325; thinks Britain would enslave America, 284; to his wife after the passage of the port bill, 351
Adams, Mrs. John, on the battle of Bunker Hill, 367; on the behavior of the French officers, 394, 395; on changes in society, 387; on the favor of Heaven to Boston, 380; on the situation of the British, 376; sermon at marriage of, 206
Adams, John Quincy, tells Jefferson that the embargo cannot be enforced in New England, 415
Adams, Nehemiah, pastor of the Essex Street Church, 447
Adams, Samuel, Sr., member of the Caucus Club, 221
Adams, Samuel, not adapted to the times after independence had been won, 402; appointed delegate to congress, 358; argues with Hutchinson, 313; asks to have the galleries cleared, 335; called Master of the Puppets, 306; brings young men forward, 262; death of, 405; defends the committee of correspondence, 347; gives the populace a cue, 314; denies the right of parliament to tax America, 278; expresses the thanks of America to the French, 395; the "famous," 393; fears the Society of the Cincinnati, 405; graduates, 235; character of, 235; habits of, 393; has great influence as clerk of the legislature, 292; influence of, in education, 442; invites some British troops to front seats, 359; keeps up the pre-revolutionary indignation, 276; labors of, 295; leaves college and prepares to practise law, 256; makes a memorable address at Cambridge, 236; opposed to toryism, 399; plan of, for committees of corre-

484 INDEX

spondence, 279, 326, 327, 334; publishes an "Appeal to the World," 338; puts Hutchinson in the wrong, 331, 332; retires from public life, 404; secretary of state, 390; sends out a circular-letter, 350; the skill of, 290, 291; warns Boston on the coming of a British fleet, 324; writes an address for Hancock, 349; writes voluminously for the press, 263
Adams and Hancock excepted from a proclamation by Gage, 365; outlaws, 383
Advertiser, Independent, the, begins a career, 264
Albany Convention of 1754, the, 243, 250
Alexandria, meeting of royal governors at, in 1755, 250
America, strange views regarding, 12
America, History of, by Winsor, 2
American empire, an, figured by some before the Revolution, 261
American Magazine, the, 476
Americans, misrepresented at court, 307; said to be poor but proud, 150; spirits of the, to be broken at all hazards, 321
Amphictyons, the, set up as models, 332
Amusements renounced on account of the presence of troops, 301
Anabaptists, fears of the, 78, 105; simply Baptists, 105
Ancient and Honorable Artillery Company, the, 88, 240
Andrew, John Albion, governor, 465; vigor of, 473
Andros, Sir Edmund, becomes governor, 164; arrested and sent to England, 170
Anniversaries, importance of, in the estimation of Adams, 293; influence of celebrations of, 294, 319
Antagonism between Bostonians and officers of the king, 261

Anthology Club, the, 478
Anthology, Monthly, the, edited by William Emerson, 476
Antinomianism, controversy about, 78
Antiquarian Club, the, 474
Anti-Slavery Society, the, founded, 463
Apthorp, Rev. East, comes to Cambridge, 273
Arbella, the ship, named in honor of Mrs. Johnson, 32
Aristides, monument of, 483
Aristocracy, a sort of established, in Boston, 84
Arms, the appeal to, advocated under certain circumstances, 265
Armstrong, Samuel T., mayor, 456
Artillery Company, the Ancient and Honorable, 88, 240
Assistants, the first court of, 42
Athenæum, the Boston, how begun, 476
Attucks, Crispus, death of, 312
Aulnay, d', wishes to trade with Boston, 99
Austin, Anne, and Mary Fisher arrive from the Barbadoes, and are sent away, 110

B

Back Bay, improvements in the, planned by Arthur Gilman, and carried out, 455
Back-Bay region, process of improving, 412
Ball, the Peace, in 1815, dress of an attendant at, 417
Balls frowned upon by Adams, 392
Bancroft, George, on the transfer of the charter, 9; History, quoted, 301, 457
Banishment, a punishment for uninvited settlers, 63; of Roger Williams, 77
Bank, a private, proposed, 208
Baptism, infant, trouble about, 104
Baptist Society, the First, in Boston, 110

INDEX. 485

Barbadoes, contest about a salary at, 226; trade with, 97
Barré calls the Bostonians Sons of Liberty, 291
Barton collection of books, 476
Bates, Joshua, gives money to the Public Library, 476
Bay Psalm Book, the, 118; specimens of the verses in, 109
Beacon Hill, the (Sentry) digging away of, 412, 454; in early days, 58; the steepness of, 454
Beecher, Henry Ward, on the character of Boston, 482
Beecher, Lyman, pastor of the church on Bowdoin Street, 447
Belcher, Jonathan, becomes governor, 228; disaffection with, 230
Belknap, Jeremy, founds the Massachusetts Historical Society, 475
Bellomont, Earl of (Richard Coote), 189; begins his rule, 196
Bernard, Governor Francis, denounced, 294; called to account for unwarranted expenditure, 271; called to London, 303; character of, 304; fears to ask for troops, 295
Bernard and Hutchinson, influence of, 325
Bible, the, furnishes the model for the Bostonian government, 84; influence of the, on England, 16; to be kissed by witnesses, 167; the mode of reading it, 180; quoted to support a Boston notion, 190; the source of early Boston laws, 119
Bible-reading in churches, 118
Bigelow, John P., mayor, 456
Bilboes, as a punishment, 63, 64
Bill, the, sent up by Judge Sewall in the Old South, 187
Bishop's palace, the, in Cambridge, occupied by Burgoyne, 389
Blackstone. See Blaxton.
Bladen, Martin, charges that Boston seeks independency, 209
Blaxton, the first settler at Boston,
38; invites Winthrop to Shawmut, 42
Blessing of the Bay, the, launched, 52
"Blockade of Boston," a play composed to enliven the British during the siege, 372
Blood, the first, spilled, 309
Boards, price of, fixed, 69
Board of Trade, the development of, 209; invites a meeting of colonists, 250
"Body of Liberties," the, prepared by Ward, 121
Bomazeen, imprisonment of, 189
Book, the first, printed in Boston, 119
Books and printing, 118
Boston accused of aiming at the sovereignty of the continent, 328; acts as though she were independent, 151; alarmed by a rumor of the return of the British, 388; alarmed by rumors of Indian war, 146; alarmed by the French Acadians, 100; alarmed when the charter was called for, 122; area of, 56; area of, enlarged, 412; aspect of, in 1631, 56, 60, 61; beauty of, 454; becomes a place governed by a few, 420; bound hand and foot, 167; carefully watched by England, 273; celebrates its coming two hundred years of age, 451; celebrates its 250th anniversary, 482; censures the governor for accepting a salary from the king, 326; changes in, after the Revolution, 397; the chief seat of opposition, 307; church, the, errors in, 79; complained of by the Board of Trade, 209; condition of, during the siege, 368, 369; condition of, after the siege, 380; in constant strife with the king's governors, 191, 192; denounces the stamp act, 285; destitute of the choice spirits that once it

knew, 387; determined to resist taxation, 308; determines to assert its rights, 297; divisions of, in early times, 397; early government of, 83; in the early times, 126; engages in the trade with China, 415; evacuated by General Howe, 375; excellences of, 385, 386; excited by the arrival of tea ships, 337; excites Hutchinson's jealousy, 321; expects liberty to be snatched away, 292; the first settlers around, 38; government of, 418; great influence of, in the public discussions, 290; hears of the declaration of independence, 384; holds an "adjourned" town-meeting, 354; holds a town-meeting about the port bill, 351; holds power through its town-meetings, 92; importance of, in the early period, 376, 378; independency of, makes an impression in England, 143; independent in the days of Cromwell, 138; influence of, among the towns, 91, 332; influence of, throughout the colonies, 249; invested by war ships, 299; the jealousy on the part of other towns disappears, 299; just before the Revolution, as drawn by Hutchinson, 323, 325; laughed at by New York, 328; living in, in early days, 145; looks toward the great West, 406; loses population during the Revolution, 397, 398; made the naval rendezvous, 322; meetings of the selectmen cease, 363; merchants support the legislature against Burnet, 226; named, 42, 44; objects to the presence of troops, 302; opposed to giving up the charter, 154; opposed to governors appointed by the king, 190; opposed to the War of 1812, 416; origin of the name, 44; Parliament thinks it ought to be destroyed, 345; a period in its existence, 376; people, not a rabble, 363; port of, closed, 346; postpones giving up the charter, 124; prepares to defend itself against the king, 123, 141; progress of, 172; customs of, 172; changes in, 173; "creeping statesmen" in, 172; tricks not to be shown in, 174; Sunday in, 175, 176; matrimony in, 178; holy days in, 178; preaching in, 180; first marriage in the Town House, 182; dwellings and mode of living in, 184; inhabitants of, 185; prosperous, 125; "prostrates" itself before Charles II., and keeps on fortifying itself, 141, 142; a purely English town, 426; receives a charter as a city, 422; rejoices at the removal of Bernard, 304; relative size of, in early days, 87; remarkable changes in its physical appearance, 469; reported bombardment of, 357; restless under Hutchinson, 327; sends letters to the other towns, 327; settles the financial policy of the province, 208; siege of, begun, 361, 364; seventeen miles from a seaport, 353; social changes in, 390; supports the Union cause in the last war, 473; terrified at the appointment of Kirke, 156, 157; threatened by a fleet, 324; trade growing up in, 97; trade interfered with by the parliament, 193; troubled by Indians, 92; troubled by Quakers, 110; widening of the interests of, 472; wishes to become a city, 419

Boston Mill Corporation, scheme of 412

Boston Public Library, the, 475

Boston and Roxbury Mill Corporation, scheme of, 410

Boston and Worcester Railroad, 450

Bostoneers, name given the inhabitants of Boston by Randolph, 198
Bostonian Society, the, object of, 474
Bostonians, called "Sons of Liberty," 291; defects of, as seen by John Adams, 385, 386; grow rich in the carrying trade, 414; mainly whigs, 262; think rapidly and to purpose, 286; uneasy in the days of Pownall, 259
Bounties offered for scalps, 201
Bowdoin, Governor, dwelling of occupied by Burgoyne, 370; gives a sentiment, 384
Bowen, Francis, "Life of Otis," by, 296
Bow-wows, the three, arrive, 363
Boyle, Robert, President of the Society for the Propagation of the Gospel, 136
Boylston, Thomas, disciplined by sundry "females," 358
Bracket's tavern, known as Cromwell's Head, 408
Bradish's tavern, now Porter's Hotel, 389
Bradstreet, Simon, at the head of Boston affairs, 169, 170
Brattle Street church, beginning of, 199
Brawls in the streets in 1768, 301, 310, 311
Breck, Samuel, dwelling of, occupied by Earl Percy, 370
Breed's Hill, battle on, 366. See Bunker's Hill
Bridge to Charlestown, building of a, 408
Bridge, the Craigie, to Cambridge, built, 409; the Harvard, building of, 409
Bridges, effect of the, when lighted, 409, 410
Brighton, annexation of, 470
Brimmer, Martin, mayor, 456
Briscoe, Nathaniel, brutally beaten, 107
British authority ended in Boston, 385

Brook Farm movement, the, plan of, 460
Browne, John and Samuel, sent to England, 64
Brown, John, comes to Boston, 466
Buckminster, Rev. Joseph Stevens, pastor of the Brattle Street church, 200
Buildings, new, on the made land, 470
Bulfinch, Charles, designs a monument to commemorate the Beacon, 453
Bullivant, Doctor, makes a repartee to Bellomont, 197
Bunch of Grapes tavern, bonfire in front of; 385; important meeting in, 406; reception of Governor Burnet at, 225
Bunker Hill, battle on, 366, 367
Burgoyne, General, arrives in Boston the first time, 363; surrender of, 389
Burnet, William, becomes governor, 223; death of, 227
Burying-place, the first, 43
Business, stagnation of, in 1814, 416
Byles, Mather, minister of the Hollis Street church, salutes Governor Burnet, 224; describes a Harvard commencement, 237

C

Cambridge, Eng., important meeting at, 1, 9
Cambridge. See New Town.
Cambridge, an army at, the day after Lexington, 364; legislature adjourns to, in 1769, 302; adjournment of the court to, 227; ferry to, 131; meetings of the provincial congress at, 358, 360; receives its name, 107; reception of Washington in, in 1789, 402
Cambridge platform, departed from, 199
Canals, beginnings of, 448

Canso, garrison at, surprised, 244
Capital offences in America and England, 121
Carpets not known in early Boston, 400
Carrying trade, prosperity of the, 414
Catholics, fear of the, 102
Caucus Club, the, 221
Caulker's Club, the, 223, 235
Celebrations, anniversaries, etc., influence of, 294
"Centennial," the first, in Boston, 231
Centennial period, the, 473, 474
Chandelier, the word attracts the attention of Gen. Putnam, 374
Channing, William E., influence of, 446; shows his sympathy with the opponents of slavery, 464
Chapman, Jonathan, mayor, 456
Charles I. grants a charter to settlers in New England, 3
Charles II. not "proclaimed" in Boston, 139
Charlestown, annexation of, 470; bridge to, built, 408
Charlton becomes the capital, 41
Charter, the Massachusetts, proposal to take it to America, 5; transfer of the, discussed, 6; the, demanded by the king, 122; differing views of the nature of, 193; the 'explanatory" (1725), 213; rights under the, 6; rights under the, proclaimed, 140; struggle for it between the king and the colonists, 151, 153, etc.
Charters, abrogation of the, advocated, 209
Chauncy, Charles, reads the Declaration of Independence in his pulpit, 385; on the union of the colonies, 355
Christ Church (Boston), lanterns hung in the steeple of, 361
Christ Church, Cambridge, 273
Church, Benjamin, brought forward, 263; delivers an oration commemorating the massacre,

332; a writer on the side of England, 325
Church green, site of the New South meeting-house, 221
Church of England, feelings of Winthrop towards, 30; the, suspected, 273
Church, the Episcopal, begins to thrive, 162
Church, the, of New England, character of, according to Hubbard, 75
Church music, 117
Church services in the early days, 180
Cincinnati, Society of the, fears about, 405
Cisterns provided for use in case of fire, 431
Citizen, an indignant, writes to the *Advertiser*, 410
City, movements toward a, 420–423
Clergy, limits to the influence of, 72; a new, sought by Randolph, 181
Club, the Anthology, 478
Club, a whig, advocates the rights of the people, in 1747, 264
Clymer, George, on liberty, 337
Cobb, Samuel C., mayor, 456
Cobbler, the Simple, of Agawam, mentioned, 26; on fashions, 138
Cochituate Lake, water obtained from, 435, 455
Codfish and cranberries sent to the king, 144
Coinage of money complained of by Randolph, 153
Coleridge, S. T., influence of, 459
Colman, Benjamin, first pastor of the Manifesto Church, 199, 200; "lashes" the Mathers, 202
Colonization of America, 1
Colonists, invited to Ireland, 125; some leave Boston, 98
Column, the, on Beacon Hill, 453;
Come-Outers, the, 459
Commencement at Harvard, as described by Byles, 237, 238

Commerce, depressed by war debts, 400; prosperity of, 449; suffered during the Revolution, 398
Commissioners from the king, expected to take the government from the people, 140, 141; arrive, but effect nothing, 142
Commissions, roving, of the king's governors, 191
Common, the Boston, owed to the influence of Winthrop, 73; cows pastured on, 438; the water that once washed its shores, 410
Concert Hall, situation of, 394
Concord, "battle" at, 361; provincial Congress formed at, 357
Confederation, the New England, of 1643, origin of, 93
Congregational Church, the, 447
Congress, of the colonies called, 351; a continental, wished by Samuel Adams, 337; the continental, delegates to, 353; the first of the colonies, 249; meets at Philadelphia, 353; a provincial, favored by the "county meeting," 356; the provincial, organized at Concord, 357; the stamp act, 280
Conscience, liberty of, 77, 106; freedom of, to be extended to users of the prayer-book, 139; should be free, thought Saltonstall, 65
Conscientiousness in early times, 219
Constitution, the new, of Massachusetts, adopted, 391, 403, 404; debate on the adoption of, 350
Constitution of the United States, ratification of the, 474
Contraction of marriage, 178
Cooper, Rev. Samuel, pastor of the Brattle Street church, 200
Cooper, Rev. William, pastor of the Brattle Street church, 200
Coote, Richard, Earl of Bellomont, 189, 196
Copp's (Windmill) Hill, 58; the burial-place of the Mathers, 213; digging away of, 413
Corn a legal tender, 98
Corn-stalks, sugar and molasses to be made from, 388, 389
Correspondence, committees of, 279; meet, 350; opposed by Hancock, 391; plan for, 326, 327, 334
Cotting, Uriah, important project of, 410
Cotton, Rev. John, arrives, 70, 130; disapproves of democracy, 83; expected by Winthrop at Groton, 28; on Roger Williams, 66, 76; overrates his clerical power; 72; prepares "Moses, his Judicials," 119
Cotton's Hill, a name of Pemberton Hill, 413
Council for New England, records of, edited by Charles Deane, 3
County meeting, a, held at Dedham and Milton, 355
Couriers, a system of, established by the county meeting, 356
Court, the Great and General, formed, 5; troubled about a sow, 89, 90; adjourns to Cambridge, 210; adjourns to Salem, 226; adjourns, hoping for some "unhappy accident," 160; meets at Salem, and appoints delegates to Congress, 352, 353, 354
Courtship in the Winthrop family, 27, 54
Coves, the, of Boston, 58
Cows pastured on the Common until 1828, 438
Cradle of Liberty, a name of Faneuil Hall, 235
Cradock, Matthew, governor of the Massachusetts Company, 5
Crafts, Thomas, reads the Declaration of Independence in Boston the first time, 384
Credit, bills of, banish coin, 208
Creeping statesmen infest Boston, 173

Cromwell invites colonists to Ireland and Jamaica, 125
Cromwell's Head tavern, 408
Cross in the flag, the, disapproved, 76, 174
Curfew bell, the, 114
Currency, paper, depreciation of, 229; troubles with, 209
Curwen, Samuel, "Journal" of, quoted, 397; remarks of, about changes in society, 387, 396
Cushing, Thomas, appointed delegate to Congress, 358
Customs, early Bostonian, 114
Cutler, Manasseh, negotiates with Congress about western lands, 408

D

Dalrymple, Col., decides to remove troops, 316
Dancing opposed in early days, 175
Dancing-school, an, established, 176
Dartmouth, the first tea-ship, appears in Boston harbor, 338
Davis, Thomas A., mayor, 456
Dawes, William, sent to Lexington, 360
Daye, Stephen, the first printer, 118
Deaf-mutes, schools for, 444
Deane, Charles, communicates to the Historical Society about John Hull's house, 162; edits the records of the Council for New England, 3; on the Council for New England, 2; on the gift of Boston to Ireland, 150
Debt, the, of England, increase of, 277
Debt, the, public, increased by the Louisburg expedition, 247
Debts incurred during the Revolution, 398, 400
Democracy, a, not intended by the founders of New England, 83; a simple, the government of Boston, 418

Diary, the, of John Winthrop, begun, 32
Dickinson, John, on the American Congress, 355
"Dippers Dipt," the, by Featley, 78
Discourse on Government, by John Winthrop, 6
Display opposed by Samuel Adams, 390
Discussion in Boston before the Revolution, 274
Distress, financial, after the wars, 208
Dorchester Heights fortified, 366, 374, 406
Dorchester Neck annexed and called South Boston, 409
Dress thoroughly studied in early Boston, 400
Drinking too much punished, 69
Druiletes, Gabriel, the Jesuit missionary, visits Boston, 103; says the first mass in Boston, 103
Dudley, Joseph, chosen governor by Charles II., 159; disappoints the expectations of Randolph, 161; made governor, 200; degeneracy of, 153; his demand for a salary, how met, 192; death of, 205
Dudley, Thomas, one of the first settlers in Boston, 20; deputy-governor, traits of, 66; receives Druiletes, the Jesuit missionary, 103
Dummer, William, governor *ad interim*, 212
Dunkirkers, dangers from, 35
Dunster, Henry, becomes president of Harvard College, 108; finds himself at odds with his church about baptism, 109; is obliged to vacate his office, 109
Duties levied on goods imported from England and the West Indies, 211
Dwellings, in early days, 115; furniture of, 400

E

Eaton, Nathaniel, is made head of Harvard College, 107; he beats his usher brutally, 107; feeds his scholars poorly, 107; is cast out, and goes to Virginia, 108
Education in early Boston, 439, 441
Election, methods of, 85
Election Sermon, the, before the artillery company, 241
Eliot, the Rev. John, apostle to the Indians, exchanges civilities with Druiletes, 103, 104, 136
Eliot, Samuel Atkins, mayor, 456
Ellis, Dr. G. E., describes the trials of the colonists, 126; on the motives of the early emigrants, 31; on the transfer of the charter, 9
Embargo, the, effect of, in Boston, 415, 416
Emerson, George B., labors to improve the school system, 456
Emerson, R. W., interested in Coleridge, 459
Emerson, William, begins the Athenæum, 476
Emigrant Aid Society, the, founded, 466
Emigration, falls off in 1631, 65; numbers who came over, 95
Endicott, Governor John, cuts the cross out of the flag, 76; goes to Salem, 2; meets Winthrop on his arrival at Salem, 37
Engines, fire, opposition to the use of, 432
England, claims America by virtue of Cabot's discovery, 1; decides to be "civil and conciliating," 144; endeavors to restrict the trade of Boston in 1785, 414; sees evidence of independence, 88; supposed to need American money to pay its debts, 255
England, Church of, discountenanced, 153
English high-school, the, 443

Episcopal Church, the, growth of 447
Episcopalians encouraged by Randolph, 161
Episcopal service held in Boston for the first time, 161
Equality of men, the, supported by Otis, 272
Evelyn, John, on the independency of Boston, 143
Everett, Edward, at the Federal Street church, 446; gives his books to the Public Library, 476; on slavery, 464
Exportations, prohibited from Boston, 415; renewed by British merchants, 307
Extent of the American continent as seen by early colonists, 3

F

Factory towns increase, 452
Falmouth, now Portland, Adams at, 362
Familists, the, errors of, 79
Famine in Boston, 52
Faneuil Hall, a business men's meeting in, in 1785, 414; important meetings in, 422; Lovejoy meeting in, 464; meeting against abolitionism, 463; meeting in, to condemn the Ursuline Convent riot, 468; meeting in, to oppose the importation of tea, 338; meetings in, to protest against extravagance, 392; occupied by troops, 300; site of, 60.
Faneuil Hall market, built, 234, 235; inadequate, 433
Faneuil, Peter, proposes to build a market-house, 234
Fast, the first, 41
Fasts and thanksgivings, 179
Father of America, the, 379
Federalist leaders receive an offer from England, 415
Federalists, the, support the Massachusetts constitution, 404
Federal Street Church, convention, in, 474

Federal Street, why so named, 404
Female Anti-Slavery Society, meeting of, 463
Ferry, a, established to Charlestown, 69
Feudalism feared on account of the formation of the Society of the Cincinnati, 405
Finances, the, of Boston retrieved from confusion by Mayor Quincy, 432
Financial distress, 208
Fines as punishments, 69
Fire, the great, of 1872, 480
Fires, confusion at, 431; provision against, in early times, 431, 478; reform in management of, 430; the notable, in Boston, 478
Fisheries, interest of Samuel Adams in, 403
Flats, contract for filling, 455, 456
Fleet, a British, comes to Boston, 324
Floors uncarpeted in early Boston, 400
Flynt, Tutor, opinion of Whitefield, 233
Fones, Priscilla, matrimonial affair of, 26
Food in early days, 62
Fort Hill, efforts to fortify, 379; now cut away, 58; levelled, 454
Fortunes made during the Revolution, 400
Foster, John, the first Boston printer, 119
Fourth of July, the noisy celebration of, owed to John Adams, 384; takes the place of other anniversaries, 319
Foxcroft, Rev. Thomas, preaches a centennial sermon, 231
France, alliance with, 394; a fictitious war with, provided against, 299
Franklin, Benjamin, colonial agent in London, 348; examined by the House of Commons, 288; in favor of paying for the tea destroyed, 354; obtains some letters of Hutchinson, 335
Franklin, James, begins a paper in Boston, 211
Franklins, the, do not reverence the Mathers, 212
Freemen, oath of the, 85; must belong to churches, 84; seek to enlarge their share in the government, 85; semi-annual meetings of, how warned, 418
Free-Soil Party, the, 465
French, the, at Acadie, relations with, 99, 100
Frog Pond, water let into, from Cochituate Lake, 455
Frothingham, O. B., quoted, 458, 460
Fugitive Slave Act, the, denounced, 466
Fuller, Margaret, and Transcendentalism, 459
Funeral, the, of the boy Schneider, 309
Funerals, how conducted, 177, 178; of the victims of the massacre, 316

G

Gage, General, arrives in Boston as governor, 351; character of, 352; collects troops, builds barracks and fortifications, 356; dissolves the general court at Salem, 354; on the Boston people, 363; recalled after the battle of Bunker Hill, 371; receives a protest against the presence of troops, 302; sends troops to Concord, 360
Gammell, Prof. William, "Life of Roger Williams," 66
Gannett, Ezra Stiles, in the Federal Street church, 446
Gardiner, Sir Christopher, banished, 64
Gardiner, S. R., "History of England," quoted, 5; on the character of Margaret Winthrop, 16; on independency in Boston, 88

Garments of men and women in early days, 218
Garrison monument, the, 467
Garrison, William Lloyd, and abolitionism, 461; dragged through the streets, 463; likened to Samuel Adams, 466; monument, 467
Gaston, William, mayor, 456
Gates, General, in command of the army about Boston, 379
George III, expresses his " unalterable" determination, 372
Germaine, Lord George, on the influence of town-meetings, 345
Gibbons, Mrs. Edward, goes to Pullen Point, 99
Gilman, Arthur, plans improvements in the Back Bay, 454
Gilman, Nicholas, makes out a "carnal" scheme, 248
Girls' high-school, the, revived, 442
Girls' Latin school, the, founded, 442
Girls, opportunities for education, 439, 440
Gloves and rings at funerals 227, 228
Gold obtained for rum, 399
Gordon, William, on the Caucus Club, 221; his " American Revolution," quoted, 277
Gorges, F., " America Painted to the Life," 4
Gorham, town of, favors liberty, 329
Gospel, intention to carry it to the Indians, 14
Gout, the, an old friend of Hancock, 350, 403
Government, a continental demanded, 381
Government of Boston, the, 418; inefficient, 420; loose methods in, 422; suffers a change, 83
Governments, local, recommended by the Continental Congress, 381
Governors, royal, number of, 195; not successful, 206; popular feeling, towards, 197; time of the, a period of constant strife, 189

Grace-cup, a, presented to Harvard College by William Dummer, 217
Grammar schools, course in the, 445
Granary burying-ground, the resting-place of the victims of the massacre, 317
Gray, Edward, begins rope-making, 310
Gray, Harrison, grandfather of Harrison Gray Otis, 310; warns a young gentleman against intemperate language, 342
Great tree, the, at Essex Street, 281, 287, 291
Green, J. R., on the condition of Puritan England, 16
Greene, Gardiner, estate of, 413; mansion of, occupied by Earl Percy, 370
Greene, Samuel A., mayor, 456
Gridley, Jeremiah, opens the case in favor of writs of assistance, 269
Griffin, E. D., pastor of the Park Street church, 447
Griffin's wharf, the tea-party at, 342
Groton, Suffolk, the home of John Winthrop, 11
Groton, sale of the homestead at, 51

H

Hair-cutting, views regarding, 215
Hair, long, not to be tolerated, 136
Hancock, J., appointed delegate to Congress, 358; arrested, 301; charged with smuggling, 296; in conflict with Washington, 402; delivers an oration written by Adams, 349, 350; dwelling of, occupied by Gen. Clinton, 370; entertains the French officers, 394; enters college, 258; "exposes" letters of Hutchinson, 335; gives a great dinner, 289; opposed to the nomination of Washington, 391; ostentation of, 402; refuses to order the

cadets to support Hutchinson, 339
Hancock and Adams, characteristics of each, 390; dissensions between and reconciliation of, 391; excepted from a proclamation by Gage, 365; outlaws, 383
Hangings, public, opposed by Quincy, 429
Hanover Square, an open space around the Liberty Tree, 291
Hart, Thomas N., mayor, 456
Hartford Convention, the, characterized, 416
Harvard Bridge, the, 409
Harvard College begins in a school, 106; commencement in early days, 237, 238; criticized by Whitefield, 232, 233; "dangerous" teachings at, 199; a nursery of seditious preachers, 182; ought to be suppressed, 182; reorganization of, by Josiah Quincy, 437; its original purpose, 439; students assert their patriotism, 300
Harvard examinations for women, 443
Harvard, Rev. John, becomes benefactor of the college, 107
Health, Board of, declares the Back-Bay region a nuisance, 412
Health-drinking, disapproved, 51
Heath, General, called upon to lend a book, 373
Henry, Patrick, draws up the Virginia resolves, 278; makes a celebrated speech against the stamp act, 280; proposes a congress, 280; provides for intercolonial correspondence, 334
Higginson, the Rev. Francis, sails for America, 4
High-school, course in the, 445; a, for girls, in Boston, 440
High and Latin school building, the, 444
Hills, the, of Boston, 58
Historic-Genealogic Society, the, 475

History, interest in, 474
Holyoke, President Edward, testifies against Whitefield, 233
Homespun goods, 399; admired, 286
Hooker, Rev. Thomas, 130; preaches a long sermon, in Cambridge, 117
Hoosac mountain to be tunnelled, 448
Hope, the ship, captured when entering Boston harbor, 380
Hosmer, J. K., "Life of Adams," quoted, 295, 329, 349
House of Correction established, 70
Howe, Estes, settles the site of the house of John Hull, 162
Howe, General, arrives at Boston, 363; on the Battle of Bunker Hill, 367
Howes, the, hatred of, 369
Hubbard, William, historian, quoted, 32; on the enemies of New England, 78
Hull, John, site of his house, 162
Humanity, the enthusiasm of, 459
Humfrey, John, an original settler, 21
Hutchinson, Anne, comes to Boston, 74; character of, 79; banned, 80
Hutchinson, Edward, sent against Philip, 147
Hutchinson, Thomas, alarmed by the action of Massachusetts towns, 330; assumes the management of affairs, 306; character of, and descent of, 265, 266; characterizes the first committee of correspondence, 327; his demand for a salary, how opposed, 192; favors extreme measures, 308; fatuity of, 330; favors a hard-money currency, 248; flees from his home, 284; his "History of Massachusetts" quoted, 4, 266; his house mobbed, 283; impotent to support the tax collectors, 339; investigates the massacre, 312; leaves for Eng-

land, 352; letters of, theatrically exposed, 335; made governor, 322; on the means used by Samuel Adams, 378; on the murder of a "poor German," 310; his power gone, 349; recall of, demanded, 226; on the second generation of statesmen in Boston, 173; surrenders the Castle to Major Dalrymple, 322; on the uneasiness of the people, 85

Hydraulion, a, purchased by Mayor Quincy, 431

I

Importations opposed by Boston, 351

Impressment of seamen, 252; on the *Romney*, 296

Independency, the aim at, traced to Governor Winthrop, 451; almost a fact in 1671, 144; an avowal of, according to Hutchinson, 334; danger of the approach of, according to Hutchinson, 330; declared, 383, 384; desire for, the controlling passion from the beginning, 275; desire for, charged to the Bostonians, 209; disavowed as an intention, 279; dreaded by the tories, 381; evidences of a feeling of, 8; the first declaration of, 10; the great topic before the Congress of 1776, 383; indicated by the coinage of money, 139; indications of, 121, 151; jealously watched by the king's governors, 191; looking towards, 87; a move towards, made by Adams, 237, 239; planned by Adams, 265; prophesied by Governor Pownall, 261; signs of, 95; the son of Liberty, 281; supported by biblical arguments, 190

Indians, gives trouble, 145; as servants, 115; shut out of Boston, 151

Indian strife, results of, 196

Indian war causes anxiety in Boston, 258; devastates the country, 201

Indies, searchers for the, who thought to go through the continent, 3

Individualism, the, of the religion of Boston, 457

Industries, the great, of Boston, 398

Informer, an, tarred and feathered, 308

Innovations in government opposed, 421

Inoculation practised by Dr. Boylston, 211

Intemperance in the olden time, 196

Ireland sends money to Boston, 150

Isms, the, of Boston, 458

J

James I. grants a charter, 2

Jamaica Pond furnishes water to Boston, 435

Jefferson, Thomas, influenced by Federalist representations, 416; on Samuel Adams, 378

Jenks, William, pastor of the Park Street church, 447

Johnson, Arbella, an original settler, 21; dies, 42

Johnson, Isaac, an original settler, 21

"Joice junior" terrifies royalists, 387

Joseph, The Selling of, tract by Sewall, 218, 463

Judges, the, to be made independent of the people, 326

Junketings of the selectmen, 419

Jury, trial by, to be refused, 277

K

Kansas, emigrants sent to, 466

Keayne, Robert, captain of the Ancient and Honorable Artillery Company, 240; and the widow's pig, 88, 89

Kidd, William, and the Earl of Bellomont, 198

Kindergartens established, 444
King, the, ignored in the freeman's oath, 87
King's Chapel built, 166
Kirke, Col. Piercy, chosen as governor of New England, 156; characterized by Mather, 158
Knowles, Commodore Sir Charles, impresses seamen, 252

L

Lamb abstained from, that there might be more sheep and wool, 285
"Land Bank" scheme, the, 230
Land titles disturbed by Randolph and Andros, 167, 169
Language, peculiar use of, by the Mathers, 214
Latin School, the, purpose of, 441; boys in the, 440
La Tour wishes to trade with Boston, 99
Laud, Archbishop, influence of, on New England, 81
Lawrence, Amos A., sends men to Kansas, 466
Laws, the early, 119
Lawyers, profession of, not admired, 206
Lectures at the Lowell Institute, 446
Lee, Arthur, opposes the importation of tea, 337, 338
Lee, Richard Henry, approves intercolonial correspondence, 334; letter of Samuel Adams to, on State sovereignty, 403
Letters of John Adams and his wife quoted, 385, 386 (See Adams, Mrs. John)
Letters, the, of Hutchinson, theatrically exposed, 335
Letters, virulent, written by the Mathers, 201
Leverett, John, governor, sends men against Philip, 147
Lexington, "battle" at, 361
Liberator, The, publication of, 461

Liberties abridged under the king's governors, 160
Liberty, not always distinguished from license, 284; movement towards, 460; threatened by a fleet, 324
Liberty Hall an open space, 287, 291
Liberty Party, the, formed, 465
Liberty Tree, the, at Essex Street, 287; cut down by the British soldiers, 371
Library, the Boston Public, 475
Licenses of tippling-houses taken away by Mayor Quincy, 430
Lincoln, F. W., Jr., mayor, 456
Lincoln monument, the, 483
Linn, Henry, whipped and banished, 64
Liverpool wharf, Tea-party at, 342
Living, cost of, after the Revolution, 386, 387; in Boston in early days, 115
Local governments recommended by the Continental Congress, 381
London, city of, loses its charter, 155; affected by Boston's restrictions on trade, 415
Long Lane, name of, changed to Federal Street, 405
Long Pond, now Lake Cochituate, used as a water-supply, 435
Lothrop, Rev. Samuel K., pastor of the Brattle Street church, 200
Loudoun, Lord, commander of the royal army, 260
Louisburg, capture of, 243, 247; iron cross from, 256
Lovejoy, killing of, meeting about, 464
Lowell, Master John, gives Faneuil Hall a name, 235, 236; imprisonment of, 369; closing of the Latin school by, 423
Lowell Institute founded by John Lowell in 1839, 446
Lowell, John, establishes the Lowell Institute, 445
Lowell railroad, the, opened, 450
Loyalists find refuge in Boston, 364

Loyalty, defined by the *Independent Advertiser*, 265 ; weakening in Boston in 1760, 260
Luxury, after the Revolution, 400 ; opposition of John Adams to, 393
Lyman, Theodore, Jr., mayor, 456

M

Mall, breezes that once blew over the, 410 ; a new, on Charles Street, 432
"Manifesto" Church, the, why so named, 199
Mann, Horace, improvements in the school system by, 456 ; influence of, in education, 442
Manufactory House, the, a place for the celebration of the massacre, 319
Manufacture, the chief, before the Revolution, 398
Manufactures, grow up in Boston, 98 ; interfered with by parliament, 194 ; the New England Society for the promotion of, 452 ; and trade, improve, 452
Market-house, designs for a new one, by Mayor Quincy, 432 ; building of a, 433
Markets, three built, and destroyed, 234
Marriage ceremony, the, in early days, 178
Marriage, the first, in the Town House, 182
Marriages solemnized by a magistrate, 177
Marsh, President, introduces the works of Coleridge, 459
Martin, Augustus P., mayor, 456
Masked ball, a, arranged by the British, 372
Mass, the first, in Boston, 103
Massachusetts becomes the Territory of Massachusetts Bay, 371 ; the chief industries of, in 1750, 398 ; colony to be broken up, 124 ; forms a local government, 356, 357, 381 ; gives up to the king under protest, 160 ; named by John Smith, 2 ; refuses to furnish troops in 1814, 417
Massachusetts Company, the, formed, 4
Massachusetts Historical Society, the purposes of, 475
Massacre, the Boston, a street riot, 276 ; how originated, 311, 312, 313 ; celebrated in 1773, 332 ; in 1775, 358, 359 ; monument to commemorate, 483
Master of the Puppets, a name given to Adams by Hutchinson, 306
Mather, Cotton, character of, 134, 135 ; on danger from fire in Boston, 480 ; on the death of Arbella Johnson, 42 ; favors inoculation, 211 ; his opinion of Williams, 76 ; prepares to be president of Harvard College, 135 ; is disappointed, 135 ; proposes to publish a tract on slavery, 218 ; on religious customs, 177
Mather dynasty, the, begins, 129
Mather, Rev. Increase, life of, 132 ; called a "bellows of sedition and treason," 184 ; characterizes the students at Harvard College, 439 ; church of, burned, 479 ; connected with the persecution of witches, 186 ; gives an opinion of a newspaper, 212 ; laments the bad times, 199 ; sent to England to plead with the king, 168 ; has some success in England, 171 ; strong words of, on the charter, 154 ; writes the first book printed in Boston, 119
Mather, Increase and Cotton, deaths of, 213
Mather, Richard, arrives, 129
Mather, Samuel, loses his library and the books of Cotton and Increase Mather, at the Battle of Bunker Hill, 367
Mather and Willard refuse the use of the Old South for Episcopal worship, 165

Mathers, the, opponents of Dudley, 201
Maverick, Samuel, at Winnisimmet, 38
Mayflower, the ship, carries emigrants to Boston, 32
Mayhew, Jonathan, denies the power of parliament over religion, 274; preaches a notable sermon, 283; writes about liberty, 281
Mayoralty, difficulty about, at the organization of the city government, 422
Mayors, the, of Boston, 438; list of, 456
Mechanics' Institute, the Boston, 452
Medford, once Mystic, 40
Meeting-house, the first, 61, 116; its second building, 179
Meeting, talking in, forbidden, 137
Memorial Association, the Boston, 474
Military companies formed upon the passage of the port bill, 351
Militia, the, in early Boston, 241; training-day for, 69
Mill Corporation, the Boston and Roxbury, scheme of, 410
Mill Cove and Creek, 58
Mill Cove, filled up with soil from Beacon Hill, 454; filling up of the, 412
Mill Creek, filling up of, 412
Mill-dam, building of the, 410
Mill Pond, limits of, in early days, 59; filling up of the, 412, 413
Ministers, influence of, 87; invited to emigrate, 25
Minot's continuation of Hutchinson's History, quoted, 398
Minute-men enrolled, 358
"Model of Christian Charity," a work by John Winthrop, 48
Molasses act, forfeitures under the, 268; the, enforced by Paxton, 254
Molasses distilled into rum by Gage, 369; price of, after the Revolution, 387
Money, the coinage of, in Boston, 139; trouble about, 208
Montreal, fall of, 259
Morning gun of the Revolution, the, 274
Morton, Thomas, of Wollaston, sent to England, 64; punished for "cheating Indians," 50
Motto of Boston city, 425
"Mr." Plastowe, to be called Josias, 69
Mugford, Captain, captures a vessel with powder, 380
Munster, excesses at, 78, 105
Music, instrumental, not relished, 200
Mutiny act, the, passed, 280

N

Naumkeag, the early name for Salem, 2
Navigation, the act of, interferes with commerce, 140
Neck, change in the width of, 456, 470
Negroes, traffic in, disliked by Sewall, 218
New England as seen by John Winthrop, 49, 51
New England, Council for, formed, 2
New England people awkward, according to John Adams, 386
New Hampshire, boundary trouble, 230; forms a local government, 381
News-Letter, ill success of the, 211
New South church, the, 222
Newspapers, origin of, in Boston, 202
Newspaper, the third, begun by James Franklin, 211
New Town (Cambridge) fortified, 69; a college to be established at, 106; once destined to be the capital, 67; becomes Cambridge, 107

New York becomes larger than Boston, 398; political principles of, 337
Non-importation agreements, 285; foretold, 278
Norcross, Otis, mayor, 456
Normal schools founded, 442
North End, the, loses its precedence, 397; outlines of, 397
North, Lord, thinks the people of Boston a "riotous rabble," 346
North meeting-house, the, pulled down for firewood, 370
Northwestern territory, plan for influencing, 406
Norton, Rev. John, of Boston, 130, 131
Norton, Rev. John, of Hingham, preaches a "flattering" sermon, 202
Nowell, John, one of the original settlers, 20

O

Oakes, Urian, president of Harvard College compliments Cotton Mather, 134
O'Brien, Hugh, mayor, 456
Offal, removal of, under Mayor Quincy, 432
Office a trust, not to be declined, 242
Olcott, A. Bronson, and Transcendentalism, 459
Old North church, burned, 479
Old South meeting-house, the, after the massacre, 313, 314; meeting in, to oppose importation of tea, 339, 340; occupied as a riding-school, 370; refused to Andros, 165
Old South lectures on American history, 474
Oliver, Andrew, obliged to resign, 281; death of, 349
Oliver, Peter, chief-justice, charges against, 348
Opinions, effect of, in acts, 173
Otis, Harrison Gray, candidate for mayor, 423; chosen mayor, 448; describes Garrison, 462; suggests a Hartford convention, 416
Otis, James, arouses enthusiasm among the Harvard students, 302; close of the active life of, 305; graduation of, 258; Life of, by Francis Bowen, mentioned, 296; moves that the Superior Court adjourn to Faneuil Hall, "on account of the presence of soldiers," 301; opens debates to the public, 295; opposed to Bernard, 270; opposes the legality of writs of assistance, 269; prepares a memorial to go to England, 279; protests against troops about the State House, 302; publishes a vindication of the house, 272; on taxation without representation, 276; traits of, 266; comes into conflict with government, 266; would not deny all parliamentary authority, 325

P

Paine, Robert Treat, appointed delegate to congress, 358
Painter, one, whipped for not having his children baptized, 105
Painter, Rev. Henry, courts Priscilla Fones, 27
Palaverers, the Two, an inn, 221
Palfrey, Rev. John G., pastor of the Brattle Street church, 200, 446; does not oppose the Union, 465; his History referred to, 73
Palinurus, the, of the Revolution, 378
Palmer, Albert, mayor, 456
Panic, a financial, in Boston, 96
Paper money, refused after the Revolution, 387; troubles from, 229
Parker, Theodore, favors the Union, 465; gives books to the Public Library, 476; and Transcendentalism, 459

Parliament, acts of, not to be executed in Boston, 322
Parliament debates the question of taxing America, 288; deems its power vindicated, 347; resolves to check the defiant spirit of Boston, 345; right of, to tax America denied, 325; suppresses a bank by a retroactive decision, 230
Parliamentary supremacy argued for by Hutchinson, 331
Parsons, Theophilus, writes an address for Hancock, 350
Parties, in early Boston, 250; political, formed in abolition times, 465
Party strife lapses in war, 207
Patent, the, Williams' views regarding, 77
Patriotism, aroused in Boston, 286; bred in the New England towns, 92
Pauperism, investigated by Josiah Quincy, 429
Paxton, Charles, surveyor of the port, enforces the sugar law, 254
Pemberton, Rev. Ebenezer, disturbed, 204
Pemberton Hill, digging away of, 413
Pennsylvania, political principles of, 337
Pepperell, William, takes command of the Louisburg expedition, 246
Pepys, Samuel, acknowledges a "blessing mighty unexpected," 144
Pequod war, the, 92, 93
Percy, Lord, retreats to Boston, 365; sent with troops to Concord, 361
Peter, Hugh, comes to Boston, 74, 81
Petersham opposed to salaries for the governor from the king, 329
Philadelphia, congress to be held at, 353; the meeting, 355; contributes to alleviate the rigors of the port bill, 353; rejoices over the Boston tea-party, 343
Philip of Mount Hope gives trouble, 145; killed, 149
Philip's war, 206
Phillips, John, chosen mayor of Boston, 424
Phillips, pastor at Watertown, disciplined, 69
Phillips, Wendell, begins his remarkable career, 465; points out his father's house, 425
Philosophy, the, of Transcendentalism, 460
Phips, Sir William, made governor, 171; career of, 187; his pugilistic traits, 188
Pierce, Henry L., mayor, 456
Piracy, efforts to extirpate, 197; honored in early times, 33
Plastowe, Josias, fined for stealing from Indians, 69
Police force, reorganization of the, 456
Politics, revolution in, after the Revolution, 397
Poor, provision for the, under Mayor Quincy, 432
Population, growth of, retarded, 206
Port bill, the Boston, 347, 350, 354, 364
Porter's hotel, formerly Bradish's tavern, 389
Pownall, Thomas, appointed governor, 258; character of, 260, 261; holds correct views about America, 325
Prayer, a political, 202
Prayer-book forms objected to, 64
Preaching with notes, 180
Prerogative, the royal, sustained by Shute, 208
Prerogative men opposed to the patriots, 250
Press, importance of, in American history, 250
Preston, Captain John, and the massacre, 312, 317, 318
Primary schools, course in, 445

Prince, Frederick O., mayor, 456
Prince, Rev. Thomas, preaches a centennial sermon, 231
Prisoners, treatment of, by the British, 368
Privateering, a means of gaining riches, 387
Prophesying in church, 118
Providence railroad, the, opened, 450
Provincial congress, the, formed at Concord, 357
Provisions in early days, 62
Psalms, the, no longer read line by line in church, 200
Psalm-singing, in early days, 117; made libellous, 204
Public, the, admitted to debates, 295
Public Library, the, 475
Publishment of marriage intentions, 178
Punishments in early days, 53, 63
Puppets, Master of the, a name given to Adams, 306
Purchase Street, home of Adams on, 295; origin of name of, 310
Puritan dress, and other matters, 218
Puritanism, tendency of, 458
Putnam, General Rufus, makes a timely call, 373; writes to Washington in regard to western immigration, 406, 407
Putnam, Israel, surprises Charlestown, 365
"Puritan Age and Rule," the, referred to, 9, 31, 126, 429
Pynchon, William, an original settler, 21

Q

Quakers, hanged on the Common, 112; punishments for, 111; trouble Boston, 110
Quality, persons of, propose to emigrate to Boston, 73
Quarters for troops, dispute regarding, 300

Quebec, fall of, 259, sends aid to Boston, 353
Queen Street, now Court, 394
Quincy, three members of the family named Josiah, 340
Quincy, Josiah, Jr., bravely appears for Preston, 317, 428; called the Boston "Cicero," 263; announces the doctrine of secession 415; asks a question about tea and salt water, 340; recommends retaliation, 307; Memoir of quoted, 325, 345, 428
Quincy, Josiah, becomes president of Harvard College, 437; career of, before becoming mayor, 428; chosen mayor, 426; on common schools, 440; correspondence of, 416; delivers a Fourth of July oration, 428; gives an account of the motives of the settlers of Boston, 451; his History of Harvard University, 439; on the independency of early Bostonians, 8; influence of, on Boston, 438; Life of, quoted, 415; method of performing his duties as mayor, 429, 430, 436; Municipal History of, 422; nominated as mayor, 423; retires from office, 436
Quincy, Josiah, eleventh mayor, 454
Quincy Market, the, building of, 433
Quo warranto, matter of the, 155

R

Radcliffe, Rev. Robert, holds Episcopal service, 161, 163, 182
Radicals, the, 459
Railways, beginnings of, 449.
Randolph, Edward, appears in Boston, 151; makes charges against the colonists, 152, 153; arrested, 169
Ratcliff, Philip, circulates scandals in England, 63

Rawson, Edward, secretary, on the condition of the colony, 158
Reformation, a, expected in England, 96
Regicides, the, escape to Boston, 139
Regiments, the "Sam Adams," 317
Religion, the, of the founders of the colony, 274
Religious character of Bostonians in early days, 177
Religious life in Boston, 446
Religious troubles at the Old South, 166, 167
Representative government established, 85
Republican party, the, formed, 465
Revere, Paul, carries a message from a Boston town-meeting to Philadelphia, 351; carries the Suffolk resolves to Philadelphia, 356; illuminates his house, 319; influences Samuel Adams by means of the mechanics, 404; sent to Concord, 330; takes to Philadelphia an account of the tea-party, 343
Revolution, the "causes" of, 275
Rice, Alexander H., mayor, 456
Richardson, the informer, who caused the death of Schneider, 309
Riedesel, General, in Cambridge, 389
Rights of the people advocated by a club, 264
Rings and gloves at funerals, 227, 228
Riot, the, on account of the seizure of Hancock's vessel, 296; caused by impressment of seamen, 252, 253; at the time of the *Romney* trouble, 297; the, at the Ursuline convent, 468
Rioters dispersed by Mayor Quincy, 430
Ripley, George, and Transcendentalism, 459, 460

Römer, Col., William Wolfgang, engineer, repairs the Castle, 219
Romney, impressment of seamen on the, 296
Rope-making in Boston, 310
Roxbury, annexation of, 470; beginnings of, 40
Royalists not accorded justice, 173
Rum, extravagant price of, 387; the chief manufacture previous to the Revolution, 398; not to be sold without a permit from Gage, 369
Ryece, Robert, a friend of Winthrop, gives him advice, 17, 18

S

Safety, a committee of, appointed, in 1770, 316; formed, 358; a council for, appointed, 171
Salaries decreased by the depreciation of the currency, 248
Salaries to be paid by the king, 346
Salary, Belcher's contest for, 229; difficulties of Bellomont in regard to, 198; contest of Burnet for, 225; not given to Dudley, 201; the, of Hutchinson direct from the king, 323; contest of Shirley for, 243; troubles of Shute regarding, 210
Salary question, the, as connected with the king's governors, 192
Salem, general court adjourned to, 226; meetings of the general court at, 352, 354; made the capital, 346
Salem witchcraft, the, 185
Saltonstall, Sir Richard, character of, 20; obliged to make restitution to Indians, 69; protests against certain acts of the early settlers, 65
Salutation Inn, and Alley, 221
Satan, the emissaries of, abroad at an early date, 119; influence of, in New England, 48; as a hard master of the Indians, 92; said to have been the instigator of the

persecution of the witches, 187; his kingdom supported by Quakers, 111

Scalps, bounties offered for, 201

Schneider, the boy, becomes the "first martyr," 309

School committee, the, how formed, 445

Schools, free and unsectarian not known in early Boston, 439; plan formed for the support of, in the West, 406

Schools in the West, 408

School Street, named for the Latin school, 408

School system, organization of, under the influence of Samuel Adams, 442

Scrupulosity, the, of Bostonians, 136; in early times, 219

Secession, first announcement of the doctrine of, 415; from a Southern point of view in 1814, 416

Secrecy of the movements of the colony company in arranging to take the charter to America, 7

Selectmen, the first appearance of, 91; the, of early Boston, 418; junketings of the, 419

Selling of Joseph, the, a tract by Judge Sewall, 218, 463

Sentry (Beacon) Hill in early days, 58

Separatism opposed by Winthrop, 31, 74

Sermon, the Election, before the Artillery Company, 241

Sermons in the heroic age, 117; strange texts for, 205, 206

Servants in Boston families, 116

Sever, Benjamin, mayor, 456

Sewall, Samuel, judge of the court that tried witches, 186; his repentance of his deeds, 187; comforts himself at the coming of Andros, 164; comments on the change in the times, 162; his home, 162; his Selling of Joseph, 218; converses about the Dudley letters, 201, 202; deals with "brother Wing," 174; gives a view of the doings of his day, 214; has scruples about the cross in the colors, 174; his opinion of the influence of Increase Mather, 215; death of, 231

Sewall, Samuel E., unites in founding the Anti-Slavery Society, 463

Shawmut becomes Boston, 43

Shays' rebellion, the, causes of, 400, 402

Shepard Memorial church, mentioned, 309

Shepard, Rev. Thomas, of Cambridge, 80

Sherman, goodwife, and her troublesome sow, 88, 89

Shirley, Thomas, expresses his opinion of Boston, 328

Shirley, William, appointed governor, 243; puts the independency of America in the distance, 261

Shurtleff, Nathaniel B., mayor, 456; his "Description of Boston," quoted, 307

Shute, Samuel, appointed governor, 208

Shylock, a lesson from, 195

Singing by note first introduced, 200

Slavery, abolished in Massachusetts, 405; Edward Everett on, 464; protests against interference with, 463; tract against, by Sewall, 218

Slaves, cost of and care of, 184; obtained for rum, 399

Small-pox in Boston, 210

Smith, Jerome V. C., mayor, 456

Smith, John, on the beauty of Boston, 38; gives names to places in New England, 2

Smith, Rev. Ralph, becomes a Separatist, 32, 74

Smuggling, seizure of the *Liberty* for, 296

Smuggling trade, the, 254

Snow, Dr. Caleb H., History of Boston, 202, 355, 409

Society, changes in, as marked by Samuel Curwen, 387 ; after the Revolution, 396
Soldiers, in the early Boston economy, 242 ; from Halifax arrive in Boston, 300 ; provision for quartering, upon towns, 346
Sons of Liberty, an organization, 291
South Boston, annexed, 409 ; (Dorchester Heights) fortified, 366
South Carolina, forms a local government, 381 ; sympathizes with suffering Boston, 353
South End, boundaries of, 397 ; in early days, 223
Sovereigns, Americans first so-called, 261
Sow, the stray, and what it brought about, 88, 89
Speculation after the Revolution, 387
Speculators punished as royalists, 387
Sprague, Charles, reads a poem, 451
Squeb, Captain, at Nantasket, 40
Stamp-act congress, the, 280 ; mentioned, 326
Stamp-act riot, the, 282 ; celebrated, 294 ; denounced, 284
Stamp act, the, passed, 280 ; repealed, 288
Stamp duties proposed by Sir William Keith, 224
Stamps deemed a mark of slavery, and not to be used, 381
Stamp tax, the, proposed, 277
State Church, the, in Boston, 178
State House, the present, begun, 452, 453
State sovereignty as interpreted by Hancock, 402, 403
Stoddard, Rev. Solomon, of Northampton, 216
Stone, Rev. Samuel, 130
Stoughton, William, acting governor, 189 ; governor, rule of, 195, 198
Streets, changes in, after the Revolution, 397 ; condition of, in early days, 59 ; improvement in the, under Mayor Quincy, 432 ; new, built by Mayor Quincy, 434
Suffolk resolves, how passed, 355, 356
Suffrage, the, and church membership, 84 ; right of, sought by women, 467
Sugar law, the, enforced by Charles Paxton, 254
Sumner, Charles, becomes a Free-Soiler, 465
Sunday customs in Boston, 115
Sunday, how kept in early days, 175, 176
Sunday services given up at the time of the battle of Bunker Hill, 367
Swearing, the terrible, in Boston in early days, 232
Synod, the, of 1637, at New Town, (Cambridge), 79

T

Table, provisions for the, 219
Taxation, arguments against, source of, 272 ; by stamp proposed, 224, 277 ; without representation tyranny, a sentiment of Otis, 276
Taxes, arbitrary, laid by Andros and Randolph, 167 ; exorbitant in Boston, 277 ; ought to be laid by representatives only, 168 ; removed, except on tea, 321
Taylor, Jeremy, on the treatment of Baptists, 106
Tea, cost of, after the Revolution, 386 ; the, destroyed at Griffin's wharf, shall it be paid for? 354 ; quality of, and quantity of, used in Boston in pre-revolutionary times, 323 ; renounced by Harvard students and others, 300, 301 ; shipments of, expected, 337 ; tax upon, levied by England, 292 ; tax upon, retained for a reason, 321 ; endangers liberty, 324, 325
Teachers, training demanded of, 444 ; women equal to men, 442

Temperance approved by Winthrop, 51
Ten Hills Farm, 52
Ten men, the, of early Boston, 418
Texts, strange, for sermons, 205, 206
Thacher, Oxenbridge, supports Adams, 278
Thanksgiving-day, the first, in Boston, 52
Theology in Boston, 446
Thompson, Benjamin, on early New England diet, 62
Thompson, George, anti-slavery agitator, 463
Thursday lecture, the, 118, 175; attendance upon, made a means of popularity, 196
Ticknor, George, gives books to the Public Library, 476
Tindale, Arthur, carries a letter to Margaret Winthrop, 46
Tobacco, laws against the use of, 137
Toleration, Williams on, 76
Tonnage of Boston in 1717, 194
Tories, estates of, confiscated, 396; the, oppose the formation of local governments, 381; ridicule the committee of correspondence, 328
Tories and whigs, rise of the names, 262
Toryism makes itself felt in 1778, 389
Town Cove in early days, 58
Town Dock, the, condition of, in 1822, 433
Town-house, the old, a scene in, 268; the first, 61
Town-meeting, a, called to censure the governor, 326; in Boston to confer with Gage, 364; highest mark of the, 329; important function of the, 378
Town-meetings, difficulties in regard to, 420; feared by England, 345; how warned, 91; not to be permitted, 346
Towns, first heard of, 91; the, about Boston arm themselves, 357; in Massachusetts express themselves, 328; the "unfortunate" power of, 91
"Townsmen," the, of early Boston, 418; refreshments for the, 419
Town system, the, a bungling one, 419
Trade, brisk, in Boston, 96; growing up in Boston, 97; intercolonial, interfered with, 194; interfered with by the Boston port bill, 352; interference with, 193; obstructed by the king, 168; policy of controlling, 208; views of English politicians regarding, 399; carrying, the, wealth gained in, 414
Trade and manufactures improve, 452
Trade, the Board of, inquires about Boston affairs, 143
Training-day for the militia, 60
Transcendentalism, History of, quoted, 458, 460
Tribulations at the coming of Andros, 164
Trick, a political, begins the municipal history of Boston, 424
Trinity Church, site of, 470
Troops, demand for their removal, 313; expected in Boston, 295, 298; goaded almost beyond endurance, 308, 310, 311; how quartered in 1770, 310; trouble in regard to quartering, 269
Tunnel, the, through the Hoosac mountain, cost of, 449
Tupper, General Benjamin, sent to the Ohio country, 407
Tyler, Moses Coit, on the influence of Laud, 81

U

Uniform, the, of the old militia, 242
Union, the first American, 93; the, of America, as seen by Dickinson, 355; plan for an Ameri-

can, presented by Church, 332;
discussed at Albany, 250; suggestions of breaking the, 415
Unitarian Church, distinguished ministers in the, 446
Ursuline convent, destruction of the, 467

V

Vane, Sir Henry, comes to Boston, 74, 81; character and influence of, 81
Vassall, William, an original settler, 20
Veils, Mather preaches on, 76
Veto power, the, of the magistrates in the general court, 90
Vice, increase of, bewailed by Cotton Mather, 196
Virginia contributes to alleviate the sufferings of Boston, 353
Virginia plan, the, for intercolonial correspondence, 334
Virginia resolves, the, drawn up by Patrick Henry, 275

W

Wainscoting, trouble about some, 67
Walford, Thomas, at Charton, or Charleton, 38
Walpole, Sir Robert, declines to tax the colonies, 224
Ward, Artemas, commands the American army, 365; again in command of the army about Boston, 379
Ward, Nathaniel, prepares the "Body of Liberties," as laws for the colony, 120; recommended as freeman, 26
Ware, Henry, chosen Hollis Professor, 446
War, the civil, 473
War of 1812, the, protests against, 416
War, Queen Anne's, 206
Warrants, "general," issued and objected to, 255

Warren, Joseph, brought into prominence, 262; delivers the address commemorating the massacre, in 1775, 358, 359; on General Gage, 352; member of a committee to treat with Hutchinson, 314; patriotism of, 326
Washington, George, appointed commander of the continental army, 371; enters Boston, 375; subscribes to aid Boston, 353; visits Boston, in 1789, 402
Washington Street, early names of, 58
Water, condition of, in the wells and cisterns in Boston, 435; not thought a strange drink in early days, 62; provision for more, desired by the first Mayor Quincy, 432, 435
Waterton, Charles, on the Boston tea-party, 344
Watertown becomes the capital, 371
Webb, Rev. John, preaches a centennial sermon, 231
Webster, Daniel, on the massacre, 319
Wells, Charles, mayor, 456
Wells, W. V., Life of Adams, quoted, 295, 403
West, the, Boston men look toward, 406
West End, boundaries of, 397; obtrusiveness of vice in, 430
Wheelright, Rev. John, banished, 80
Whigs, a club of, in 1747, 264
Whigs and tories, rise of the names, 262
Whipping as a punishment, 64, 69
Whitefield, George, visits Boston, 232
Whitman, Zachariah, G., mentioned, 241
Wig, the, of Josiah Willard, 215
Wigglesworth, Michael, on the inhabitants of America, 12

Wightman, Joseph M., mayor, 456
Wilkins, Richard, bookseller, altercation in shop of, 215
Willard, Josiah, cuts off his hair, 215
Willard, Rev. Samuel, President of Harvard College, 135 ; preaches on the bad times, 199
William Henry, Fort, fall of, 258
Williams, Roger, comes over, 65 ; banished, 77 ; Life of, by W. Gammell, 66 ; opinions of, 76 ; views regarding the Church of England, 31, 74 ; will not persecute Quakers, 111
Wilmington, N. C., sends aid to Boston, 353
Wilson, Rev. John, chosen first pastor, 41
Windmill Hill (Copp's) 58
Wine at funerals, 228 ; furnished the populace, 289
Winsor, Justin, "History of America," 2 ; "Memorial History of Boston," by, 101, 344, 398, 410, 418, 433, 442, 479
Winthrop, Fones, wishes to marry Ursula Fones, 27
Winthrop, Forth, and Deane sail for America, 55
Winthrop, Henry, death of, 46
Winthrop, John, appears in connection with the Boston colony, 6 ; aims of, according to Mayor Quincy, 451 ; character of, 127 ; chosen governor, 24 ; dwelling of, probably demolished by the British, 370 ; gives up the use of tobacco, 137 ; home of, 59, 60 ; lost in the woods, 53 ; motives of, 11 ; ordered to give up the charter, 123 ; removes his dwelling to Boston, 67 ; rotated out of office, 72 ; statue of, 482 ; tender letters of, 28, 30 ; tries to keep his courage up, 48 ; troubled by a financial panic, 97 ; dies, 114, 127 ; his "Model of Christian Charity," 34
Winthrop and Dudley fall out, 67
Winthrop, John, Jr., agrees with his father about America, 23 ; invents a windmill, 28
Winthrop, Margaret, correspondence with her husband, 16 ; sails for America, 55 ; character of, 114 ; dies, 114
Winthrop, Robert Charles, Speaker of the House, 465
Witchcraft delusion, the, 185
Woman's Club, the New England, 468
Woman's Journal, The, 468
Woman suffragism, rise of, 467
Women, education of, 439, 441 ; examinations for, at Harvard College, 443 ; fashions of, in early days, 138 ; garments of, in early times, 218 ; voters, work of, 467 ; wish to complete a good English education, 442, 443
"Wonder-Working Providence," The, of Edward Johnson, 41
Worcester, railway to, 450
Worship, forms of, 64 ; religions, in families, 177
Writs of assistance, legality of, questioned, 268, 270

Y

Yorktown, victory at, gives joy to Boston, 395
Young, Thomas, makes an address, 319

The Story of the Nations.

MESSRS. G. P. PUTNAM'S SONS take pleasure in announcing that they have in course of publication a series of historical studies, intended to present in a graphic manner the stories of the different nations that have attained prominence in history.

In the story form the current of each national life will be distinctly indicated, and its picturesque and noteworthy periods and episodes will be presented for the reader in their philosophical relation to each other as well as to universal history.

It is the plan of the writers of the different volumes to enter into the real life of the peoples, and to bring them before the reader as they actually lived, labored, and struggled—as they studied and wrote, and as they amused themselves. In carrying out this plan, the myths, with which the history of all lands begins, will not be overlooked, though these will be carefully distinguished from the actual history, so far as the labors of the accepted historical authorities have resulted in definite conclusions.

The subjects of the different volumes will be planned to cover connecting and, as far as possible, consecutive epochs or periods, so that the set when completed will present in a comprehensive narrative the chief events in the great STORY OF THE NATIONS; but it will, of course not always prove practicable to issue the several volumes in their chronological order.

The "Stories" are printed in good readable type, and in handsome 12mo form. They are adequately illustrated and furnished with maps and indexes. They are sold separately at a price of $1.50 each.

The following is a partial list of the subjects thus far determined upon :

THE STORY OF *ANCIENT EGYPT. Prof. GEORGE RAWLINSON.
" " " *CHALDEA. Z. A. RAGOZIN.
" " " *GREECE. Prof. JAMES A. HARRISON,
Washington and Lee University.
" " " *ROME. ARTHUR GILMAN.
" " " *THE JEWS. Prof. JAMES K. HOSMER,
Washington University of St. Louis.
" " " *CARTHAGE. Prof. ALFRED J. CHURCH,
University College, London.
" " " BYZANTIUM.
" " " *THE GOTHS. HENRY BRADLEY.
" " " *THE NORMANS. SARAH O. JEWETT.
" " " *PERSIA. S. G. W. BENJAMIN.
" " " *SPAIN. Rev. E. E. and SUSAN HALE.
" " " *GERMANY. S. BARING-GOULD.
" " " THE ITALIAN REPUBLICS.
" " " *HOLLAND. Prof. C. F. THOROLD ROGERS.
" " " *NORWAY. HJALMAR H. BOYESEN.
" " " *THE MOORS IN SPAIN. STANLEY LANE-POOLE.
" " " *HUNGARY. Prof. A. VÁMBÉRY.
" " " THE ITALIAN KINGDOM. W. L. ALDEN.
" " " *MEDIEVAL FRANCE. Prof. GUSTAVE MASSON.
" " " *ALEXANDER'S EMPIRE. Prof. J. P. MAHAFFY.
" " " THE HANSE TOWNS. HELEN ZIMMERN.
" " " *ASSYRIA. Z. A. RAGOZIN.
" " " *THE SARACENS. ARTHUR GILMAN.
" " " *TURKEY. STANLEY LANE-POOLE.
" " " PORTUGAL. H. MORSE STEPHENS.
" " " *MEXICO. SUSAN HALE.
" " " *IRELAND. HON. EMILY LAWLESS.
" " " PHŒNICIA.
" " " SWITZERLAND.
" " " RUSSIA.
" " " WALES.
" " " SCOTLAND.
" " " *MEDIA, BABYLON, AND PERSIA.
Z. A. RAGOZIN.

* (The volumes starred are now ready, November, 1888.)

G. P. PUTNAM'S SONS
NEW YORK   LONDON
27 AND 29 WEST TWENTY-THIRD STREET   27 KING WILLIAM STREET, STRAND

THE SCRIPTURES,

HEBREW AND CHRISTIAN.

ARRANGED AND EDITED AS AN INTRODUCTION TO THE STUDY OF THE BIBLE.

Rev. EDWARD T. BARTLETT, D.D.,
Dean of the Divinity School of the P. E. Church in Philadelphia, and Mary Wolfe, Prof. of Ecclesiastical History.

Rev. JOHN P. PETERS, Ph.D.,
Professor of Old Testament Literature and Language in the Divinity School of the P. E. Church in Philadelphia, and Professor of Hebrew in the University of Pennsylvania.

} Editors.

The work is to be completed in three volumes, containing each about 500 pages. Vols. I. and II. now ready.

Vol. I. includes Hebrew story from the Creation to the time of Nehemiah, as in the Hebrew canon.

Vol. II. is devoted to Hebrew poetry and prophecy.

Vol. III. will contain the selections from the Christian Scriptures.

The volumes are handsomely printed in 12mo form, and with an open, readable page, not arranged in verses, but paragraphed according to the sense of the narrative.

Each volume is complete in itself, and will be sold separately at $1.50.

The editors say in their announcement: "Our object is to remove stones of stumbling from the path of young readers by presenting Scriptures to them in a form as intelligible and as instructive as may be practicable. This plan involves some re-arrangements and omissions, before which we have not hesitated, inasmuch as our proposed work will not claim to be the Bible, but an introduction to it. That we may avoid imposing our own interpertation upon Holy Writ, it will be our endeavor to make Scripture serve as the commentary on Scripture. In the treatment of the Prophets of the Old Testament and the Epistles of the New Testament, it will not be practicable entirely to avoid comment, but no attempt will be made to pronounce upon doctrinal questions."

The first volume is divided into four parts:

Part I.—Hebrew Story, from the Beginning to the Time of Saul.
" II.—The Kingdom of all Israel.
" III.—Samaria, or the Northern Kingdom.
" IV.—Judah, from Rehoboam to the Exile.

The second volume comprises:

PART I.—HEBREW HISTORY FROM THE EXILE TO NEHEMIAH.
" II.—HEBREW LEGISLATION.
" III.—HEBREW TALES.
" IV.—HEBREW PROPHECY.
" V.—HEBREW POETRY.
" VI.—HEBREW WISDOM.

The third volume will comprise the selections from the New Testament, arranged as follows:

I.—THE GOSPEL ACCORDING TO ST. MARK, PRESENTING THE EVANGELICAL STORY IN ITS SIMPLEST FORM; SUPPLEMENTED BY SELECTIONS FROM ST. MATTHEW AND ST. LUKE.
II.—THE ACTS OF THE APOSTLES, WITH SOME INDICATION OF THE PROBABLE PLACE OF THE EPISTLES IN THE NARRATIVE.
III.—THE EPISTLES OF ST. JAMES AND THE FIRST EPISTLE OF ST. PETER.
IV.—THE EPISTLES OF ST. PAUL.
V.—THE EPISTLE TO THE HEBREWS.
VI.—THE REVELATION OF ST. JOHN (A PORTION).
VII.—THE FIRST EPISTLE OF ST. JOHN.
VIII.—THE GOSPEL OF ST. JOHN.

Full details of the plan of the undertaking, and of the methods adopted by the editors in the selection and arrangement of the material, will be found in the separate prospectus.

"I congratulate you on the issue of a work which, I am sure, will find a wide welcome, and the excellent features of which make it of permanent value."—Rt. Rev. HENRY C. POTTER, Bishop of New York.

"Should prove a valuable adjunct of Biblical instruction."—Rt. Rev. W. E. STEVENS, Bishop of Pennsylvania.

"Admirably conceived and admirably executed. . . . It is the Bible story in Bible words. The work of scholarly and devout men. . . . Will prove a help to Bible study."—Rev. HOWARD CROSBY, D.D.

"We know of no volume which will better promote an intelligent understanding of the structure and substance of the Bible than this work, prepared, as it is, by competent and reverent Christian scholars."—*Sunday-School Times.*

G. P. PUTNAM'S SONS

NEW YORK:
27 AND 29 WEST 23D STREET

LONDON:
27 KING WILLIAM ST., STRAND

PUBLICATIONS OF G. P. PUTNAM'S SONS.

The Story of the City of Washington. By CHARLES BURR TODD, author of "The Story of the City of New York." Octavo, cloth, with many illustrations and maps. (No. 2 in the series of the *Great Cities of the Republic*) . . $1 75

WASHINGTON, ABOUT 1800.
(From "The Story of the City of Washington.")

"It is well to remember that a nation's capital may fairly be considered as an index to a nation's character, and that the outcome of our institutions will be studied by critical strangers in the city on the banks of the Potomac."—*From Author's Preface.*

"It is peculiarly happy in its focus, complete in its scope, patriotic in its tone, and graphic in its style."—*Boston Journal of Education.*

"This is a copious guide-book to the capital city of the United States, as well as an interesting record of its history, its political and oratorical events, and its civic growth."—*Portland Press.*

"So valuable do we regard this book that we express the hope that it may find its way into the hands of every boy and girl in this country."—*Journal of Pedagogy.*

"Its perusal is worth even more than a flying trip to Washington, and should, in fact, precede such a journey."—*Philadelphia Ledger.*

G. P. PUTNAM'S SONS, NEW YORK AND LONDON

PUBLICATIONS OF G. P. PUTNAM'S SONS

Story of the City of New York. By CHARLES BURR TODD, author of "Life and Letters of Joel Barlow." A history of the city from the discovery of the island by Verrazano till the present time. Profusely illustrated, cloth $1 75

THE BATTERY IN 1663.
(From "The Story of the City of New York.)

"Will be found in all respects a convenient, accurate, and comprehensive record of the city's development for three hundred years."—*New York Independent.*

"Mr. Todd has managed his material with much skill, and he succeeds excellently in putting before the reader very striking pen-pictures of the different phases of civic development. The book is pleasantly written and we have found it very readable."—*Philadelphia Telegraph.*

G. P. PUTNAM'S SONS, NEW YORK AND LONDON.

Robert Fulton and Steam Navigation. By THOS. W. KNOX, editor of "The Travels of Marco Polo," author of "Boy Travellers in the East," etc., etc. One large 12mo volume, profusely illustrated . $1 75

This book tells the story of a life of constant activity and usefulness, and describes the rise and progress of steam navigation in a manner most remarkable and clear. It is free from technical terms of all description, and is written in that charmingly narrative and picturesque form for which Mr. Knox is so justly famous.

The book is composed of 500 pages, and contains 82 elegant engravings, which go to emphasize its usefulness.

The early struggles of Fulton to get recognition for his inventions, his perseverance, and his dogged determination to succeed, are depicted forcefully and sympathetically. All the great ocean, war, and river steamers of the century, their principles of construction, the gradual evolution of speed by means of improved application of the original idea, and the development of the original crude machinery, are described and exemplified by numerous illustrations.

G. P. PUTNAM'S SONS, NEW YORK AND LONDON.

PUBLICATIONS OF G. P. PUTNAM'S SONS

Life of Abraham Lincoln. By NOAH BROOKS. Crown octavo, with many illustrations. $1 75

LINCOLN'S WRESTLE WITH ARMSTRONG.
(Reduced from "Life of Abraham Lincoln.")

"In writing this brief biography, I have been moved by a desire to give the generation of young people, who will never know aught of Abraham Lincoln but what is traditional, a life-like picture of the man as many men knew him. . . . Many things relating to his early life herein set down were derived from his own lips, often during hours of secluded companionship."—*From Author's Preface.*

"An excellent and timely book."—*New Albany Ledger.*
"An admirably written book."—*Buffalo Christian Advocate.*
"It is a capital book."—*Pittsburgh Chronicle.*
"A more interesting biography we have not read."—*Hartford Times.*

G. P. PUTNAM'S SONS, NEW YORK AND LONDON

www.ingramcontent.com/pod-product-compliance
Lightning Source LLC
Chambersburg PA
CBHW020857020526
44116CB00029B/336